LANDMARK CASES IN INTERNATIONAL REFUGEE PROTECTION

This volume examines judicial decisions that have shaped the law of asylum and refugee protection.

Each chapter analyses a single judicial decision and locates it in a wider legal, political and policy context, tracing its subsequent impact on refugee law and policy. Some of the decisions analysed in this collection were foundational in establishing the reach of refugee law, particularly in defining the scope of the refugee definition. Others engage with key areas of refugee rights in contexts which indicate a critical turning point in state refugee policy, such as interdiction of boats at sea, encampment and extraterritorial asylum processing mechanisms. The contributions demonstrate how refugee protection is shaped by the intersection of different fields of law, including refugee law, human rights law, and domestic constitutional provisions.

Reflecting this complexity, the collection explores decisions from the UK, Canada, USA, Kenya, Australia and Papua New Guinea, as well as regional courts including the European Court of Human Rights, the Inter-American Court of Human Rights, the Court of Justice of the European Union, and decisions of the United Nations Human Rights treaty bodies. Authors include leading academics and practitioners in refugee and human rights law from a range of jurisdictions.

This book offers compelling insights for anyone with an interest in international refugee protection, human rights, and the development of international refugee law.

Landmark Cases in International Refugee Protection

International Jurisprudence on the Rights of Refugees

Edited by
Kirsten McConnachie
and
Sarah Singer

•HART•
OXFORD • LONDON • NEW YORK • NEW DELHI • SYDNEY

HART PUBLISHING
Bloomsbury Publishing Plc
Kemp House, Chawley Park, Cumnor Hill, Oxford, OX2 9PH, UK
1385 Broadway, New York, NY 10018, USA
Bloomsbury Publishing Ireland Limited, 29 Earlsfort Terrace, Dublin 2, D02 AY28, Ireland

HART PUBLISHING, the Hart/Stag logo, BLOOMSBURY and the Diana logo are trademarks of Bloomsbury Publishing Plc

First published in Great Britain 2026

A catalogue record for this book is available from the British Library.

A catalogue record for this book is available from the Library of Congress.

Library of Congress Control Number: 2025949154

ISBN: HB: 978-1-50998-133-5
ePDF: 978-1-50998-135-9
ePub: 978-1-50998-134-2

Typeset by Compuscript Ltd, Shannon

ACKNOWLEDGEMENTS

Convening an edited volume is not the work of a single person or persons but a collective endeavour, and accordingly one which entails a great debt of thanks to all involved. We would firstly like to thank all our contributing authors for so enthusiastically taking up the task set to them and producing what we trust readers will find to be fascinating and valuable accounts of the landmark cases they discuss and the key themes of refugee protection law and policy they have brought to the fore.

We would like to thank our institutions – the School of Law at the University of East Anglia, and the Refugee Law Initiative at the School of Advanced Study, University of London – for granting us the time to work on this publication.

We of course also owe a great debt of thanks to Hart for taking on this project, and particularly to Sasha Jawed, Verity Stuart, Victoria Broom and Linda Goss for their support during the drafting and production processes.

On a personal note, we would like to thank our colleagues, friends and family for their support and encouragement throughout this endeavour. Sarah would like to thank her partner Tiago Cunha, her father Gwilym Colenso, and her colleagues at the Refugee Law Initiative including David Cantor and Nick Maple. Kirsten would like to thank her family, including Margaret and Sandy, Ranald and Kathryn McConnachie, and colleagues at UEA including Karina Aveyard, Caitlin Scott and Maren Duvendack.

We would like to dedicate this collection to the memory of Mark Chelvan-Stanmore, and to the work of everyone engaged in law and litigation to protect the rights of refugees.

CONTENTS

PART C
FUTURE DIRECTIONS IN REFUGEE PROTECTION

CONTRIBUTORS

Bruce Burson sits on the New Zealand Immigration and Protection Tribunal and has written many of its leading decisions, including *Teitiota*. For 20 years he has worked with UN agencies and the International Federation of Red Cross and Red Crescent Societies on issues surrounding human (im)mobility, climate change and disasters. He has co-authored many technical reports and guides. He was special advisor on climate mobility to the New Zealand Ministry of Foreign Affairs and Trade (2020–2024). He has been involved with a number of technical committees including the ILA Committee on International Law and Sea-Level Rise, the Nansen Initiative and the Platform on Disaster Displacement.

S Chelvan, Barrister of the Inner Temple, BSC (SocSci) Politics and Law (First class) (Soton), LLM (Harvard), PhD (Research) (KCL), and DUniv (OU). Chelvan was called to the Bar in October 1999 and is Head of Immigration and Public Law at 33 Bedford Row Chambers and Adjunct Professor at Southampton Law School. He has a global and international reputation in refugee protection claims based on sexual identity, litigating case up to and including the European Court of Human Rights. Chelvan's focus on refugee and LGBTQ+ rights is primarily as a strategic litigation lawyer, with the additional strands as an academic, policy advisor and media legal commentator.

Elspeth Guild holds a Global Chair in Social Justice at the University of Liverpool and is Emerita Professor at Radboud University, Nijmegen, Netherlands. She is also a visiting professor at the College of Europe, Bruges. She holds a PhD in law from the Radboud University and a PhD honoris causa from the University of Lund. In 2022 she assisted the Council of Europe Parliamentary Assembly with an analysis of the EU Pact on Migration and Asylum, resulting in resolution 2416 (2022). Her most recent book is entitled *Monitoring Border Violence in the EU: Frontex in Focus* (Taylor & Francis, 2023).

Liliana Jubilut is Professor of the Postgraduate Programme in Law at Universidade Católica de Santos, where she coordinates the institution's De Mello Chair in partnership with the United Nations High Commissioner for Refugees (UNHCR) and the Research Group 'Human Rights and Vulnerabilities'. She holds a PhD and a Master's degree in International Law from Universidade de São Paulo and a LLM in International Legal Studies from NYU. She was Visiting Scholar at Columbia Law School and Visiting Fellow at the Refugee Law Initiative, and has had summer school experiences at the University of Oxford and Harvard University. She is Co-Chair of the Global Academic

Interdisciplinary Network (GAIN), from the Global Compact on Refugees, a part of the International Organization for Migration's Migration Research Leaders' Syndicate and is a Migration Research and Publishing High-Level Adviser for the Organization as well.

Camila Marques Gilberto is Professor of the Graduate Programme in Law at Universidade Católica de Santos. She is part of the Research Group 'Human Rights and Vulnerabilities' and De Mello Chair. She holds a PhD in International Environmental Law from Universidade Católica de Santos, a Master's degree in International Law from Universidade Católica de Santos and a LLM in International Law from University College of London.

Kirsten McConnachie is Professor of Socio-Legal Studies at the University of East Anglia, a Research Associate at the University of Oxford's Refugee Studies Centre, a Senior Research Associate of the University of London's Refugee Law Initiative and a trustee of the UK Socio-Legal Studies Association. Her primary area of teaching and research is refugee law from a socio-legal and interdisciplinary perspective. She has a regional interest in displacement in and from Myanmar and has published on areas including the governance of refugee camps, legal pluralism and informal governance in refugee situations, legal anthropology, and forced migration in southeast Asia.

Paul McDonough is a research fellow at the Department of Political and Social Sciences at the University of Bologna, working on the European Research Council-funded project 'Gatekeepers to International Refugee Law? – The Role of Courts in Shaping Access to Asylum (ACCESS)'. He was previously a Lecturer in Law at Cardiff University and a Max Weber fellow at the law department of the European University Institute.

Stephen Meili is the James H Michael Professor of International Human Rights Law at the University of Minnesota Law School. He has authored *The Constitutionalization of Human Rights Law: Implications for Refugees* (Oxford University Press, 2022) as well as numerous articles and book chapters. His research takes a comparative and empirical approach, and lies at the intersection of human rights treaty effectiveness, refugee law, and cause lawyering. Much of his work focuses on asylum law in the Global South. He also supervises students in the Law School's Immigration and Human Rights Clinic, which represents asylum seekers from a variety of countries.

Maria O'Sullivan is an Associate Professor at the Deakin Law School in Melbourne, Australia and is the author of a number of international and national publications on the subject of human rights, public law and refugee law. Her work focuses on the importance of power in the formulation and implementation of the law and she has recently published commentary on concepts of vulnerability and the lived experience of those subject to the law. She is currently undertaking research on permanent pathways for temporary protection status, the right of non-citizens to protest and automation of refugee decisions.

Flávia Oliveira Ribeiro is a PhD candidate and Research Assistant at the Academy for European Human Rights Protection at the University of Cologne. She holds a Master's and a Bachelor's degree in Law from the Universidade Estadual Paulista. She is part of the Research Group 'Human Rights and Vulnerabilities' at the Universidade Católica de Santos. She attended the International Refugee Law Course at the Sanremo International Institute of Humanitarian Law and the Pre-College Programme in International Politics and Law at Boston University. She has been assisting the Global Academic Interdisciplinary Network (GAIN) for the last two years.

Christel Querton is a Senior Lecturer in Law at the University of the West of England, Bristol. Her research focuses on international refugee law, particularly persons fleeing armed conflicts and refugee women. Christel founded and is the co-convener of the Women in Refugee Law Network, aiming to recentre refugee women within refugee law, policy and practice. Christel was an immigration and human rights barrister and previously worked at Asylum Aid and Wilson Solicitors LLP. She was a founding Trustee of the Asylum Research Centre Foundation.

Sarah Singer is Professor of Refugee Law at the Refugee Law Initiative, School of Advanced Study, University of London. She is an internationally recognised expert on criminality and asylum, has led major collaborative interdisciplinary research projects in the refugee protection field, and is a recognised expert on postgraduate online education. She is inaugural Programme Director of the distance-learning Master's in Refugee Protection and Forced Migration Studies and co-convenes the 'Refugees in the 21st Century' MOOC (Coursera). She is Joint Editor-in-Chief of the *International Journal of Refugee Law* (Oxford University Press).

Dallal Stevens is Professor of Refugee Law and Deputy Head of the School of Law, University of Warwick. She has published over 60 books, peer reviewed journal articles, book chapters and reports on UK, EU and Middle Eastern asylum and refugee law and policy. Dallal has collaborated on projects on refugee policy in the Arab World; data and displacement of internally displaced people; and UK asylum law. Dallal is Associate Editor of the *Journal of Immigration, Asylum and Nationality Law* and formerly Book Review Editor for the *International Journal of Refugee Law* (2019–2024).

Hugo Storey is retired judge of the Upper Tribunal (UK) and honorary president of IARMJ-Europe. In an academic capacity, he is Honorary Professor, Refugee Law Initiative, University of London and Adjunct Professor, Kaldor Centre, University of New South Wales, Sydney and has published widely on human rights, refugee law, international law and European law issues. His book on *The Refugee Definition in International Law* was published by Oxford University Press in October 2023.

Nikolas Feith Tan is Senior Lecturer at Melbourne Law School where he researches in the field of international refugee law. Nikolas' monograph, *Transnational Asylum*, was published with Routledge in 2025. Nikolas is also Senior

Protection Officer at UNHCR. The views expressed in this chapter are those of the author and do not necessarily reflect those of the United Nations or UNHCR. In 2025, Nikolas was appointed as a Member to the Australian Administrative Review Tribunal. Nikolas is a member of the board of the *International Journal of Refugee Law*. He holds affiliations with the University of Copenhagen, University of London's Refugee Law Initiative and the Kaldor Centre for International Refugee Law, UNSW.

Evangelia (Lilian) Tsourdi is Professor and Jean Monnet Chair in European Migration Law and Governance at the Law Faculty of Maastricht University and the Maastricht Centre for European Law. She is currently (2025–2029) PI of the SoftEn (Soft Enforcement of EU Migration Law) project supported by a European Research Council Starting Grant, as well as WP leader in the ongoing (2023–2026) collective Horizon Europe ENSURED project on global governance and the EU's role in defending multilateralism. Lilian is also the joint Editor-in-Chief of the *International Journal of Refugee Law* and an Editorial Board member of the *Maastricht Journal of European and Comparative Law*.

Samuel Woldemariam is lecturer at the University of Newcastle, NSW, Australia. He was awarded a PhD from the University of Newcastle in 2021 for his higher degree research on the topic of 'Forced Human Displacement, the State and International Law: A Critical Look from the South'. Samuel is a lawyer by profession and has received legal education in Ethiopia and the USA. He graduated from the LL.M in US Law program, magna cum laude, at the University of St Thomas School of Law in Minneapolis in 2016. He received an LL.B degree, magna cum laude, from an Ethiopian Law School in 2012. Samuel worked at the International Legal Affairs Department of the Ethiopian Ministry of Foreign Affairs from 2012–2015.

Natasha Yacoub has worked for two decades for UNHCR, where she has been posted since 2001 in conflict and peacetime settings in Egypt, Sudan, Ireland, UN Headquarters New York, Myanmar, Australia and the Pacific Island States (including Nauru and Papua New Guinea). She served as a decision-maker on the Refugee Review Tribunal and Migration Review Tribunal in Australia from 2012 to 2014. She is a doctoral scholar at the Kaldor Centre for International Refugee Law at the University of New South Wales. Her thesis is titled: 'Gendering the International Law Criteria for Return of Refugees: The Case of Sudan'.

TABLE OF CASES

Note: Numbers in bold refer to a chapter dedicated to the case in question. Unless otherwise indicated, cross-references are to cases in the same section of the Table.

International Courts and Tribunals

Court of Justice of the European Union

European Court of Human Rights

Human Rights Committee

Inter-American Commission on Human Rights

Inter-American Court of Human Rights

Human Rights Committee

Inter-American Commission on Human Rights

Inter-American Court of Human Rights

International Court of Justice

National Courts and Tribunals

Australia

Canada

Papua New Guinea

United Kingdom

United States

Introduction

KIRSTEN McCONNACHIE AND SARAH SINGER

I. Introducing Landmark Cases in International Refugee Protection

We are delighted to introduce *Landmark Cases in International Refugee Protection*, a collection exploring judicial decisions that have shaped the rights of refugees. Recent years have seen refugee protection operating under increased pressure as many states apply ever stricter border controls and evade or ignore their obligations to refugees seeking asylum. In this climate, judicial scrutiny is a vital check on state power and a crucial tool for preserving the integrity of asylum.

Each chapter in this volume analyses a single judicial decision and locates it in a wider legal, political and policy context. Cases explore the law of refugee *protection*, in recognition that this is a distinctive field of legal practice that engages multiple bodies of law and operates at multiple jurisdictional scales. The cases that we have included apply provisions from refugee law, human rights law and domestic constitutional law, determined by national courts (in Australia, Canada, Kenya, Papua New Guinea, the United Kingdom (UK) and the United States (US)), regional courts (European Court of Human Rights (ECtHR), Inter-American Court of Human Rights (IACtHR), Court of Justice of the European Union (CJEU)) and United Nations (UN) treaty bodies (the Human Rights Committee (HRC), overseeing implementation of the International Covenant on Civil and Political Rights (ICCPR).

The body of law that protects refugee status and rights is broader than refugee law alone but the cornerstone is undoubtedly the 1951 Convention relating to the Status of Refugees (1951 Refugee Convention).[1] With 146 contracting State Parties, the Refugee Convention is one of the world's most widely ratified treaties and establishes a truly global framework for the recognition and protection of refugees. International protection under the Convention requires that refugees be afforded fundamental freedoms such as freedom of religion and freedom of movement, as well as entitlements such as access to courts, access to social welfare and access to education. Safety in the country of asylum is preserved by principles

[1] UN General Assembly, 1951 Convention relating to the Status of Refugees, United Nations, Treaty Series, 189:137, 28 July 1951 (1951 Refugee Convention).

of non-penalisation for illegal entry to the country of asylum (Article 31) and the cardinal protection of *non-refoulement* (Article 33).

The contributions to this volume demonstrate the vital role of courts in upholding Convention rights and shaping the contours of their application. Dauvergne has described the definition of a refugee in Article 1A(2) of the Refugee Convention as 'one of the most relentlessly hermeneutic pieces of international law', noting that:

> Few international legal texts are interpreted more frequently. The refugee definition is interpreted and applied with every asylum decision made [...] It is not an exaggeration to say that this international legal text was considered and applied a million times in 2011. This is a conservative estimate.[2]

In this respect, the 'judicial pillar' of international refugee law has been 'indispensable'[3] in shaping the field.[4] Goodwin-Gill notes:

> The growth in national refugee status determination procedures and the judicialization of process have led the 1951 Convention to be one of the most litigated treaties at the domestic level, with courts and tribunals around the world engaged almost daily in a common purpose – elucidating the meaning of and applying the refugee definition and other Convention provisions relevant to admission, non-penalization by reason of irregular entry or presence, residence, non-removal, and protection at large.[5]

Despite these credible claims for core principles of refugee law as among the most widely applied provisions of international law, this is also a field of considerable legal and jurisdictional complexity. Litigation of the rights of refugees faces a range of challenges including varying levels of incorporation by states, intersecting fields of applicable law (particularly refugee and human rights law, and potentially also international humanitarian law), and a range of possible courts before which refugees' rights may be heard, each with its own mandate, specific areas of competence and rights of standing.[6]

Applying Refugee Convention rights in domestic courts naturally requires incorporation of those rights in that territory. Almost 50 Member States of the UN General Assembly have not ratified the Refugee Convention, while the 146 contracting states have not uniformly incorporated its provisions into domestic law. For example, the UK, as a dualist legal order, does not automatically apply international treaties in domestic law. It has partially incorporated the 1951 Refugee Convention with a general statement of compliance rather than the

[2] C Dauvergne, 'Refugee Law as Perpetual Crisis' in S Singh Juss and C Harvey (eds), *Contemporary Issues in Refugee Law* (Elgar, 2013) 13–30, 22–23.

[3] H Storey, *The Refugee Definition in International Law* (Oxford University Press, 2023) 51.

[4] JC Hathaway, 'A Forum for the Transnational Development of Refugee Law: The IARLJ's Advanced Refugee Law Workshop' (2003) *International Journal of Refugee Law* 15(3) 418–421, 418.

[5] GS Goodwin-Gill, 'The Lawyer and the Refugee' (2021) *Berkeley Journal of International Law*, 14 39(1) 1–17, 14.

[6] S Fatima, *Using International Law in Domestic Courts* (Hart Publishing, 2005); A Roberts, 'Comparative International Law? The Role of National Courts in Creating and Enforcing International Law' (2011) *International and Comparative Law Quarterly* 60: 57–92.

full adoption of Convention rights in a manner that can be directly litigated by refugees.[7] The US has a similarly complex position, having acceded to the 1967 Protocol to the 1951 Convention but not ratified the 1951 Convention itself. The Refugee Act 1980 incorporates elements of the 1951 Refugee Convention into domestic law (notably the refugee definition) but again does not adopt the original text in its entirety. This is further complicated by a legal culture that has been cautious, or indeed resistant, to the use of international law in domestic courts.[8] In his chapter contribution, Meili observes that the US Supreme Court's decision in *Sale v Haitian Centers Council*[9] was based almost entirely on domestic US statutory interpretation to the exclusion of international sources. This approach resulted in a limited and restrictive interpretation of US obligations under the Refugee Convention. Meili argues that, '*Sale* is a compelling example of the way in which supposedly objective, content-neutral methods of legal analysis like statutory construction and legislative interpretation can nonetheless rob international refugee law of its humanitarian purpose'.[10]

Depending on the status of national accession to or incorporation of the 1951 Refugee Convention, the most relevant applicable law in a case turning on refugees' rights might be domestic constitutional and public law principles, potentially supplemented with reference to refugee law or human rights law to the extent applicable in that jurisdiction (as evidenced in the chapter contributions on *Kituo Cha Sheria*[11] and *Namah v Pato*).[12] Human rights law and refugee law emerged as distinct tracts of international law but are now so closely interrelated that it is impossible to apprehend the scope of refugee protection without also considering the application of human rights law.[13] The 'multifaceted intermingling'[14] between refugee and human rights law operates at multiple levels. A 'human rights-based

[7] Section 2 of the UK's Asylum and Immigration Appeals Act 1993 provides: 'Nothing in the immigration rules … shall lay down any practice which would be contrary to the Convention'.

[8] G Born, 'International Law in American Courts' in PB Stephan and SA Cleveland (eds), *The Restatement and Beyond: The Past, Present and Future of US Foreign Relations Law* (Oxford University Press, 2020); M Fullerton, 'Stealth Emulation: The United States and European Protection Norms' in H Lambert, J McAdam and M Fullerton (eds), *The Global Reach of European Refugee Law* (Cambridge University Press, 2013) 201–24.

[9] *Sale v Haitian Centers Council, Inc, et al* (509)U S 155 (1993).

[10] Stephen Meili, 'Refugee Rights Adrift: Haitian Interdiction and the Long Term Effects of *Sale v Haitian Centres Council* (1993)' in ch 7 of this volume at 128.

[11] The Kenyan High Court in *Kituo Cha Sheria and Others v Attorney General* [2013] eKLR (High Court of Kenya) was notable for its reliance on Kenyan constitutional protections to support its interpretations of the rights of refugees. See Samuel Woldemariam, '*Kituo Cha Sheria and Others v Attorney-General* 2013: Betwixt Executive Opposition and Judicial Affirmation of Refugee Rights' in ch 10 of this volume.

[12] Reliance on domestic protections was particularly important in *Namah v Pato* [2016] PGSC 13 (Papua New Guinea Supreme Court) as, despite its accession in 1986, there was no domestic implementation of the 1951 Convention in Papua New Guinea at the time. See Maria O'Sullivan, '*Namah v Pato* [2016]: Constitutional Challenges in Offshore Destination States' in ch 13 of this volume.

[13] V Chetail, 'Are Refugee Rights Human Rights? An Unorthodox Questioning of the Relations between Refugee Law and Human Rights Law' in R Rubio-Marín (ed), *Human Rights and Immigration* (Oxford University Press, 2014) 19–72.

[14] ibid, 72.

approach'[15] to the interpretation of the Refugee Convention has been extremely influential in informing the scope of application of the Convention[16] and the nature of substantive Convention rights.[17] Human rights law has also become an important source for elucidating aspects of refugees' rights on which the Convention is silent. Most notably, human rights norms have been drawn upon to inform applicable procedural standards attached to refugee status determination processes, and in areas such as administrative detention and expulsion.[18] These have in many instances served as vital safeguards in ensuring refugees' access to the courts.

Human rights law also serves as an independent source of rights. Although not specific to refugees, human rights standards addressing key areas of import for refugees including *non-refoulement*, freedom of movement, and the right to liberty and security of the person have become pivotal in informing refugees' rights before domestic courts. In the absence of an international enforcement regime for the Refugee Convention, international and regional human rights regimes have also become key enforcement channels for refugees' rights.[19] Beyond domestic courts, other courts that might have jurisdiction over the rights of refugees include regional and supranational fora such as the ECtHR, the IACtHR, the African Court on Human and Peoples' Rights (ACtHPR), and the CJEU. Each of these courts has a distinct jurisdictional scope and judicial capacity.

The ECtHR was established in 1959 by the Council of Europe to oversee the European Convention on Human Rights (ECHR).[20] It can hear applications from individuals or Member States alleging violation of their rights by an ECHR Member State. All domestic remedies must have been exhausted before an application may be made to the ECtHR. The Court does not have competence to directly interpret the terms of the 1951 Refugee Convention or other refugee law instruments. Instruments of European Union (EU) law such as the legislation comprising the Common European Asylum System (CEAS) fall within the jurisdiction of the CJEU. However, this does not prevent the ECtHR from referring

[15] The human rights approach to the interpretation of the 1951 Refugee Convention was influenced in no small part by the Canadian Supreme Court's decision in *Canada (Attorney General) v Ward* [1993] 2 SCR 689. See the contribution in this volume where Hugo Storey also notes the influence of the then-recently adopted Canadian Charter of Rights and Freedoms on the interpretation advocated by the Canadian Supreme Court. Hugo Storey, '*Canada (Attorney General) v Ward* [1993]: Refugee Law's Parthenon' in ch 1 of this volume.

[16] As explored in several chapter contributions to this volume on the refugee definition. See chs 2, 3 and 5.

[17] Most notably *non-refoulement* under 1951 Refugee Convention, Art 33(1).

[18] As explored in Liliana Jubilut, C Marques Gilberto and F Oliveira Ribeiro, '*Pacheco Tineo Family v Bolivia* (2013): Human Rights and Procedural Guarantees for Refugees in the Americas' in ch 12 of this volume.

[19] B Gorlick, 'Human Rights and Refugees: Enhancing Protection through International Human Rights Law' UNHCR New Issues in Refugee Research working paper no 30, UNHCR, October 2000.

[20] Council of Europe, European Convention on Human Rights, as amended by Protocols Nos 11, 14 and 15, ETS No 005, 4 November 1950.

to other international sources as appropriate, as can be seen in the relevant chapter contributions of this volume.[21]

The role of the IACtHR is examined in this volume by Jubilut, Gilberto and Ribeiro in relation to its judgment in *Pacheco Tineo Family v Bolivia*. In contrast to the ECHR, and indeed the 1951 Refugee Convention, the American Convention on Human Rights explicitly includes the right to 'seek and be granted' asylum. The IACtHR's competence to interpret this provision in light of a broad range of regional and international sources enables the Court to consider both refugee law norms and human rights law norms.[22] This special mandate enables the Court to advance a 'normative convergence' between international refugee law and international human rights law.[23] The similarly broad mandate of the ACtHPR to interpret the right to 'seek and obtain' asylum as provided in the regional African Charter on Human and Peoples' Rights means there is great potential for this regional body to similarly advance developments in the field.[24] The space given to decisions of regional human rights courts in this volume is indicative of the value of strong regional human rights courts in advancing refugee protection. This is particularly so for the standard setting decisions of the ECtHR, of which we have included three judgments, which is more than we have included from any other single court but many fewer than we could have chosen.

The CJEU is a regional court with very different scope. Created in 1952, the CJEU exists to harmonise interpretation of EU law throughout Member States. It has a mandate to interpret EU law in its entirety, including (but certainly not limited to) the instruments which comprise the CEAS, many of which seek to harmonise interpretation of the provisions of the 1951 Refugee Convention. The Court has competence to interpret these instruments in light of the EU's Charter of Fundamental Rights and broader principles of EU law.[25] In this sense, the Court may be considered to both indirectly interpret the terms of the 1951 Refugee Convention (through its interpretation of the EU Qualification Directive[26])

[21] See, eg, chs 9 and 12 of this volume, which detail the Court's engagement with Law of the Sea and International Humanitarian Law, respectively. Elspeth Guild, '*Hirsi Jamaa and others v Italy* (2012) and the Prohibition on Pushbacks' in ch 8 of this volume; Christel Querton, 'Protection from Conflict: *Sufi and Elmi v UK* [2011]' in ch 11 of this volume.

[22] Organization of American States (OAS), American Convention on Human Rights, 'Pact of San Jose', Costa Rica, 22 November 1969, Art 22.7.

[23] Jubilut, Marques Gilberto and Oliveira Ribeiro (n 18), 222–224.

[24] Organization of African Unity (OAU), African Charter on Human and Peoples' Rights, CAB/LEG/67/3 rev. 5, 21 ILM. 58 (1982), 27 June 1981, Art 12(3). However, Sharpe notes that access to the Court by individuals and non-governmental organisations (NGOs) is severely limited by the strict rules on standing, and 'Indeed, the only refugee issue to ever come before the African Court was ruled inadmissible because the defendant State had not filed an article 34(6) declaration.' M Sharpe, 'Regional Refugee Regimes: Africa' in C Costello, M Foster and J McAdam (eds), *The Oxford Handbook of International Refugee Law* (Oxford University Press, 2021) 290–91.

[25] European Union, Charter of Fundamental Rights of the European Union, 2012/C 326/02, 14 December 2007.

[26] Council Directive 2004/83/EC of 29 April 2004 on minimum standards for the qualification and status of third country nationals or stateless persons as refugees or as persons who otherwise need international protection and the content of the protection granted [2004] OJ L304/12.

and to do so in light of binding human rights standards. This unique mandate gives the CJEU a special status in the judicialisation of international refugee protection, and its decisions are increasingly cited not only by EU Member States but also further afield including in guidance of the United Nations High Commissioner for Refugees (UNHCR). As Stevens explains in her chapter contribution on *Nawras Bolbol v Bevándorlási és Állampolgársági Hivatal*,[27] the CJEU's decision in this case prompted the UNHCR to revise its guidance on the interpretation of Article 1D of the 1951 Refugee Convention.[28] However, note must also be made of the CJEU's special status as a court of referral. Cases are referred to the CJEU by national courts, and the CJEU's decision is then referred to the domestic court to be applied within the national legal system. This reference procedure prioritises EU Member States and does not lead to non-parties to the domestic case, other than other EU Member States, having a right of audience.[29]

The role of courts in norm-setting is particularly important for the 1951 Refugee Convention, given that there is no treaty body with a mandate to provide authoritative interpretation of its provisions.[30] The Statute of the UNHCR provides the agency with a supervisory responsibility for the Refugee Convention[31] while Articles 35 and 36 of the 1951 Refugee Convention establish a corollary obligation on states to co-operate with UNHCR in the exercise of its functions.[32] In practice, UNHCR monitors implementation of Convention responsibilities by states,[33] issues guidance on the appropriate interpretation of Convention rights,[34]

[27] *Nawras Bolbol v Bevándorlási és Állampolgársági Hivatal* [2010] ECR I 5539, Case C-31/09 (CJEU).

[28] Dallal Stevens, '*Bolbol v Bevándorlási és Állampolgársági Hivatal* [2010]: When is a Palestinian Refugee a Convention Refugee?' in ch 4 of this volume.

[29] G Gilbert, 'UNHCR and Courts: Amicus Curiae. Sed Curia Amica Est?' (2016) 28 *International Journal of Refugee Law* 623, 632.

[30] As per Art 38 of the 1951 Refugee Convention, State Parties may refer a dispute about the interpretation or application of the Convention to the International Court of Justice, but this mechanism has never been used and is unlikely to be employed in future. McAdam notes that UNHCR supervisory role 'does not extend to a mandate to provide authoritative rulings or opinions on the meaning of particular treaty terms, and accordingly the UNHCR can only issue *guidance* on the 1951 Convention's interpretation through the UNHCR *Handbook on Procedures*, UNHCR guidelines, and its notes on international protection'. J McAdam, 'Interpretation of the 1951 Convention' in A Zimmerman (ed), *The 1951 Convention Relating to the Status of Refugees and Its 1967 Protocol: A Commentary* (Oxford University Press, 2011) 75–116, 79.

[31] See para 8 of the Statute of the UNHCR: 'The High Commissioner shall provide for the protection of refugees falling under the competence of his Office by: (a) promoting the conclusion and ratification of international conventions for the protection of refugees, supervising their application and proposing amendments thereto ….' UN General Assembly, 1950 Statute of the Office of the United Nations High Commissioner for Refugees, A/RES/428(V), 14 December 1950.

[32] See also Art II of the 1967 Protocol relating to the Status of Refugees, UNTS 606:267, 31 January 1967; Art VIII of the Organization of African Unity (OAU) 1969 Convention Governing the Specific Aspects of Refugee Problems in Africa (OAU Convention), 1001 UNTS 45, 10 September 1969.

[33] See, eg, UNHCR, *UNHCR Updated Observations on the Nationality and Borders Bill, as amended*, January 2022, available at www.refworld.org/legal/natlegcomments/unhcr/2022/en/123993; UNHCR, *UNHCR Legal Observations on the Illegal Migration Bill*, 22 March 2023, available www.refworld.org/legal/natlegcomments/unhcr/2023/en/124244.

[34] Notably through the UNHCR Handbook and Guidelines on International Protection (GIPs). UNHCR, *Handbook on Procedures and Criteria for Determining Refugee Status and Guidelines on International Protection Under the 1951 Convention and the 1967 Protocol Relating to the Status of*

and seeks to influence compliance with Convention obligations through (inter alia) participation in relevant litigation before national, regional and international courts, often as amicus curiae. This role is often given specific judicial mention. In the recent UK case of *AAA v SSHD*, while the Divisional Court considered that UNHCR's evidence 'carried no overriding weight', the Supreme Court emphatically disagreed, finding that 'particular importance' should attach to UNHCR's evidence due to the agency's 'undoubted expertise … and unrivalled practical experience'.[35] Nevertheless, UNHCR's supervisory function falls far short of the mandates of treaty bodies that can receive and consider individual complaints, issue conclusions and authoritatively interpret treaty terms. This includes the HRC, the treaty body for the ICCPR,[36] whose views in the complaint raised by Ioane Teitiota against New Zealand is considered in chapter 15. The HRC addressed *non-refoulement* as protected under the ICCPR rather than any parallel consideration under refugee protection instruments as had been undertaken in the earlier New Zealand domestic decisions. As the UN treaty body to the ICCPR, the views of the HRC are persuasive but non-binding on States, which is another way this body differs from the other decision-makers featured in this volume.[37]

This collection recognises the key role played by judicial decisions in shaping the field of refugee protection. However, such cases do not simply 'appear' before decision-makers, nor are decision-makers the only actors that are instrumental in developing this field of law. As Gilbert has noted, 'international refugee law is developed through continual interaction between the courts and those arguing for the asylum seeker'.[38] This is most directly realised through the legal practitioners who represent asylum seekers and refugees before domestic and international decision-makers. Yet the vital contributions of practitioners in developing lines of legal argumentation and strategically focusing on (or anticipating) the key issues to be resolved are often obscured or hidden in the final decision itself. Our collection seeks to recognise the impact and value of these contributions, and of the decision-makers who hand down such judgments, by including perspectives from judges and practitioners. In chapter 3, S Chelvan reflects on his role as legal

Refugees, HCR/1P/4/ENG/REV. 4, April 2019, available at www.refworld.org/policy/legalguidance/unhcr/2019/en/123881. The Guidelines on International Protection can be accessed via www.refworld.org/.

[35] *R (on the application of AAA and others) v Secretary of State for the Home Department* [2023] UKSC 42 [70]; [68]. See chapter 14 in this volume. Notably, UNHCR acted as amicus or intervener in many of the cases examined in this volume. See also chapters 1, 7, 8, 10 and 12.

[36] UN General Assembly, *International Covenant on Civil and Political Rights*, UNTS 999:171, 16 December 1966.

[37] There are mixed views on the 'success' of States' compliance with the views of human rights treaty bodies, particularly the HRC. However, as argued by Rodley, 'The outcomes of the [Human Rights] committees' procedures (concluding observations, general comments, and jurisprudence) are not per se legally binding, but they have real legal significance' through the normative impact they have on development of law at the international and domestic levels. NS Rodley, 'The Role and Impact of Treaty Bodies' in D Shelton (ed), *The Oxford Handbook of International Human Rights Law* (Oxford University Press, 2013) 621–48, 639.

[38] Gilbert (n 29), referring to GS Goodwin-Gill, 'The Dynamic of International Refugee Law' (2013) 25 *International Journal of Refugee Law* 651, 657.

counsel in *HJ (Iran) and HT (Cameroon)*[39] and provides a glimpse into the world of a strategic litigation lawyer. In charting his own professional and personal engagement with strategic Sexual Orientation and Gender Identity asylum litigation, we see the work involved in bringing such cases before decision-makers and situational context of this work within the legal and LGBT+ communities.

Providing insight on the legal thinking that goes into deciding leading cases, Bruce Burson, a judge on the New Zealand Immigration and Protection Tribunal (IPT) who heard Mr Teitiota's appeal against his denial of international protection, reveals what may be seen as an example of strategic *judicial* decision-making in his contribution in chapter 15. While the New Zealand tribunal decision (subsequently endorsed by the HRC) did not itself entail a protection outcome for Mr Teitiota, Burson points out that the decision played an important role in 'critically examining the status quo' as it stood at the time, and made important advancements in challenging conventional thinking about the approach to those displaced due to the effects of disasters and climate change. The case thus laid the groundwork for future domestic consideration of protection issues in disaster contexts, as was recognised by the New Zealand Supreme Court. It also paved the way for consideration of this issue by the HRC. As Burson notes:

> There can be little doubt that the single most important significant outcome of this litigation has been to move the legal paradigm from one in which it was generally understood that international protection law does not apply to the disaster and climate context to one where it is now broadly accepted as doing just that; indeed, this was the primary ambition of the author of this chapter in writing the [tribunal] decision in *AF (Kiribati)*.[40]

Strategic action in such litigation is not limited to legal practitioners and decision-makers. Judicial rules on standing and admissibility, and the particularities of refugee-related litigation, have often necessitated a broader strategic approach to refugee litigation by civil society groups and other actors. It is notable that several cases considered in this volume were pursued by non-governmental organisations (NGOs) or other actors on behalf of refugees and asylum seekers.[41] Public interest actions brought by NGOs and other stakeholders alongside or on behalf of those

[39] *HJ (Iran), and HT (Cameroon) v Secretary of State for the Home Department* [2010] UKSC 31, [2011] 1 AC 596.

[40] Bruce Burson, '*Ioane Teitiota v New Zealand* (2020): Meeting the Challenge of Climate Change Through International Protection Law' in ch 15 of this volume.

[41] For example, Woldemariam explains that the *Kituo Cha Sheria* litigation was a consolidated petition from Kituo Cha Sheria, an NGO, and seven refugees. As non-citizens, refugees and asylum seekers in Kenya are excluded from full participation in the political life of the State, and in this context the NGO acting on behalf of refugees filled a gap. Strikingly, the lead plaintiff in the *Namah v Pato* litigation was the then leader of the political opposition in Papua New Guinea. Again, having the standing to bring this action on behalf of those subject to an offshore processing regime, as O'Sullivan notes, this 'illustrates the importance of utilising various avenues for redress in relation to offshore detention, and also the need for liberal standing rules which allow for representative complaints (individuals or groups acting as litigation representatives in the public interest)'. Woldemariam (n 11) 191; O'Sullivan (n 12) 238.

most affected are an important means for navigating restrictions on legal standing and the resource and other constraints so commonly faced by refugees and asylum seekers in a host country.[42] They also play a large role in bringing cases at crucial moments in time.

Of course, strategic litigation (or indeed any litigation) does not necessarily result in the outcome that refugee rights advocates have hoped and worked for. Some of the cases discussed in this collection are landmark for establishing important precedents on the approach to refugees' substantive and procedural rights at the regional level (*Pacheco Tineo*) or overturning a harmful line of interpretation. However, others are notable for an unhelpfully rigid interpretation of fundamental concepts, particularly of *non-refoulement*. This includes the US Supreme Court decision in *Sale v Haitian Centers Council* (examined by Meili in chapter 7) or the ECtHR in *ND and NT v Spain*[43] (which we were unable to include in this collection due to lack of space but which is discussed by Guild in chapter 8, on *Hirsi Jamaa).* As this collection went to press, the judgment of the ECtHR in *SS & Others v Italy* was issued.[44] This long-awaited decision held that the Court had no jurisdiction over Italy for 'rescue operations' carried out by Libyan vessels in co-operation with Italian authorities. This decision effectively provides a 'green light' for European States to outsource responsibility for maritime governance, regardless of the rights consequences for doing so.

II. What is a 'Landmark Case'?

Presenting a collection of landmark cases inevitably begs the question of what constitutes or designates a 'landmark case'. Our goal in this collection is to analyse cases of enduring significance to refugee protection and reflect on their contribution to the development of this field of law. We sought to profile cases addressing fundamental concepts in refugee protection, derived both from refugee law and the wider ambit of related human rights law and international law provisions. Our case selection therefore includes judicial decisions from diverse legal fora considering the most fundamental provisions of refugee law and associated protective rights, and addressing different aspects of refugees' conditions and protection needs.

In addition to thematic considerations of case selection, it was of course also essential that each case is legitimately a 'landmark' in its own right. Each case in

[42] Public interest groups have also played a significant role in much of this litigation as interveners. See, eg, the involvement of such organisations noted in chapters 1, 7, 8 and 10 of this volume.

[43] Case of *ND and NT v Spain* ECLI:CE:ECHR:2020:0213JUD000867515.

[44] *SS and Others v Italy* App no 21660/18 (ECtHR, 20 May 2025).

this volume addresses legal issues that have profound implications for the meaning and application of refugee protection; many engage with multiple rights and areas of law. These are judicial decisions that represent important moments in the development and implementation of international refugee protection. They are cases that have had significant impact within their own jurisdiction but also in most cases have generated a high degree of transnational judicial dialogue or academic commentary such that they have transcended a single jurisdiction to become truly international judgments.

Clearly, the indicia that we used to identify landmark cases could be applied to many more decisions than we have included in this volume. Required by the publisher to limit the collection to 15 cases, we had to be ruthless in our selection. Inevitably this entailed setting aside many other important cases. Ultimately, while we recognise that this is not an exhaustive set of 'landmark cases', we hope that the final selection nevertheless provides valuable insight into the different legal regimes shaping refugee protection, the diverse policies and practices that have come under legal scrutiny, and the vital role of the judiciary in giving meaning to the legal rights of refugees.

We have structured the collection in three parts: (A) The Refugee Definition, (B) Rights of Refugees and (C) Future Directions in Refugee Protection (covering concepts that push the parameters of refugee protection). This structure reflects the reality that much litigation in refugee protection clusters around a small number of provisions, notably the definition of refugee status under Article 1, the principle of *non-refoulement* in Article 33 of the Refugee Convention and in human rights law (particularly the prohibition of torture and cruel, inhuman or degrading treatment). Our case selection reflects the importance of these provisions while also considering other rights of refugees, such as the protection from penalisation for illegal entry (Article 31 of the 1951 Convention), deprivation of socio-economic rights, the realisation of rights in encampment, and procedural guarantees attached to refugee status determination and expulsion processes.

A. Part A: The Refugee Definition

Some of the decisions analysed in this collection were foundational in establishing the reach of refugee law, particularly in defining the scope of application of Article 1. This includes cases such as *Ward v Canada* and *Pushpanathan v Canada*,[45] each of which defined an interpretative approach to the application of the refugee definition that was subsequently adopted widely elsewhere (regarding the 'inclusion' definition under Article 1A(2) of the 1951 Refugee Convention and the scope of exclusion under Article 1F respectively).[46] These

[45] *Canada (Attorney General) v Ward* [1993] 2 SCR 689; *Pushpanathan v Canada (Minister of Citizenship and Immigration)* [1998] 1 SCR 982.

[46] The latter case building on the approach to the exclusion clauses laid down in *Ward*. Sarah Singer, '*Pushpanathan v Canada (Minister of Citizenship and Immigration)* [1998]: Excluding (Suspected) Criminals From Refugee Protection' in ch 5 of this volume; Storey (n 15).

were pivotal decisions in what might be considered the 'early days' of the judicial pillar of the refugee regime, when litigation of refugee law was relatively new and there was arguably greater scope to judicially define central concepts.

However, the boundaries of legal interpretation are continually evolving in response to new challenges in refugee protection. More recent 'landmark judgments' with a profound impact on the scope of refugee status include *HJ (Iran) and HT (Cameroon)* (on consideration of claims on the basis of sexual orientation), *Minister for Immigration and Multicultural Affairs v Khawar*[47] (on determining refugee claims from those fleeing gender-based persecution) and *Bolbol* (on the circumstances wherein Palestinian refugees formerly in receipt of care and assistance from the United Nations Relief and Works Agency for Palestine Refugees in the Near East can benefit from refugee status).[48] In the course of preparing this volume, important decisions handed down concerning refugee claims on gender-related persecution (*AH and FN*[49]) and sexual orientation-based persecution (*MI v Switzerland*[50]) continue to demonstrate that the scope of Article 1 is by no means conclusively settled and continues to both need and benefit from judicial clarification.

B. Part B: Rights of Refugees

Part B of this collection addresses significant areas of refugee rights, which have often been litigated in the context of key areas of executive refugee policy. Most notably these have arisen in relation to border control operations, and include consideration of protection against penalisation for irregular entry under Article 31 of the Refugee Convention (*Adimi*),[51] and states' *non-refoulement* obligations in the context of maritime interdictions (*Sale v Haitian Centres Council*; *Hirsi Jamaa*).[52] Contributions also consider refugees' rights in-country in the face of encampment policies (*Kituo Cha Sheria*), and the extent of *non-refoulement* obligations in the context of socio-economic rights deprivations (*MSS v Belgium and Greece*).[53]

These landmark cases speak to key areas of executive policy which continue to reverberate today. Accessing asylum remains a real challenge for many. The increasing trend towards engaging in bilateral and regional agreements

[47] *Minister for Immigration and Multicultural Affairs v Khawar* [2002] 14 HCA.

[48] S Chelvan, 'The Diary of a UK-based Strategic Litigation Lawyer. *HJ (Iran) and HT (Cameroon) v SSHD* [2010]: Beacon of Hope, or Template for Exclusion' in ch 3 of this volume; Natasha Yacoub, '*Minister for Immigration and Multicultural Affairs v Khawar* [2002]: Protection for Refugee Women through Transnational Jurisprudence and Feminist Advocacy in ch 2 of this volume; Stevens (n 28).

[49] *AH, FN, v Bundesamt für Fremdenwesen und Asyl*, C 608/22 & C 609/22, ECLI:EU:C:2024:828, EU: CJEU, 4 October 2024, discussed by Yacoub, ibid 48.

[50] *MI v Switzerland* App no 56390/21 (ECtHR, 12 November 2024), discussed by Chelvan (n 48) 67–69.

[51] *R v Uxbridge Magistrates Court and another ex parte Adimi* [1999] EWHC Admin 765.

[52] *Sale* (n 9); *Hirsi Jamaa and Others v Italy* ECLI:CE:ECHR:2012:0223JUD002776509. See chs 7 and 8.

[53] *Kituo Cha Sheria and Others v Attorney General* [2013] eKLR (High Court of Kenya); *MSS v Belgium and Greece* (2011) 53 EHRR 2. See chs 9 and 10.

with third states to pursue migration 'containment' strategies continues to push the limits of the *non-refoulement* principle as elucidated by the ECtHR in *Hirsi Jamaa*. Maritime governance and interdiction at sea continue to raise significant legal questions regarding state responsibility for human rights violations committed 'at a distance' and by third parties.[54] The corollary trend towards increasing securitisation, or even closure, of borders further limits the asylum space.[55] Criminalisation of irregular entry through the imposition of new penalties in Europe and elsewhere, and even outright denial of access to asylum through 'inadmissibility' processes, calls into question adherence to the Refugee Convention regime, including Article 31(1) and the principle of non-penalisation for unlawful entry by a refugee to the country of refuge. The expansion of such approaches has prompted UNHCR to issue authoritative *Guidelines on the Interpretation and Application of Article 31*, in which the agency emphasises that Article 31 is 'central to the object and purpose of the 1951 Convention and its 1967 Protocol because it ensures that refugees can gain access to international protection effectively, without being penalised for breaches of immigration and other laws' and clarifying also that penalties prohibited under Article 31(1) include criminal sanctions but also fines, restrictions on economic or social rights, and 'any discriminatory treatment or procedural detriment to the refugee'.[56] These developments are discussed by McConnachie in chapter 6 on the case of *Adimi*.[57]

The socio-economic conditions of refugees continue to be of grave concern. Significant cuts in the humanitarian funding landscape globally, in conjunction with a rise in nationalist political sentiment in the Global North and elsewhere, are driving deteriorating conditions for many refugees which may present new directions of litigation building on the holdings in cases such as *MSS v Belgium and Greece*, and *Sufi and Elmi*.[58]

C. Future Directions in Refugee Protection

Part C of this collection considers 'future directions' in refugee protection, profiling some more recent cases that have further redrawn the boundaries of protection, by clarifying the scope and application of asylum rights and procedural guarantees

[54] *SS and Others v Italy* (n 44).

[55] See, eg, *Case of ND and NT v Spain* (n 43), discussed by Guild (n 21).

[56] UNHCR, 'Guidelines on International Protection No. 14: Non-penalization of refugees on account of their irregular entry or presence and restrictions on their movements in accordance with Article 31 of the 1951 Convention relating to the Status of Refugees', HCR/GIP/24/14, 23 September 2024, paras 3 and 28.

[57] Kirsten McConnachie, '*R v Uxbridge Magistrates Court and another ex parte Adimi* [1999]: "Article 31 Must Henceforth be Honoured"' in ch 6 of this volume.

[58] *Sufi and Elmi v UK* [2011] ECHR 1045; *MSS v Belgium and Greece* (n 52). See discussion by Querton (n 21) and Evangelia (Lilian) Tsourdi and Paul McDonough, '*MSS v Belgium and Greece* (2011): The Interplay between Non-Refoulement and Refugee Protection' in ch 9 of this volume, respectively.

(Pacheco Tineo),[59] examining the extent to which 'conflict refugees' and 'climate refugees' can benefit from protection under human rights and refugee law frameworks (*Sufi and Elmi*; *Teitiota*),[60] addressing controversial policies for externalisation of asylum determination and hosting responsibilities (*Namah v Pato; AAA v SSHD*),[61] and developing new jurisdictional directions in strategic litigation by using the courts in one country to challenge policies that originate in another (*Namah v Pato*). This jurisprudence speaks to the continued relevance of refugee litigation in responding both to contemporary drivers of forced migration, and also new and emerging forms of state practice which seek to address such movements.

The import of judicial decisions in this field is set only to continue as we consider challenges to refugee protection for the future. Already, increasing practices of (and state responses to) the 'instrumentalization' of refugees and other migrants raise concerns about states' adherence to *non-refoulement* and other fundamental norms of refugee protection.[62] Developments in the use of Artificial Intelligence (AI) and other technologies to regulate refugee status determination and border management processes raise new challenges with regard to procedural standards, non-discrimination and the rights to privacy and data protection for affected individuals.[63] Further, the role of states in advancing the socio-economic rights of refugees will take on ever more significance in the context of global funding cuts shrinking the space of UN agencies and other humanitarian actors to directly support refugees in-country. This may be expected to fuel further state interest in third country processing and hosting arrangements. Set against the backdrop of changing global political, environmental and institutional precarities, the importance of judicial scrutiny of key and emerging issues of refugee protection will continue to act as a vital check on state action.

III. Landmark Cases in Context

One of the main contributions of this volume is the space to explore the long-term influence of a judicial decision. This approach allows recognition of the impact of

[59] See ch 12.

[60] See chs 11 and 15.

[61] *R (on the application of AAA (Syria) and others)* (n 35). See chs 13 and 14.

[62] 'Instrumentalization' as a term has been used to describe 'movements of persons which are forced, encouraged or facilitated with the aim of disrupting essential State functions'. UNHCR, *Legal Considerations on Asylum and Non-refoulement in the Context of 'Instrumentalization'*, 26 September 2024, 1, available at www.refworld.org/policy/legalguidance/unhcr/2024/en/148736.

[63] N Kinchin and D Mougouei, 'What Can Artificial Intelligence Do for Refugee Status Determination? A Proposal for Removing Subjective Fear' (2022) *International Journal of Refugee Law* (34)3-4, 373–97; M Pasquale Amoroso, 'Intelligent Borders: Exploring the Suitability of Artificial Intelligence Systems in Refugee Status Determination Under International Law' (2024) 43(4) *Refugee Survey Quarterly* 410–26; M Ineli Ciger, 'Artificial Intelligence and Resettlement of Refugees: Implications for the Fundamental Rights', EUI, RSC, Working Paper, 2023/44, Migration Policy Centre, available at https://cadmus.eui.eu/entities/publication/f86356ad-00c2-58e8-9abd-754aef7ccbf2.

a case beyond its legal reasoning, revealing the underlying 'stories' of these landmark cases, the influence of different actors both within and outside the court room, and the impact the decisions have had on key areas of refugee policy.

Even with the benefit of hindsight, however, the impact of a judicial decision is not always easy to pinpoint. It is certainly relevant to consider the extent to which legal reasoning in these cases has endured, whether that is demonstrated in judicial or academic citations, UNHCR guidance or other commentary. It is perhaps even more important to consider whether or to what extent the legal reasoning *should* have endured. In some cases, a judgment that was viewed as progressive at the point of issuance can be seen to have had a different impact in hindsight. Storey comments on the 'transformative' impact of many aspects of the Canadian Supreme Court's decision in *Ward*, which continues to be widely cited, remains authoritative on multiple issues, and 'furnish[es] important reference points for ongoing attempts to build a more coherent body of international refugee law'. However, Storey notes that as the case has aged 'cracks in the structure are now more evident' and '[p]aradoxically, one of the main achievements for which it was hailed at the time, namely its 'protected characteristics' approach to particular social group, now appears unduly constraining'.[64] He ponders whether the best way to celebrate this case is 'to more vigorously address weaknesses that, over time, have become more visible'.[65] Examples of such 'cracks' may also be seen in the influence of the Canadian Court's conclusions in *Pushpanathan*, which have been relied on by a range of bodies to significantly expand the personal scope of the 1951 Convention's exclusion clause in the context of the global War on Terror.[66] Tan takes a similarly nuanced view of the impact of the *AAA* judgment of the UK Supreme Court. Whilst noting the decision 'was a good day for the international protection system', Tan also notes that the Supreme Court's narrow approach in its reasoning ultimately 'raises more questions than it answers' with regard to safe third country arrangements. Indeed, Tan argues the decision has left the door open to future third country arrangements, for which there remains significant interest in Europe.[67]

Other decisions were less immediate in their impact but have matured in influence over time. Woldemariam notes that although the *Kituo Cha Sheria* decision had minimal immediate impact in driving tangible changes in refugee policy in Kenya, the decision *did* succeed in unsettling the status quo by 'promoting an alternative human rights-based approach that the judiciary, refugees, human rights advocates, non-governmental organisations and international organisations can hold onto to continue their advocacy'. This impact

[64] Storey (n 15) 37.
[65] ibid 37.
[66] Singer (n 45) Section IV.
[67] Nikolas Feith Tan, '*R (on the application of AAA and others) v Secretary of State for the Home Department* [2023]: The Limits of Externalisation and the Failed UK-Rwanda Arrangement' in ch 14 of this volume.

in shifting the national discourse has had a gradual, yet profound, influence on policy change in Kenya.[68]

Other cases have arguably yet to achieve their full potential to reshape the protection landscape. The *Teitiotia* decision was negative in relation to the individual claimant, but by recognising that cases of conflict and disaster-related displacement could engage *non-refoulement* and protection obligations in principle, has laid the groundwork for legal examination of the issue by major international agencies, academia, and opened doors to future litigation. As Burson notes in relation to the initial New Zealand tribunal decision, '[t]he decade since *AF (Kiribati)* was decided has seen an explosion in academic interest' in protection claims in this area, and the reasoning of the tribunal[69] has become central to a 'paradigm shift' in legal examination among lawyers, decision-makers and judges. Thus, Burson argues, '[a]s much as this claimant failed, the litigation provides an architecture for future claims to succeed'.[70] Similarly, Querton considers the potential for further impact to emerge from the ECtHR decision in *Sufi and Elmi*. Whilst Querton is ambivalent on the impact of the decision to date for conflict-related international protection claims in Europe, she concludes that perhaps 'the true potential of the judgment is yet to be fully realised', including its potential application in the context of international protection from returns to dire socio-economic conditions including those resulting from conflict, climate and disaster-related displacement.

'Landmark cases' arise when they offer clarity on a significant legal problem, whether that be one of interpretive uncertainty or of state non-compliance. In refugee law, these tend to be cases that are not only legally important but also politically impactful, and often entail judicial determination of the lawfulness of controversial policies. Several cases in this collection engage with forms of state practice that indicate a critical turning point in refugee policy, such as interdiction of boats at sea (*Sale*; *Hirsi Jamaa*) or extraterritorial asylum processing mechanisms (the Supreme Court of Papua New Guinea in *Namah v Pato*; the Supreme Court of the UK in *AAA v SSHD*).

Contrary to the doctrinal fiction of legal objectivity, these decisions often explicitly recognise the political context of their decision. In the UK case of *Adimi*, the Divisional Court demanded that the Government take action to prevent the prosecution of refugees for false document offences ('It must be hoped that these challenges will mark a turning point in the Crown's approach to the prosecution of refugees for travelling on false passports. Article 31 must henceforth be honoured'). Similarly, in the landmark *AAA* decision, in assessing the UK-Rwanda asylum arrangement, the UK Supreme Court made a pointed critique of the unduly deferential approach shown in the High Court's earlier decision.[71] Yet both of these cases were followed by subsequent executive action to reduce their impact. The Nationality and Borders

[68] Woldemariam (n 11) 181.
[69] Referring to the identification of factual scenarios.
[70] Querton (n 21) 211.
[71] Tan (n 66) 257.

Act 2022 was adopted with the explicit intention to 'confine the scope' of Article 31 non-penalisation obligations,[72] while the Safety of Rwanda Act 2024 avoided the Supreme Court's ruling by creating a legal fiction that Rwanda was a safe third country and every decision-maker, court and tribunal 'must conclusively treat' it as such.[73]

At the other end of the spectrum of relations between executive and judiciary, Meili comments that, seen in its political, social and racial context, the US *Sale* decision provides a 'sobering glimpse' of how courts have shaped restrictive national refugee policies. Concerning an early example of 'exploitative bilateral agreements between countries of the Global North and Global South', the US Supreme Court did not see its role as to challenge the US maritime interdiction policy, and rather took a deferential approach to executive action framed as a national security initiative.[74] Demonstrating the direct impact of legal decisions on policy design, Meili notes that the US Supreme Court's decision in *Sale* has 'created juridical cover for a range of new mechanisms designed to allow states to deny access to the asylum determination process' and 'helped foster an atmosphere of tolerance for a range of externalization of border measures most likely not contemplated in the early 1990s'.[75]

A markedly different approach to the role of the courts and the application of jurisdiction in maritime interdiction policies was taken by the ECtHR in *Hirsi Jamaa*. In that case, concerning arrangements between Italy and Libya, the Court found that Italy's *non-refoulement* obligations *did* extend to its interdiction activities, and Italy could not evade its own responsibility by relying on the bilateral agreements between the countries. The decisions in *Sale* and in *Hirsi Jamaa* demonstrate opposing judicial interpretations of the parameters of *non-refoulement* and the lawfulness of maritime interdictions. However, while the *Hirsi Jamaa* decision was immensely significant in clarifying states' obligations to refugees and in this respect 'changed the political and legal landscape of Europe', Guild notes how European states reacted with a variety of measures to avoid the full impact of the decision. Thus, while the *Hirsi* judgment stopped Italy's practice of 'pushbacks' (in which migrant boat passengers were brought on board Italian flag vessels in the Mediterranean and returned to their port of departure in Libya) it did not stop the practice of interdiction at sea and return to Libya. Rather, it led Italy and other European states to 'outsource' the return process to Libyan authorities to conduct 'pull backs' on Europe's behalf. This practice became the subject of further litigation to the ECtHR, in the case of *SS & Others v Italy* – which, as noted above, is another landmark decision on maritime governance by the European Court, this time unfortunately by applying a restrictive interpretation of jurisdiction and state responsibility.[76]

[72] M Gower, *Article 31 of the Refugee Convention* (House of Commons Library Research Briefing 2021); UK Parliament, *Nationality and Borders Act Explanatory Notes* at 21, 23, 161.

[73] Safety of Rwanda (Asylum and Immigration) Act 2024, s 2.

[74] Meili (n 10) 128–129.

[75] ibid 142.

[76] *SS and Others v Italy* (n 44).

Similarly contradictory consequences can be seen in relation to another ECtHR decision, *MSS v Belgium and Greece*. By determining that states' *non-refoulement* obligations are engaged in cases of extreme socio-economic deprivation, and by refuting the use of a 'blind' presumption of trust between EU Member States, the Court established the need for judicial scrutiny of 'Dublin' transfers between EU Member States under the CEAS. This had an immediate impact in halting transfers to Greece and was affirmed in subsequent EU legislation. However, Tsourdi and McDonough argue that the decision in *MSS* also left many questions unanswered, which has had a damaging effect on refugee protection in subsequent litigation and carries the risk of fragmenting human rights obligations towards asylum seekers between EU Member States and wider Council of Europe members.

These decisions touch not only on domestic political policies but address important areas of global geopolitics. This is particularly evident for areas of policy involving what might be viewed as exploitative refugee arrangements between developing nations and more powerful neighbours in the Global North. The case of *Namah v Pato* is unusual (thus far) as litigation seeking redress in an offshore 'destination' state rather than the sending state. O'Sullivan's analysis shows that the decision might be considered to demonstrate both the value and limitations of this approach. In challenging a bilateral agreement between Papua New Guinea (PNG) and Australia implementing Australia's offshore processing policy, the PNG Supreme Court sought to address an accountability gap[77] and bind not only the PNG but also the Australian Government. The decision ultimately 'had no legal implications for the constitutional and legislative underpinnings of the offshore processing regime operated under the authority of Australian law'. However, considered against the context of power and international relations between the Global North and Global South, the decision has considerable symbolic value. O'Sullivan comments that, in its (post)colonial context it 'could be said that the decision in *Namah* represents an act by a colonised state (PNG) to push-back on the power and influence by its former coloniser (Australia)'.[78] Ultimately however, whilst the PNG Supreme Court's decision led to the closure of the Manus Island detention centre, detainees were transferred to transit accommodation centres elsewhere in PNG rather than transferred back to Australia. In this respect, whilst a positive and valuable decision in utilising constitutional provisions to protect the rights of asylum seekers and refugees, 'one could question whether the decision resulted in a substantial improvement of the conditions of the detained asylum seekers'.[79]

O'Sullivan's conclusion resonates across many of the analyses in this volume and speaks to both the opportunities and limits of the legal process. However impactful a judicial decision is at its point of adoption, as Storey tells us, '[s]ooner

[77] O'Sullivan notes numerous legal challenges to the offshore policy within Australia had been unsuccessful. O'Sullivan (n 12) 232.

[78] ibid 247.

[79] ibid 242.

or later, all landmark cases become ruined temples'.[80] Even the most powerful cases eventually diminish in influence, whether because they are overturned, revoked by legislation or superseded by changing societal context. The struggle between judiciary and executive is a recurring theme in the analyses in this volume, reflecting both the intrinsic character of law as a site of struggle and the politically febrile nature of refugee law and policy. And yet, however flawed and fragile it may be, as this collection demonstrates, the rule of law and an independent judiciary remains one of the strongest tools for the protection of refugees.

[80] Storey (n 15) 25.

PART A

The Refugee Definition

1

Canada (Attorney General) v Ward [1993]: Refugee Law's Parthenon

HUGO STOREY*

I. Introduction

It is hard to think of a refugee law case more landmark than *Canada (Attorney-General) v Ward* (hereafter *Ward*).[1] It accelerated a step-change in

* The author would like to thank James Simeon, Lorne Waldman and Sarah Singer for their suggestions and comments on an earlier draft.

[1] *Canada (Attorney General) v Ward* (hereafter *Ward*) [1993] 2 SCR 689. Key materials relating to *Ward* (in chronological order) include: J Hathaway, *The Law of Refugee Status* (Butterworths, 1991) (hereafter Hathaway, 1991); DBN Bagambire, 'Terrorism and Convention Refugee Status in Canadian Immigration Law. The Social Group Category according to Ward v. Canada' (1993) 5 *International Journal of Refugee Law* 183; LE Tranter, 'A Step Forward in Protecting Human Rights: *Canada v. Ward*' (1993) 13:4 *Refuge* 16 at 16; N Mawani, 'Introduction to the Immigration and Refugee Board of Canada Guidelines on Gender-Related Persecution' (1993) 5 *International Journal of Refugee Law* 240; for the text of the Guidelines, see 5 (1993) *International Journal of Refugee Law* 278; A Macklin, 'Canada(Attorney-General) v Ward: Review Essay' (1994) 6 *International Journal of Refugee Law* 3, 362–81; R Shacter, 'The Cases of Ward and Chan' (Fall/Winter 1997) *Osgood Hall Law Journal* 35.3/4, 723–36; J Carlier et al, *Who Is a Refugee? A Comparative Case Law Study* (Brill, 1997); GS Goodwin-Gill, 'Judicial Reasoning and "Social Group" after Islam and Shah' (1999) 11 *International Journal of Refugee Law* 538; P Zambelli, 'Problematic Trends in the Analysis of State Protection and Article 1F(a) Exclusion in Canadian Refugee Law' (2011) 23 *International Journal of Refugee Law* 252; A Fortin, 'The Meaning of Protection in the Refugee Definition (2000) 12(4) *International Journal of Refugee Law* 548; H Lambert, 'The Conceptualisation of 'Persecution' by the House of Lords: Horvath v SSHD' (2001) 13 *International Journal of Refugee Law* 16 at 20; K Daley and N Kelley, 'Particular Social Group: A Human Rights Approach in Canadian Jurisprudence' (2002) 12(2) *International Journal of Refugee Law*; TA Aleinikoff, 'Protected Characteristics and Social Perceptions: An Analysis of the Meaning of "Membership of a Particular Social Group"' in E Feller, V Türk, and F Nicholson (eds), *Refugee Protection in International Law: UNHCR's Global Consultations on International Protection* (Cambridge University Press, 2003); M Bossin and L Demirdache, 'A Canadian Perspective on the Subjective Component of the Bipartite Test for 'Persecution': Time for Re-evaluation' (2004) 22(1) *Refugee: Canada's Journal on Refugees* 108; E Arbel, 'The Culture of Rights Protection in Canadian Refugee Law: Examining the Domestic Violence Cases' (2013) *Refuge* 58:3. C Dauvergne, 'How the Charter Has Failed Non-citizens in Canada: Reviewing Thirty Years of Supreme Court of Canada Jurisprudence' (2013) *McGill Law Journal* 58:3; R Zinn and B Perryman, 'The Impact of International Law and Domestic Human Rights Law on Canada's Judicial Supervision of the 1951 Refugee Convention' in JC Simeon (ed), *The UNHCR and the Supervision of International Refugee Law* (Cambridge University Press, 2013); I Greene, The

international understanding of the inclusion clauses of the 1951 Convention relating to the Status of Refugees (Refugee Convention).[2] It is one of very few cases to transcend national and regional boundaries.[3] It is perhaps most oft-cited for its statements about particular social group, but its scope and legacy go far beyond that. It brought to the fore the notion of surrogacy as an overarching principle. It identified non-discrimination as one of the Convention's primary objects and purposes. It provided the first proclamation at a supreme court level of the human rights approach to the refugee definition. It also had important things to say about most of the key elements of the Refugee Convention's inclusion clauses: nationality, persecution, protection, Convention reasons, and the individual reasons of particular social group and political opinion. It also laid down an important marker for the proper approach to the exclusion clauses.

The *Ward* case also exemplifies some of the major internal constituents of a foundational judgment: the Court made sure it had before it not only materials from the United Nations High Commissioner for Refugees (UNHCR), but also decisions from other countries, and a wide range of academic sources, including the three most influential monographs of the time: studies by Grahl-Madsen, Goodwin-Gill and Hathaway;[4] there was no dispute about the facts (the Court found Ward an entirely credible witness); there were interveners (the Canadian Council of Refugees,[5] and UNHCR (the latter in written form)). Externally, it has been and still is one of the most frequently cited cases in both the case law

Charter of Rights and Freedoms: 30+ Years of Decision that Shaped Canadian Life (James Lorimer & Co Ltd, 2014); S Meili, 'When do Human Rights Treaties Help Asylum Seekers?' (2014) 51 (2) *Osgood Hall Law Journal*; J Hathaway and M Foster, *The Law of Refugee Status*, 2nd edn (Cambridge University Press, 2014) 295–96; 303–306; SY Kneebone, 'Refugees as Objects of Surrogate Protection: Shifting Identities' in SY Kneebone, D Stevens, and L Baldassar (eds), *Refugee Protection and the Role of Law: Conflicting Identities* (Routledge, 2014); B Burson B and D Cantor, 'Introduction: Interpreting the Refugee Definition via Human Rights Standards' in B Burson and D Cantor (eds), *Human Rights and the Refugee Definition* (Brill Nijhoff, 2016); J Simeon, 'The Human Rights Bases of Refugee Protection in Canada' in Burson and Cantor (eds), ibid; D Cantor, 'Defining Refugees: Persecution, Surrogacy and the Human Rights Paradigm' in Burson and Cantor (eds), ibid; L Waldman, *The Definition of Convention Refugee*, 2nd edn (Lexis Nexis, 2019); P Zambelli, 'Knowing Persecution: Non-State Actors and the Measure of State Protection' (2020) 32(1) *International Journal of Refugee Law* 28; H Storey, 'The Human Rights Approach: Rising Sun or Falling Star' (2021) 33(3) *International Journal of Refugee Law* 379; GS Goodwin-Gill and J McAdam, *The Refugee in International Law*, 4th edn (Oxford University Press, 2021); H Storey, *The Refugee Definition in International Law* (Oxford University Press, 2023).

[2] UN General Assembly, 1951 Convention relating to the Status of Refugees, United Nations, Treaty Series, 189:137, 28 July 1951.

[3] eg cited with approval by the UK House of Lords in *Horvath v Secretary of State for the Home Department* [2000] UKHL 37 and by the Australian High Court in *S152/2003* (2004) 222 CLR 1. In correspondence with the author, judges from several civil law countries, including Germany, have related that even though the case is not cited in their national judicial decisions, it was often discussed during deliberations on asylum cases.

[4] *Ward* (n 1) 14–15; A Grahl-Madsen, *The Status of Refugees in International Law. Volume II: Asylum, Entry and Sojourn* (Sijthoff, 1972); GS Goodwin-Gill, *The Refugee in International Law*, 1st edn (Oxford University Press, 1983); Hathaway, 1991 (n 1).

[5] See further Shacter (n 1).

(certainly in the common law world)[6] and the wider literature. It is truly thus refugee law's Parthenon.

This chapter proceeds with an outline of the (unusual) facts of the *Ward* case and then moves on to consider some of the background reasons why such a case came to be decided at apex court level in Canada when it did, and what was happening at the time in refugee law globally.

There is then interrogation of the decision in a contemporary context, it being noted that despite the efflux of time, there are several key aspects that continue to provide at least important reference points today. These points are then critically examined in turn: the principle of surrogacy; the human rights approach, including to defining persecution; the approach to protection; the bipartite approach to well-founded fear; the approach to the Convention reasons of particular social group and political opinion; multiple nationality; and exclusion.

After a brief reflection on what would be the position of a *Ward*-type applicant were he to apply for asylum in Canada today, the chapter offers overall conclusions, arguing that whilst remaining mindful of its enduring strengths, the best way to celebrate this case should be to more vigorously address its weaknesses.

II. Summary of the *Ward* Case and Decision

An ardent republican, Ward had been convicted in 1982 in Northern Ireland by a special court for possessing firearms, conspiracy to convey things unlawfully into Northern Ireland and contributing to acts of terrorism. In 1983 he joined the Irish National Liberation Army (INLA), a para-military terrorist group that had broken away from the IRA. Shortly after, INLA had assigned him to guard two hostages. When he heard the group's leadership had decided to execute the hostages, he felt driven by his conscience to help secure their escape. After delivering the hostages to a police station, he went back to Northern Ireland. When he returned to the Republic for a wedding, the INLA kidnapped him. After being tortured and court-martialled by the group's leadership, he managed to escape and sought police protection. The Irish police charged him for his part in the hostage incident and sentenced him to three years in jail. Towards the end of his prison sentence, Ward sought the assistance of a prison chaplain for protection from INLA members. The chaplain, with co-operation of police, obtained a Republic of Ireland passport for him and airline tickets to Canada. He arrived in Toronto in December 1985.

In Canada Ward's claim for refugee status was rejected, but he was successful on appeal to the Immigration Appeal Board (IAB). That decision was set aside by the Federal Court of Appeal (FCA) in 1990, but in 1993 the Canadian Supreme

[6] Hathaway and Foster (n 1) 294.

Court (SC) overruled the FCA. Allowing Ward's appeal, the SC held: (1) that persecution 'includes situations where the state is not in strictness an accomplice to the persecution but is simply unable to protect its citizens'; (2) Ward had not established a Convention ground of particular social group; (3) he had, however, established a Convention ground of imputed political opinion; and (4) Ward having conceded dual nationality, the Board had erred in failing to address this matter properly, therefore his case had to go back to the Board for it to investigate whether he was unable or unwilling to avail himself of the protection of both countries of nationality.

It should be mentioned that around the time Ward had been sentenced by the Irish courts for being involved in forcibly detaining hostages, the INLA abducted his wife and children. They were eventually released upon his assurance that he would not himself turn 'supergrass' with respect to the kidnapping of the other hostages.

The SC decision to send his case back to the IAB (now the Immigration and Refugee Board (IRB)) did not go well for Ward. In 1994 the IRB decided that as he would be safe in his second country of nationality (within England), he did not qualify as a Convention refugee. There then followed a drawn-out series of challenges to removal orders made against him. Eventually, on 7 January 1997, the FCA concluded that there was no risk that he would suffer irreparable harm in England. Upholding execution of the deportation order, the Court noted, inter alia, that after 12 appearances before various courts and tribunals, he had exhausted all possible arguments.[7]

III. Decision in Context

Despite being an unusual case on the facts (Ward claiming to fear persecution in two western democracies, Ireland and the United Kingdom (UK)),[8] the SC saw fit to raise several general issues relating to the refugee definition. Why a case of such panoramic scope emerged in Canada when it did, is a question of some interest. Factors likely include: that at that time Canada was strongly internationalist in outlook, having ratified all major UN human rights treaties[9] and having also enacted the Canadian Charter of Rights and Freedoms in 1982; and that in 1985, in the *Singh* case, the SC had interpreted the 1951 Refugee Convention's framework of rights in light of the Charter.[10] Canada had also become internationally known for a positive approach to refugees. Its legislation required Refugee Status

[7] *Ward v Canada* (MCI) [1997] FCJ No 86.

[8] In *Zalzali* Can FCA, 1991 at 611, Decary J appeared to think that the facts in *Ward* (then at the FCA level) were too 'exceptional' to resolve general questions, including the complicity issue.

[9] For list of Canadian ratifications, see Simeon, 2016 (n 1) 90.

[10] *Singh v Canada (Minister of Employment and Immigration)* [1985] 1 SCR 177, 17 DLR (4th) 422, 58 NR 1.There had been an earlier SC decision, *Kwiatkowsky v Minister of Employment and Immigration* [1982] 2 SCR 856, dealing with the standard of proof applicable in refugee cases.

Determination (RSD) to uphold Canada's 'humanitarian tradition'.[11] A few years earlier, in 1986, the Canadian people had been awarded the Nansen Medal in recognition of the support for refugees fleeing the Southeast Asian Refugee Movement and Humanitarian Response. In the same year as the *Ward* judgment, the IRB had formally recognised that gender can ground a claim for refugee status, and released its ground-breaking Guidelines on this subject.[12] The SC judge who penned the decision, Justice La Forest, was a notable scholar in his own right.[13]

Ward was not the first major case in refugee law. In Europe and in several other countries, courts and tribunals had already begun to carve out a new role as interpreters of the 1951 Refugee Convention, and to lay the foundation stones for what has become the 'judicial pillar', to stand alongside the UNHCR pillar, the latter which, through its 1979 Handbook, had previously been the only significant source of interpretive guidance on the refugee definition.[14] And even though it was the first case on the refugee definition dealt with by the Canadian SC, its 1985 decision in the *Singh* case had ruled that refugees have fundamental rights in Canada.[15] In addition, other levels of the Canadian court system, aided by the IAB (the predecessor to the IRB), had started to develop a significant body of case law, which meant that the SC already had multiple reference points. There were already a significant number of Canadian FCA cases and Board decisions seeking to draw on international human rights and Canadian Charter standards and to push for different interpretations of various elements of the refugee definition drawing on these.[16] The SC too had also begun to identify ways in which the Canadian Charter could impact on the rights of non-citizens.[17]

In the wider world, the collapse of the Soviet Union in 1991 was causing major realignments; in developed countries, liberalism was in the ascendant.

IV. Reflecting on the *Ward* Decision Today

Sooner or later, all landmark cases become ruined temples. Few major cases in refugee law age particularly well. That is a tribute to the dynamic state of this area

[11] The Immigration Act 1976, para 3(g) recognises Canada's need to fulfil its 'international legal obligations with respect to refugees and to uphold its humanitarian tradition with respect to the displaced and persecuted'.

[12] IRB Guidelines Issued by the Chairperson Pursuant to s 65(4) of the Immigration Act: Guideline 4 – *Women Refugee Claimants Fearing Gender-Related Persecution*, 9 March 1993; Mawani (n 1); for the text of the Guidelines, see ibid, 278.

[13] See www.scc-csc.ca/media-medias/new-nouveautes/2025-06-13-3/.

[14] Storey, 2021 (n 1) 51–53.

[15] *Singh* (n 10). Refugee Rights Day in Canada is celebrated on 4th April each year to recognise the *Singh* decision. According to James Simeon, in a communication with the author, this decision led to the establishment of the IRB of Canada.

[16] Hathaway, 1991 (n 1) 60, 113 furnishes a number of examples, including in relation to persecution and state protection. Mention should also be made of two other cases, both landmark in their own right, *Zalzali* (n 8) and *Zolfagharkhani v Canada (MEI)* [1993] FCJ No 584 (CA).

[17] *Andres v Law Society British Columbia* [1989] 1 SCR 143, 56 DLR (4th).

of law and is what should be expected, given the constant need to reconsider issues in the light of new situations. Academic commentators at the time hailed the *Ward* decision as 'laudably progressive in many respects' but noted also that:

> Like any judicial pronouncement, however, the Ward decision is reactive, dependent on the particular facts of the case, and reflects the orientation of the specific and collective judicial mindset from which it emerges. As such, it is not free from ambiguity, problematic pronouncements, and acute gaps in reasoning.[18]

Nevertheless, within Canada the *Ward* case is still heavily cited[19] and, more widely, certain key aspects of the *Ward* case still either hold up to scrutiny or continue to provide at least relevant reference points. When setting these out, I will also offer some observations about their respective efficacy.

A. Principle of Surrogacy

Drawing on the analysis of James Hathaway, whose seminal book, *The Law of Refugee Status*, had been published two years earlier,[20] La Forest concluded that:

> International refugee law was formulated to serve as a back-up to the protection owed a national by his or her state. It was meant to come into play only in situations where that protection is unavailable, and then only in certain situations. The international community intended that persecuted individuals be required to approach their home state for protection before the responsibility of other states becomes engaged.[21]

La Forest saw this principle as 'permeat[ing] the interpretation of the various terms requiring examination'.[22] There has since, of course, been significant disagreement with the identification of such a principle,[23] but whether or not such disagreement is well-founded, this proclamation in *Ward* was to gain wider endorsement in the UK case law,[24] eg in *Horvath*,[25] and *HJ(Iran)*;[26] and it quite likely had an influence on the apparent adoption of this principle by the European Union (EU) Commission and by the Court of Justice of the European Union (CJEU) in

[18] Macklin (n 1) 373.

[19] See IRB, 2020 Interpretation (n 1) chapters 1, 3, 4, 5, 6. At 1.4 they list 14 items of general interpretation that came out of *Ward*.

[20] Hathaway, 1991 (n 1).

[21] *Ward* (n 1) 33–34.

[22] ibid 33–34.

[23] See, eg, Goodwin-Gill and McAdam (n 1) 8–9; GS Goodwin-Gill, 'Current Challenges in Refugee Law' in J-P Gauci et al (eds), *Exploring the Boundaries of Refugee Law* (Brill Nijhoff, 2015) 11–12. See further Storey, 2023 (n 1) 149–50, 163–65, 194.

[24] Lord Keith had already endorsed it in *R v Secretary of State for the Home Department, Ex parte Sivakumaran* [1988] 1 AC 958, 992–93.

[25] *Horvath* (n 3) (per Lord Hooper, 3 and Lord Clyde, 17).

[26] *HJ(Iran) and HT(Cameroon) v Secretary of State for the Home Department* [2010] UKSC 31 (per Lord Hope, 13, per Lord Rodger, 52).

Abdullah and *LW*.[27] The underlying position taken is that applicants cannot expect to be granted international protection if they can avail themselves of national protection.

B. Human Rights Approach

Again, with reference to Hathaway (and Goodwin-Gill), La Forest went on to state that the boundaries of 'many' of the elements of the refugee definition were set by the underlying theme of human rights. He wrote:

> 'Persecution', for example, undefined in the Convention, has been ascribed the meaning of 'sustained or systemic violation of basic human rights demonstrative of a failure of state protection'; see Hathaway, *supra*, at pp. 104–105 …

The Court also identified the object and purpose '[u]nderlying the Convention [to be] the international community's commitment to the assurance of basic human rights without discrimination'.

Such observations constituted the first known statement at supreme court level of a human rights approach to the refugee definition. In so framing things, however, La Forest was not operating in a vacuum. The SC in *Singh* (as noted earlier) had construed the Refugee Convention rights in terms of Canadian Charter norms;[28] and both the Board and the FCA in some cases had begun referencing human rights norms as the applicable standard for assessing persecution and/or the Convention reasons;[29] albeit never in such programmatic or framework terms. Even though La Forest did not expressly apply a Vienna Convention on the Law of Treaties (VCLT) approach to interpretation, his analysis reveals a strong emphasis on the Convention's context and object and purpose as reflected in the 1951 Convention's preambular reference to human rights. *Ward* was undoubtedly a major influence upon the UK House of Lords's decision several years later in *Horvath* to endorse

[27] See, eg, Commission Proposal (2001) COM (2001) 510, 18; Joined Cases C-175/08, C-176/08, C-178/08 *Abdullah* ECLI:EU:C:2010:105, in which the CJEU stated at [68] that 'the circumstances which demonstrate the country of origin's inability or, conversely, its ability to ensure protection against acts of persecution constitute a crucial element in the assessment which leads to the granting of, or, as the case may be, by means of the opposite conclusion, to the cessation of refugee status'. In Case C-91/20 *LW v Bundesrepublik Deutschland* [2021] ECLI:EU:C:2021:898 [33], the same Court ruled that 'an applicant who is a national of more than one third country is considered to be deprived of protection only if he or she cannot or, because of the fear of being persecuted, does not wish to avail himself or herself of the protection of any of those countries'. In [32] it described this as an 'expression of the principle of the subsidiarity of international protection'.

[28] See *Singh* (n 10).

[29] Hathaway, 1991 (n 1) himself submitted at 108 that 'refugee law ought to concern itself with actions that deny human dignity in any key way', and that the sustained and systemic denial of core human rights is the appropriate standard was a position that 'has been specifically endorsed in the Canadian case law'. He cited as examples *Felix Salatiel Nunez Veloso*, IAB Decision 79-1017, Aug 24 1979; *Jose del Rosario Perez Gomez*, IAB Decision M79-1179, June 2, 1980; and *Jose Mariano Aguilar Vides*, IAB Decision M83-1009, Feb 3, 1983.

the same approach;[30] and also upon the drafting of the EU Qualification Directive of 2004 and its 2011 recast,[31] whose Article 9 defines acts of persecution in human rights terms.

The Court's adoption of a human rights approach has rightly been hailed by numerous commentators.[32] The decision did not of course address the specificities of this approach, but by expressly approving Hathaway's formulation, the Court appeared to send a clear message to decision-makers to have close regard to the latter's more detailed development of it.

However, in terms of subsequent Canadian case law, three things stand out. First, in actual fact very little of the pre-*Ward* Canadian case law applied a human rights understanding of persecution, featuring instead reliance on dictionary definitions,[33] or the 'circumstantial' or enumerative approach adopted by the 1979 UNHCR Handbook.[34] Second, case law post-*Ward* has rarely applied the human rights approach in any express way, save in clear cases of violations of non-derogable human rights.[35] The same can indeed be said for UK case law post-*Horvath*, and indeed to this day the only country to have systematically applied a human rights approach is New Zealand.[36] Third, the human rights approach has nevertheless become, world-wide, the dominant approach.[37] These features are best further analysed by reference to the approach to persecution.

C. Human Rights Approach to Persecution

The failure of Canadian decision-makers who had endorsed *Ward*'s human rights approach to apply it in systematic fashion to persecution is worth reflecting on. It conveys perhaps that its enunciation was felt too programmatic and unqualified to be workable.[38] So much is suggested by, for example, the subsequent position

[30] *Horvath* (n 3) 3, 6.

[31] Directive 2011/95/EU of the European Parliament and of the Council of 13 December 2011 on standards for the qualification of third-country nationals or stateless persons as beneficiaries of international protection, for a uniform status for refugees or for persons eligible for subsidiary protection, and for the content of the protection granted (recast) (QD(recast)) [2011] OJ L337/9.

[32] See, eg, Tranter (n 1) 16.

[33] *Rajudeen v MEI* (1984) 55 NR 129 133; *Arguello-Garcia v Canada (MEI)* [1991] FCJ No 635, 21 Imm L R (2d) 285 (TD).

[34] UNHCR, *Handbook on Procedures and Criteria for Determining Refugee Status and Guidelines on International Protection under the 1951 Convention and the 1967 Protocol Relating to the Status of Refugees* (Geneva, 1979, reissued in 2019) para 52.

[35] As noted by Meili (n 1) 627–72 and Simeon, 2016 (n 1) 106–108; this also appears borne out by the IRB, 2020 Interpretation (n 1) survey.

[36] Storey, 2023 (n 1) 146, 175.

[37] ibid 135, 140.

[38] The suggestion made here is similar to the first and third of four reasons proffered by Meili (n 1) 632–51: (to paraphrase) lack of awareness, resources or time; focus on the Convention itself; 'human rights fatigue'; and greater robustness of the Refugee Convention. Among others, Simeon, 2016 (n 2) 107–108, considers that once the influence of domestic human rights law is factored in, it remains that Canadian case law 'rests firmly on human rights law'.

struck in both the Canadian, UK and Australian case law regarding the requirement that the denial of core human rights had to be 'sustained and systemic'; this was seen to be too onerous a test, since persecution could arise without it necessarily being sustained or systemic.[39] Further, Article 9 of the EU Qualification Directive does not rely on Hathaway's 1991 four-fold hierarchical model of obligations; and Hathaway himself went on to renounce his 1991 approach.[40] Outside of the EU, there remain diverse approaches to the use, or extent of the use, of human rights norms for interpreting persecution.[41] That said, the Canadian SC in a 2023 decision reaffirmed that international norms are essential interpretive aids in administrative decision-making.[42]

D. Approach to Protection

La Forest closely linked the issue of protection with the 'well-founded fear of being persecuted' limb of the definition. He made clear that for acts to constitute persecution, it was not enough that they inflicted serious harm; it had also to be shown that they did so in ways that demonstrated a failure of state protection. Again, this was not a novel position in Canada,[43] but it co-existed with contrary approaches (which required state complicity); and prior attempts to give it a clear analytical underpinning struggled to find a way to ground such an understanding in the wording of Article 1A(2).[44] This understanding of there being a close interrelationship between persecution and protection has gained wide acceptance.[45] La Forest was also adamant that whatever combined reading was given to the 'unable' and 'unwilling' criteria, the key issue was what the state could provide internally by way of protection.[46]

The SC's take on the accepted facts in Ward necessitated a reconceptualisation of the notion of protection: after all, its ratio was that there could be some individuals (such as Ward) whom even democratic states could not protect.

Also notable was that the Court in *Ward* expressly rejected the view that in order to establish inadequate state protection, claimants had to show they had

[39] IRB, 2020 Interpretation (n 1) ch 3.6. For the UK and Australian case law, see Storey, 2023 (n 1) 388–99.

[40] Hathaway and Foster (n 1) 203.

[41] Cantor (n 1) 378–91; Storey, 2023 (n 1) 150–51, 166–68.

[42] *Mason v Canada (Citizenship and Immigration)* 2023 SCC 21 [72].

[43] Hathaway, 1991 (n 1) 129 mentions, inter alia, the case of *Surujpal v MEI* (1985) 60 NR 73 (FCA). At 129–32 he also cites *Rajudeen* [(n 24)] in support and the dissenting opinion of MacGuigan in the FCA decision in *Ward*.

[44] See *Zalzali* (n 8) 612–13 (another pre-*Ward* case in which Hathaway was cited with approval).

[45] See Lambert (n 1) 16 at 20; Hathaway and Foster (n 1) 295–96, 303–306. See also Case C- 255/ 19 *Secretary of State for the Home Department v OA* [2021] ECLI:EU:C:2021:36 [57]. For the opposing view, see Storey, 2023 (n 1) 424–42.

[46] *Ward* (n 1) 34–36, 45–51. The Court referenced the analysis of Justice Decary in *Zalzali* (n 8) which made clear at 614 that the concept of being 'unable' could potentially apply to a significant range of circumstances.

exhausted all domestic remedies. That, observed La Forest, went too far and he approved the more qualified test set out by Hathaway of whether state protection 'might reasonably be forthcoming'.[47] There is now a preponderance of authority that is in agreement and *Ward* is indeed oft cited as a case clearly recognising this.[48] Yet it seems the contrary view has nevertheless dogged some Canadian case law since and remains a sometimes fraught issue more widely.[49] Perhaps illustrative of the fact that precedents do not, however, always rule the roost even in common law countries, Hathaway and Foster note that notwithstanding *Ward*, reliance on an exhaustion of domestic remedies rule has been 'strikingly prevalent' in Canada.[50]

With hindsight, *Ward* can be seen to have sounded the death knell for what is known as the 'accountability' approach, according to which persecution could only arise if there was some involvement of the state, direct or indirect.[51] What is particularly interesting about La Forest's rejection of the majority view at the FCA level (for whom persecution required state complicity) is his analysis of how this position, under pressure because it left obvious protection gaps, had already had to shift to effectively empty the complicity requirement of any substantive meaning. Although a significant number of countries, including Germany, France, the Netherlands, Austria and Switzerland continued for some years to cleave to the accountability approach,[52] *Ward*'s carefully crafted reasons for rejecting it, alongside the position already expressed by the courts in the United States,[53] saw opinions shift to such an extent that within Europe, by 2004 the Qualification Directive included a specific recognition in Article 6 of non-state actors of persecution.[54]

At the same time, the conception of state protection advanced in *Ward* remained locked in a state-centric mind-set. For La Forest the principle that a state should normally be expected to protect its own citizens entailed that there should be a presumption of state protection, which claimants had to rebut. This was stated to require (except where there was no functioning government) 'clear

[47] *Ward* (n 1) 56.

[48] ibid; Hathaway and Foster (n 1) 324.

[49] Hathaway and Foster (n 1) 324, although their survey of the case law does note a number of cases rejecting such a proposition. Waldman (n 1) 280–86 cites several cases that have applied this presumption in a restrictive way.

[50] Hathaway and Foster (n 1) 324.

[51] R Marx, 'The Notion of Persecution by Non-State Agents in German Jurisprudence' (2001) 15 *Georgetown Immigration Law Journal* 447, at 453.

[52] See *R v SSHD, ex p Adan* [2001] 2 AC 477 (UKHL); *TI v United Kingdom* App no 43844/ 98 (ECtHR, 7 March 2000); W Kalin, 'Non-State Agents of Persecution and the Inability of the State to Protect (2001) 15 *Georgetown Immigration Law Journal* 415; C Phuong, 'Persecution by Non-State Agents: Comparative Judicial Interpretations of the 1951 Refugee Convention' (2003) 4 *European Journal of Migration & Law* 521; European Council on Refugees and Exiles, 'Research Paper on Non-State Agents of Persecution' (*European Legal Network on Asylum*, 1998, updated 1 September 2000), cited Hathaway and Foster (n 1) 303–304.

[53] Hathaway and Foster (n 1) 306.

[54] QD(recast) (n 31).

and convincing proof of a state's inability to protect …', thus creating an evidentiary as well as a legal burden.[55] As Waldman among others have noted, reliance on a presumption of state protection still persists in Canadian case law (sometimes tied to the issue of the extent to which the country of origin is a democracy),[56] although there is now more focus on whether protection is effective in the individual case.[57]

Also evident in La Forest's opinion is a disinclination to reject outright the position that a state can be considered to protect if it is doing its best. It is interesting that Lod Clyde in the UK House of Lords in *Horvath* drew on *Ward* to support his view that the focus should be on whether a state shows 'reasonable willingness' to operate a machinery for detection, prosecution and punishment through the criminal law of acts constituting persecution; or takes reasonable steps to protect (a view that can be seen to have influenced the wording of Article 7 of the 2004 Qualification Directive). Zambelli, among others, has noted that even post-*Ward*, Canadian jurisprudence has seen broad protective measures taken in a state's legislation to 'trump police inaction, neglect or even ridicule in the cases of battered women from the Caribbean, homosexuals from Mexico, Roma from Hungary and Shia Muslims from Pakistan, respectively'.[58] Put another way, *Ward* reads as a decision that has not fully understood the importance of the need for protection to be effective.[59] And indeed, in Europe at least, it was only in 2011, in response to complaints that the 2004 Directive was leading some countries to reject claims of persecution purely on the footing that the state in question was 'doing its best', that the recast Qualification Directive expressly introduced the requirements of effectiveness and non-temporariness.[60]

E. Bipartite Approach to Well-Founded Fear

According to what has become known as the bipartite approach, an applicant cannot establish well-founded fear unless able to show both a subjective and an objective fear. Although it played no effective part in the Court's decision in *Ward*

[55] *Ward* (n 1) 59; see also *Carrillo* (Can FCA, 2008) at 638.

[56] See, eg, *Canada (Minister of Citizenship and Immigration) v Kadenko* (1996) 143 DLR (4th) 532 (FCA) and further discussion in IRB, 2020 Interpretation (n 1) 6.1.7.3.1.

[57] Waldman (n 1) 273–74 seeks to argue, with reference to *Carrillo v Canada* (MCI) [2008] FCJ No 399, 2008 FCA 94, that the presumption does not add to the evidentiary threshold of balance of probabilities. Hathaway and Foster (n 1) 320 note the observation by the FCA in *Mendoza v Canada (Minister of Citizenship and Immigration* [2010] C 119 (Can FC 119) at 28 that there 'is a wealth of jurisprudence on the required elements of state protection which is essentially based on the Supreme Court of Canada; decision in [*Ward*]'. See further IRB, 2020 *Interpretation* (n 1) 6.1.7.3.2.

[58] Zambelli, 2011 (n 1) 266, cited in Hathaway and Foster (n 1) 311; see also Zambelli, 2020 (n 1) 28 at 31–36.

[59] In *A v MIMA* (1999) 53 ALD 545 at 554 the Full Federal Court of Australia stated that the 'presumption of protection' advocated in *Ward* is 'a presumption without a basic fact'. Waldman (n 1) 274–80 views the case law in Canada to have nevertheless embraced the centrality of effectiveness of protection.

[60] See QD (recast) (n 31) Art 7.

(because there was no dispute that Ward had shown both a subjective and objective fear), Ward expressly endorsed a bipartite approach to well-founded fear. For the SC, the subjective component relates to the existence of the fear of persecution in the mind of the refugee and is assessed with reference to the claimant's subjective condition. The objective component, in contrast, requires that the refugees fear be evaluated objectively to determine if there is a valid basis for that fear.[61]

It seems that as a result of *Ward*'s endorsement at the apex court level of the bipartite approach,[62] the Canadian courts have never sought to re-examine this issue. It appears that previous Canadian case law had sought to take the sting out of this test already, by equating it with a positive credibility assessment, but the SC endorsement (and re-endorsement in *Chan*),[63] has been drawn on in subsequent FCA decisions to reiterate it; and in particular to make a close link between the bipartite approach and the Convention concept of 'unwillingness'.[64] But despite the case law before and after seeking to ameliorate the plainly unpalatable features of this approach,[65] it cannot be excluded that this decision has encouraged at least some courts elsewhere in the world to apply the test without such amelioration. For example, in Australia some of the case law continues to view failure to show subjective fear as a valid reason to reach a negative decision.[66] It further appears that (erroneously in this author's view) some decision-makers in both Australia and the UK eye the recently imposed statutory definitions of well-founded fear as confirming the consequentiality of the subjective element.[67] This has to be seen as a baleful effect of *Ward* and to be one of the reasons why international refugee law has not reached consensus instead on a purely objective test that simply considers subjective elements in the context of the principle of individual assessment.[68]

F. Approach to Particular Social Group

According to Audrey Macklin, the *Ward* decision adopts a relatively expansive interpretation of the term 'particular social group' by linking the designation to concepts of anti-discrimination in Canadian and international law, and section 15 of the Charter in particular, thus 'neatly dispos[ing] of at least some of the

[61] *Ward* (n 1) 54–55, citing *Rajudeen* (n 33).

[62] This position was long-standing in Canadian case law: see, eg, *Rajudeen* (n 33) and *Adjei v Canada(MEI)* [1989] FCJ No 67, 7 Imm LR (2d) 169 (TD); see further Waldman (n 1) ch 3.

[63] *Chan v Canada (MEI)* [1995] 3 SCR 593.

[64] eg *Sukhu v Canada (MCI)*[2008] FCJ No515, 2008 FC 427.

[65] See, eg, *Ramirez-Osorio v Canada* (MCI) [2013] FCJ No 492, 2013 FC 461.

[66] eg *Iyer v MIMA* [2000] FCA 1788; *MIC v SZJGV* (2009) 238 CLR 642 at [53].

[67] *Guide to Refugee Law in Australia* (Administrative Review Tribunal, October 2024) ch 5, p 23 states that s 5J(1)(a) of the Migration Act (which requires that the person 'fears being persecuted' for one of the stated reasons) 'appears to incorporate the need for subjective fear, consistent with the Australian courts' interpretation of 'well-founded' fear in art 1A(2) of the Convention'. In relation to s 32 of the Nationality and Borders Act 2022, see *JCK v Secretary of State for the Home Department (Botswana)* [2024] UKUT 100 (IAC) [17].

[68] See discussion in Storey, 2023 (n 1) 682–704.

juridical constraints that have cramped the contours of the "particular social group" category'. Chief among these impediments were the requirement of self-conscious affiliation and an oblique notion that the group had to be numerically 'manageable'.[69]

By alighting on the underlying principle of non-discrimination, *Ward* offered a coherent basis rooted in the Convention's objects and purposes for analysing this and indeed all the Convention reasons, since La Forest was clearly in agreement with the *euisdem generis* approach – also known as the 'protected characteristics' approach – advocated by Hathaway and already promoted by the US case of *Acosta*.[70] Drawing on *Acosta* and two Canadian cases,[71] he identified three possible categories:

> (1) groups defined by an innate or unchangeable characteristic; (2) groups whose members voluntarily associate for reasons so fundamental to their human dignity that they should not be forced to forsake the association; and (3) groups associated by a former voluntary status, unalterable due to its historical permanence.

Thereby *Ward* can be said to have legitimised understanding particular social group to encompass a wide range of groups based on, for example, gender, age, sexual orientation, disability, or lineage. La Forest helpfully offered several examples of cases coming within each category.[72]

It is beyond doubt that the approach taken in *Ward* towards interpretation of the particular social group reason had a progressive effect in subsequent case law both in Canada and more widely,[73] especially in relation to recognition of gender-specific social groups.[74] However, it would be wrong to evaluate *Ward*'s pronouncements on particular social group in isolation from the rest of the decision. If the Court had not first rejected the state accountability approach, there would have continued to be decision-makers routinely rejecting claims on the basis that the claimant's fear was only of 'private persecution' and thereby not persecution under the refugee definition; and it was especially in 'private persecution' cases that women were the victims.[75]

[69] Macklin (n 1) 371.

[70] *Matter of Acosta* [1985] A- 24159781.

[71] *Cheung v Minister of Employment and Immigration* [1993] FCJ No 309 (QL) Appeal No A-785-91; *Mayers v Canada (Minister of Employment and Immigration)* (1992) 97 DLR (4th) 729.

[72] *Ward* (n 1) 79: the first category 'would embrace individuals fearing persecution on such bases as gender, linguistic background and sexual orientation'; the second 'would encompass, for example, human rights activists'; the third 'is included more because of historical intentions …'.

[73] See, eg, *Immigration Appeal Tribunal and Another, ex parte Shah (AP)* [1999] UKHL 20.

[74] In relation to Canadian case law, see Macklin (n 1) 372–73; Hathaway and Foster (n 1) 436–42.

[75] Significantly, one of the Interveners, the Canadian Council for Refugees *via* Parkdale Community Legal Services, considered that it was the combination of the Court rejecting the notion of state complicity (and its corollary that private persecution is not persecution) and the adoption of the human rights-derived notion of non-discrimination that resulted in an approach able to recognise women in particular as meeting the particular social group requirements. See Shacter (n 1) 725, 730. For analysis of the treatment in Australia of the notion of 'private persecution', see Natasha Yacoub, '*Minister for Immigration and Multicultural Affairs v Khawar* [2002]: Protection for Refugee Women through Transitional Jurisprudence and Feminist Advocacy' in ch 2 in this volume.

Even so, the historical reception of *Ward* as being progressive on the topic of particular social group needs revisiting. Indeed it could be said to be paradoxical because in adopting this approach it clearly rejected the more sociological FCA approach which was manifestly more liberal.[76] It has to be asked whether La Forest and subsequent proponents fully understood that the tripartite test set out in *Acosta* can have a narrowing effect in certain types of cases and is in tension with the more sociological approach as set out by Goodwin-Gill and others.[77] Its arguably straitjacketing effect has been commented upon plentifully in the literature. Since its category 1 is confined to immutable characteristics and category 3 is derivative of 1, category 2 operates as the only bolthole for all particular social group cases not based on innate characteristics. Intriguingly, it might well be said that La Forest's own application of the *Acosta* test illustrates how this overreliance on category 2 can have a narrowing effect. For La Forest, Ward's membership of the INLA put him out with category 2 because the group's view that killing political opponents was legitimate could not be seen as a matter of conscience.[78] Not only did this rejection sit somewhat uncomfortably with his earlier assertion that particular social groups can include terrorist and criminal groups (pointing out that they may well, however, be caught by the exclusion clauses).[79] It is also at odds with the broad approach taken in most of the literature towards the other four Convention reasons. In relation to three of them at least, a non-evaluative approach has been taken – eg it is plainly not required, in order to show one has a Convention reason of race or religion or nationality; that one has a particular set of values; and case law is increasingly giving a non-evaluative reading to the political opinion reason also.[80]

Alternatively, assuming La Forest was correct about this, it might still be asked why he did not accept that Ward could qualify by reference to a particular social group comprising *former* INLA members,[81] since then Ward's decision to spare the lives of hostages would have been quintessentially a matter of fundamental beliefs and conscience.

As regards La Forest's assessment that Ward could not rely on not being able to change his association,[82] it might be thought that that was the nub of his predicament – that he could not escape his past because the INLA would not let him.

La Forest's further reason for rejecting that Ward could show membership of a particular social group was his view that he was being persecuted for what he did

[76] Hathaway, 1991 (n 1) 159–60 considers the FCA approach, which was to define particular social group simply as a group of persons 'associated, allied, combined' and 'united in a stable association with common purposes' … to be a 'liberal attempt' that has 'gone too far'.

[77] Goodwin-Gill (n 1) 538.

[78] *Ward* (n 1) 86–87.

[79] ibid 79–84.

[80] Storey, 2023 (n 1) 651–52.

[81] *Ward* (n 1) 85.

[82] ibid 86–87.

rather than who he belonged to,[83] but that rather flew in the face of the evidence that the INLA's own internal rules included a court-martialling procedure for the punishment of specific categories, namely those who were disaffected members – supergrasses, traitors, etc.

Of course, a more pressing contemporary concern when it comes to particular social group assessment is that some countries have now adopted a cumulative requirement, according to which no particular social group arises unless a claimant can show not only that he has a 'protected characteristic' within the *Acosta/Ward* framework but also that he has a 'social perception' characteristic of being set apart from society. One cannot avoid speculating that if the *Acosta/Ward* approach had not sought to demarcate itself so much from more sociological approaches, a more flexible synthesis may have been found.[84]

G. Political Opinion

Re-reading *Ward*, its reasoning in relation to this Convention reason is remarkably prescient. First, it builds on existing understandings that this reason covers thoughts as well as acts (which was of some relevance to the facts of the *Ward* case).[85] Second, it made clear that the definition of political, although it had to be related to the machinery of government, was not confined to it; the INLA, albeit a non-state actor, was clearly recognised as capable of seeking to persecute someone (Ward) for their political opinion. As expressed by La Forest, 'a claimant may be seen as a threat by a group unrelated, and perhaps even opposed, to the government because of his or her political viewpoint, perceived or real'.[86] The INLA, he observed, would view Ward as a 'political traitor'.[87] Given that at the relevant time (the late 1980s) the Irish continent was heavily affected by conflicts, sometimes armed, between Catholics and Protestants and those in favour of and those opposed to Irish reunification, that made very good sense. Third, the decision contains a powerful affirmation of the doctrine of attribution, which is now, of course, codified in the Qualification Directive and its 2011 recast.[88]

H. Multiple Nationality

Ward is one of the important early decisions adding judicial weight to the opinion already expressed by the UNHCR Handbook that persons with more than one

[83] ibid 87.
[84] See further Storey, 2023 (n 1) 624–32.
[85] *Ward* (n 1) 89, 92.
[86] ibid 88–89.
[87] ibid 92.
[88] ibid 89–90. QD (recast) (n 31) Art 10(2).

nationality are required to establish a well-founded fear of persecution in each of them. But it also made this subject (correctly in this author's view) to the clear exception set out in the second paragraph of Article 1A(2), so that for La Forest the key issue was whether it was the case or not that the Great Britain area of the UK could protect Ward, given suggestions that, apart from anything else, the authorities there might not admit him.[89]

I. Exclusion

The SC did not address the issue of exclusion as such but it did usefully admonish those who tried to read exclusion criteria into the particular social group ground.[90] La Forest did venture, obiter, that Ward would not have been caught by the exclusion clauses anyway because he had served his sentence.[91] So far as concerns Article 1F(b), that remains a controversial position in much of the existing literature.[92]

V. *Ward* Today

Perhaps symptomatic of the extent to which access to procedures has come to dominate the contemporary landscape of refugee law, if Ward (or a *Ward*-type applicant) were to apply for international protection in Canada today, he would be routed into an inadmissibility procedure, by virtue of his terrorist past.[93]

VI. Conclusion

Like all landmark cases of a certain vintage, *Ward* is now a 'ruined temple', although in Canada it continues to be widely cited and remains authoritative on multiple issues. Landmark cases are always very context-specific and are always cases on the road to where were are now. From today's vantage-point, *Ward*, more than other key cases of its era, continues to furnish important reference points for ongoing attempts to build a more coherent body of international refugee law. Its adoption of a human rights approach to the refugee definition generally was transformative.

[89] *Ward* (n 1) 95–101.See further, Storey, 2023 (n 1) 230–34.

[90] *Ward* (n 1) 79–84. See further Sarah Singer, '*Pushpanathan v Canada (Minister of Citizenship and Immigration)* [1998]: Excluding (Suspected) Criminals from Refugee Protection' in ch 5 in this volume.

[91] *Ward* (n 1) 94.

[92] J Rikhof, *Exclusion and Refoulement: Criminality in International and Domestic Refugee Law* (Irwin Law, 2023) 583 (where he notes that expiation has for the most part been rejected by the judiciary in the context of Art 1F(b) of the Convention).

[93] International Refugee Protection Act, SC 2001 c 27, s 34(1)(c).

By bringing this approach to bear to achieve a better understanding of the concept of persecution and by construing it as closely interrelated with lack of protection, *Ward* helped refugee law break free from the shackles of an 'accountability' approach that had promoted the misplaced notion of 'private persecution'. Its broad approach to the political opinion ground has proved prescient. But cracks in the structure are now more evident. Paradoxically, one of the main achievements for which *Ward* was hailed at the time, namely its 'protected characteristics' approach to particular social group, now appears unduly constraining. Its adoption of a bipartite approach to 'well-founded fear' has had a baleful effect. The tension within the decision between on the one hand viewing state protection as a presumption and on the other hand requiring protection to be effective in the individual case, is still palpable in Canadian jurisprudence today and also in certain other jurisdictions. Holding fast to its strengths, the best way to celebrate this case must surely be to more vigorously address weaknesses that, over time, have become more visible.

2

Minister for Immigration and Multicultural Affairs v Khawar [2002]: Protection for Refugee Women Through Transnational Jurisprudence and Feminist Advocacy

NATASHA YACOUB

I. Introduction

The landmark decision of the High Court of Australia (High Court) in *Minister for Immigration and Multicultural Affairs v Khawar* (*Khawar*)[1] was part of a transnational development to expand refugee protection for women and a reminder of ongoing gender inequality in international refugee law. While the drafters of the 1951 Convention relating to the Status of Refugees (1951 Refugee Convention)[2] omitted sex as a ground for discrimination in the treaty's text, the High Court in *Khawar* 'shaped'[3] the international refugee definition to include women's experiences where it had been historically excluded.[4] The High Court's precedent-setting decision found, first, that the state's failure to protect women from family violence could constitute persecution and, second, that women could form a 'particular social group' within the refugee definition.

The High Court in *Khawar* rejected earlier Australian jurisprudence that international refugee law was not designed to protect women from 'private' harms.

[1] *Minister for Immigration and Multicultural Affairs v Khawar* [2002] 14 HCA.

[2] UN General Assembly, 1951 Convention relating to the Status of Refugees, United Nations, Treaty Series, 189:137, 28 July 1951 (hereafter 1951 Refugee Convention).

[3] National courts play a dual role in international law development both to 'create and shape international norms' as well as to 'impartially enforce international law'. A Roberts, 'Comparative International Law? The Role of National Courts in Creating International Law' (2011) 60 *ICLQ* 57, 60.

[4] The 1951 Refugee Convention contains no explicit mention of sex or gender, and the international refugee definition includes persons forced to leave their country owing to persecution 'for reasons of race, religion, nationality, membership of a particular social group or political opinion' (Art 1A(2)). For further detail, see section II below.

Feminist scholars highlight the ways that the public/private distinction entrenches gender inequality in international law because:

> the public realm of the work place, the law, economics, politics and intellectual and cultural life, where power and authority are exercised, is regarded as the natural province of men; while the private world of the home, the hearth and children is seen as the appropriate domain of women.[5]

The protection of women from violence in their homes was, until *Khawar*, minimised and not included within the meaning of 'persecution' in the international refugee definition in Australian jurisprudence, echoing earlier similar developments in other parts of the world.

However, the significance of *Khawar* lies beyond the outcome of extending refugee protection to those fleeing family violence, since the decision illuminates the possibilities and challenges of using international refugee law to protect women from gendered harm. Such harm pervades all aspects of women's displacement: from their reasons for fleeing,[6] to difficulties crossing borders,[7] experiences in asylum countries,[8] and access to permanent solutions.[9] The *Khawar* case was part of a 'transjudicial communication' between regulators, legislators and judges[10] to include gender in the refugee definition, especially with the United Kingdom (UK) following the landmark case of *Islam (AP) v Secretary of State for the Home Department; R v Immigration Appeal Tribunal and Another, Ex Parte Shah (AP)* (*Shah and Islam*).[11] Notably, international human rights law was used in New Zealand in the 1990s to make visible the types of harm women fled from within the meaning of the refugee definition where they had previously been ignored.[12]

[5] In this seminal text on feminist approaches to international law, the authors draw on feminist critiques of the public/private distinction from the 1980s. H Charlesworth, C Chinkin and S Wright, 'Feminist Approaches to International Law' (1991) 85 *American Journal of International Law* 613, 626.

[6] For example, D Dankey, 'Gendered Experiences of Subsistence Harms: A Possible Contribution to Feminist Discourse on Gendered Harm?' (2015) 24 *Social and Legal Studies* 1 24–45, 24.

[7] S P and B Cochrane, 'Irregular Border-Crossing Deaths and Gender: Where, How and Why Women Die Crossing Borders' (2012) 17 *Theoretical Criminology* 27, 33.

[8] For example, asylum country practices exposing refugee women to gendered violence: S Vasefi and S Dehm, 'Refugee Women and the Gendered Violence of Australia's Extraterritorial Asylum Regime on Nauru' (2022) 41 *Refugee Survey Quarterly* 3, 529.

[9] For example, inequality in integration on account of gender and sexuality: A Güler, M Shevtsova and D Venturi (eds), *LGBTI Asylum Seekers and Refugees from a Legal and Political Perspective: Persecution, Asylum and Integration* (Springer, 2018).

[10] A-M Slaughter, 'A Typology of Transjudicial Communication' [1994] 29 *University of Richmond Law Review* 99. Slaughter later theorised that international relations are conducted by a 'disaggregated state' consisting of regulators, judges and legislators. See: A-M Slaughter, *A New World Order* (Princeton University Press, 2004) 12–22.

[11] In particular, a landmark UK House of Lords decision was handed down in the same year as Ms Khawar's application for judicial review to the Federal Court: *Islam (AP) v Secretary of State for the Home Department; R v Immigration Appeal Tribunal and Another, Ex Parte Shah (AP)* [1999] UKHL 20 (*Shah and Islam*).

[12] Among several jurisdictions including 'gender-based persecution' in the refugee definition, New Zealand took groundbreaking steps to incorporate a sophisticated perspective of gender in its case law for its time. See: the excellent report: R PG Haines, 'Gender-Based Persecution: New Zealand Jurisprudence' (UNHCR Geneva, 1996), available at www.refugee.org.nz/Reference/ref.htm.

These cases followed a decade of feminist engagement challenging international law's exclusion of women.[13]

This chapter first explains the historical exclusion of 'sex' and 'gender' by the drafters of the 1951 Refugee Convention and the progressive development in the 1960s by states emerging from colonial rule, the Asian-African Legal Consultative Committee (AALCC),[14] to explicitly include sex discrimination in refugee law standards, and the Bangkok Principles on the Status and Treatment of Refugees (Bangkok Principles), reaffirmed in 2001. Next, the chapter explores the significance of *Khawar* and related decisions, including gendered harm in the international refugee definition. The chapter then sets out the success of *Khawar* as part of transjudicial communication, highlighting the influence of feminist scholarship and advocacy in the 1990s to strengthen the protection of women's rights in international law. The chapter qualifies the success of Khawar however, concluding with reflections on the ongoing gender inequality excluding women from refugee protection.

II. Historical Blindness to Women, Gender and Sexual Inequality

In international refugee law scholarship, *Khawar* is one of several significant cases among a series that included considerations of gender-related persecution in the international refugee definition where they had been historically excluded. The 1951 Refugee Convention, according to Edwards, at the time of drafting, was characterised by a 'complete blindness to women, gender, and issues of sexual inequality'.[15] This blindness is common in international laws, as Charlesworth, Chinkin and Wright explain, since they are drafted and interpreted by men, interpreted by male-dominated institutions and exclude or minimise women's experiences.[16] The 1951 Refugee Convention drafting process exemplifies this male bias.

[13] An important part of feminist approaches to international law is the inclusion of diverse knowledge systems to interpret the law, see Charlesworth, Chinkin, Wright (n 5). For examples of this knowledge from diverse regions, see: M Jolly, 'Re-membering Oceanic Masculinities' (2008) 20 *The Contemporary Pacific* 1; A Mama, 'African Feminist Thought' in *Oxford Research Encyclopedia of African History* (Oxford University Press, 2019) 1–29; and A Pitts, M Ortega, J Medina (eds), *Theories of the Flesh: Latinx and Latin American Feminisms, Transformation, and Resistance* (Oxford University Press, 2020).

[14] Several Association of Southeast Asian Nations (ASEAN) Member States developed inter-regional refugee standards in the 1960s under the auspices of the Asian-African Legal Consultative Committee (AALCC), now called the Asian-African Legal Consultative Organisation (AALCO), a grouping that emerged from the Conference between African and Asian states, most of which were newly independent, in Bandung in Indonesia in 1955. Its objective, stated in Art 1 of its Statute, includes: 'to serve as an advisory body to its Member States in the field of international law and as a forum for Asian-African co-operation in legal matters of common concern …', including common asylum standards.

[15] A Edwards, 'Transitioning Gender: Feminist Engagement with International Refugee Law and Policy 1950–2010' (2010) 29 *Refugee Survey Quarterly* 2, 21–45, at 21.

[16] Charlesworth, Chinkin, Wright (n 5) 623.

The significance of *Khawar* is its role, along with legal developments in countries elsewhere, to remedy the omission of sex discrimination by men drafting the 1951 Refugee Convention. A proposal by the Yugoslav delegate to include 'sex' as a prohibited ground of discrimination, in Article 3 of the Convention, was unsuccessful.[17] The working documents reveal that the drafting body's Committee President said he 'doubted *strongly* whether there would be any cases of persecution on grounds of sex' (emphasis added).[18] One drafter took offence to the implication that sex discrimination exists in certain countries.[19] While these views may not have been uncommon in the 1950s, they diverge from the position of the drafters of the 1950 Universal Declaration of Human Rights that did include 'sex' as a ground for discrimination.[20]

In the decades before *Khawar*, the most groundbreaking developments to expand refugee protection for women were in regional refugee laws. In the 1960s, states emerging from colonial rule formed the AALCC and agreed on the Bangkok Principles on the Status and Treatment of Refugees (Bangkok Principles), reaffirmed in 2001. An expanded refugee definition in the Bangkok Principles was reinforced in regional refugee laws in Africa[21] and Latin America.[22] Not only do these instruments expand the international refugee definition to include women fleeing generalised harm, such as civil war, but the Bangkok Principles also explicitly include persecution on account of gender.[23] While the Bangkok Principles are non-binding on Member States, historical state practice in the post-World War Two years does reveal protections of refugee women, for example in certain countries in South East Asia.[24]

Similar developments were to take place in other countries to increase protection for refugee women, including Australia, after the issuance in 1991 of guidelines on the protection of refugee women by the United Nations High Commissioner for Refugees (UNHCR),[25] followed by further guidance to states elaborating on the

[17] The delegate from Yugoslavia suggested an amendment to the non-discrimination clause in Art 3 of the 1951 Refugee Convention to prohibit 'sex' discrimination since the 1950 Universal Declaration of Human Rights referred to sex in Art 2 concerning non-discrimination. A/CONF.2/SR.5, 9.

[18] ibid 10.

[19] The French delegate said that the inclusion of 'sex' as a ground for discrimination would imply that certain countries practice such discrimination but '[s]uch was not the case'. A/CONF.2/SR.5, 9.

[20] United Nations General Assembly, *Universal Declaration of Human Rights* (1948) 217 A (III) (UDHR).

[21] Convention Governing the Specific Aspects of Refugee Problems in Africa (1969) 1001 UNTS 45 (1969 OAU Convention).

[22] Declaración de Cartagena sobre Refugiados (1984) (1984 Cartegena Declaration).

[23] Article 1(1) of the Bangkok Principles 2001 defines a refugee as a person who, 'owing to persecution or a well-founded fear of persecution for reasons of race, colour, religion, nationality, ethnic origin, gender, political opinion or membership of a particular social group: (a) leaves the State of which he is a national, or the Country of his nationality, or, if he has no nationality, the State or Country of which he is a habitual resident; or, (b) being outside of such a State or Country, is unable or unwilling to return to it or to avail himself of its protection …'.

[24] For an example of Thailand's protection of Vietnamese refugees in the 1950s, see: NE Yacoub, 'A New History of Refugee Protection in Post-World War Two Southeast Asia: Lessons from the Global South' (2023) 13 *Asian Journal of International Law* 2, 220.

[25] United Nations High Commissioner for Refugees (UNHCR), *Guidelines on the Protection of Refugee Women* (Geneva 1991).

legal contours of gender persecution in the refugee definition.[26] The next section elaborates on the significant ways *Khawar* read gender into the 1951 Refugee Convention definition.

III. The *Khawar* Decision: Including Gender Considerations in the Refugee Definition

Ms Naima Khawar and her three daughters arrived in Australia from Pakistan in 1997 and applied for refugee 'protection visas'.[27] Whilst in Pakistan, Ms Khawar had experienced increasing levels of violence perpetrated by her husband and his brother, which she reported to police four times. The first time she was told 'if [the police] had to do something about all the similar complaints it would take all their time' and she was ignored.[28] The next time, the police took no action when she reported that her husband threatened to throw hot oil on her. When she returned home, her husband's brother beat her so badly she was hospitalised for seven days.[29] The third time, the police wrote something 'grossly inaccurate' about a beating by her husband and took no action.[30] The last time, she reported that her husband and his brother poured petrol on her and the police stated that 'women always tried to blame their husbands for problems of which they were the real cause and that she should sort out her "own work"'.[31] Fearing for her life, she fled Pakistan with her children.

The first two decisions on Ms Khawar's protection application in Australia reproduced the historical blindness of refugee law to gender, overturned on appeal as part of transnational developments. The two decisions at first instance and on

[26] UNHCR subsequently issued guidelines elaborating on the nature of gender-related persecution in the refugee definition. UNHCR, *Guidelines on International Protection No 1: Gender-Related Persecution within the Context of Article 1A(2) of the 1951 Convention and/or its 1967 Protocol relating to the Status of Refugees* (HCR/GIP/02/01, 2002) ('UNHCR Gender-Related Persecution Guidelines'). Several states issued gender guidelines in refugee status determination: for example, Immigration and Refugee Board of Canada, *Chairperson Guidelines 4: Women Refugee Claimants Fearing Gender-Related Persecution 1996*; US Guidelines, *Office of International Affairs, Immigration and Naturalization Service, Regarding Adjudicating Asylum Cases on the Basis of Gender* (26 May 1996); UK Visas and Immigration, *Gender Issues in the Asylum Claim* (2010).

[27] According to the Australian Migration Act 1958 (Commonwealth) (Migration Act), a protection visa may be granted by the Minister for Immigration and Multicultural Affairs (the Minister) if a non-citizen is a person 'to whom Australia has protection obligations under 1951 Refugee Convention and its 1967 Protocol'. Section 65 of the *Migration Act* provides that, after considering a valid application for a visa, the Minister may grant a protection visa where the criteria are met to satisfy Australia's protection obligations in the 1951 Refugee Convention (clause 866.221 of Schedule 2 to the Migration Regulations 1994).

[28] Statutory declaration, Ms Khawar, dated 22 September 1997. Cited in *Khawar v Minister for Immigration & Multicultural Affairs* [1999] FCA 1529 (5 November 1999), 168 ALC 190 [7], available at www.austlii.edu.au/cgi-bin/viewdoc/au/cases/cth/FCA/1999/1529.html?context=1;query=khawar%20;mask_path=.

[29] ibid [8].

[30] ibid [9].

[31] ibid [10].

review denied Ms Khawar protection on the basis that family violence is private in nature, does not comprise 'persecution', and is not linked to a Convention ground.[32] At the time of the review decision and appeal to the Federal Court of Australia in November 1999,[33] the landmark UK decision *Shah and Islam* had been handed down[34] and was applied to find an error in the review decision's failure to identify a particular social group.[35] An appeal to the Full Court of the Federal Court on 23 August 2000[36] was dismissed,[37] also citing *Shah and Islam*.[38] An appeal to the High Court, Australia's last appellate level, led to the groundbreaking precedent challenging the law's historical exclusion of women.[39]

An important factor in the High Court's progressive decision in *Khawar* was the composition of judges who were willing, for the first time in its history, to draw on international human rights to interpret Australian law.[40] The reasoning in the decision of Justice Michael Kirby, a champion of including international human rights law within Australian law, shaped the meaning of 'persecution' in refugee law to protect women. He drew on the International Covenant on Civil and Political Rights and the Committee on the Elimination of Discrimination against

[32] The Refugee Review Tribunal found '[s]he was not persecuted because she was a member of a particular family. She was harmed because the applicant's husband's family were angry or shamed by the fact that he married her for love when he was already engaged to a relative and because she brought no dowry to the family. She was also seen as being responsible for her husband being estranged from his family for five years'. *Re Khawar* [1999] RRTA 5980 (23 November 1999). ibid [12].

[33] *Khawar* (n 28).

[34] Similar to the facts of Ms Khawar's case, *Shah and Islam* concerned two women from Pakistan, Syeda Shah and Shahanna Islam, who were subjected to serious physical abuse by their husbands and feared further family violence from which the Pakistan state would not protect them, as well as a fear of punishment arising from adultery allegations. The House of Lords recognised, for the first time in the UK, that gender is a protected characteristic and women comprise a particular social group within the meaning of Art 1A(2) of the 1951 Refugee Convention. *Shah and Islam* (n 11).

[35] The Refugee Review Tribunal (RRT) decision is a 'judicially reviewable decision' under s 475(1)(b) of the Migration Act to the Federal Court that assesses whether there has been an 'error of law' (not a de novo hearing). The Court found an error, relying on UNHCR's 1991 *Guidelines on the Protection of Refugee Women* (to include women fleeing sexual violence or other gender-related persecution in the refugee definition. Federal Court decision, per Branson J, [39].

[36] *Minister For Immigration & Multicultural Affairs v Khawar* [2000] FCA 1130, (2000) 101 FCR 501.

[37] Full Court of the Federal Court [2000], [160].

[38] Lindgren J noted that the formula was taken from the *Gender Guidelines for the Determination of Asylum Claims* in the UK, published by the Refugee Women's Legal Group in July 1998. Full Court of the Federal Court [2000] [132]. A dissenting judgment by Justice Hill found that *Shah and Islam* was not applicable law in an Australian court since it conflicted with a decision of the High Court defining a particular social group in *Minister For Immigration & Multicultural Affairs v Khawar* (n 36), ie 'a group which existed independently of and which was defined other than by reference to the discriminatory treatment or persecution which they feared'. Full Court of the Federal Court [2000].

[39] The two questions the appellant put before the High Court were answered in the affirmative: 'The first issue is whether the failure of a country of nationality to provide protection against domestic violence to women, in circumstances where the motivation of the perpetrators of the violence is private, can result in persecution of the kind referred to in Art 1A(2) of the Convention. The second issue is whether women or, for the present purposes, women in Pakistan may constitute a particular social group within the meaning of the Convention.' *Khawar* (n 1) per Gleeson CJ, [5]–[6].

[40] H Charlesworth, 'Australia and the International Human Rights System' in HV Bonavita (ed), *Human Rights: A Fair Go For All* (Curtin University of Technology, Brisbane, 2001) 159–64.

Women to explain the importance of 'expressing the concept of women's equality before the law and the unacceptability of the state and its agencies discriminating unjustly against women solely by reason of their sex'.[41] Over many years on the High Court, Justice Kirby sought to ensure compliance of domestic laws with international human rights law obligations.[42]

Khawar aligned Australian law with international human rights law in two key ways. First, the High Court's decision is significant because it included within the refugee definition violence by non-state actors,[43] Ms Khawar's husband and his brother, in light of the police's failure to protect her as a woman. The majority found that persecution may be constituted by 'both a risk of serious harm to the applicant from human sources and a failure on the part of the state to afford protection'.[44] The Court drew on the UK *Shah and Islam* decision and reiterated the formula 'Persecution = Serious Harm + The Failure of State Protection'.[45] This test acknowledged that persecution could arise not only from direct state action but also from the state's discriminatory inaction to protect certain groups.[46]

The High Court's approach represented a significant departure from earlier decisions' characterisation of 'domestic violence' as a private matter. Instead, it recognised that state failure to protect women from this violence could itself constitute persecution when such failure occurred on a discriminatory basis.[47] This interpretation aligned with the groundbreaking approach in *Shah and Islam*, where the House of Lords had established that family violence combined with state failure to protect could constitute persecution.[48] The High Court recognised that while the immediate perpetrators might act for personal motives, the state's discriminatory failure to protect women comprised persecution within the refugee definition.[49] In doing so, the High Court departed from the Australian precedent excluding domestic violence from the meaning of persecution. Moreover, it connects 'private' violence to 'public' harm of state inaction viewed as part of a system of power in Pakistan creating the conditions in which persecution may occur.

Second, the High Court's decision to recognise women in Pakistan as a 'particular social group' under the Refugee Convention marked another fundamental shift in Australian refugee law. In reaching this conclusion, the High Court

[41] *Khawar* (n 1) [111], per Kirby J.

[42] M Kirby, 'Domestic Courts and International Human Rights Law: The Ongoing Judicial Conversation' (2010) *Utrecht Law Review* 168–81. LAH Johns, Justice Kirby, Human Rights and the Exercise of Judicial Choice' (2001) *Monash University Law Review* 27(2), 290–318.

[43] W Kälin, 'Non-State Agents of Persecution and the Inability of the State to Protect' (2001) 15 *Georgetown Immigration Law Journal* 415.

[44] In so finding, the High Court distinguished between mere inability to provide protection and systematic discriminatory withdrawal of protection, High Court of Australia [2002] [115].

[45] ibid [118] referring to *R v Immigration Appeal Tribunal; Ex parte Shah* [1999] 2 AC 629, 653; *Horvath v Secretary of State for the Home Department* [2001] 1 AC 489, 515–16.

[46] ibid [27]–[29].

[47] ibid.

[48] ibid [30].

[49] ibid.

drew extensively on the reasoning in *Shah and Islam*, where the House of Lords had concluded that 'women in Pakistan' constituted a particular social group.[50] Not defining women as a particular group on the basis of the persecution they faced, the High Court found that 'their distinctive attributes and characteristics exist independently of the manner in which they are treated, either by males or by governments' since women 'would exist as a group even if such violence were to disappear entirely'.[51] Addressing potential criticism that the decision essentialises women's experience, the High Court of Australia also found that women are a cognisable group but need not be cohesive.[52]

This development in the jurisprudence in Australia reflected an understanding of how gender intersects with other factors as a basis for persecution. The High Court recognised that the systematic denial of state protection to women could evidence their recognition as a particular social group within their society. In doing so, the High Court moved beyond the harmful public-private binary that led to the exclusion of 'private' violence, instead recognising that it cannot be distinguished from the 'public' violence resulting from gender discrimination in state institutions that refuse to protect women. This alignment of Australian law with international standards and jurisprudence, including UNHCR guidance[53] and the *Shah and Islam* decision, represented a crucial step forward in Australia's approach to refugee protection for women fleeing gendered harm.

IV. The Success of *Khawar*: Increased Refugee Protection Through Transnational Women's Rights Movements

Feminist scholarship, women's rights advocacy and regional refugee law developments to include gender issues in international refugee law are an important part of *Khawar's* bigger success story and lesson for future strategic litigation to improve the protection of refugee women. A rich body of scholarship on gender and international refugee law in the 1990s laid important groundwork for *Khawar* and similar jurisprudential developments.[54] As well as gendered harm, this scholarship highlights persecution on intersecting grounds as relevant for the refugee definition. For example, queer theory has been applied to show how flawed constructions of 'homosexuality', as a particular identity or acts, can result

[50] ibid [31].

[51] ibid [35].

[52] The High Court observed that 'Some particular social groups are notoriously lacking in cohesiveness', ibid [33].

[53] UNHCR Guidelines 1991 (n 25).

[54] For example, L Cipriani, 'Gender and Persecution: Protecting Women Under International Refugee Law' (1993) 7 *Georgetown Immigration Law Journal* 11.

in the denial of refugee protection.[55] This scholarship paves the way for increased protection from persecution on account of sexuality in refugee law.[56]

Similarly, women's rights activists played an important role in the jurisprudential developments that led to *Khawar*. For example, Honkala documents the active role of women's rights advocates in *Shah and Islam*.[57] In the lead-up to *Shah and Islam*, the House of Lords relied on national guidelines on gender and refugee status determination of 1997 prepared by UK women's rights advocates,[58] also cited by the High Court in *Khawar*. These advocates communicated with the United States' (US) legal team in the groundbreaking US case, *In re Fauziya Kasinga*,[59] an impressive tale of advocacy and principled decision-making.[60] *Kasinga* overturned on review a decision denying refugee protection to a woman fearing the 'private' act of female genital cutting.[61] Although a great leap forward in refugee protection for women fleeing gendered harm in the US at the time,[62] many setbacks for

[55] For example, J Wessels, *Concealment Controversy* (Cambridge University Press, 2022); M Dustin, N Ferriera, 'Improving SOGI Asylum Adjudication: Putting Persecution Ahead of Identity' (2021) 40 *Refugee Survey Quarterly* 3, 315; I Manganini, 'The Refugee Status Determination of Transgender Asylum Seekers: A Queer Critique' (Global Migration Center Research Paper Series N° 978-2-8399-2956-12020), available at www.graduateinstitute.ch/sites/internet/files/2020-06/Research%20Paper%20Series%20 Manganini24_0.pdf; A Güler, M Shevtsova, D Venturi (eds), *LGBTI Asylum Seekers and Refugees from a Legal and Political Perspective: Persecution, Asylum and Integration* (Springer, 2018).

[56] Wessels (n 55).

[57] N Honkala, 'Islam v Secretary of State for the Home Department, R v Immigration Appeal Tribunal and Another, ex parte Shah' in E Rackley and R Auchmuty, *Celebrating the History of Women and Law in the UK and Ireland* (Hart Publishing, 1999).

[58] Canadian Immigration and Refugee Board, 'Guidelines on Women Refugee Claimants Fearing Gender-Related Persecution' (9 March 1993, updated November 1996) (hereafter Canadian Guidelines); US Immigration and Naturalization Service, 'Considerations For Asylum Officers Adjudicating Asylum Claims From Women' (26 May 1995) (hereafter US Guidelines); Australian Department of Immigration and Multi-Cultural Affairs, 'Guidelines on Gender Issues for Decision-Makers, July 1996' (hereafter Australian Guidelines). These explained to adjudicators not only how to approach gender claims but also the legal framework for assessing them.

[59] *In re Fauziya Kasinga*, 3278, United States Board of Immigration Appeals, 13 June 1996. *Kasinga* attracted significant media attention, for example: CW Dugger, 'US Grants Asylum to Woman Fleeing Genital Mutilation Rite' *New York Times* (14 June 1996); AM Rosenthal, 'On My Mind; To the Clintons and the Doles' *New York Times* (28 May 1996); and P Constable, 'Full Immigration Board Hears Female Genital Mutilation Case' *Washington Post* (3 May 1996).

[60] These developments were influenced by activism at the United Nations (UN) to prevent female genital cutting, women's rights advocacy in the US, media attention and the positive role of the decision-makers on the Board of Immigration Review. Sincere thanks to Ms Kasinga's lawyers, Layli Miller-Muro and Karen B Musalo, and former immigration appellate judge Lory Rosenberg and Paul Schmidt, involved in Ms Kasinga's case, for their communication with the author. Thanks also to the applicant herself whose strength and tireless advocacy were a critical component of this landmark case.

[61] For a detailed articulation of the refugee definition and its implementation, see F Khan and T Schreier (eds), *Refugee Law in South Africa* (Juta & Co, 2014).

[62] *In Re Kasinga: A Big Step Forward for Gender-Based Asylum Claims*, 73 Interpreter Releases, 853 (1 July 1996) and *Ruminations on In re Kasinga:The Decision's Legacy*, 7 U.S.C. Review of Law and Women's Studies 357 (1998); and K Musalo, 'A Short History of Gender Asylum in the United States: Resistance and Ambivalence May Very Slowly Be Inching Towards Recognition of Women's Claims' (2010) 29 *Refugee Survey Quarterly* 2.

gender equality in refugee law in the US followed,[63] denying protection to refugee women.[64] Notwithstanding ongoing challenges, Khawar shows how opportunities arise to overcome gender inequality in refugee law as part of transnational developments.

Since *Khawar*, there have been significant developments influenced by women's rights activists to challenge gender inequality in regional refugee law. In Africa, the Protocol to the African Charter on Human and People's Rights on the Rights of Women in Africa (Maputo Protocol) expands protections for refugee women, defining violence against women as both public and private.[65] Among progressive national asylum laws, South Africa extends refugee protection, albeit imperfectly,[66] to 'transgender-identified' refugees. In Latin America, many national asylum laws explicitly recognise gender as a ground for persecution.[67]

The groundbreaking decision of the Court of Justice of the European Union (CJEU) in 2024 strengthened the reasoning in *Khawar*, extending refugee protection to women fleeing structural, serious discrimination on account of their membership of a particular social group as Afghan women.[68] The applicants, two Afghan nationals, were denied refugee status in Austria because the gendered harm they feared by the Taliban regime was not found to be sufficiently severe to comprise persecution. The applicants' appeal to the CJEU made two findings. First, women from Afghanistan endure systematic and serious discrimination which amounts to persecution.[69] Second, the judgment found that women from Afghanistan can be a particular social group constituted by gender alone.[70] These developments to expand women's refugee protection after *Khawar*, however, must be understood in light of pervasive gender inequality in refugee law, explored below.

[63] L Frydman and K Seelinger, 'Kasinga's Protection Undermined? Recent Developments in Female Genital Cutting Jurisprudence' (2008) 18 *Bender's Immigration Bulletin* 1073.

[64] Almost three decades after the *Kasinga* decision, Musalo laments that it has since 'become almost impossible for women and girls to rely upon the particular social group ground because of current requirements that social groups not only be defined by immutable or fundamental characteristics, but also be socially distinct and have particularity', K Musalo, 'Aligning United States Law with International Norms Would Remove Major Barriers to Protection in Gender Claims' (2024) 36 *International Journal of Refugee Law* 1–2, 20.

[65] Article 1 defines violence against women as: '"Violence against women" means all acts perpetrated against women which cause or could cause them physical, sexual, psychological, and economic harm, including the threat to take such acts; or to undertake the imposition of arbitrary restrictions on or deprivation of fundamental freedoms in private or public life in peace time and during situations of armed conflicts or of war'. African Union, *Protocol to the African Charter on Human and People's Rights on the Rights of Women in Africa* [2003] (Maputo Protocol).

[66] B Camminga, '"Gender Refugees" in South Africa: The "Common-Sense" Paradox' (2018) 53 *Africa Spectrum*, *1*, 89–112.

[67] For detailed analysis, see O Hammoud-Gallego, 'A Liberal Region in a World of Closed Borders? The Liberalization of Asylum Policies in Latin America, 1990–2020' [2017] 56 *International Migration Review* 1, 63–96.

[68] C-608/22 & C-609/22 *AH, FN, v Bundesamt für Fremdenwesen und Asyl* ECLI:EU:C:2024:828.

[69] ibid [49]–[59].

[70] ibid [74].

V. The Limits of *Khawar*: Protection within an International Legal Framework with Gender Inequality at its Foundations

The success of *Khawar* and subsequent developments are qualified by feminist critiques,[71] providing important insights for refugee women, scholars, advocates and law-makers seeking to address ongoing gender inequality in refugee law. Three feminist critiques will be outlined next to argue that, despite improvement in the protection of women following *Khawar*, the refugee definition continues to be interpreted using distinctions that ignore women's experiences, perpetuate racial and gender stereotypes and makes a 'finite' improvement for the protection of refugee women in international refugee law that is gender unequal at its foundations.

First, it is argued that *Khawar* does not do enough to change the harmful public-private distinction in refugee law.[72] The decision continues to distinguish between 'private' domestic violence and 'public' state action. Wood argues that the public-private binary in *Khawar* must be revisited because it is based on the assumption that Ms Khawar is a private individual owned by her husband and therefore outside the scope of municipal law.[73] Further, Wood argues that the notion of formal equality of men and women in the law must be abandoned to acknowledge that women's oppression is masked in formalist legal language.[74] In this sense, Khawar obscures the role of legal methodology and jurisprudence, 'maintaining and legitimating a patriarchal status quo privileging male power over women, all the while employing a rhetoric of justice, neutrality and objectivity'.[75] This framing therefore perpetuates the public-private distinction to the detriment of women.

Second, *Khawar's* framing of gender persecution is critiqued as part of jurisprudence that perpetuates racial stereotypes of harm perpetrated by 'brown men against brown women'.[76] The refugee definition has been interpreted to include gendered harm by focusing primarily on violence perpetrated from within Global South communities.[77] Another critique is the attention to claims of rape and other forms

[71] For insightful analysis of the limitations of the category of 'gender' asylum claims, see C Querton, 'Gender and the Boundaries of International Refugee Law: Beyond the Category of Gender-Related Asylum Claims' (2019) 37 *Netherlands Quarterly of Human Rights* 4, 379. See also K Ogg, 'The Future of Feminist Engagement with Refugee Law: From the Margins to the Centre and Out of the "Pink Ghetto"?' in S Harris Rimmer and K Ogg (eds), *Research Handbook on Feminist Engagement with International Law* (Edward Elgar Publishing, 2019).

[72] A Roberts, 'Gender and Refugee Law' (2002) 22 *Australian Yearbook of International Law* 160, 161.

[73] A Wood, 'Legal Theories of the State and Membership 2002 – Case Analysis: Minister for Immigration and Multicultural Affairs v Khawar' (2002) 11 *Griffith Law Review* 497, 504.

[74] ibid 504.

[75] ibid 498.

[76] H Crawley, 'Saving Brown Women from Brown Men? "Refugee Women", Gender and the Racialised Politics of Protection' (2022) 41(3) *Refugee Survey Quarterly* 355, 355.

[77] J Middleton, 'Barriers to Protection: Gender-Related Persecution and Asylum in South Africa' in E Burman, K Chantler, P Kiguwa, and I Palmary (eds), *Gender and Migration: Feminist Interventions* (Zed Books, 2010) 78.

of sexual violence that fetishise women.[78] This framing is criticised, for example, for perpetuating the stereotypes of women in the Muslim world that Akram describes as 'neo-Orientalism'.[79] Feminist scholars have called for broader framing of gender persecution to include 'structural injustice',[80] for example for women experiencing gender barriers to access land or livelihoods. Scholarship focused on the strengths of refugee women subvert dominant narratives of vulnerability.[81]

Third, it is argued that *Khawar* improved the protection of women seeking asylum but within the context of gender discrimination in asylum law and policies that prevent women from leaving[82] or accessing territorial asylum.[83] For example, restrictions on movement due to laws requiring approval of male guardians to travel, as well as difficulties gaining entrance to countries to seek asylum through gender and racial discrimination in visa categories.[84] Therefore, *Khawar* has 'claimed a place for refugee women within protective rights mechanisms', according to Oswin, as a 'small portion of what is already extremely finite territory'.[85] Indeed, Dauvergne warns that 'the past three decades of feminist work in refugee law advocacy stand as a cautionary tale' because 'what began with a huge burst of energy and creativity in the final decade of the twentieth century has stalled spectacularly'.[86] The process to remove gender inequality from refugee law may not be linear but it is far from over.

VI. Conclusion

The *Khawar* decision demonstrates how moments of broader social and legal transformation to make women's rights more visible in international law, as seen in the 1990s, can create opportunities to develop international refugee law

[78] R Kapur, *Erotic Justice: Law and the New Politics of Postcolonialism* (Routledge, 2005).

[79] S Musarrat Akram, *Orientalism Revisited in Asylum and Refugee Claims.* Available at SSRN: https://ssrn.com/abstract=237371.

[80] S Parekh, 'Does Ordinary Injustice Make Extraordinary Injustice Possible? Gender, Structural Injustice, and the Ethics of Refugee Determination' (2012) 8(2–3) *Journal of Global Ethics* 269, 275.

[81] U Sunata and S Özsoy, 'Feminization of Refugee: Intersectionality, Solidarity, Resistance' (2022) 61(1) *International Migration* 273; A Khoday, 'Protecting Those Who Go Beyond the Law: Contemplating Refugee Status for Individuals Who Challenge Oppression Through Resistance' (2011) 25(3) *Georgetown Immigration Law Journal* 571.

[82] Most women may be unable to flee their country of origin due to lack of resources or freedom to move. For example, see J Bhabha, 'Border Rights and Rites: Generalizations, Stereotypes and Gendered Migration' in S van Walsum and T Spijkerboer (eds), *Women and Immigration Law: New Variations on Classical Feminist Themes* (Routledge-Cavendish, 2007) at 15.

[83] N Yacoub, 'Feminism' in V Chetail (ed), *Elgar Concise Encyclopedia of Migration and Asylum Law* (Edward Elgar Publishing, 2025) 170–79.

[84] Many women in the Global South cannot leave their countries to claim protection due to racial and gendered barriers. N Oswin, 'Rights Spaces: An Exploration of Feminist Approaches to Refugee Law' (2001) 3 *International Feminist Journal of Politics* 347, 348.

[85] ibid.

[86] C Dauvergne, 'Women in Refugee Jurisprudence' in C Costello, M Foster and J McAdam (eds), *The Oxford Handbook of International Refugee Law* (Oxford University Press, 2021).

to improve protection for refugee women. The case emerged during significant feminist scholarship and activism exposing gender inequality in international law, alongside evolving approaches by states and international organisations to incorporate gender considerations in refugee status determination. These developments laid the foundation for the Australian High Court to address women's historical exclusion from refugee protection through its progressive legal reasoning.

Yet *Khawar's* success remains qualified. While establishing an important precedent for recognising gender-based persecution, the decision operates within an international legal system that continues to marginalise women's experiences and creates barriers to accessing protection. Ongoing feminist engagement with international refugee law must move beyond the refugee definition.[87] It has the potential to challenge and transform states' interpretation of fundamental international law principles which exclude refugee women's rights, including in practices such as interception at sea[88] and externalisation.[89] Recent developments, including regional refugee standards on gender and climate,[90] as well as the Global Compacts on Migrants and Refugees,[91] provide some opportunities to advance this work. The journey of refugee law that *Khawar* represents – from the minimisation of women's experiences to their recognition – remains unfinished.

[87] N Yacoub, 'Feminist Approaches to Recenter Humanity in International Migration Law' (ch 24) in J Jarpa Dawuni, N Grossman, J Ramji-Nogales and H Ruiz Fabri (eds), *The Oxford Handbook of Women and International Law* (Oxford University Press, 2025).

[88] For a critique of states' exclusion of gendered violence in customary principles of law of the sea and international refugee law, see N Yacoub, N Errington, WW Nu and A Robinson, 'Rights Adrift: Sexual Violence Against Rohingya Women on the Andaman Sea' (2021) 2(1) *Asia-Pacific Journal on Human Rights and the Law* 96.

[89] S Vasefi and S Dehm, 'Refugee Women and the Gendered Violence of Australia's Extraterritorial Asylum Regime on Nauru' (2022) 41 *Refugee Survey Quarterly* 3, 529.

[90] For example, the African Union *Convention on Ending Violence Against Women and Girls* 2025 addresses violence against women presenting concerns of future displacement for women.

[91] Future feminist engagement remains critical, since there continues to be a perception that migration is 'to stay within Global South countries or people are turned away from state borders as they approach the Global North'. J Hyndman and J Reynolds, 'Introduction: Beyond the Global Compacts' [2020] 63 *Refuge: Canada's Journal on Refugees* 1, 66–74, 67.

3

The Diary of a Strategic Litigation Lawyer. *HJ (Iran) and HT (Cameroon)* [2010]: Beacon of Hope, or Template for Exclusion*

S CHELVAN

I. Introduction

If I point a gun towards you, do you run towards the gun or away from the gun?**

On 7 July 2010, a round of applause followed the end of Lord Hope's reading of the summary judgment of the UK Supreme Court in the case of *HJ (Iran) and HT (Cameroon) v Secretary of State for the Home Department.*[1] In allowing the appeals of two gay men, this landmark judgment rejected a prior canon of case law that applied a test of 'reasonably tolerable discretion' to asylum applicants who were denied

* Elements of this chapter are drawn from my PhD thesis for King's College London (2019), *At the End of the Rainbow: Where Next for the Queer Refugee – Understanding Queer Refugees' Lives, Moving from Sexual Conduct to Identity on Sexual Orientation/Identity Asylum Cases in England and Wales* (not published). My PhD thesis is dedicated to my now late-husband Mark Chelvan-Stanmore (6 October 1963–13 March 2024). We commenced our relationship meeting on his birthday in 2001, whilst I was in my last six weeks prior to completion of pupillage. As the spouse, and soulmate of a strategic litigation lawyer, I was always indebted to Mark and publicly recognised the role he has had in my career, not just building and maintaining our home life so I could concentrate on my career, to becoming personal friends of former clients, to the devastating timing of his death, two weeks before his retirement and next chapter of our then nearly 23 years, including nearly 18 years of marriage. Drafting this chapter has been an emotional journey, both memory and loss triggers and I am greatly indebted to our co-editors of the volume, Professors Kirsten McConnachie and Sarah Singer for their immense support and guidance. 'Your passion' the description of what motivated former clients when describing my approach to the law, following 'Passion, compassion, intelligence' on why Mark was in love with me, grounds why I am committed to representing refugees and migrants and their right to love, as in my lifetime I have experienced what it is to love, and be loved.

** A presentational learning tool used by the author since 2006 to provide a non-legal analogy with respect to the impact and lack of real choice the majority of refugee applicants have when faced with persecution.

[1] *HJ (Iran) and HT (Cameroon) v Secretary of State for the Home Department* [2010] UKSC 31, [2011] 1 AC 596 (hereafter *HJ and HT*).

refugee protection on the basis they had failed to establish that it would not be reasonably tolerable for them to adopt 'discretion' on return, to conceal their sexual orientation and evade an accepted well-founded fear of persecution. In doing so, the judgment reaffirmed the underlying protection rationale of the 1951 Convention relating to the Status of Refugees (1951 Refugee Convention)[2] regime, highlighted by Lord Rodger as the right to 'live openly and freely without that fear' of persecution, whether the applicant is 'black, or the descendants of some former dictator, or gay […]'[3] thereby re-elevating 'fear' as the determinative factor in refugee and human rights protection status determination in the United Kingdom (UK).

In recognising that 'no straight person would find discretion reasonably tolerable', the Supreme Court recognised that 'discretion reasoning' was disproportionately applied to gay and lesbian appellants. Evidence of this was first clear in the body of the Court of Appeal's judgments from 2004[4] and was confirmed by statistical evidence of systemic bias against gay asylum applicants (with the UK Lesbian and Gay Immigration Group finding a 98–99 per cent Home Office decision refusal rate based solely on the discretion test for gay applicants, compared to a uniform 73 per cent refusal rate for non-gay asylum claims).[5]

However, while the judgment in *HJ and HT* is generally perceived as a breakthrough in the protection of gay refugees in the UK, it failed to remove discretion reasoning entirely. As discussed below, Lord Rodger's binding guidance for fact-finding Tribunals retains discretion-reasoning in its final conduct 'limb'. According to this guidance, where an applicant would be returning to a country where it is accepted that there is a well-founded fear of persecution of those who are openly gay, and where it is found that that applicant would act discreetly on return, protection will be denied where this discretion is found to arise for reasons of personal choice or social pressure. This final limb of the judgment retains discretion reasoning as part of the asylum claim assessment and thus provides a template for exclusion, rather than a beacon of hope to those who have made the physical and emotional journey to seek sanctuary in the UK. Even where those asylum claimants have successfully navigated the evidential maze to 'prove' that they are gay and to establish objective country evidence of real risk of harm on return to those who are open, such applicants can nevertheless be returned based on the presumption they will be 'successfully' discreet and avoid persecution. This single finding on their behaviour on return leads to refusal of asylum, notwithstanding making a protection claim which is based on well-founded fear of harm (the central core litigation point required to initiate the asylum claim in the UK proceedings). After return, discretion must be maintained not for one day, or one week, but for the rest of their lives.

[2] UN General Assembly, 1951 Convention relating to the Status of Refugees, United Nations, Treaty Series, 189:137, 28 July 1951 (1951 Refugee Convention).

[3] *HJ and HT* (n 1) [53].

[4] *Z v Secretary of State for the Home Department* [2004] EWCA Civ 1578, [2005] Imm AR 75 (hereafter *Z*).

[5] L Millikin Gray, *Failing the Grade* (UK Lesbian & Gay Immigration Group (UKLGIG), April 2010), analysing data based on asylum claims brought to the attention of UKLGIG from 2005 to 2009.

As a UK-based strategic litigation lawyer, called to the Bar by the Inner Temple in October 1999, I have been specialising in Queer Refugee cases and policy development in the UK for over 20 years, litigating cases before the UK Courts and Tribunals (pre- and post-*HJ and HT*), up to and including the UK Supreme Court, and the European Court of Human Rights (ECtHR).

My role as a barrister is firstly as a story-teller, creating a safe-space for my clients' voice, that is recorded in their statements and their evidence. My role is also that of an interpreter, interpreting their words into the foreign language we call 'the law'. This requires understanding and believing in the law as a driver of positive change, even where at times it is applied as a straitjacket of binding precedent. The art of a strategic litigation lawyer is to identify the gaps, as these may one day form legal bridges in the form of the causative nexus. As I now share with my post-graduate students, a positive precedent is applied to your case, a negative precedent is distinguished on the facts, and a binding precedent faces 'litigation, litigation and litigation' to locate the gaps and enable the court to revisit earlier judgments. The Supreme Court, adopting the same reasoning of the earlier House of Lords, makes clear in the Court's Procedure Rules that it will revisit binding decisions 'when it appear[s] right to do so'.[6] In the canon of 'discretion' reasoning in asylum cases that time must be now. As this chapter highlights in its final section, an end to the application of discretion reasoning now appears imminent following the ECtHR judgment in *MI v Switzerland*, in conjunction with ongoing litigation following the Court of Appeal's judgment in *Secretary of State for the Home Department v PG*.[7]

II. From *Binbasi* [1989] to *XY (Iran)* [2008]: The UK's Fixation with Gay Sex and Reasonably Tolerable Discretion

Persecution based on identification of 'difference' is embedded at the core of the 1951 Refugee Convention. The horrific images of those incarcerated and murdered within Nazi camps should never be forgotten. Those who were persecuted were those perceived as different, who were rendered visible by badges highlighting their convergent narratives of 'difference', including Jews (Star of David) but also gay men (inverted pink triangles) and lesbians (inverted black triangles).

Despite the evident persecution of Queer people at this time, Refugee Convention signatory countries would exclude Queer refugee applicants from refugee protection,

[6] UK Supreme Court, Practice Direction 3.5, available at https://supremecourt.uk/how-to-appeal/practice-directions.

[7] *Secretary of State for the Home Department v PG* [2025] EWCA Civ 133. Unreported elsewhere. Permission application refused by the Supreme Court on 5 August 2025 (UKSC/2025/0078), available at https://supremecourt.uk/cases/uksc-2025-0078. Court of Appeal 18 February 2025 Order remits *PG's* appeal back to the Upper Tribunal, to be substantively reconsidered on Art 3 ECHR grounds.

highlighting a protection-gap and reflecting their own continued persecution of this marginalised group whose 'difference' arises from the social construction of otherness. Queerness is constructed as a deviation from heteronormative gender and sex-roles, giving rise to stigma, shame, harm and persecution.

The Netherlands was the first Refugee Convention signatory country to positively recognise sexual orientation as a protection ground (in 1981).[8] It took many more years for the UK to reach a similar point. In 1989, the Queen's Bench Division in *Binbasi*[9] refused Convention protection to even those labelled (sexually-)'active homosexuals'. The UK would not afford this group Convention protection where there existed a lack of persecution of those who refrain from sexual conduct. *Binbasi* drew on the earlier political opinion case of *Mendis*[10] in finding that where there exists an opportunity to refrain from an act that would give rise to persecution, the applicant who refuses to refrain from that conduct places himself outside Convention protection.[11] *Binbasi* established a fixation on sexual conduct in asylum claims of gay men, which continued up to and including *XY (Iran)* in 2008,[12] a line of legal argumentation characterised by Millbank as the British 'preoccupation with perversion'.[13]

In 1999, the House of Lords in *Shah and Islam* drew on international case law to support its conclusion that gender was an 'immutable characteristic' and therefore women could be considered a 'particular social group' and eligible for Convention protection if they suffer persecution for that reason.[14] In doing so, the House of Lords corrected a historical wrong: the failure to include 'sex' (as in 'gender') as a protected Convention ground in Article 1A(2). In the most important obiter breadcrumbs from the judicial table, Lord Steyn in *Shah and Islam* additionally found that 'practising homosexuals', due to their distinct status as a discriminated social group, who share 'an innate and immutable characteristic',[15] may also be protected as a 'particular social group'.[16]

[8] *Afdeling rechtspraak van de Raad van State* (Judicial Division of the Council of State, 13 August 1981), (unreported) *Rechtspraak Vreemdelingenrecht* 1981, 5, *Gids Vreemdelingenrecht (oud)* D12-51 cited in S Jansen and T Spijkerboer, 'Fleeing Homophobia: Asylum Claims Related to Sexual Orientation and Gender Identity in Europe' (Amsterdam, 2011) 19, fn 36, available at www.refworld.org/docid/4ebba7852.html.

[9] *R v Secretary of State for the Home Department ex parte Zia Mehmet Binbasi* [1989] Imm AR 595.

[10] *Mendis v Secretary of State for the Home Department* [1989] Imm AR 6.

[11] *Binbasi* (n 9) at 599.

[12] *XY (Iran) v Secretary of State for the Home Department* [2008] EWCA Civ 911 (unreported elsewhere).

[13] J Millbank, 'A Preoccupation with Perversion: The British Response to Refugee Claims on the Basis of Sexual Orientation 1989-2003' (2005) 14(1) *Social & Legal Studies* 115.

[14] In this case, defined variously as 'women of Pakistan' and 'Pakistani women … accused of transgressing social mores'. *R v Immigration Appeal Tribunal ex part Shah* and *Islam v Secretary of State for the Home Department* [1999] 2 AC 629. See further N Yacoub, '*Minister for Immigration and Multicultural Affairs v Khawar* [2002]: Protection for Refugee Women through Transitional Jurisprudence and Feminist Advocacy' in ch 2 of this volume.

[15] See also *In re Costa* (1985) 19 I. & N 211 cited in *Shah and Islam* (n 14) [641B] and [643C-E] (Lord Steyn).

[16] *Shah and Islam* (n 14) [643C-E] (Lord Steyn).

Within the year, relying on this reasoning, the Court of Appeal in *Jain*[17] afforded male homosexuals[18] Convention protection against persecution in their home countries as members of a 'particular social group'. However this protection was limited in scope by considering persecution as prosecution (ie criminalisation of the 'sex act') rather than constructing a continuum of treatment on which to place sexual identity asylum claims.

This slither of hope for eventual recognition of non-discriminatory protection for Queer refugees would be cast back into the shadows. The concept of voluntary discretion was deployed as a legal tool to exclude positive refugee status determination for Queer refugees, who were instead returned to countries where they must live a lie to evade detection and persecution, in all likelihood for the rest of their lives.

The canon of 'discretion test' case law, embedded and developed by the Court of Appeal from 2004 to 2009, commenced in December 2004 in *Z*[19] with a misguided interpretation of the 2003 Australian High Court judgment in *Appellants S395/S396*.[20] The requirement to show discretion voluntarily adopted by the Queer refugee was in itself persecutory, with the required intensity or duration (a life and lifetime), effectively rendering the home to act as a cage with sexual conduct to be limited to the presumed safety of the bedroom. In the UK, this 'discretion test' was systematically and disproportionally applied to Queer refugee claims and developed through a succession of cases to the 'reasonably tolerable discretion test' in 2006 in *J*.[21] In February 2009, the Court of Appeal expanded the reach of the test with additional judicial deference to bigotry in its decision in *HJ (Iran) and HT (Cameroon)*,[22] by including consideration of the underlying cultural, religious and social mores that underpin persecutory conduct in its assessment of what should be considered as reasonably tolerable discretion. Per Pill LJ:

> The need to protect fundamental human rights transcends national boundaries but, in assessing *whether there has been a breach of such rights, a degree of respect for social norms and religious beliefs in other states is in my view appropriate*. Both in Muslim Iran and Roman Catholic Cameroon, strong views are genuinely held about homosexual practices. *In considering what is reasonably tolerable in a particular society, the fact-finding Tribunal is in my view entitled to have regard to the beliefs held there. A judgment as to what is reasonably tolerable is made in the context of the particular society*. Analysis

[17] *Sham Jain v Secretary of State for the Home Department* [2000] INLR 71.

[18] As the judicial reasoning is focussed on criminal legislation prohibiting (male) same-sex conduct then it cannot be assumed that the courts at this time provided equal surrogate protection to lesbians. This is irrespective of the fact as of June 2025, around 40 out of the 63 countries specifically criminalise same-sex conduct between women, see International Lesbian and Gay Association (ILGA) (2025), available at https://database.ilga.org/criminalisation-consensual-same-sex-sexual-acts.

[19] *Z* (n 4).

[20] *Appellant S395/2002 v Minister for Immigration and Multicultural Affairs*; *Appellant S* [2004] INLR 233 (hereafter *Appellants S395/S396*).

[21] *J v Secretary of State for the Home Department* [2006] 1238, [207] Imm AR73 (hereafter *J*).

[22] *HJ (Iran) and HT (Cameroon) v Secretary of State for the Home Department* [2009] EWCA Civ 172, [2009]Imm AR 600 (hereafter *HJ and HT*).

> of in-country evidence is necessary in deciding what an applicant can expect on return and cannot, in my view, be ignored when considering that issue.' (Emphasis added.)[23]

This approach placed the UK in the position of de facto enforcer of these norms[24] contrary to its Convention obligations to protect against these forms of discrimination historically known to lead to persecution.

III. *HJ and HT*: A Narrative of Litigation and a Case Study in Perseverance

Millbank highlights the use of discretion reasoning in asylum claims as being 'extraordinarily widespread, resistant to challenge and strongly associated with high rejection rates for lesbian, gay and bisexual refugee claims'.[25] *HJ and HT* marks a seminal landmark case with respect to the analysis of discretion, and one which I was associated with personally and professionally due to my instruction as Counsel to represent HT.

The procedural history for HT was exceptionally problematic. In September 2008 I was contacted by Sebastian Rocca, then Executive Director of the UK Lesbian and Gay Immigration Group. The request was to provide urgent assistance to a gay man from Cameroon, who was subject to removal and had exhausted his in-country appeal rights, subject to removal directions in 11 days. One of HT's supporters had contacted the charity requesting urgent assistance due to the imminent real risk of removal.

HT's factual narrative was unusual within the context of asylum claims based on sexual identity at that time. Even though he had suffered past persecution, the UK courts held that he could internally relocate within Cameroon, where he could be voluntarily discreet. In September 2006, following being seen kissing his boyfriend in his back garden and then identified as a 'homosexual', HT was ridiculed and subjected to a mob attack. The police participated in the attack rather than provided protection, and HT required two months of hospitalisation to treat the injuries he suffered during the attack.

HT fled Cameroon and arrived in the UK with plans for onward travel to Canada. In January 2007, he was apprehended at Gatwick airport prior to boarding a flight to Canada and informed that the passport he was travelling on was false. He was arrested, prosecuted and (having entered a guilty plea) sentenced to a term of imprisonment of just over 12 months. Having been convicted of a criminal offence, HT was then served with a decision notifying him of his liability for deportation. This

[23] ibid [32] (Pill LJ).

[24] *Refugee Appeal No 74655/03* [2005] INLR 68 [114] (RPG Haines QC).

[25] J Millbank, 'The Right of Lesbians and Gay Men to Live Freely, Openly, and on Equal Terms Is Not Bad Law: A Reply to Hathaway and Pobjoy' (2012) 44 *NYU Journal of International Law and Politics* 497, 506.

prompted him to make his application for asylum arising from his clear past narrative and future fear of persecution as a gay man from Cameroon.

HT is, and was accepted at all material times by the UK authorities as, a gay man. Born in 1974, his sexual identity was known to him for a decade prior to his arrival in the UK, with relationships in Cameroon conducted clandestinely for fear of discovery and harm. This acceptance of HT's sexual identity without intrusive or inappropriate questioning reflected the default position of the then-UK Border Agency with respect to the majority of asylum claims based on sexual identity: accept the sexual identity of the applicant and then refuse asylum on the *J* test (reasonable tolerability of discretion).[26]

The Secretary of State's August 2007 decision in refusing HT's protection claim made the following findings of fact, which would form the basis of the administrative and judicial proceedings, up to and including the Supreme Court's judgment, nearly three years later in July 2010:

> It is accepted that you have been assaulted in the past for your sexual orientation and the Police joined in with this attack. However, as stated above it would be possible for you to practice homosexuality in private and not come to the attention of the authorities. The option exists for you to relocate to an area of Cameroon where you are not known and therefore your sexual orientation would not be widely known … it is therefore reasonable to expect you to be able to relocate to another part of Cameroon where you are not known and can practise homosexuality in private.

HJ[27] the conjoined appellant with *HT* when both appeals were substantively heard by the Court of Appeal in February 2009, concerned a gay Iranian man. The Asylum and Immigration Tribunal found he had held barbeques with his boyfriend in his back garden in Tehran without difficulties. His ability to form relationships with other gay men through work colleagues was considered by the Tribunal

[26] See Millikin Gray (n 5).

[27] On appeal from *HJ (homosexuality: Reasonably tolerating living discreetly) Iran* [2008] UKAIT 00044. Maurice Kay LJ, who in his lead judgment in *J* provided the 'reasonable tolerability' test held, in granting permission in September 2008, the Tribunal had arguably misapplied the test. He also gave permission in *AM (Syria)* on the papers on the same point, finding that conduct was influenced by his 'respect for the law' where the evidence showed criminal sanctions for consensual adult same-sex conduct. The appeal was consented out by the Secretary of State for the Home Department within 14 days prior to the Court of Appeal litigation (C5/2008/1760) (20 January 2009), case cited by Rix LJ at [22] of the judgment who with Carnworth LJ granted permission to appeal, subject to the jurisdiction point *HT (Cameroon) v Secretary of State for the Home Department* [2008] EWCA Civ 1288 (22 October 2008) (hereafter *HT*). *AM's* appeal on asylum/Art 3 grounds allowed by offer of remittal to Tribunal by the Secretary of State, due to a lack of finding on Art 8 European Convention on Human Rights (May 2010). In hindsight, noting the approach of the Supreme Court in *HJ*, as criminal sanctions in Syria were applied, then as modification was directly related to a persecutory law, this would have been a strong fact case, making the Secretary of State's position in defending three appeals more difficult. *HT* had a strong factual case, where he had suffered past-persecution at the hands of state and non-state agents, probative of future risk on return ([339K], *Demirkaya v Secretary of State for the Home Department* [1999] EWCA Civ 1654; 1999 Imm AR 498 applied. I was instructed as sole Counsel for *AM (Syria)* in both the proceedings before the Court of Appeal and remitted Upper Tribunal, where the appeal was allowed, and *AM (Syria)* was granted asylum.

(and later by the Court of Appeal) as an indicator that his life in Iran had not entailed harm (bar earlier problems when at school) and therefore that living discreetly in Iran on return, even in the knowledge of the risk, would be 'reasonably tolerable'.

As explained above, the Court of Appeal judgment in *HJ and HT* introduced 'cultural relativism' to the 'reasonably tolerable discretion' test, whereby the social and religious norms of a country should also be considered when determining whether discretion was 'reasonably tolerable'.[28] This approach disproportionately extended exclusion of Queer refugees by embedding the perception of a homophobic and unjustifiably discriminatory approach to sexual identity asylum claims.[29]

The subsequent appeal of *HJ and HT* to the Supreme Court marked a positive fundamental shift from a focus on conduct to a partially identity-based analysis. The judgment struck down the Court of Appeal's 'reasonably tolerable discretion test'[30] as an immeasurable yardstick to measure and one that would ordinarily result in a lifetime of invisibility to evade persecution. The *HJ and HT* judgment also included in the first limb of Lord Rodger's guidelines a perception category, a fundamental mirror category in Convention-reason group membership, but one with greater significance in Queer refugee claims in emphasising that 'perception is key'. This enabled later case law to develop consideration of the significance of non-heteronormative conformity identity triggers, based on 'difference', that lead to serious harm from a potential persecutor.

IV. *HJ (Iran) and HT (Cameroon)* Supreme Court Judgment and Reasoning

It was clear to the Supreme Court in *HJ and HT* that the test of whether discretion is 'reasonably tolerable' is intrinsically difficult to measure and fundamentally flawed. No straight person would accept such discretion, which is in effect, for a lifetime.[31] Lord Rodger held that such a test undermines the very rationale of the Convention which protects an ability to live 'openly and freely',[32] and to form relationships without fear of persecution. Where the home state does not protect, the international community steps in to provide surrogate protection.[33] The Secretary of State's submission that even Anne Frank would not be a refugee if she presented

[28] *HJ and HT* (n 22) 32.

[29] Millikin Gray (n 5).

[30] *J* (n 21) 80 [16]–[17] (Maurice-Kay LJ). The test was held to be a misinterpretation of the guidance set by the High Court of Australia in *Appellants S395/S396* (n 20) [40], accepted as arguable by Maurice-Kay LJ when granting permission to appeal to the Court of Appeal, on the papers, to *HJ (Iran)* and another appellant *AM (Syria)* (n 27).

[31] *HJ and HT* (n 1) 596, 645, [75]–[76] (Lord Rodger).

[32] ibid 596, 637–638, [53] (Lord Rodger).

[33] *Horvath v Secretary of State for the Home Department* [2001] 1 AC 489.

herself to a UK court having escaped the confines of the attic, failing to establish that her life in the attic had reached the high threshold of persecution, was held by the Court to be 'absurd and unreal'.[34]

The sub-heading on the reported case refers to the guidance of Lord Hope as 'the test' and of Lord Rodger's guidelines as 'the approach to be followed by Tribunals'.[35] However, it is clear from reading the judgment that Lord Hope's 'test' does not provide the binding guidance, as firstly, all three other Justices support Lord Rodger's guidelines.[36] Further, the reference to rejection of a claim based on simply voluntary discretion 'in response to social pressures or for cultural and religious reasons of his own choosing' has a direct causative nexus to the emanation of persecution, reaffirming the cultural relativism test of Pill LJ in the Court of Appeal, rejected by Lord Dyson, MR ('Master of the Rolls') in *HJ and HT*.[37] On this basis, contrary to the Secretary of State's current published policy position,[38] the binding guidance is that of Lord Rodger.

Lord Rodger's guidelines on 'The approach to be followed by Tribunals' are:

(a) First limb – Is the Appellant gay, or will s/he/they be perceived to be gay on return;
(b) Second limb – Do 'openly' gay people have a well-founded fear of persecution on return (not an assessment of risk to the general gay population, as invisibility would be how the majority would act due to fear of persecution);
(c) Third limb – Will the individual be open on return (identifiable through positive act or negative omission)? – if so, they are a refugee; if not;
(d) Fourth limb – What is the reason for 'voluntary discretion' on return (conduct in the UK is immaterial)? – *if it is simply through personal choice or social pressure then they are not a refugee*; if a material reason for voluntary discretion is a fear of persecution, then they are a refugee (emphasis added).[39]

A fact-finding Tribunal's first step is to establish an individual is gay, lesbian or bisexual, or will be perceived to be, on return to their country of origin. This importantly recognises the risk to those who do not live what I term a 'heterosexual narrative', ie living, or being perceived to live, a straight life, by engaging in a socially expected heterosexual gender-sex role.[40]

Second, an assessment will be required of what would occur to a gay, lesbian, or bisexual person, if they lived 'openly and freely' in the country of origin. If, as a result of living openly, there would be persecution, then the fear is well-founded.

Third, if it is found that they will live 'openly' then on the basis of having established persecutory harm to those who are open, they are entitled to refugee status.

[34] *HJ and HT* (n 1) 596, 655, [107] (Lord Collins).
[35] ibid at [35] for Lord Hope's test and [82] for Lord Rodger's guidance.
[36] ibid 596, 653 and 661, [98], [100] and [132] (Lord Walker, Lord Collins and Lord Dyson).
[37] ibid 596, 660–61, [128]–[130] (Lord Dyson JSC).
[38] Home Office, 'Asylum Policy Instruction on Sexual Orientation Issues in Asylum Claims (version 6)' (August 2016) 38. The published policy does not record Lord Hope's name, but it does record the offending cultural relativism reference within [35 (d)] of *HJ and HT* (n 1) 596, 631.
[39] *HJ and HT* (n 1) 596, 647–48 [82] (Lord Rodger).
[40] See for further analysis on this point, S Chelvan, 'SB (Uganda) – Case Comment' (2010) 24 (2) *Journal of Immigration, Asylum and Nationality Law* 191.

It is the fourth 'limb' of the guidance that retains a consideration of a gay refugee's ability to 'live discreetly'. If the *only* reason for being discreet is 'simply' family or social disapproval or personal choice, then the individual is not entitled to refugee status. This does not ignore the many cases of honour killing as a result of family disapproval, for this is a recognised form of persecutory harm. The Court recognises in the final limb that there can be a multitude of reasons for fearing return, but fear of persecution does not have to be the 'primary' fear. If a material reason for (voluntary) discretion includes fear of persecution, then the individual is a refugee.

Persecution requires attainment of a high threshold. Contrary to a knee-jerk and highly ill-informed Migration Watch press statement issued on the day of the handing down of the judgment (declaring that anyone from a country where homosexuality is criminalised with a lack of social and political equality will be able to successfully claim asylum),[41] the Court of Appeal had already held in *OO (Sudan) and JM (Uganda)*[42] that mere criminalisation without enforcement does not amount to persecution. This approach was subsequently approved by the Court of Justice of the European Union in *XYZ v Germany.*[43]

Following the Supreme Court's judgment, *HT* was rightly granted refugee status in November 2010 by the Secretary of State, without the need for a further Tribunal hearing.[44] *HJ* was granted Indefinite Leave to Remain in January 2010, prior to the May 2010 hearing. His remitted appeal before the Upper Tribunal was finally abandoned in June 2012, following his grant of British citizenship, nullifying any appeal on asylum grounds.[45]

V. Critique of the Judgment – Historical Rights and Wrongs

Outright rejection of the lawfulness of the *HJ and HT* judgment, for different reasons, were advanced and circulated as early as 2011. In a critique entitled 'Queer Cases Make Bad Law', James Hathaway and Jason Pobjoy (now KC) characterised the Supreme Court's approach as undermining the Convention by enabling protection to a category of refugees who are granted asylum without establishing future risk at the requisite intensity of harm (ie persecution).[46] The challenge advanced

[41] See H Mitchell QC, 'Homosexuals, Asylum and the Supreme Court' (*Migration Watch*, 7 July 2010).

[42] *OO (Sudan) and JM (Uganda) v Secretary of State for the Home Department* [2009] EWCA Civ 1432, [2010] All ER (D) 17 (Jun).

[43] Case C-199/12 to C-201/12 *Ministr voor Immigratie en Asiel v X, Y and Z* [2014] 3 WLR 770.

[44] Email communication with Russell Blakely, *HT*'s solicitor, Wilson Solicitors LLP, 22nd November 2010.

[45] Email communications with Deirdre Sheahan, *HJ*'s solicitor, Paragon Law, 24th January 2011 and 31st March 2017.

[46] J Hathaway and J Pobjoy, 'Queer Cases Make Bad Law' (2011–12) 44 (2) NYJ of *International Law & Politics* 315.

by them centres on categorising the risk of persecution as rendered implausible when living with discretion, thus requiring psychological internal harm to establish Convention protection where there exists no external harm (when living with discretion or concealing identity). They argue that concealment for reasons of persecution that does not have a real risk of materialising should not lead to positive status determination. This point of academic analysis is directly analogous to the 'double persecution' arising from the 'reasonably tolerable discretion' test which was specifically rejected by the Supreme Court in *HJ and HT*.

The *Opinos Juris* blog website subsequently published a set of responses by academics and practitioners to Hathaway and Pobjoy's article.[47] Goodwin-Gill whole-heartedly rejected the Hathaway and Pobjoy criticism of *HJ and HT* as over-reaching the limits of the Refugee Convention, making clear the definition 'protects those who fear persecution, because of who they are, and who should not lose that protection if, fearing persecution, they might seek to conceal their "true" identity'.[48] Anker and Ardalan argued that Hathaway and Pobjoy 'do not fully acknowledge the importance of the rights to equal treatment and non-discrimination',[49] while Millbank concluded that even if 'Hathaway and Pobjoy [are] correct in every particular [argument] of theirs, it is impossible to accept that *HJ and HT* could inflict a greater harm than the one it has remedied'.[50]

The fundamental flaw with the Hathaway and Pobjoy approach is firstly the omission of the precursor to the harm, the 'well-founded fear' component, which does not require the applicant to show *actual* harm will be faced on the hypothetical return to country of origin, but that there is a 'real risk' of future harm. Secondly, the implausibility of harm due to discretion as the central tenet did not address the possibility of lack of success, or even the drastic steps that must be deployed in order to 'prove straight' and not be identified as gay. In my own contribution to the *Opinio Juris* collection, I made clear that,

> [i]t is the identification of difference, with the consequent attachment of requisitioned stigma based on social/religious/cultural norms that results in the harms. This provides

[47] The Hathaway and Pobjoy article was then published by the New York University journal in a special edition (Winter 2012) with a collection of articles addressing their position taken against *HJ and HT* including Millbank (n 25); D Anker and S Ardalan, 'Escalating Persecution of Gays and Refugees Protection: Comment on Queer Cases Make Bad Law' *NJU Journal of International Law and Politics* 44: 2, 529 Online Symposium (9 March 2012), available at https://nyujilp.org/wp-content/uploads/2010/06/44.2-Anker-Ardalan.pdf and J Tobin, 'Assessing GLBTI Refugee Claims: Using Human Rights Law to Shift the Narrative of Persecution Within Refugee Law' *NJU Journal of International Law and Politics* 44: 2, 447 Online Symposium (9 March 2012), available at https://nyujilp.org/wp-content/uploads/2010/06/44.2-Tobin.pdf. S Chelvan, 'Queer Cases: Great Law: S Chelvan Responds to Jenni Millbank and Gugleilmo Verdirame' *NJU Journal of Internation Law and Politics* 44: 2 Online Symposium (9 March 2012), available at http://opiniojuris.org/2012/03/09/queer-cases-great-law-s-chelvan-responds-to-jenni-millbank-guglielmo-verdirame/. *HJ and HT* (n 1) 596, 645 [75] (Lord Rodger).

[48] GS Goodwin-Gill, 'The Dynamic of International Refugee Law' (2013) 25 *International Journal of Refugee Law* 651, 662.

[49] Anker and Ardalan (n 47) 529, 539.

[50] Millbank (n 25) 497, 527.

> a correct focus not on 'protected and unprotected activities' but on 'protected status'. This is what the Supreme Court protects in *HJ [and HT]*.'[51]

However, noting the international expertise and respect that Hathaway commands as a leading academic in the field of refugee law, when Counsel for the respondent Home Secretary submitted to the Supreme Court in *RT (Zimbabwe)*[52] an acceptance of *HJ and HT* as being correctly decided, a palpable sigh of relief was heard in the court room.[53]

VI. The Immediate Response: Having to Explain British Humour

As US lawyers must have felt in 2003, when their Supreme Court struck down anti-sodomy laws in *Lawrence and Grant v Texas*,[54] and again in 2015 with the *Obergefell v Hodges*[55] ruling on equal marriage rights for same-sex couples, my own reflection on the initial impact of *HJ and HT* was summarised in the following emotions: 'the United Kingdom's Supreme Court's judgment [...] marked a phenomenal day, not just for LGBTI[56] asylum law, but also for asylum law, LGBTI rights, and British justice!'[57] Queer jurisprudential activists sang in praise of the judgment, whilst not at all times fully appreciating the unique sense of British humour underpinning the late Lord Rodger's focus on difference and protection – leading to the case's unique sub-heading as 'the Kylie concert case'.

Yes, my comments above were published in an article entitled 'Put Your Hands Up if You Feel Love'– the title to the third track of Kylie's 2010 *Aphrodite* album. Yes, my cocktail *du jour* at the time was the Porn Star Martini. And, yes, I have a coterie of female friends who are assembled to discuss the joys and faults of the male of the species. So, having collected the *HJ and HT* judgment that morning, on the afternoon of 7 July 2010, with other activists at the University of Greenwich's conference on Lesbian, Gay, Bisexual, Transgender and Intersex (LGBTI) asylum, I laughed with joy, as did everyone else, when I shared with the delegates Lord Rodger's comments on gay men being entitled to go to a Kylie concert, drink exotically coloured cocktails, and discuss 'boys' with their straight female mates:

> What is protected is the applicant's right to live freely and openly as a gay man. That involves a wide spectrum of conduct, going well beyond conduct designed to attract

[51] Chelvan (n 47).

[52] *RT (Zimbabwe) and anor v Secretary of State for the Home Department* [2012] UKSC 38, [2013] 1 AC 152.

[53] I attended the hearing while a PhD student at King's College London.

[54] *Lawrence and Grant v Texas* (2003) 539 US 558.

[55] *Obergefell et al v Hodges, Director, Ohio Department of Health et al* (2015) 576 US.

[56] Whilst the Supreme Court did not address asylum claims based on gender identity, it would be inconceivable that the guidelines would not also apply to Trans or Intersex claims.

[57] S Chelvan, 'Put Your Hands Up if You Feel Love' (2011) 25 *Journal of Immigration, Asylum and Nationality Law* 55–86, at 56.

> sexual partners and maintain relationships with them. To illustrate the point with trivial stereotypical examples from British society: *just as male heterosexuals are free to enjoy themselves playing rugby, drinking beer and talking about girls with their mates, so male homosexuals are to be free to enjoy themselves going to Kylie concerts, drinking exotically coloured cocktails and talking about boys with their straight female mates.* Mutatis mutandis – and in many cases the adaptations would obviously be great – the same must apply to other societies. In other words, gay men are to be as free as their straight equivalents in the society concerned to live their lives in the way that is natural to them as gay men, without the fear of persecution.[58] (Emphasis added.)

The above paragraph would identify the case in legal, but also in contemporary culture, to be ever known as the 'Kylie concert case' as a mark not of any homophobic views or unnecessary comment,[59] but in my opinion a mark of the great British (Scottish) humour of the late Lord Rodger.

The inability of a straight man to 'indulge openly in the mild flirtations which are an enjoyable part of heterosexual life'[60] provided the comparator,[61] and an illustration of why the jurisprudence surrounding the 'reasonably tolerable' test (which resulted in LGB asylum seekers being returned to their home countries to live a life of perpetual lies) was so fundamentally flawed. No individual wakes up gay or lesbian, with an 'on' and 'off' switch between 'gay' and 'not gay'. The journey undertaken will be specific to the individual, as is in some instances termed a 'coming out' process. What is common to the narrative of LGB asylum seekers is the core narrative of *difference* (emphasis added). This marks the individual as separate from the majority in society and also identifies them to the potential persecutor.[62]

Language is vitally important, and the fact that the Court referred to 'gay men', 'lesbians' and (for the first-time in a higher court decision relating to asylum) 'bisexuals'[63] was a significant positive contribution to international refugee jurisprudence. This was reflected in *HT*'s legal team's written submissions that the term 'homosexual' was no longer acceptable.[64] The use of these positive identity terms

[58] *HJ and HT* (n 1) 596, 645–46 [78] (Lord Rodger).

[59] Email from Jenni Millbank to the author (14 July 2010): 'Great result in HJ – and amazing to see the lords say not only "gay" but "straight" too. Could have done without the Kylie reference but all in all such a good judgment, streets ahead of s395.'

[60] *HJ and HT* (n 1) 596, 645 [77] (Lord Rodger).

[61] See also C Dauvergne and J Millbank, 'Applicants S396/2002 and S395/2002, a Gay Refugee Couple from Bangladesh' (2003) 25 *Sydney Law Review* 97, 107.

[62] *HJ and HT* (n 1). The limitation of the group to LGB, rather than LGBTQ+ is used deliberately, as discretion-reasoning for trans claims was not, to my knowledge, relied upon by the Home Office when determining gender identity refugee applicants, where trans or non-binary gender identity is accepted as credible under the first limb of *HJ and HT*. When subsequently addressing the final third and fourth conduct limbs, the applicant will succeed under the 'open on return' third limb. As the returnee's affirmed expression of gender identity will not align with the potential persecutor's stereotyped perception of the gender expression of the returnee recorded in their state identification document and/or records in their (dead) name and/or natal biological identity, this difference will result in them being able to fail to 'prove cisgender', thereby resulting in the well-founded fear of persecution they have successfully established by traversing the second to third limb of *HJ and HT*.

[63] *HJ and HT* (n 1) 596, 647 [76] (Lord Rodger).

[64] Inserted in fn 1 of the skeleton argument filed on behalf of *HT* was the following 'The word "gay" is preferred to the word "homosexual" for much the same reasons as the word "black" is preferred

marks a clear shift in correcting a historical wrong where lesbian and bisexual claimants were invisible, while gay men were presented in a purely sexual deviant role. This should, at last, end the references to 'buggery' and 'sodomy',[65] in connection with '(male) (practising) (active) homosexuals' that were associated with the 'conduct' approach.[66] That such terms were used in Tribunal decisions should be seen as vulgar, completely wrong, and unlawful.

Further, and more importantly, the use of more appropriate language, such as Lesbian, Gay and Bisexual, has enabled and empowered the post-*HJ and HT* non-straight and non-cisgender terminologies. This includes Trans, Intersex, Queer, Asexual, and Plus, LGBT, LGBT+, LGBTI, LGBTQ+ an ever-increasing rainbow spectrum, as well as increasing prevalence of the umbrella term Queer Refugees. In my own practice I have in the past year had a demi-sexual client, and a polyamorous bisexual asylum client and in the immigration context I have been instructed by a client in a throuple relationship. The Queerness of *HJ and HT* is that it thrusts the decision-maker out of the closet door in the bedroom and into the 'outside world', a sphere which straight people inhabit without having to lie to everyone they meet due to fear. It also recognises the need, if not a core right, to be who one is as a human being and to express this in ways not confined solely to the sexual act. Whilst lower courts[67] and tribunals[68] grappled with what constituted sexual identity, it took the Supreme Court to recognise that British society has 'caught-up'. Lord Hope highlighted the pledge of the British Government to resolve 'one of the most demanding social issues of our time'.[69] Such hope should not be misplaced.[70]

VII. Closing the *HJ and HT* Discretion-Gap

Whilst the judgment in *HJ and HT* is a breakthrough in the protection of gay refugees in the UK by removing blanket application of discretion, the judgment failed to remove discretion reasoning entirely. Currently, those who fall at the penultimate conduct limb test (ie their discreet behaviour on return being through 'personal choice or social pressure') are refused asylum and returned to a country where they have established a well-founded fear of persecution. After return, 'discretion' must be maintained not for one day, or one week, but for the rest of their lives.

This discretion-gap is based on what is in reality a legal fiction. The Supreme Court made it clear that the adoption of discretion is based on the knowledge of

to the word "negro" for descriptive purposes of a particular sexual orientation as for a particular race or ethnicity.' Skeleton argument for *HT (Cameroon)* for the Supreme Court, dated 24 March 2010, Monica Carrs-Frisk, QC and Peter Jorro.

[65] *Z v Secretary of State for the Home Department* (01TH02634) (8 November 2001).

[66] See *Binbasi* (n 9).

[67] *J* (n 21).

[68] *MN (Findings on Sexuality) Kenya* [2005] UKIAT 00021.

[69] *HJ and HT* (n 1) 596, 618 [3] (Lord Hope).

[70] *SB (India) and CB (India) v Secretary of State for the Home Department* [2016] EWCA Civ 451, [2016] 4 WLR 103.

a risk of persecution to those who are open. As outlined by Lord Rodger, 'unless he were minded to swell the ranks of gay martyrs, when faced with a real threat of persecution, the applicant would have no real choice: he would be compelled to act discreetly'.[71] By virtue of undertaking the asylum claim process to the stage of completing the limbs of the *HJ and HT* guidance, the applicant has established a well-founded fear of persecution to those who are openly gay and thus in their own mind also established knowledge of a 'real threat of persecution'. This knowledge cannot subsequently be undone. Thus, any applicant who is returned and lives discreetly cannot be said to do so *only* for reasons of social pressure or personal choice. They are inevitably doing so to avoid the real risk of persecution that they now categorically know faces those who are openly gay in that country. Thus, living with discretion in terms of the fourth limb of the *HJ and HT* guidance is a legal fiction, for even those who adopt 'voluntary discretion' in part due to personal choice or social pressure will inevitably also now be acting in part with a fear of persecution (and therefore should be recognised as a refugee, in terms of the *HJ and HT* guidance).

Since the *HJ and HT* judgment, I have spent nearly 15 years of my professional life identifying cases to close the gap of discretion reasoning in Queer refugee claims in the UK. This has arguably been achieved following the 12 November 2024 judgment of the ECtHR in *MI v Switzerland*.[72] In a poetic example of legal karma, one of the two Swiss advocates for MI was Stephanie Motz – who as my first pupil barrister, assisted me in 2009 when I was Junior for *HT* in the proceedings before the Court of Appeal. Here in *MI*, leading Haydée Dijkstal at my chambers at 33 Bedford Row, and instructed by Jacqui McKenzie of Leigh Day Solicitors for the gay and refugee charities African Rainbow Family and Stonewall, was an opportunity to end discretion reasoning in protection claims.[73]

The domestic Swiss authorities did not accept MI's past narrative of fear arising from his family, and despite having accepted that he is a gay man known to the LGBT community in Iran, failed to undertake any Article 3 European Convention on Human Rights (ECHR) assessment of future risk on return. The national authorities rejected MI's claim on the basis that he had in the past successfully lived in Iran without risk by exercising discretion and could return to this life, exercising the same discretion that he had previous employed. In contrast, the Strasbourg Court drew upon various country background reports (including the July 2022 UK Home Office Country Policy and Information report on Iran) to determine that there is a real risk of Article 3 ECHR torture for gay men in Iran. In finding for the applicant, the Strasbourg Court extended its reasoning in *IK v Switzerland*[74] and *B and C v*

[71] *HJ and HT* (n 1) [59].

[72] *MI v Switzerland* App no 56390/21 (Article 3–(Prohibition of Torture: Third Section)) [2024] ECHR 862.

[73] Written submissions for the Interveners, 21 October 2022, available at www.33bedfordrow.co.uk/upload/files/ECHR%20MI%20v%20Switzerland%20Written%20Comments%20of%20Intervenors%20African%20Rainbow%20Family%20and%20Stonewall%20Application%20no%2056390.21%20as%20filed%20on%2021%20October%202022.pdf.

[74] *IK v Switzerland* App nos 21417/17 (ECtHR, 19 December 2017).

Switzerland,[75] where it rejected reliance on discretion where this is due to a fear of persecution. It noted that the factual matrix of discretion in *MI* was not connected to any accepted fear of state or non-state agents, but made clear that discretion-reasoning should not be applied in assessment of the real risk of harm on return, as it is not guaranteed to be life-long, and cannot be guaranteed and on this basis cannot be applied to an Article 3 ECHR risk assessment in protection claims.

My 15 years as a strategic litigation lawyer includes the core commitment to close the discretion-gap for Queer asylum claimants in the UK, in which *HJ and HT* is applied as a template of exclusion. For UK domestic law, a breakthrough equivalent to *MI* appeared imminent with the case of *PG*. In 2023, the Upper Tribunal allowed PG's appeal on Article 3 ECHR grounds arising from the concealment of his identity, holding that a climate of 'fear of societal disapproval that he will deny his sexuality by the way he lives his life and the constant hypocrisy, needed to ensure safety, is more than this appellant should seek to bear'.[76] The key legal submission adopted by the Upper Tribunal was that 'the claimant could only function by living discreetly which in his case meant living contrary to his wishes',[77] and citing ECtHR jurisprudence in establishing that to *act against his will or conscience … [constitutes] … inhuman or degrading treatment*'.[78] Unfortunately, a 4 August 2025 Order of the Supreme Court refused *PG* permission to appeal, finding 'no arguable point of law'. The earlier Court of Appeal hearing read the *MI* judgment and heard detailed submissions on that case but made clear that only the Supreme Court could address any alleged divergence. By refusing permission to appeal, the Supreme Court retains consistency with *HJ and HT*, but by what crossing can a refugee applicant cross the Rubicon, where the ECtHR has made clear there should be no discretion-reasoning in Article 3 ECHR protection claims?

As the arguments put forward in section III of this chapter indicate, the solution may lie within the *HJ and HT* test itself. As I argue in that section, any individual who has established that they have a well-founded fear of persecution in their country of origin as an openly gay person must thereafter be acting with that knowledge. Any decision to 'act discreetly' after return is necessarily informed by that fear of persecution and a person who lives in this way cannot be considered to be acting wholly voluntarily through personal choice or social pressure. The memory of 'facing the gun' can never be erased from their memory, noting at a minimum this knowledge is gained through the successful engagement of the first two limbs of the *HJ and HT* guidance required to be granted sanctuary in the UK. As such, a fear of persecution is inescapably a material factor in any decision to live with discretion. In this light, the fourth limb of the Supreme Court's test (on whether the reason for discretion on return simply through personal choice or

[75] *B and C v Switzerland* App nos 889/19 and 43987/16 (ECtHR, 17 November 2020).

[76] *PG* (n 7) [123].

[77] ibid [75].

[78] *East African Asians v the UK* [1973] ECHR 2 (24 December 1973), see [195].

social pressure) is redundant, as *all* claims decided under the final two conduct limbs are protection claims and will lead to positive grants of protection, therefore aligning to the ECtHR's reasoning in *MI v Switzerland* excluding discretion-reasoning from determination of a protection claim. Therefore, an applicant or appellant who fulfils the first and second limbs of the test (gay or perceived as gay in a country where openly gay people have a well-founded fear of persecution) must be considered a refugee, establishing *HJ and HT*, once again, as a beacon of hope.

4

Nawras Bolbol v Bevándorlási és Állampolgársági Hivatal [2010]: When is a Palestinian Refugee a Convention Refugee?

DALLAL STEVENS

I. Introduction

The case of *Bolbol*[1] is regarded as a landmark judgment as it was the first before the Court of Justice of the European Union (CJEU)[2] to address long-standing uncertainty surrounding the interpretation of Article 1D of the 1951 Convention relating to the Status of Refugees (Refugee Convention).[3] It provided a foundation for further case law and legal analysis in the European Union (EU) and before national courts, as well as contributing significantly to the understanding of this major provision. The case is of further significance and interest in that it provides an example of the substantive examination of the facts and law by – and consequent impact – of the Advocate General's (AG) opinion, rather than the actual final judgment, which accepted her advice fully.[4] Thus, in assessing its significance, account must be taken of both the AG's advisory opinion and the Court's judgment.

Article 1D of the 1951 Refugee Convention explains that certain individuals who are under the care (assistance and protection) of United Nations (UN) bodies other than the United Nations High Commissioner for Refugees are outside the

[1] Case C-31/09 *Nawras Bolbol v Bevándorlási és Állampolgársági Hivatal* [2010] ECR I 5539 [Court of Justice of the European Union (CJEU)].

[2] The CJEU deals with requests for preliminary rulings from national courts, actions for annulment and appeals. It does not try the facts of a case but interprets the law and can be seen as engaging in a type of vertical dialogue with national courts.

[3] UN General Assembly (UNGA), 1951 Convention relating to the Status of Refugees, United Nations, Treaty Series, 189:137, 28 July 1951.

[4] The Advocate General's (AG) Opinion is not binding on the CJEU. The role of the AG is to write an impartial and independent opinion on a certain case, thereby proposing a legal solution for the CJEU to consider (Art 252, Consolidated version of the Treaty on the Functioning of the European Union OJ C 202, 7.6.2016). The AG's opinion is frequently followed but not always.

ambit of the Refugee Convention. However, where this care ceases, such persons must be considered refugees under the Convention. It states:

> This Convention shall not apply to persons who are at present receiving from organs or agencies of the United Nations other than the United Nations High Commissioner for Refugees protection or assistance.
>
> When such protection or assistance has ceased for any reason, without the position of such persons being definitively settled in accordance with the relevant resolutions adopted by the General Assembly of the United Nations, these persons shall ipso facto be entitled to the benefits of this Convention.

Perhaps more than any other provision of the Refugee Convention, this Article has proved controversial. Despite the universality of the language, it was introduced during drafting of the Convention to tackle the unresolved issue of refugees from Palestine. To clarify their position internationally, various questions as to the correct interpretation of Article 1D have persisted over time. These questions include the following:

- Does Article 1D(1) apply only to Palestinians who were receiving protection or assistance on 28 July 1951 (the date on which the Convention was opened for signature)?[5]
- Should the words 'at present receiving' in Article 1D(1) be interpreted in their historical context with due regard to the fact that states in 1951 did not anticipate a protracted refugee situation?
- Do the words 'such protection or assistance has ceased for any reason' in Article 1D(2) mean that all assistance by United Nations Relief and Works Agency for Palestine Refugees in the Near East (UNRWA) must have ceased – that is, UNRWA's mandate has been ended by the UN?[6]
- Is Article 1D an inclusion clause contingent upon certain events, such as inability to return to their former country of residence, rather than an exclusion clause?
- Is Article 1D(1) an exclusion clause, while Article 1D(2) is an inclusion clause? Do Palestinian refugees who leave UNRWA's area of operations, and are without protection and not in receipt of assistance, fall automatically within the Convention, without a need to determine that they qualify as refugees with a well-founded fear of persecution?

This chapter opens with a brief exploration of the history of Article 1D. It moves on to a summary of the facts of the case, the crucial opinion of AG Sharpston, the judgment of the CJEU in *Bolbol* and subsequent case law. It concludes with further reflections on why *Bolbol* is a landmark case, namely that it influenced the

[5] See for discussion on this point, *El-Ali v Secretary of State for the Home Department* [2002] EWCA Civ 1103.

[6] ibid.

interpretation of Article 1D, prompting the United Nations High Commissioner for Refugees (UNHCR) to revise its Note on the applicability of Article 1D to Palestinian Refugees and leading to further cases before the CJEU, with consequent implications for national courts and, more critically, for the protection of Palestinian refugees.

II. A Long Historical Legacy

To understand the *Bolbol* judgment, it is necessary to consider the intentions of the drafters concerning Article 1D, and reference must therefore be paid to the drafting history of both the 1950 UNHCR Statute and the 1951 Refugee Convention.[7]

A useful starting point is the Ad Hoc Committee on Statelessness and Related Problems, established to consider revising and consolidating a convention relating to the international status of refugees and stateless persons. In early discussions, in January 1950, on the definition of the term 'refugees', the United States proposed a definition containing 'neo-refugees' that did not include Palestinian refugees.[8] Rather, an exception for Palestine refugees was introduced: '[t]he United States Government did not consider that certain groups should be included within the framework of the convention, such as the approximately 600,000 Arab refugees for whom the United Nations had made special arrangements …'[9]

By November 1950, during final negotiations on the definition of the term 'refugee' to be applied by the High Commissioner for Refugees in the 1950 UNHCR Statute, greater consideration was being given to refugees from Palestine. The delegate for Lebanon discussed a joint amendment offered by Egypt, Lebanon and Saudi Arabia, which included an additional paragraph that read: 'The mandate of the High Commissioner's Office shall not extend to categories of refugees at present placed under the competence of other organs or agencies of the United Nations.'[10] This, he said, would be necessary if the General Assembly (GA) adopted a broad definition of a 'refugee'. The delegations concerned were thinking of the Palestine

[7] UNGA, 1950 Statute of the Office of the United Nations High Commissioner for Refugees, A/RES/428(V) 14 December 1950; FP Albanese and L Takkenberg, *Palestinian Refugees in International Law*, 2nd edn (Oxford University Press, 2020) s 3.2.

[8] UNHCR, 'Ad Hoc Committee on Statelessness and Related Problems, First Session: Summary Record of the Third Meeting Held at Lake Success, New York, on Tuesday, 17 January 1950, at 3 p.m.' para 45, available at www.refworld.org/legal/leghist/ahcrsp/1950/en/32388.

[9] ibid para 38.

[10] UNGA, Fifth Session, Third Committee 328th Meeting, Lake Success, New York, Monday 27 November 1950, at 3.30p.m., Refugees and stateless persons (A/1385, A/1396, A/C.3/528, AjC.3j538, A/C.3/540, A/C.3/547, E/1850 and E/1850/Annex) (continued), A/C.3/SR.328, 355. 358., para 45 (Mr Azkoul).

refugees, 'who differed from all other refugees'.[11] The Saudi Arabian representative added that the 'problem of Palestine refugees was characterized by certain peculiarities', one of which was

> the fact that no other group of refugees constituted such a high percentage of the total population as did the Palestine refugees: some 700,000 to 800,000 – that is, 60 to 70 per cent – of the total of 1,250,000 Palestine Arabs were living outside their homeland.[12]

His concern was that if the GA included refugees from Palestine in a general definition of refugees, 'they would become submerged and relegated to a position of minor importance'.[13] In the view of the Arab States, the only real solution to their problem was repatriation,[14] and pending a proper settlement of the matter, Palestinian refugees should continue to be granted a separate and special status.[15] The proposed amendments of the Arab delegations were accepted and, consequently, when the UNHCR Statute was adopted on 14 December 1950, it contained the following paragraph 7(c): 'the competence of the High Commissioner ... shall not extend to a person: ... Who continues to receive from other organs or agencies of the United Nations protection or assistance'.

Concerning the Refugee Convention, the *travaux préparatoires* reveal that Palestinian refugees received further scrutiny and debate. The draft Convention included a clause akin to paragraph 7(c) of the UNHCR Statute, thereby excluding refugees from Palestine from the remit of the proposed Refugee Convention. There was some difference of opinion on whether the exclusion of Palestinian Arabs was permanent or temporary, and, consequently, the Egyptian representative submitted an amendment to ensure possible future inclusion of Palestinians within the Convention.[16] Already, at this early point, the question of whether Arab refugees were covered by the Convention was controversial: on the one hand, for example, the United Kingdom (UK) representative thought that Palestinians were permanently excluded from the benefits of the Convention; on the other hand, the Egyptian representative considered the opposite to be true.[17] To address any

[11] Note that there is a difference of opinion regarding the reality of Palestinian exceptionalism and the 'UN responsibility theory' – see pro: S Akram and GS Goodwin-Gill, 'Brief Amicus Curiae on the Status of Palestinian Refugees under International Law' (2000/2001) 11 *The Palestine Yearbook of International Law* 185; GS Goodwin-Gill and J McAdam, *The Refugee in International Law*, 4th edn (Oxford University Press, 2021) para 4.2.3; contra: M Kagan, 'The (Relative) Decline of Palestinian Exceptionalism and its Consequences for Refugee Studies in the Middle East' (2009) 22 *Journal of Refugee Studies* 417.

[12] UNGA (n 10) para 49 (Mr Baroody).

[13] ibid para 52.

[14] ibid.

[15] ibid para 55.

[16] A/CONF.2/13 (Bey Mostafa); see UNGA, *Conference of Plenipotentiaries on the Status of Refugees and Stateless Persons: Summary Record of the Twenty-ninth Meeting*, A/CONF.2/SR.29, UN Conference of Plenipotentiaries on the Status of Refugees and Stateless Persons, 28 November 1951.

[17] ibid.

possible misunderstanding, Egypt submitted a further amendment to the text, as follows:

> When such protection or assistance has ceased for any reason, without the position of such persons being definitively settled in accordance with the relevant resolutions adopted by the United Nations General Assembly, they shall *ipso facto* be entitled to the benefit of this Convention.[18]

As can be seen, this is almost identical to the final agreed version that became Article 1D(2).

Albanese and Takkenberg note that the amendment reflected the circumstances at the time: three years had passed since the events of 1948 that had caused Palestinians to flee and the Arab delegates at the Conference were beginning to wonder if the solution for the Palestinian refugees, contained in GA Resolution 194 (III), was unlikely to be realised.[19] They were concerned that Palestinian refugees should be protected in the long-term if they no longer benefited from the protection or assistance provided by the organs or agencies of the UN because they had ceased to function.[20] Yet, despite the fact that a close reading of the *travaux préparatoires* reveals the clear intention behind the drafting of Article 1D, the provision has suffered from ambiguity[21] and 'continues to raise interpretative challenges'.[22]

The *Bolbol* case considered some of these interpretative challenges for the first time in the EU, and in a supranational court.[23] The activity of the CJEU in relation to Article 1D can arguably be related to the provision's incorporation in EU law and the increase in references to the Court on its meaning and application in Member States (MS).

III. Summary of Case

The EU incorporated Article 1D almost verbatim into its legislation on who qualifies for refugee status/international protection in MS. This legislation comprises the 2004 Qualification Directive (QD)[24] and the 2011 recast Qualification

[18] UNGA, *Draft Convention Relating to the Status of Refugees. Egypt: Amendment to Article 1*, A/CONF.2/13, UN Conference of Plenipotentiaries on the Status of Refugees and Stateless Persons, 3 July 1951, available at www.refworld.org/legal/leghist/cpsrsp/1951/en/29546. This was draft Art 1C(2) to the Convention (eventually, Art 1D(2)).

[19] Albanese and Takkenberg (n 7) 82.

[20] See Bey Mostafa (Egypt) (n 16).

[21] GS Goodwin-Gill and J McAdam, *The Refugee in International Law*, 3rd edn (Oxford University Press, 2007) 152.

[22] ibid para 4.2.2.

[23] National case law on Art 1D is limited. An early UK example is *El-Ali* (n 5).

[24] Council Directive 2004/83/EC of 29 April 2004 on minimum standards for the qualification and status of third country nationals or stateless persons as refugees or as persons who otherwise need international protection and the content of the protection granted [2004] OJ L304/12.

Directive (recast QD).[25] In the QD and recast QD, which applies currently to most MS, Article 12, which concerns 'exclusion', states that:

> 1. A third-country national or a stateless person is excluded from being a refugee if:
>
> (a) he or she falls within the scope of Article 1(D) of the Geneva Convention, relating to protection or assistance from organs or agencies of the United Nations other than the United Nations High Commissioner for Refugees. When such protection or assistance has ceased for any reason, without the position of such persons being definitely settled in accordance with the relevant resolutions adopted by the General Assembly of the United Nations, those persons shall ipso facto be entitled to the benefits of this Directive.[26]

Bolbol, which was decided by the Grand Chamber of the CJEU on 17 June 2010, was the first reference to the Court on Article 12. Nawras Bolbol was a stateless Palestinian who travelled on a visa from the Gaza Strip to Hungary with her husband. On arrival, she applied for – and was granted – a resident permit from the immigration authority. On 21 June 2007, she applied for asylum to Bevándorlási és Állampolgársági Hivatal (the 'BAH'; Immigration and Citizenship Office). Her reasons for so doing were that she considered the situation in the Gaza Strip, which faced daily clashes between Fatah and Hamas, to be unsafe. Ms Bolbol based her application on Article 1D(2) of the Refugee Convention, pointing out that she was a Palestinian residing outside UNRWA's area of operations and that her only family member who remained in the Gaza Strip was her father, who worked as a university lecturer.

It was accepted by both parties that Ms Bolbol had not availed herself of the protection or assistance of UNRWA. She claimed, however, that she was *entitled* to such protection and assistance, and produced an UNRWA registration card issued to the family of her father's first cousin. BAH did not accept the existence of a family connection without further documentary evidence, and despite the steps taken by Ms Bolbol at UNRWA, she was unable to establish her right to be registered based on family connections. On 14 September 2007, BAH refused Ms Bolbol's application for refugee status, but prohibited her expulsion with a *non-refoulement* order 'on the grounds that the readmission of Palestinians was at the discretion of the Israeli authorities and Ms Bolbol would be exposed to torture

[25] Council Directive 2011/95/EU of The European Parliament and of The Council of 13 December 2011 on standards for the qualification of third-country nationals or stateless persons as beneficiaries of international protection, for a uniform status for refugees or for persons eligible for subsidiary protection, and for the content of the protection granted (recast) [2011] OJ L337/9. Note that new legislation will apply from 1 July 2026: Regulation 2024/1347 of The European Parliament and of The Council of 14 May 2024 on standards for the qualification of third-country nationals or stateless persons as beneficiaries of international protection, for a uniform status for refugees or for persons eligible for subsidiary protection and for the content of the protection granted, amending Council Directive 2003/109/EC and repealing Directive 2011/95/EU of the European Parliament and of the Council.

[26] Art 12(1)(a) is identical in the 2004 and 2011 Qualification Directives.

or inhuman and degrading treatment in the Gaza Strip on account of the critical conditions there'.[27]

Ms Bolbol challenged BAH's decision to reject her application for refugee status before the Fővárosi Bíróság (Budapest Municipal Court). She argued that Article 1D(2) provided a separate basis for recognition as a refugee, and that she met the conditions laid down in that provision, and was therefore entitled to recognition as a refugee irrespective of whether she qualified as a refugee under Article 1A. Ms Bolbol asserted that the purpose of Article 1D was to make it clear that, a person registered – or entitled to be registered – with UNRWA who resides, for any reason, outside UNRWA's area of operations and who, for good reason, cannot be expected to return, should automatically be granted refugee status.[28] She stated that she was entitled to be registered with UNRWA through her father, and because she was residing in Hungary, and was consequently outside UNRWA's area of operations, she should be recognised as a refugee with immediate effect.[29]

The defendant maintained that Ms Bolbol's application for refugee status was unfounded as she had not left Gaza for any of the reasons set out in Article 1A (that is, she had not left owing to fear of persecution for reasons of race, religion, nationality, or political opinion) and that Article 1D did not automatically grant a basis for refugee status, but was 'merely a provision concerning the Convention's scope *ratione personae*'.[30] Consequently, in BAH's view, Palestinians were entitled to refugee status only where they met the definition of 'refugee' in accordance with Article 1A, and this needed to be determined on a case-by-case basis.

Fővárosi Bíróság decided to stay the proceedings and refer three questions to the CJEU for a preliminary ruling:

> For the purposes of Article 12(1)(a) of Council Directive 2004/83/EC:
>
> 1. Must someone be regarded as a person receiving the protection and assistance of a United Nations agency merely by virtue of the fact that he is entitled to assistance or protection or is it also necessary for him actually to avail himself of that protection or assistance?
> 2. Does cessation of the agency's protection or assistance mean residence outside the agency's area of operations, cessation of the agency and cessation of the possibility of receiving the agency's protection or assistance or, possibly, an objective obstacle such that the person entitled thereto is unable to avail himself of that protection or assistance?
> 3. Do the benefits of the directive mean recognition as a refugee, or either of the two forms of protection covered by the directive (recognition as a refugee and the grant of subsidiary protection), according to the choice made by the

[27] *Bolbol* (n 1) [30].
[28] ibid [31].
[29] ibid.
[30] ibid [32].

> Member State, or, possibly, [does it mean] neither automatically but merely [lead to] inclusion [of the person concerned within] the scope ratione personae of the Directive?[31]

IV. AG Sharpston's Opinion

AG Eleanor Sharpston provided an opinion on 4 March 2010.[32] This was a significant opportunity for the CJEU to clarify some of the uncertainty that had long troubled Article 1D, and she seized the chance. Following a brief overview of the Refugee Convention, she referred to relevant UN Resolutions affecting Palestinians[33] and to the definition of people who met UNRWA's Palestine Refugee criteria (for registration), namely 'persons whose normal place of residence was Palestine during the period 1 June 1946 to 15 May 1948 and who lost both home and means of livelihood as a result of the 1948 conflict'.[34] She clarified that others who did not meet UNRWA's Palestinian Refugee criteria were also eligible to receive UNRWA's services.[35] Further, some Palestinians were eligible to receive UNRWA services without being registered in UNRWA's Registration System. These included 'non-registered persons displaced as a result of the 1967 and subsequent hostilities' and 'non-registered persons who live in refugee camps and communities'.[36] The AG drew attention to UNHCR's non-binding contributions (UNHCR Handbook; and the 2002 and 2009 statements on Article 1D) on the approach to be adopted to Article 1D, one of which – the 2009 statement – she elected, rather unusually, to treat as an unofficial *amicus curiae* brief.[37] Crucially, she rehearsed the background to the Qualification Directive and the history of the

[31] ibid [35].

[32] Opinion of Advocate General Sharpston delivered on 4 March 2010 in Case C-32/09 *Nawras Bolbol v Bevándorlási és Állampolgársági Hivatal* ('AG, *Bolbol*'), available at curia.europa.eu/juris/document/document_print.jsf;jsessionid=CBFA976C1C2AEEE4977D38DEF29787F1?pageIndex=0&docid=79353&doclang=EN&text=&cid=4922600#Footref14.

[33] Resolution 181 (II) on the partitioning of Palestine, 29 November 1947; Resolution 212 (III) establishing the UN Relief for Palestinian Refugees, 19 November 1948; Resolution 302 (IV), establishing the UN Relief and Works Agency for Palestine Refugees in the Near East (UNRWA) after the 1948 conflict, 8 December 1949.

[34] UNRWA, *Consolidated Eligibility and Registration Instructions* (CERI) (1 January 2009) point IIIA(1), available at www.unrwa.org/resources/strategy-policy/consolidated-eligibility-and-registration-instructions.

[35] These are 'persons who at the time of original registration did not satisfy all of UNRWA's Palestinian Refugee criteria, but who were determined to have suffered significant loss and/or hardship for reasons related to the 1948 conflict in Palestine; they also include persons who belong to the families of Registered Persons' (CERI, ibid, point IIIA(2). Although registered with UNRWA, such persons are not counted as part of the official Registered Refugee population of the Agency.

[36] CERI, ibid, para IIIB.

[37] AG, *Bolbol* (n 32) [16]. UNHCR, *UNHCR Revised Statement on Article 1D of the 1951 Convention 1 Issued in the context of the preliminary ruling reference to the Court of Justice of the European Communities from the Budapest Municipal Court regarding the interpretation of Article 12(1)(a) of the Qualification Directive*, October 2009 ('UNHCR's 2009 Statement'), available at www.unhcr.org/sites/default/files/legacy-pdf/4add88379.pdf.

drafting of the Refugee Convention, and Article 1D in particular, finally arriving at a point where she stated:

> Although it is a short provision, Article 1D is replete with unanswered questions. At least four broad areas of opacity can be distinguished – two arising from the first sentence and two from the second – that must be resolved in order to answer the questions referred to the Court in the present proceedings.[38]

The AG's decision to posit four of her own questions arguably reinforces the value of the case; through such a method, she addressed the confusion that had long surrounded the interpretation of Article 1D and paid credence to the drafting history.

Regarding her first question (what is meant, in a geographical and/or temporal sense, by 'persons who are at present receiving … protection or assistance'?), Sharpston argued that, to receive protection or assistance from a UN organ or agency other than the UNHCR, a person must be in a place where such protection and assistance is physically available. Assistance from UNRWA is obtainable only in the UNRWA zone. Consequently, a person will only come within Article 1D(1) when she is resident in the UNRWA zone. The AG felt that neither of the two sentences that comprise Article 1D is limited geographically. It was simply the realities of receiving UNRWA assistance that produced the apparent geographical limitation in Article 1D(1). Consequently, an individual who leaves the UNRWA zone should be able to invoke the specific rights conferred by Article 1D(2), wherever she may be.[39]

As far as limitation of time was concerned – arising from the words 'at present' – while the AG accepted that in 1951 the drafters were probably thinking of those who were already receiving protection or assistance from other 'organs and agencies' of the United Nations (such as UNRWA), she noted that many additional persons (both the descendants of those originally displaced and new displaced persons) had been assisted and protected by UNRWA.[40] Logically, therefore, an overly restrictive reading of Article 1D(1), which determines that 'at present' refers only to 1951, should not be applied (as had occurred in the UK in the case of *El-Ali*)[41] especially when mindful of the special consideration given by the UN to displaced Palestinians.[42] She preferred balance when interpretating Article 1D and it therefore followed that some limitation in time was necessary: 'at present receiving' protection or assistance in Article 1D(1) meant, at any particular point in time, 'persons who are currently receiving protection or assistance from UN organs or agencies other than the UNHCR'. Such persons were excluded from the Convention because they did not need its protection.[43]

[38] AG, *Bolbol* (n 32) [46].
[39] ibid [59]–[61].
[40] ibid [66].
[41] *El-Ali* (n 5).
[42] AG, *Bolbol* (n 32) [68].
[43] ibid [70].

As to the second question (do persons 'who are at present receiving … protection or assistance' have to be in actual receipt of protection or assistance, or does it suffice that they would be entitled to receive it?), the AG argued that only those who had actually availed themselves of the protection or assistance of an organ or agency other than the UNHCR fell within the scope of Article 1D.[44] In disagreeing with the interpretation put forward by the UNHCR, that displaced Palestinians and their descendants by their presence in an UNRWA area of operation should be included,[45] she claimed she was guided primarily by the text of the provision, which had not been amended in over 50 years. Certainly, UNHCR's approach had 'the advantage of eliminating most evidentiary problems associated with the first sentence', but, in her opinion, it did so by excluding many more potential refugees from the scope of the Refugee Convention.[46]

Turning to the third enquiry – assessment of circumstances in which 'such protection or assistance has ceased for any reason' – the AG disagreed with Ms Bolbol's suggestion that if *either* protection *or* assistance ceases, Article 1D(2) is triggered.[47] Rather, the two sentences of Article 1D were to be read consecutively. The phrase 'protection or assistance' – used in both sentences – should be read as meaning protection or assistance provided by any one of the 'organs or agencies of the United Nations' other than the UNHCR. The word 'ceased' meant that Article 1D(2) is triggered if that same person is no longer able to benefit from protection or assistance from any such agency.[48] Crucially, 'ceased' did not require the total cessation of UNRWA's activities throughout the UNRWA zone.[49] What was important to determine was whether the individual concerned had ceased to receive protection or assistance.[50]

On this point, the AG also considered whether the reason for the cessation of UNRWA assistance mattered. Specifically, she asked, whether Article 1D(2) would be triggered if a person voluntarily removed herself from the UNRWA zone, making it impossible for her to continue to receive UNRWA's assistance? Or did 'cessation for any reason' mean simply 'whatever the reason why UNRWA has ceased to provide assistance to a particular person'?[51] In trying to 'unpick this Gordian knot', it was crucial to look at both the consequences of a particular reading and at the underlying rationale behind the provision. She distinguished between those who remove themselves *voluntarily* from the UNRWA zone, and thereby from UNRWA's assistance, and those who find that *external events beyond their control* have meant that UNRWA ceases to continue to aid them.[52] This analysis helped her resolve her fourth question.

[44] ibid [72].
[45] See UNHCR's 2009 Statement (n 37) 6–7 for its position.
[46] ibid.
[47] AG, *Bolbol* (n 32) [77].
[48] ibid [78].
[49] ibid [79].
[50] ibid [80].
[51] ibid [81].
[52] ibid [81]–[82].

People in the first category are no longer excluded from the scope of the Refugee Convention; since they are not 'at present receiving … protection or assistance', they can request individual refugee assessment under Article 1A(2). However, the benefits of the Convention are not automatic, as they have chosen to place themselves in a situation in which UNRWA's assistance is no longer available to them, though UNRWA is still willing to provide such assistance. Those in the second category are different. Their previous situation (in which, although excluded from the Convention by Article 1D(1), they were being cared for by UNRWA) has been altered through no fault of theirs. UNRWA has ceased to provide such assistance to them and, as a result, Article 1D(2) must step in to address their needs; they are *ipso facto* entitled to the benefits of the Convention, which means an automatic grant of refugee status without further individual assessment.[53]

Having dealt in detail with her own questions, AG Sharpston considered briefly the three questions referred by Fővárosi Bíróság and concluded her opinion by suggesting that the Court answer them as follows:

> 1) A person comes within the scope of the first sentence of Article 12(1)(a) of Council Directive 2004/83/EC of 29 April 2004 only if he has actually availed himself of the protection or assistance of a United Nations agency other than the UNHCR. Mere entitlement to such protection or assistance does not suffice to trigger that provision.
> 2) The words 'cessation of the agency's protection or assistance' mean that the person concerned is no longer in the relevant geographical area and has ceased, otherwise than of his own volition, to benefit from the protection or assistance that he enjoyed immediately before leaving that geographical area.
> 3) The words 'the benefits of this directive' mean recognition as a refugee and the automatic grant of refugee status.[54]

V. The Judgment of the Court

A noteworthy feature of this case is the influence that the AG exerted.[55] The Court accepted her reasoning fully and agreed that the application of Article 1D 1951 RC/Article 12(1)(a)QD was not limited to Palestinians who became refugees due to the 1948 conflict and included 'non-registered persons displaced as a result of the 1967 and subsequent hostilities'.[56] It accepted the AG's conclusion, stating that

> [i]t follows from the clear wording of Article 1D of the Geneva Convention that only those persons who have actually availed themselves of the assistance provided by UNRWA come within the clause excluding refugee status set out therein, which must,

[53] ibid [83]–[84], 89.
[54] ibid [111].
[55] See n 4.
[56] *Bolbol* (n 1) [45].

> as such, be construed narrowly and cannot therefore also cover persons who are or have been eligible to receive protection or assistance from that agency.[57]

Persons who have not actually availed themselves of protection or assistance from UNRWA, prior to their application for refugee status, were entitled to have their asylum application examined.[58] On the issue of evidence, the CJEU noted that

> [w]hile registration with UNRWA is sufficient proof of actually receiving assistance from it, … such assistance can be provided even in the absence of such registration, in which case the beneficiary must be permitted to adduce evidence of that assistance by other means.[59]

The Court ruled that for the purposes of the first sentence of Article 12(1)(a) of the Qualification Directive, a person receives protection or assistance from a UN agency, other than UNHCR, when that person has actually availed himself of that protection or assistance. As Ms Bolbol had not availed herself of protection or assistance from UNRWA, the Court did not consider it necessary to reply to the other questions referred, thereby avoiding answering the fundamental second question as to when and how protection of assistance can be said to have ceased for any reason, and leaving the matter for future cases to resolve.

VI. *Bolbol's* Legacy

Bolbol was followed by a few key cases before the CJEU. In the first, *El Kott et al*,[60] the Court tackled some unresolved issues. The three applicants had left UNRWA refugee camps in Lebanon due to threats to their security and claimed asylum in Hungary. Like Ms Bolbol, they were refused refugee status, but in *El Kott*, it was ordered that they not be returned to Lebanon (in accordance with Article 21(1) of the 2004 Qualification Directive), and one party (Ismail) and his family members were granted subsidiary protection. All three appealed refusal of refugee status and their cases were joined for the purpose of the main proceedings by the referring court. The applicants argued that, since UNRWA protection had ceased (on account of the security issues), they were automatically entitled to recognition as refugees under Article 1D(2).[61] Fővárosi Bíróság referred two questions that were almost identical to those (2 and 3) referred to in the *Bolbol* case.[62]

[57] ibid [51].
[58] ibid [54].
[59] ibid [52].
[60] C-364/11 *Mostafa Abed El Karem EL Kott, Chadi Amin A Radi, Hazem Kamel Ismail v Bevandorlasi es Allampolgarsagi Hivatal (BAH)* 19 December 2012, [2012] EU:C:2012:826.
[61] To which the second sentence of Article 1D/Article 12(1)(a) refers.
[62] *El Kott* (n 60) [41].

The AG was the same: Sharpston.[63] This time, the CJEU answered the questions, since the three Palestinians concerned had received UNRWA protection, in contrast to Ms Bolbol. The Court held that Article 1D(1), and the words who 'are at present receiving' could not be construed as meaning that 'mere absence or voluntary departure from UNRWA's area of operations would be sufficient to end the exclusion from refugee status laid down in that provision'.[64] The Court went on to consider the interpretation of Article 1D(2) and decided that the cessation of protection or assistance from agencies such as UNRWA 'for any reason' was not brought about by the abolition of UNRWA alone, but also included the situation in which it was impossible for UNRWA to carry out its mission.[65] In other words, it included circumstances in which a person who, after actually availing himself of such protection or assistance, ceases to receive it for a reason beyond her control and independent of her volition.[66] It was for the MS examining the asylum application to determine whether the person was forced to leave the operational area of the relevant agency; and this would be established where personal safety was at serious risk and it was impossible for the agency to guarantee that his living conditions would be commensurate with the mission entrusted to the agency.[67]

Insofar as the thorny question regarding the meaning of 'shall *ipso facto* be entitled to the benefits of [the] Directive' was concerned, the Court was very clear: such words permitted persons 'to benefit "as of right" from the regime of the convention and the "benefits" conferred by it'.[68] For the avoidance of doubt, it stated that a person who is *ipso facto* entitled to the benefits of the 2004 Qualification Directive is not necessarily required to show that she has a well-founded fear of being persecuted, but must apply for refugee status to the responsible MS. In examining the application, the authorities must verify not only that the applicant actually sought assistance from UNRWA,[69] and that the assistance has ceased, but also that the applicant is not caught by any of the grounds for exclusion laid down in the Directive, which are the same as in the Refugee Convention.[70]

In subsequent cases, MS seemed particularly keen to limit their obligations to Palestinians by reverting responsibility to Middle Eastern countries in which UNRWA operates. In *Alheto*,[71] for example, the Court considered the case of an UNRWA-registered woman of Palestinian origin, who left the Gaza Strip for Jordan

[63] Opinion of Advocate General Sharpston delivered on 13 September 2012 in Case C-364/11, *Mostafa Abed El Karem El Kott, Chadi Amin A Radi, Hazem Kamel Ismail v Bevándorlási és Állampolgársági Hivatal ENSZ Menekültügyi Fıbiztosság (intervening)(Reference for a preliminary ruling from the Fıvárosi Bíróság (Hungary)*.

[64] *El Kott* (n 60) [49].

[65] ibid [56].

[66] ibid [82].

[67] ibid [63].

[68] ibid [71].

[69] See, in that regard, *Bolbol* (n 1) [52].

[70] *El Kott* (n 60) [76].

[71] C-586/16 *Serin Alheto v Zamestnik-predsedatel na Darzhavna agentsia za bezhantsite* [CJEU] 25 July 2018, ECLI:EU:C:2018:584.

and stayed for a short time before travelling to an EU MS, where she lodged an application for international protection. It determined that the authorities should first examine whether she enjoyed effective protection or assistance from UNRWA in Jordan. If so, she could not obtain asylum in the EU; and further, subsidiary protection was not an option if personal safety was not at serious risk in the Gaza Strip; or, alternatively, if Jordan were prepared to readmit her to its territory and grant her the right to stay in dignified living conditions for as long as necessary in light of the risks in the Gaza Strip. Equally, in *XT*,[72] the CJEU considered whether, for the purposes of Article 1D and cessation of protection or assistance, UNRWA's area of protection comprises the last actual residence, or all other UNRWA areas of operation. The Court determined that national authorities should consider all UNRWA's areas of operation that a stateless Palestinian could access safely, and it was for the national court to verify the circumstances.[73] While the emphasis was again on the MS to make the determination, the CJEU noted that XT's departure from UNRWA's area of operations was not voluntary, due to his inability to obtain a residence permit in Lebanon, and increased expulsions.[74]

This need by MS to examine all circumstances is seen once more in *NB and AB*. NB was living in the UK with her husband and their five minor children, including AB, who was severely disabled.[75] All family members (excluding the youngest) had previously resided in the Al Bass refugee camp in Lebanon and were registered with UNRWA. The applicants sought refugee status under Article 1D, arguing that protection and assistance had ceased because of the inability of UNRWA to assist seriously disabled children, the severe discrimination to which AB was exposed in Lebanon, the lack of access to education or appropriate medical assistance and the particularly precarious living conditions in the camp. The asylum claim was refused, and they appealed. The First-tier Tribunal referred four questions to the CJEU on the interpretation of Article 1D. The Court held that in order to assess whether protection or assistance from UNRWA had ceased, so that a person could claim *ipso facto* 'refugee status', account must be taken of the relevant circumstances as they existed at the time of departure from the UNRWA area, and also at the time when the MS authorities considered an application for refugee status or during the appeal hearing. Where the person concerned has been forced to leave the UNRWA area for reasons beyond her control and wishes, the MS must establish whether she would receive effective protection or assistance if returned. The Court found that the applicant is not required to prove that there was any intentional infliction of harm, or intentional deprivation of assistance by UNRWA; and, when assessing whether the protection or assistance from UNRWA had ceased, account must be taken of any assistance provided to that person by civil society actors, such as non-governmental organisations, provided that UNRWA has a formal relationship of

[72] C-507/19 *Bundesrepublik Deutschland v XT* [CJEU] 13 January 2021, ECLI:EU:C:2021:3.
[73] ibid [82].
[74] ibid [79].
[75] C-349/20 *NB, AB v Secretary of State for the Home Department* [CJEU] 3 March 2022, ECLI:EU:C:2022:151.

co-operation with them, of a stable nature, in which they assist UNRWA in carrying out its mandate.[76]

This tranche of cases since *Bolbol* focuses on where UNRWA protection or assistance is available, where it has ceased, and, to some extent, the nature of that protection or assistance. But there is, in fact, much that remains unclear. In the *El Kott* case, for example, as Ogg points out, '[a]t no point in the judgment [of *El Kott*] does the CJEU consider what the words "protection" and "assistance" in article 1D mean'.[77] By limiting the test to personal safety and living conditions, the Court adopted too narrow an approach that 'skewed understanding of the meaning of the words "protection" and "assistance"'.[78] There is no discussion of why the focus was personal safety and living conditions or why they are prioritised over other rights.[79] Further, the demand that living conditions have to be commensurate with the 'mission' entrusted to the agency raises a question as to the identification of such a mission and takes no account of the often dire conditions in UNRWA's areas of operations, or when such a mission cannot be carried out.[80] Having stipulated that national authorities must 'consider all circumstances' or establish that assistance in an UNRWA area had ceased, no guidance is provided on how to carry out such verification, giving rise to potential inconsistency of approach between MS. Finally, it still remains unclear as to when a Palestinian is *ipso facto* entitled to refugee status under Article 1D(2).

At the time of writing in March 2025, the conflict in the Gaza Strip has been perpetrated for over 17 months. Repeated statements by UNRWA Commissioner-General Philippe Lazzarini, and UNRWA, suggest that UNRWA in Gaza is no longer able to provide humanitarian assistance.[81] Notwithstanding the comments of the Commissioner-General, UNRWA has suggested that general hardship is insufficient to end its mandate. Arguably, though, there is a case to be made that UNRWA cannot fulfil its mission in part of the Middle East. As confirmed in *El Kott*, protection and assistance will be found to have ceased where it is 'impossible for [UNRWA] to guarantee that … living conditions in that area will be commensurate with the mission entrusted to that organ or agency'.[82] It is indisputable that Palestinians living in Gaza are currently exposed to threats to life,

[76] ibid [85].

[77] K Ogg, 'New Directions in Article 1D Jurisprudence: Greater Barriers for Palestinian Refugees Seeking the Benefits of the Refugee Convention' in S Singh Juss (ed), *Research Handbook on International Refugee Law* (Edward Elgar, 2019) Ch 23, 358–73, 365.

[78] ibid 366.

[79] ibid.

[80] On this point, see Albanese and Takkenberg (n 7) 117.

[81] UNRWA, 'Remarks by UNRWA Commissioner-General Philippe Lazzarini to the United Nations General Assembly Fourth Committee' (13 November 2024), available at www.unrwa.org/newsroom/official-statements/remarks-unrwa-commissioner-general-philippe-lazzarini-united-nations-general-assembly-fourth-committee; UNRWA, 'UNRWA Commissioner-General Philippe Lazzarini Remarks on the Situation in the Gaza Strip' (15 October 2023), available at www.unrwa.org/newsroom/official-statements/unrwa-commissioner-general-philippe-lazzarini%E2%80%AF-remarks%E2%80%AF-situation-gaza-strip.

[82] *El Kott* (n 60) [82(1)].

physical integrity, security and freedom.[83] In accordance with *El Kott*, it might be assumed that Palestinians arriving in the EU and UK, who claim asylum and who were previously registered with UNRWA in the Gaza Strip should be entitled *ipso facto* to protection under the Refugee Convention.

The question of conditions in the Gaza Strip and the cessation of UNRWA's protection or assistance was addressed in *SN and LN*, promulgated on 13 June 2024 in the CJEU.[84] The Court considered whether, within the meaning of the QD, UNRWA protection or assistance has ceased when UNRWA finds itself unable to ensure dignified living conditions for whatever reason, including the general situation prevailing in an UNRWA area of operation. The CJEU held that protection or assistance must be considered to have ceased in an UNRWA area of operation when: (i) UNRWA finds itself unable to ensure to a stateless person dignified living conditions, consistent with its mission, considering, where applicable, her state of vulnerability. Further, there is no need for the individual concerned to demonstrate that she is specifically targeted by the general situation by reason of elements specific to her personal situation; and (ii) the stateless Palestinian would find herself, if she were to return to that sector, in a state of serious insecurity, taking into account her state of vulnerability.[85]

Consequently, asylum adjudicators must consider the wider situation pertaining in Gaza (and possibly the West Bank and Lebanon) and consider factors such as access to food, drinking water, electricity, health services and medicine when evaluating if UNRWA's protection has ceased. While the ruling eases the burden of proving an individualised risk, it still requires an assessment of individual vulnerability, and, consequently, the likelihood of divergent practices at the state level is high. Interestingly, any fear by European states that thousands of Palestinian asylum cases would be lodged, on the ground that the extreme circumstances in Gaza and deteriorating conditions in UNRWA's areas of operations signalled UNRWA's inability to protect refugees, has not materialised.[86] In 2024, there were six million Palestinian refugees under UNRWA's mandate,[87] but the number of applications from Palestinians in the EU in November 2024 was stable at 1,137, with the majority (56 per cent) lodged in Belgium followed by Greece at 24 per cent.[88] Despite the overall recognition rate for Palestinians being high at 94 per cent (refugee status 82 per cent), having increased from 71 per cent in December 2022,

[83] See for an analysis of the situation in Gaza, Home Office, *Country Policy and Information Note Occupied Palestinian Territories: Security Situation in Gaza*, Version 1.0, November 2024.

[84] *SN and LN* v *Zamestnik-predsedatel na Darzhavna agentsia za bezhantsite* C-563/22 [CJEU], 13 June 2024, ECLI:EU:C:2024:494.

[85] ibid [90(2)].

[86] It is worth noting that if Art 1D inclusion applied, UNHCR would also have a mandate for Palestinian refugees, and therefore could focus on durable solutions, which would be a much more significant outcome. (My thanks to Kirsten McConnachie for this point.).

[87] UNHCR, *Global Trends Forced Displacement in 2023*, 2, available at www.unrefugees.org.uk/wp-content/uploads/2024/06/global-trends-report-2023-ukforunhcr.pdf.

[88] European Union Agency for Asylum, *Latest Asylum Trends* (November 2024), available at https://euaa.europa.eu/latest-asylum-trends-asylum.

it would seem, at least for the present, that a mass arrival of Palestinians is unlikely, due to the inability to leave (in the case of Gaza) or adherence to the right of return to Palestine and resistance to perceived ethnic cleansing.

VII. Why is *Bolbol* a Landmark Case?

Prior to the judgment, certain European countries, and the Council of Ministers, had adopted a restrictive approach to Article 1D, refusing the application of the Refugee Convention to Palestinian refugees who had voluntarily removed themselves from UNRWA's area of operations. For example, the 1996 Council's (non-binding) Joint Position on the definition of 'refugee', advised that

> Any person who deliberately removes himself from the protection and assistance referred to in Article ID of the Geneva Convention is no longer automatically covered by that Convention. In such cases, refugee status is in principle to be determined in accordance with Article 1A.[89]

According to Albanese and Takkenberg,

> Already at the time of the first edition [of *Palestinian Refugees in International Law*, 1998], European authorities were wary of an interpretation of Article 1D that could offer Palestinian refugees the choice between UNRWA and an alternative protection arrangement, and suggested an interpretation, beyond the letter of the 1951 Convention, which would discourage what they considered as 'unjustified' access to the benefits of the 1951 Convention.[90]

Article 1D was regarded as an exclusion clause (and, indeed, the Qualification Directives and Regulation 2024/1347 continue to include Article 1D under 'Exclusion').[91]

Bolbol arguably started to move the discourse away from an overly restrictive interpretation of Article 1D and allowed for a degree of harmonisation on the approach to be adopted by EU MS. It clarified that, in order to fall within the exception under Article 1D(2), refugees needed to have availed themselves of the assistance of UNRWA. AG Sharpston provided an opinion that explored the historical background to the provision and confirmed that Article 1D(1) was not time limited to 1951. She addressed important issues that were subsequently adjudicated upon by the Court in *El Kott*; namely in relation to the meaning of cessation of protection and assistance, and of *ipso facto* entitlements to the benefits

[89] Joint Position of 4 March 1996 defined by the Council on the basis of Article K.3 of the Treaty on European Union on the harmonized application of the definition of the term 'refugee' in Article 1 of the Geneva Convention of 28 July 1951 relating to the status of refugees (96/196/JHA), para 12.

[90] Albanese and Takkenberg (n 7) 107.

[91] See ibid 83, fn 114, for the suggestion that delegates were concerned about the correct order of the parts of Art 1: 'Certainly, placing present art. 1D among the clauses that excluded the status of refugee has been the source of significant confusion. … However, as the conference came under considerable pressure to complete the drafting within the time available, there was not time to address the matter.'

of the Convention. The cases of *Alheto*; *XT*; *NB and AB*; *and SN and LN* have provided additional clarification as to the scope of Article 1D. While there remains some difference of opinion as to the direction taken by the Court in *Bolbol* – in particular its conclusion that Palestinians who had 'actually availed' themselves of the protection or assistance of UNRWA (as opposed to also those who are eligible) would be considered to fall within Article 1D(1) – there is no doubt that it has had a profound impact on the rights of Palestinians to receive refugee protection in a host state once they have left UNRWA areas of operation.

The *Bolbol* judgment impacted international refugee law in three key ways thereby confirming its position as a landmark case: (i) as the first judgment on the provision – albeit one that did not deliver on all questions referred to the Court – it exercised a direct and significant influence on the interpretation of Article 1D; (ii) it prompted the UNHCR to revise its Note on the applicability of Article 1D to Palestinian Refugees; and (iii) it opened the door for further references to – and interpretative clarification by – the CJEU, with consequent implications for national courts and, more critically, for the protection of Palestinian refugees.[92]

[92] Note on UNHCR's Interpretation of Article 1D of the 1951 Convention relating to the Status of Refugees and Article 12(1)(a) of the EU Qualification Directive in the context of Palestinian refugees seeking international protection, May 2013. In 2017, the UNHCR published Guidelines on International Protection No 13: Applicability of Article 1D of the 1951 Convention relating to the Status of Refugees to Palestinian Refugees, December 2017.

5

Pushpanathan v Canada (Minister of Citizenship and Immigration) [1998]: Excluding (Suspected) Criminals from Refugee Protection

SARAH SINGER

I. Introduction

States have long been concerned about protecting their borders from potential criminal outsiders. Indeed, the exclusion of suspected serious criminals from refugee protection is an issue that has permeated the modern international refugee protection regime since its inception, and is reflected in Article 1F of the 1951 Refugee Convention relating to the Status of Refugees (1951 Refugee Convention).[1] Article 1F of the 1951 Refugee Convention excludes certain categories of individuals from the benefits of refugee status: those for whom there are 'serious reasons for considering' have committed a crime against peace, war crime or crime against humanity (Article 1F(a)); a serious non-political crime (Article 1F(b)), or; under paragraph (c), 'been guilty of acts contrary to the purposes and principles of the United Nations'. An individual who falls within one or more of the limbs of this provision is excluded from the scope of the 1951 Refugee Convention per se, and all rights and privileges contained therein, despite having a well-founded fear of persecution in their country of origin.[2]

This is an area in which one sees the intersection of refugee law with international criminal and humanitarian law and, increasingly, measures taken in the fight against terrorism at both domestic and international levels. Nowhere is this complex intersection more prevalent than in Article 1F(c)'s reference 'acts contrary to the purposes and principles of the United Nations'. In the *Pushpanathan* decision,

[1] UN General Assembly, 1951 Convention relating to the Status of Refugees, United Nations, Treaty Series, 189:137, 28 July 1951 (1951 Refugee Convention).

[2] This does not mean, however, that an excluded individual will cease to benefit from the rights and benefits contained in other international instruments, human rights treaties in particular.

the Canadian Supreme Court addressed the meaning of this vague and uncertain ground of exclusion, and defined the parameters of the acts which could be considered to fall within its scope.[3] As the first authoritative and detailed examination of the meaning of this exclusion clause, the case was significant in establishing a high threshold for the crimes which may be considered to constitute 'acts contrary to the purposes and principles of the United Nations' for the purpose of Article 1F(c). The Court's interpretive approach, underpinned by the human rights character of the 1951 Refugee Convention, has in turn been globally influential in setting a high benchmark for the interpretation of all the limbs of Article 1F.

At the same time, the Supreme Court's approach has been criticised as being both over- and under-inclusive, and in many ways superseded by developments in international law.[4] Furthermore, the Court's determination that non-state actors could, in certain circumstances, fall within the scope of Article 1F(c), has been relied on by a number of states to support the exclusion of non-state actors from refugee status under the provision. This has been particularly important in the context of the global 'War on Terror', as more frequent resort has been made to employing Article 1F(c) to exclude non-state actors from refugee status for suspected involvement in terrorist activities, significantly expanding the scope of the provision. Indeed, though not a substantive part of the judgment, it is notable that Mr Pushpanathan himself was eventually excluded from refugee status on the basis of suspected terrorist activity when his claim was subsequently reconsidered by the Refugee Division.

Handed down in a fraught domestic climate characterised by increasing concern about 'bogus' asylum seekers and an influx of migrants with criminal profiles affecting the security of the Canadian state,[5] the *Pushpanathan* decision prompted public outcry and significant political debate about hosting serious criminals in Canada. The case raises important broader questions about how states address asylum seekers and refugees with suspected criminal profiles.

Section II of this chapter outlines the facts of the case and the Canadian Supreme Court's approach to interpreting Article 1F, and Article 1F(c)'s 'acts contrary to the purposes and principles of the United Nations'. Section III evaluates the Court's interpretive approach and its enduring relevance today. Section IV considers the Court's inclusion of non-state actors within the scope of Article 1F(c), and the influence this has had in paving the way for more expansive approaches to the exclusion of non-state actors for terrorist-related activity. Section V reflects on broader questions of the 'other tools' states may use to deny access to protection to refugees and asylum seekers with criminal profiles, or who are considered to pose a security risk to the host state. It is argued that an unintended consequence of the *Pushpanathan* decision, and other cases which have established a

[3] *Pushpanathan v Canada (Minister of Citizenship and Immigration)* [1998] 1 SCR 982 (hereafter *Pushpanathan* SCC).

[4] See discussion in section III below.

[5] A Pratt and M Valverde, 'From Deserving Victims to "Masters of Confusion": Redefining Refugees in the 1990s' (2002) 27(2) *Canadian Journal of Sociology / Cahiers canadiens de sociologie* 135–61.

high threshold benchmark for the interpretation of Article 1F, has been increased resort by a number of states to other means to exclude 'undesirable' individuals from protection.

II. The Supreme Court's Interpretation of Article 1F and 'Acts Contrary to the Purposes and Principles of the United Nations'

The *Pushpanathan* case concerned a Sri Lankan asylum seeker who was convicted of conspiracy to traffic drugs in Canada. Following a term of imprisonment, Mr Pushpanathan filed a claim for Convention refugee status. The Refugee Determination Division of the Immigration and Refugee Board (the Refugee Division) decided he was not a refugee by virtue of the exclusion clause in Article 1F(c) of the 1951 Refugee Convention, which provides that the Convention does not apply to a person for whom there are 'serious reasons for considering' has been 'guilty of acts contrary to the purposes and principles of the United Nations'. Since Mr Pushpanathan's crime occurred within Canada, it could not fall within Article 1F(b), the 'common crimes' limb of Article 1F which excludes from refugee status those for whom there are 'serious reasons for considering … have committed a serious non-political crime *outside the country of refuge* …' (emphasis added). The Refugee Division's determination, upheld by the Federal Court, was that the commission of serious narcotics offences in Canada did however fall within the scope of Article 1F(c) which was not geographically limited, and Mr Pushpanathan was therefore excluded from refugee status. Mr Pushpanathan appealed this decision to the Supreme Court.

The Supreme Court's decision in the *Pushpanathan* case has considerable value within domestic administrative law in Canada for its contributions to determining the standard of review of such decisions.[6] However, the key contribution to the field of refugee protection is the detailed consideration given by the Court to interpreting the terms of Article 1F, and in particular the terms of Article 1F(c), and accordingly, whether Mr Pushpanathan's act of drug trafficking in Canada fell within the scope of the provision.

Bastarache J, writing for the majority,[7] took considerable inspiration from the Supreme Court's earlier *Ward* decision[8] in prescribing an interpretive approach to Article 1F which drew on the rules of treaty interpretation laid out in the 1969 Vienna Convention on the Law of Treaties and the 'overarching and clear human rights object and purpose' of the 1951 Refugee Convention, which should form a

[6] D Lemiuex, 'Judicial Deference in Canadian Administrative Law: The Pragmatic and Functional Approach, Pushpanathan v. Canada (1998) 1 S.C.R 982' (2002) 54 *Administrative Law Review* 757.

[7] Majority comprised of L'Heureux-Dubé, Gonthier, McLachlin and Bastarache JJ.

[8] *Canada (Attorney General) v Ward* [1993] 2 SCR 689. See also Hugo Storey, '*Canada (Attorney General) v Ward* [1993]: Refugee Law's Parthenon' in ch 1 in this volume.

background for the interpretation of any individual provisions.[9] This mandated a restrictive approach to the interpretation of Article 1F, as a 'drastic exception' to a treaty whose purpose is the protection of human rights.[10]

In a significant contribution, the Court stated the rationale of Article 1F is that 'those who are responsible for the persecution which creates refugees should not enjoy the benefits of a Convention designed to protect those refugees'.[11] In the Court's view, this connection between persecution and the international refugee protection regime was what justified exclusion under Article 1F(a) and 1F(c).[12] Since, at the time of drafting, Article 1F(a) addressed war crimes and crimes against humanity committed during conflicts,[13] the differentiated scope of Article 1F(c) was 'to exclude individuals responsible for serious, sustained or systemic violations of fundamental human rights which amount to persecution in a non-war setting'.[14] Article 1F(c) was therefore considered a residual clause to address acts of a similarly egregious character to the international crimes listed in Article 1F(a), but would not otherwise fall within the scope of the provision. The Court used this standard to inform it's approach to the interpretation of 'acts contrary to the purposes and principles of the United Nations' for exclusion under Article 1F(c).

The proper interpretation of the phrase 'acts contrary to the purposes and principles of the United Nations' has been contentious since, unlike the first two limbs of Article 1F which refer to international and domestic crimes for which guidance may be sought from international and domestic criminal law, respectively, the purposes and principles of the UN are not so clearly ascertained. The purposes and principles of the UN, as set out in the Preamble and Articles 1 and 2 of the Charter of the United Nations (UN), include such purposes as maintaining international peace and security, developing friendly relations among nations and promoting and encouraging respect for human rights, and principles such as the sovereign equality of all states, fulfilling obligations under the Charter in good faith and settling disputes by peaceful means.[15] These are broad general statements that are difficult to interpret in the refugee exclusion context. Indeed, as Hathaway and Foster note, '[t]o describe the purposes and principles of the United Nations as broad-ranging is surely an understatement'.[16] Given the vague and amorphous nature of the phrase, there has been considerable concern that states may use this

[9] *Pushpanathan* SCC (n 3) 57.
[10] ibid 74.
[11] ibid 63.
[12] ibid 74.
[13] At the time the definitions of these international crimes were drawn from the London Charter and emerging international jurisprudence. It has since been recognised that crimes against humanity can be committed during peacetime – see discussion below.
[14] *Pushpanathan* SCC (n 3) 64.
[15] Charter of the United Nations (24 October 1945) 1 UNTS XVI (UN Charter).
[16] J Hathaway and M Foster, *The Law of Refugee Status*, 2nd edn (Cambridge University Press, 2014) 590.

provision to exclude *bona fide* refugees from protection.[17] In the *Pushpanathan* decision itself, the Court drew attention to the fact that during the drafting debates, '[t]he Canadian, Chilean and Pakistani delegates all expressed concern that the vague and potentially overbroad exclusionary clause would undermine the primary purpose of the Convention, and give states a means to easily reject individuals who deserved protection'.[18] Given these concerns, the Supreme Court's guidance in *Pushpanathan* is particularly valuable in establishing a principled approach to interpretation of this phrase.

As the first authoritative and detailed examination of the meaning of Article 1F(c), the Canadian Supreme Court gave valuable guidance on the parameters of this clause. In a key passage of the judgment, Bastarache J outlined the general approach:

> .... The guiding principle is that where there is consensus in international law that particular acts constitute sufficiently serious and sustained violations of fundamental human rights as to amount to persecution, or are explicitly recognised as contrary to the purposes and principles of the United Nations, then article 1F(c) will be applicable.[19]

Thus, the Court considered that certain acts could be considered to constitute acts contrary to the UN's purposes and principles for the purpose of Article 1F(c) where they are explicitly recognised as such, and this recognition represents a reasonable consensus of the international community.

The Court considered that where a 'widely accepted international agreement or United Nations resolution explicitly declares that the commission of certain acts is contrary to the purposes and principles of the United Nations' this would be a 'strong indication' that such acts fall within Article 1F(c).[20] The Court drew attention to such international agreements as the Declaration on the Protection of All Persons from Enforced Disappearance,[21] the Declaration on the Protection of All Persons from Being Subjected to Torture and Other Cruel, Inhuman or Degrading Treatment or Punishment,[22] and the Declaration to Supplement the 1994 Declaration on Measures to Eliminate International Terrorism,[23] which all explicitly designate certain acts as contrary to the purposes and principles of the UN. Where, as in these cases, such declarations or resolutions represent a reasonable consensus of the international community, then in the Court's opinion that

[17] M Zard, 'Exclusion, Terrorism and the Refugee Convention' (2002) 13 *Forced Migration Review* 32–34; B Saul, 'Protecting Refugees in the Global "War on Terror"' (University of Sydney, Legal Studies Research Paper No 08/130, 2008); P Mathew, 'Resolution 1373 – A Call to Pre-empt Asylum Seekers?' in J McAdam (ed), *Forced Migration, Human Rights and Security* (Portland, 2008) 49–58; GS Goodwin-Gill, 'Forced Migration: Refugees, Rights and Security' in McAdam, ibid 1–17.

[18] UN Doc E/AC.7/SR.166, 22 August 1950, at 4 (cited in *Pushpanathan* SCC (n 3) at 59).

[19] *Pushpanathan* SCC (n 3) 65.

[20] ibid 63.

[21] UN General Assembly (UNGA) Res 47/133, 18 December 1992, Art 1(1).

[22] UNGA Res 3452, 9 December 1975, Art 2.

[23] UNGA Res 51/210, 16 January 1997, Annex, Art 2.

designation should be considered determinative.[24] The Court also drew attention to other sources of international law which may be relevant to such a conclusion, including determinations by the International Court of Justice.[25]

In the instant case, despite co-ordinated efforts of the international community to stop trafficking in illicit substances, there had not been any explicit declaration that drug trafficking is contrary to the purposes and principles of the UN which the Court considered could serve as an expression of the international community's judgment that such acts should qualify as such.[26] Accordingly, Mr Pushpanathan's actions did not fall within the scope of Article 1F(c) under this limb of the Supreme Court's approach.

The Court gave further guidance on a second category of acts which could be considered to fall within the scope of Article 1F(c): those which the Court is able, for itself, to characterise as serious, sustained and systemic violations of fundamental human rights constituting persecution. The Court noted that such an assessment would involve a factual and legal component: the Court must assess the status of the rule which had been violated, with particular attention to whether it is 'very near the core of the most valued principles of human rights' and 'recognized as immediately subject to international condemnation and punishment'.[27] In such a case, even an isolated violation could lead to exclusion under Article 1F(c). The status of the violated rule as a universal jurisdiction offence would be a compelling indication of such. A serious and sustained violation of human rights amounting to persecution might also arise from a particularly egregious factual situation.[28]

In the Court's opinion, in the instant case, 'there was simply no indication that drug trafficking comes close to the core, or even forms a part of the corpus of fundamental human rights'.[29] Even though international trafficking in drugs was an extremely serious problem that the UN had taken extraordinary measures to eradicate, in the absence of clear indications that the international community recognised drug trafficking as a sufficiently serious and sustained violation of fundamental human rights as to amount to persecution, in the Court's opinion individuals should not be deprived of the essential protections contained in the 1951 Refugee Convention for having committed those acts.

The Court considered that this approach to interpreting Article 1F(c) complemented Article 1F(a)'s focus on serious human rights violations committed in the context of armed conflicts, and also avoided Article 1F(c)'s overlap with 'the precisely drawn scope of Article 1F(b)', which addresses serious non-political crimes committed outside the country of refuge. In the Court's view, such crimes

[24] *Pushpanathan* SCC (n 3) 66.
[25] ibid 67.
[26] ibid 69.
[27] ibid 70.
[28] ibid 71.
[29] ibid 72.

committed in the host state, including those considered to pose a danger to the host state, were more properly addressed by a separate provision of the Convention – Article 33(2), the exception to protection against *refoulement*.[30] Accordingly, Mr Pushpanathan's conspiracy to traffic in narcotics was not considered a violation of Article 1F(c) and the case was remitted for reconsideration by the Refugee Division.

III. Both under- and Over-Inclusive? Unpacking the Supreme Court's Approach to Article 1F and 'Acts Contrary to the Purposes and Principles of the United Nations'

The Court's significant contribution to interpreting 'acts contrary to the purposes and principles of the United Nations' for the purpose of Article 1F(c) has been considered to be a 'useful approach',[31] which 'rightly emphasises the importance, in international law, of agreement among States on what acts are sufficiently serious'[32] as to fall within the terms of Article 1F(c). The Court made clear that not every serious crime could amount to an act contrary to the UN's purposes and principles for the purpose of the exclusion clause. Rather, a high threshold had to be met. As such, the Supreme Court's two-pronged test has been considered to provide a 'basic outline' of a framework which 'offers a useful basis for analysis and assessment of serious human rights violations'.[33]

Indeed, the immediate impact of the decision within Canada was marked. Prior to the Supreme Court's decision in *Pushpanathan*, Article 1F(c) had been used to exclude persons who had committed drug trafficking offences in Canada from refugee status.[34] The Supreme Court's decision in *Pushpanathan* effectively put an end to this practice,[35] and Article 1F(c) has since been used in Canada only sparingly.[36] It is notable that the Supreme Court's reasoning has been influential in guiding Canadian domestic courts in excluding certain acts – such as domestic violence – from the scope of Article 1F(c) where they are not considered to meet the Supreme Court's threshold test.[37] Similarly, courts in other jurisdictions have

[30] See further discussion of Art 33(2) in section IV below.

[31] S Sivakumaran, 'Exclusion from Refugee Status: The Purposes and Principles of the United Nations and Article 1F(c) of the Refugee Convention' (2014) 26(3) *International Journal of Refugee Law* 352.

[32] GS Goodwin-Gill and J McAdam, *The Refugee in International Law*, 4th edn (Oxford University Press, 2021) 223.

[33] ibid 223.

[34] J Rikhof, *Exclusion and Refoulement: Criminality in International and Domestic Refugee Law* (Irwin Law, 2023) 547.

[35] Interview with Mr Pushpanathan's legal representative Lorne Waldman, 15 July 2024.

[36] Rikhof (n 34) 552. Rikhof also notes that in all the jurisdictions under his review, Art 1F(c) is used sparingly and primarily in relation to human rights violations and acts of terrorism (or not at all for the United States and New Zealand).

[37] See, eg, Rikhof (n 34) 552–53.

referred to the *Pushpanathan* decision when limiting the range of acts that may be considered to fall within the scope of Article 1F(c).[38] The Court's exclusion of drug trafficking from the scope of Article 1F(c) was endorsed by the United Nations High Commissioner for Refugees (UNHCR) in its 2003 Background Note on the Application of the Exclusion Clauses.[39] Although not explicitly cited, the decision also clearly influenced UNHCR's reference to 'serious and sustained violations of human rights' as an example of acts that would fall within 1F(c) in its 2003 guidance on the interpretation of the exclusion clauses.[40] The Supreme Court's approach to interpreting Article 1F(c) may therefore be considered to have set an important parameter in avoiding overly expansive interpretations of the type of acts which may fall within the provision.

The high threshold established for Article 1F(c) acts, and the Canadian Court's interpretive approach to Article 1F grounded in the 'human rights character' of the 1951 Refugee Convention, has also been influential in setting a high benchmark for the interpretation of the other limbs of Article 1F. In numerous interventions, UNHCR has relied on the Supreme Court's characterisation of Article 1F as a 'drastic exception' to the purposes of the Convention to advocate a restrictive approach to interpreting the provision.[41] The case has been relied on by domestic courts in a number of jurisdictions to support a restrictive approach to the interpretation of the acts to be included within the scope of the different limbs of Article 1F,[42] and differentiating that clause from the national security concerns addressed in Article 33(2).[43]

However, despite this positive influence, the Court's approach to interpreting Article 1F has not been immune from critique. It has been criticised as being both over- and under-inclusive in scope, and largely superseded by developments in international law. The stated rationale of Article 1F to exclude those who are

[38] For example, the UK Supreme Court in *Al-Sirri* held that Art 1F(c) is applicable to acts which, even if they are not covered by the definitions of crimes against peace, war crimes or crimes against humanity as defined in international instruments within the meaning of Art 1F(a), are nevertheless of a comparable egregiousness and character. *Al-Sirri v Secretary of State for the Home Department* [2012] UKSC 54.

[39] United Nations High Commissioner for Refugees (UNHCR), 'Background Note on the Application of the Exclusion Clauses: Article 1F of the 1951 Convention relating to the Status of Refugees' (4 September 2003) ('UNHCR Background Note') 18: 'Moves to apply this provision more broadly, for example to activities such as drug trafficking or smuggling/trafficking of migrants, are also misguided.' (citing *Pushpanathan* SCC (n 3)).

[40] UNHCR, 'Guidelines on International Protection No. 5: Application of the Exclusion Clauses: Article 1F of the 1951 Convention relating to the Status of Refugees' (4 September 2003) ('UNHCR Exclusion Guidelines') 17.

[41] See, eg, UNHCR intervention before the Supreme Court of the United Kingdom in the cases of Yasser Al-Sirri v. Secretary of State for the Home Department and DD (Afghanistan) v. Secretary of State for the Home Department, para 5; UNHCR intervention before the Supreme Court of the United States in the case of Immigration and Naturalization Service v. Aguirre-Aguirre, p 6.

[42] See, eg, *SRYYY v Minister for Immigration & Multicultural & Indigenous Affairs* [2005] FCAFC 42 (concerning Art 1F(a)); *FTZK v Minister for Immigration and Border Protection* [2014] HCA 26 (concerning Art 1F(b)); *KK (Article 1F(c), Turkey)* [2004] UKIAT 00101 (concerning Art 1F(c)).

[43] *DOB18 v Minister for Home Affairs* [2019] FCAFC 63.

'responsible for the persecution which creates refugees' has been considered too limiting, since it does not encapsulate serious international crimes which do not give rise to refugee-producing situations, nor account for Article 1F(b)'s focus on serious common crimes.[44] It has also been cautioned that the Court's reference to 'persecution' here, while evocative of the reference to 'persecution' in the inclusion refugee definition encapsulated in Article 1A(2) of the 1951 Refugee Convention, should not be limited to discriminatory persecution as that concept is.[45] As noted by Sivakumaran, 'it would be severely (and overly) limiting were Article 1F(c) not to include particularly serious and systematic instances of torture and the like that are not conducted on discriminatory grounds'.[46]

The Supreme Court's characterisation of Article 1F(c) in particular has been similarly critiqued. In a powerful and lengthy dissenting opinion in the *Pushpanathan* case, Cory and Major JJ argued that the category of acts contrary to the UN purposes and principles should not be restricted to those expressly declared as such, nor limited to serious or systematic violations of human rights, since these only spoke to one area of the UN purposes and principles. Cory J, delivering the dissenting opinion, contended that 'there are some matters which are the subject of such grave concern and such intense and continuing activity that it may be inferred that they are fundamentally connected to the goals of the UN'.[47]

Such criticisms appear to be well-founded. In the first instance, it may be contended that focus on explicit characterisation of a range of acts as 'contrary to the purposes and principles of the UN' should not be determinative for the purpose of Article 1F(c). Indeed, Sivakumaran rightly points out that acts are rarely explicitly characterised as contrary to the purposes and principles of the UN in international instruments, as international bodies do not generally have international refugee law in mind when concluding such instruments. Similarly, characterisation as such in an international instrument, while a relevant factor to be considered, should not be determinative of an acts' status for the purpose of the exclusion clause.[48]

The Canadian Supreme Court's approach may also be considered outdated. As Hathaway and Foster note, the Court's reference to serious and sustained violations of human rights which amount to persecution in a non-war setting 'was predicated on the now-doubtful view that non-war related acts cannot

[44] Sivakumaran (n 31).

[45] The Art 1A(2) definition of a refugee refers to those who have a 'well-founded fear of being persecuted for reasons of race, religion, nationality, membership of a particular social group or political opinion…'.

[46] Sivakumaran (n 31) 353.

[47] *Pushpanathan* SCC (n 3) (Dissenting Opinion) 125. Hathaway and Foster also make this point: 'More generally, the focus on acts capable of generating refugee flows may be thought an inordinately specific understanding of "purposes and principles of the United Nations", focused as it is on only one relevant phenomenon.' Hathaway and Foster (n 16) 595.

[48] Sivakumaran (n 31) 371. Sivakumaran also notes that drug trafficking, the very act in issue in *Pushpanathan*, has since been characterized as contrary to the purposes and principles of the UN.

amount to crimes against humanity and thus the basis for exclusion under Article 1(F)(a)'.[49] Given that it is now generally accepted that crimes against humanity can occur during peacetime, such acts should now be considered under Article 1F(a) when these issues arise.[50] This is in line with the 'residual' nature of Article 1F(c).

Similarly, developments in international criminal law appear to have overtaken the Court's focus on those acts explicitly declared to be contrary to the purposes and principles of the UN. Rikhof notes that, of the five specific activities mentioned in the Supreme Court decision – torture, terrorism, apartheid, forced disappearance and hostage taking – four are now included as crimes against humanity or war crimes in the Statute of the International Criminal Court.[51] Aside from terrorism (considered further in section IV below), the acts specified by the Canadian Supreme Court have thus been largely subsumed under international criminal law and fall within the scope of Article 1F(a). The Supreme Court therefore appears to have pre-empted developments of international criminal law and the categories of crimes considered so heinous as to give rise to exclusion under Article 1F. However, this early effort to define a differentiated and distinct role for Article 1F(c) may now be considered outdated and largely overtaken by developments in international criminal law.

Indeed, the current approach outlined by UNHCR to interpreting Article 1F(c) is not limited to serious and sustained violations of human rights,[52] nor is characterisation in an international instrument considered determinative.[53] Rather, UNHCR adopts an approach which mandates a high threshold for Article 1F(c) crimes, but focuses on the impact of the activity in question rather than its characterisation by the international community:

> Article 1F(c) is only triggered in extreme circumstances by activity which attacks the very basis of the international community's coexistence. Such activity must have an international dimension. Crimes capable of affecting international peace, security and peaceful relations between States, as well as serious and sustained violations of human rights, would fall under this category.[54]

This more refined approach to interpreting the provision may be considered to overcome many of the limitations of the Supreme Court's approach. This formulation undoubtedly though owes a great debt to the Canadian Supreme Court's

[49] Hathaway and Foster (n 16) 595. Indeed, reviewing the development of international criminal and transnational law since the *Pushpanathan* decision was handed down, it is notable that it is now generally accepted that crimes against humanity are not confined to conflict contexts. See, eg, Statute of the International Criminal Court 2187 UNTS 3, Art 7.

[50] Rikhof (n 34) 571.

[51] ibid 571. Torture, apartheid, and forced disappearance are included in crimes against humanity, while hostage taking is included as a war crime.

[52] Though this is given as an example, alongside 'crimes capable of affecting international peace and security'. UNHCR Exclusion Guidelines (n 40) 17.

[53] UNHCR intervention in the cases of *Yasser Al-Sirri* (n 41) 20.

[54] UNHCR Exclusion Guidelines (n 40) 17. See also UNHCR Background Note (n 39) 18.

earlier decision,[55] which can be credited with mandating a high threshold to the types of activities which may be considered to fall within the scope of the exclusion clause.

Perhaps the most significant legacy of the *Pushpanathan* case, however, relates to the Court's approach to considering the status of actor who may fall within the scope of Article 1F(c), as considered in the following section.

IV. Non-State Actors and Exclusion for Terrorist-Related Activity

A key area that was given attention by the Supreme Court in *Pushpanathan* was the status of persons who could fall to be excluded under Article 1F(c). This was an area of particular importance given the traditional view that, given the purposes and principles enshrined in the UN Charter are directed to states, violators of such purposes and principles must be persons 'in a position of power in a member State and instrumental to his State's infringing those principles'.[56] While respecting this view, in the Court's opinion, '[a]lthough it may be more difficult for a non-state actor to perpetrate human rights violations on a scale amounting to persecution without the state thereby implicitly adopting those acts, the possibility should not be excluded *a priori*'.[57] This passage has been relied on in a number of jurisdictions to support the proposition that non-state actors can fall within the scope of Article 1F(c).[58] UNHCR has also since changed its position on this issue.[59] This recognition that non-state actors could be brought within the scope of Article 1F(c) has had significant implications for the application of the provision. As noted by Hathaway and Foster, 'Once it became accepted that anyone could fall afoul of this exclusionary rule, the risk of grounding an understanding of UN purposes and principles in the nearly boundless list of the Charter's Preamble and Arts. 1 and 2 became apparent'.[60] In the early twenty-first century this was particularly the case for those suspected of terrorist-related activity.

[55] As can be seen in the extent the *Pushpanathan* decision is referred to in the UNHCR intervention in the cases of *Yasser Al-Sirri* (n 41).

[56] See, eg, UNHCR, 'Handbook on Procedures and Criteria for Determining Refugee Status and Guidelines on International Protection Under the 1951 Convention and the 1967 Protocol Relating to the Status of Refugees', HCR/1P/4/ENG/REV. 4, April 2019, 163.

[57] *Pushpanathan* SCC (n 3) 68.

[58] See, eg, BVerwG 10 C 2.10 (31 March 2011) 39; *KK (Article 1F(c), Turkey)* (n 42) 20.

[59] '[I]n addition to persons in positions of State authority, individuals acting in a personal capacity, including as leaders of a group responsible for "acts of terrorism" which are contrary to the principles and purpose of the United Nations, could also be capable of falling under Article 1F(c), where they are found to possess individual responsibility based on the requisite tests.' UNHCR, Statement on Article 1F of the 1951 Convention (July 2009) 29.

[60] Hathaway and Foster (n 16) 591.

Terrorism was one of the categories of acts considered by the Canadian Supreme Court to constitute 'acts contrary to the purposes and principles of the United Nations' under Article 1F(c), since it had been explicitly declared as such in the UN General Assembly's Declarations on Measures to Eliminate International Terrorism.[61] This theme has since been taken up with enthusiasm by a range of states, particularly following the 9/11 terrorist attacks on the United States (US) in 2001 and the ensuing global 'War on Terror'. Yet, this category of acts has proven particularly problematic in the refugee context given the politically charged nature of determinations of acts, or groups, as 'terrorist' in nature, and the absence of a universally agreed definition of such. This again gives rise to concerns about overly wide application of the exclusion clause.[62]

Indeed, it is notable that Mr Pushpanathan himself was eventually excluded from refugee status on the basis of suspected terrorist activity when his claim was subsequently reconsidered by the Refugee Division. While his domestic drugs offences had been deemed by the Supreme Court not to fall within the scope of Article 1F(c), the Refugee Division focused on the allegation that he had been using the proceeds of his drugs activities to finance a designated Sri Lankan terrorist organisation – the Liberation Tigers of Tamil Eelam (LTTE).[63] On appeal, following the Supreme Court's approach to interpreting Article 1F(c), the Federal Court agreed with the Refugee Division that terrorism *did* fall within the scope of Article 1F(c), and Mr Pushpanathan was therefore excluded from refugee status on this basis.[64] The pivot of focus in Mr Pushpanathan's case towards the 'terrorist' nature of his activities foreshadowed the international preoccupation with terrorism which gripped the international community in the first decades of the twenty-first century.

Following the 9/11 terrorist attacks on the US and President Bush's response of a purported 'War on Terror',[65] language connecting refugees with the threat posed by international terrorism became much more forceful and entrenched in international discourse. UN Security Council Resolutions 1373 and 1377, adopted immediately following the 9/11 terror attacks, called on Member States to '[e]nsure … that refugee status is not abused by the perpetrators, organizers or facilitators of terrorist acts'.[66] Both resolutions firmly declared that 'acts, methods, and practices

[61] UNGA Res 51/210 (n 23) Annex, Art 2. See also UNGA Res 49/60, 17 February 1995, Annex, Art 2. Cited in *Pushpanathan* SCC (n 3) 66.

[62] See n 17 and accompanying text.

[63] As mentioned in the appeal hearing *Pushpanathan v Canada (Minister of Citizenship and Immigration)*, 2002 FCT 867 (CanLII) 16–18. The Refugee Division's decision is unfortunately not publicly available, but is described as 'an extensive, detailed document, reflecting the six (6)-part hearing'.

[64] The Refugee Division and the Federal Court found Mr Pushpanathan was excluded under Art 1F(a) and Art 1F(c) for crimes against humanity and his complicity in terrorist activities associated with the LTTE.

[65] The White House, 'Address to a Joint Session of Congress and the American People' (20 September 2001), available at https://georgewbush-whitehouse.archives.gov/news/releases/2001/09/20010920-8.html.

[66] UN Security Council resolution (UNSC Res) 1373, 28 September 2001, UN Doc S/RES/1373, para 3(g).

of terrorism are contrary to the purposes and principles of the United Nations and that knowingly financing, planning and inciting terrorist acts are also contrary to the purposes and principles of the United Nations'.[67] These resolutions – and later similar enunciations by the UN Security Council[68] – prompted legislative changes in the asylum frameworks of a number of countries and regions, and increased focus on the exclusion of suspected terrorists under Article 1F.[69]

Reference to these UN resolutions in interpreting Article 1F(c) was embedded in the European Union's Qualification Directive.[70] The *Pushpanathan* decision was also explicitly relied on by senior courts across a range of jurisdictions to support the exclusion of non-state actors from refugee status under Article 1F(c) for terrorist-related activities.[71] As such, the *Pushpanathan* decision appears to have been influential in shaping the practice of reliance on international declarations and resolutions on terrorism in the characterisation of Article 1F(c) acts, and the application of the clause to non-state actors.[72]

This expansion of application of Article 1F(c) to non-state actors has, in the view of some, turned the provision into 'something of a ravenous omnivore'.[73] As argued by Hathaway and Foster:

> Not only is everyone (not just leaders) potentially "guilty of" acts contrary to the purposes and principles of the UN, but more importantly an extraordinarily broad definition of purposes and principles derived from the UN Charter and pronouncements of the General Assembly and Security Council has been invoked to swallow up the carefully conceived limits to protection set by Art. 1(F)(a), Art. 1(F)(b), and even Art. 33(2).[74]

This somewhat concerning legacy of the *Pushpanathan* case speaks to expansive state approaches to excluding individuals from refugee status on the basis of ill-defined charges of involvement with 'terrorist' activity.[75] Free of the temporal and geographical restrictions of Article 1F(b), and the more clearly defined parameters of the crimes (rather than 'acts') that fall within its scope, Article 1F(c) may be increasingly used to address acts committed in the host country which do not

[67] UNSC Res 1373, para 5; UNSC Res 1377, 12 November 2001, UN Doc S/RES/1377, preamble, para 5.

[68] Including the adoption of the UNSC Res 1624 following the 7/7 terror attacks on London in 2005. UNSC Res 1624 (14 September 2005), UN Doc S/RES/1624, see preamble, paras 7 and 8.

[69] S Singer, 'Refugee Law and the War on Terror' in S Juss (ed), *Research Handbook on International Refugee Law* (Edward Elgar Publishing, 2019) 374–89.

[70] Council Directive 2004/83/EC of 29 April 2004 on minimum standards for the qualification and status of third country nationals or stateless persons as refugees or as persons who otherwise need international protection and the content of the protection granted [2004] OJ L304/12; E Guild and M Garlick, 'Refugee Protection, Counter-terrorism, and Exclusion in the European Union' (2010) 29(4) *Refugee Survey Quarterly* 63–82. See also Singer (n 69) on judicial consideration by the Court of Justice of the European Union.

[71] See n 58.

[72] Hathaway and Foster, *The Law of Refugee Status* (n 16) 591–92.

[73] ibid 594.

[74] ibid 594.

[75] Singer (n 69).

amount to crimes[76] or which would be more properly addressed via domestic criminal law enforcement.

As considered in the following section, another perhaps unintended consequence of the *Pushpanathan* decision, and later jurisprudence mandating a high threshold for the range of acts which fall within Article 1F, is the increasing tendency for states to resort to 'other tools' to exclude individuals from protection. In some cases these can go far beyond the terms of Article 1F. Indeed, concerns regarding what measures could be used to address the potential threat posed by Mr Pushpanathan himself was a key focus in the aftermath of the Supreme Court's decision, as considered immediately below.

V. Other Tools: *Refoulement*, Inadmissibility and Denial of Access to Protection

Handed down in a context of increasingly restrictive domestic asylum and immigration law and policy, and a fixation among some elements of the Canadian popular press on 'violent foreign criminals',[77] the Supreme Court's *Pushpanathan* decision attracted immediate political and media attention.[78] The case was seized on by Parliamentarians and gave rise to no less than four questions in the House of Commons the following day.[79] Concerns were raised by Members of the right-wing Reform Party about the efficacy of Canadian immigration legislation to deport persons convicted of serious offences. The Supreme Court decision was described as 'unprecedented and bizarre', a 'bad' decision which would have 'repercussions around the world and undoubtedly leaves every criminal with intent to use Canada as a safe haven with a notion that we are very easy to access'.[80] It was demanded: 'When will the minister take action so this drug dealer can be kicked out of Canada like he should be?'[81] In response, the Minister of Citizenship and Immigration drew attention to the importance of respect for the rule of law and the Supreme Court's proper role. However, she also repeatedly stressed that there were 'other avenues' and 'other tools' available in domestic legislation 'for intervening and ensuring that this kind of individual is never allowed to stay in Canada'.[82]

[76] See, eg, C-573/15 *Commissaire général aux réfugiés et aux apatrides v Mostafa Lounani* [2017] ECLI: EU: C: 2017: 71.

[77] Pratt and Valverde (n 5).

[78] A report in the *Toronto Star* that week ran the headline 'Minister Vows to Deport Refugee Drug Dealer'. Cited in *Pushpanathan v Canada (Minister of Citizenship and Immigration)* [1999] 4 FC 465 (hereafter 'Pushpanathan danger order').

[79] Official Report (Hansard) of the House of Commons Debates [Vol 135, 1st Sess, 36th Parl, 1998].

[80] ibid, Mr John Reynolds (West Vancouver – Sunshine Coast, Ref) 1120.

[81] ibid. See also similar demands raised by Mr Deepak Obhrai (Calgary East, Ref) at 1130, Mr Jason Kenney (Calgary Southeast, Ref) at 1140 and Mr Leon E Benoit (Lakeland, Ref) at 1145.

[82] ibid, Hon Lucienne Robillard (Minister of Citizenship and Immigration, Lib) 1120–30. These comments were the subject of a press report in the *Toronto Star* the following day (see n 78).

Indeed, perhaps anticipating the backlash that might ensue against the decision that Mr Pushpanathan was not excluded by virtue of Article 1F, in the *Pushpanathan* decision itself Bastarache J was careful to note that 'my determination of the scope of Article 1F(c) of the Convention … does not preclude the Minister from taking appropriate measures to ensure the safety of Canadians.'[83] Bastarache J considered that any danger posed to the Canadian society could be addressed by Article 33(2) of the 1951 Refugee Convention, which provides for an exception to the *non-refoulement* obligation outlined in Article 33(1) where there are 'reasonable grounds' to consider an individual to pose a danger to the security of the country of refuge or, having been convicted of a particularly serious crime, a danger to the safety of the community. Thus, while Mr Pushpanathan was not considered to be excluded from refugee status by virtue of Article 1F, the Supreme Court left open the door to loss of protection against *refoulement* by virtue of Article 33(2) of the Convention and his removal from Canada. Bastarache J had no qualms about stating that 'Acts which fall short of persecution may well warrant *refoulement* under Article 33.'[84]

The Court's focus on Article 33(2) of the 1951 Refugee Convention as distinct from Article 1F is notable, given there has been a tendency for states to conflate the terms of the provisions and exclude individuals from refugee status on the basis of the security concerns referred to in Article 33(2), which go beyond the parameters of Article 1F.[85] In fact, the two provisions are distinct; Article 1F mandates loss of refugee status, whilst Article 33(2) entails loss of protection against *refoulement* only, for 'refugees who become an extremely serious threat to the country of asylum due to the severity of crimes perpetrated by them.'[86] Article 33(2) refers to those for whom there are 'reasonable grounds to consider', which is comparable to Article 1F's standard of proof 'serious reasons for considering', but is a forward-looking assessment of the risk the individual is considered to pose to the security of the host state. Yet the provisions are often conflated in practice. As Gilbert and Bentajou note, 'States often regard these provisions as a suite of measures enabling the deportation of refugees.'[87] Notwithstanding, it is important to note that exclusion from the protection against *refoulement* under either provision does not mean that the individual will cease to benefit from the protections against *refoulement* offered by other international instruments, particularly human rights instruments which are absolute permitting no criminality or security exceptions.

[83] *Pushpanathan* SCC (n 3) 75.

[84] ibid 74.

[85] See, eg, EU Qualification Directive (n 70) Art 14; S Singer, 'National Security, Criminality and Exclusion from Refugee Protection under the EU Qualification Directive: Expanding the Grounds of Exclusion by the Back Door' (2018) 32(3) *Journal of Immigration, Asylum and Nationality Law* 284–300; G Gilbert, 'Exclusion and Evidentiary Evidence' in G Noll, *Proof, Evidentiary Assessment and Credibility in Asylum Procedures* (Martinus Nijhoff, 2005) 161–78.

[86] UNHCR Background Note (n 39) para 10.

[87] G Gilbert and AM Bentajou, 'Exclusion' in C Costello, M Foster and J McAdam (eds), *The Oxford Handbook of International Refugee Law* (Oxford University Press, 2021) 713. Referring also to Art 32 on expulsion of refugees.

This means that in practice those excluded from refugee protection under either provision may nevertheless be non-removable on human rights grounds.[88]

Loss of protection against *refoulement* was addressed in a later case concerning Mr Pushpanathan, heard before the Federal Court the year after the Supreme Court decision was handed down.[89] This case concerned a power within the Immigration Act by which the Minister could preclude determination of a refugee claim by a person who has been convicted of a criminal offence carrying a stipulated penalty if 'the Minister is of the opinion that the person constitutes a danger to the public in Canada'. Such a danger opinion could be determinative in a removal assessment, leaving an individual at risk of *refoulement*.[90] Although in that case the application was dismissed,[91] this trajectory is significant in hinting at what has become a dominant feature of Canadian administrative law regarding asylum seekers and refugees with suspected criminal connections. That is, administrative denial of access to the asylum system via Canada's inadmissibility regime.

Canada's contemporary inadmissibility regime provides for denial of access to the asylum system on grounds which overlap with Article 1F, but also go much further to encompass those with 'tenuous links with certain organizations and non-serious criminality'.[92] Recent research has shown that resort to inadmissibility to address asylum applicants with suspected criminal profiles appears to have surpassed resort to Article 1F determinations, and is in many cases being deliberately chosen as an avenue for review given the lower standards of the inadmissibility process compared with Article 1F.[93] This concerning finding unfortunately has echoes in other parts of the world, where refugee applicants are being excluded from access to protection via processes which go far beyond the strict terms of Article 1F.[94] The expansion of such practices appears to be an unintended consequence of the largely positive jurisprudence of senior courts in *Pushpanathan* and later judicial developments in Canada which have served to limit the scope of Article 1F and mandate a restrictive approach to its interpretation

[88] S Singer, 'Undesirable and Unreturnable Migrants in the United Kingdom' (2017) 36(1) *Refugee Survey Quarterly* 9–34.

[89] Pushpanathan danger order (n 78).

[90] Bond notes that as per s 115 of the of the Immigration and Refugee Protection Act (SC 2001, c 27), Canada's commitment to *non-refoulement* may be outweighed by a danger opinion, resulting in removal to risk. J Bond, 'Unwanted but Unremovable: Canada's Treatment of "Criminal" Migrants Who Cannot Be Removed' (2017) 36 *Refugee Survey Quarterly* 168.

[91] As the state, at the last minute, submitted evidence that no danger opinion had in fact been made.

[92] D Dogar, 'Unrecognizing Refugees: The Inadmissibility Scheme Replacing Article 1F Decisions in Canada' (2023) *International Journal of Refugee Law* 35(4) 382. Canada's inadmissibility regime is currently regulated under ss 33–43 of the Immigration and Refugee Protection Act (n 90).

[93] Dogar, ibid 370.

[94] See, eg, S Blum and N Morag, 'Terrorist Victim Or Perpetrator?: Foreign Solutions to Challenges Posed by the U.S.'s Terrorist Bars to Asylum' (2019–2020) 3 *Policy & Ethics Law Review* 591; D Dogar, 'The Use and Misuse of Immigration and Refugee Law for National Security Risks and Punitive Ends by Canada and the Netherlands' (Thesis, 2022, McGill University); S Juss, 'Detention and Delusion in Australia's Kafkaesque Refugee Law (2017) *Refugee Survey Quarterly* 36(1) 146–67.

and application,[95] properly limiting the scope of this 'drastic exception' to the 1951 Refugee Convention.

VI. Conclusion

The Canadian Supreme Court's decision in *Pushpanathan* was a landmark case in the law of exclusion from refugee status on the basis of suspected criminality. The decision was important in establishing a high threshold bar for the acts which could be considered to fall within the scope of the provision, and mandating an interpretive approach grounded in the human rights character of the 1951 Refugee Convention. However, the Court's approach has also been critiqued as being inconsistent with a proper reading of the provision, and to have lost much of its contemporary meaning having been superseded in large part by developments in international criminal law.

Perhaps the most significant contribution of the decision, however, is the determination by the Supreme Court that non-state actors could, in certain circumstances, fall within the scope of the third limb of Article 1F: Article 1F(c). This has had significant repercussions, and been relied on by jurisdictions across the globe as a basis for the exclusion of private individuals for terrorist-related activity, a practice which has taken on increased significance in the early part of the twenty-first century following the 9/11 terrorist attacks on the US and the concordant global 'War on Terror'.

The *Pushpanathan* case also raises important broader questions about how states address asylum seekers and refugees with criminal profiles, or considered to pose a threat to the security of the host state. In many ways an unintended consequence of the *Pushpanathan* decision, and other cases which have established a high threshold for Article 1F, has been increased resort by states to other means of excluding individuals from access to protection. A clear example is the development of the 'inadmissibility' regime we see in Canada today which goes far beyond the terms of Article 1F.

[95] Such as *Ezokola v Canada (Citizenship and Immigration)* [2013] 2 SCR 678 (concerning Art 1F(a)); Dogar (n 92) 374.

PART B

Rights of Refugees

6

R v Uxbridge Magistrates Court and Another ex parte Adimi [1999]: 'Article 31 Must Henceforth be Honoured.'

KIRSTEN McCONNACHIE

I. Introduction

R v Uxbridge Magistrates Court and another ex parte Adimi[1] is a foundational decision in the jurisprudence on Article 31(1) of the 1951 Convention Relating to the Status of Refugees (Refugee Convention).[2] Article 31 contains the principle of non-penalisation of refugees for unlawful entry to the country of refuge, which has been described by Lord Bingham in *Asfaw* as one of the three 'broad humanitarian aims' of the Refugee Convention and by the United Nations High Commissioner for Refugees (UNHCR) as 'central to the object and purpose of the 1951 Convention'.[3]

The protection afforded by Article 31 has become increasingly important as stricter border regimes and a growing entanglement of criminal law in migration policy have resulted in large numbers of refugees facing criminal and other penalties in precisely the circumstances that Article 31 prohibits. *Adimi* was one of the first decisions to engage with the consequences of such policies and as such can be seen as an early warning of emerging tensions between Refugee Convention obligations and state border controls. Over subsequent decades this clash has come to dominate political and legal discourse throughout much of the Global North. It is now exemplified in the widespread criminalisation of migration but also in procedures that seek to regulate access to a state's asylum system through externalisation

[1] *R v Uxbridge Magistrates Court and another ex parte Adimi* [1999] EWHC Admin 765 (hereafter *Adimi*).

[2] UN General Assembly, 1951 Convention relating to the Status of Refugees, United Nations, Treaty Series, 189:137, 28 July 1951.

[3] *R v Asfaw* [2008] UKHL 31 [9]; United Nations High Commissioner for Refugees (UNHCR) (2024), *Guidelines on International Protection No.14: Non-penalization of refugees on account of their irregular entry or presence and restrictions on their movements in accordance with Article 31 of the 1951 Convention relating to the Status of Refugees*. HCR/GIP/24/14 23 September 2024 (hereafter UNHCR GIP 14 (2024)).

agreements, safe third country regimes, country of first asylum and safe country of origin policies – practices that directly implicate Article 31 protection.[4]

The full text of Article 31 is:

> 31(1) The Contracting States shall not impose penalties, on account of their illegal entry or presence, on refugees who, coming directly from a territory where their life or freedom was threatened in the sense of Article 1, enter or are present in their territory without authorization, provided they present themselves without delay to the authorities and show good cause for their illegal entry or presence.
>
> 31(2) The Contracting States shall not apply to the movements of such refugees restrictions other than those which are necessary and such restrictions shall only be applied until their status in the country is regularized or they obtain admission into another country. The Contracting States shall allow such refugees a reasonable period and all the necessary facilities to obtain admission into another country.

Adimi was concerned with Article 31(1), a provision that raises several interpretive questions. The central obligation ('Contracting States shall not impose penalties, on account of their illegal entry or presence, on refugees') requires interpretation as to both personal scope (who is a refugee) and substantive application (what is a penalty). This is followed by three further clauses or conditions of entitlement: 'coming directly from a territory where their life or freedom was threatened'; 'present themselves without delay to the authorities' and 'show good cause for their illegal entry or presence'.[5] These phrases were scrutinised by the Court in *Adimi*, in a decision that exposed a significant gap in United Kingdom (UK) incorporation of the 1951 Refugee Convention and led directly to the adoption of section 31 of the Immigration and Asylum Act 1999 (providing refugees who have been charged with a range of false documentation offences with a statutory defence). *Adimi* was a decision by the Divisional Court of the High Court rather than the more senior Court of Appeal or apex Supreme Court, but is nevertheless a landmark case for its comprehensive analysis of the scope of Article 31 protection and its realisation in UK domestic law. Twenty-five years later, UNHCR Guidance on Article 31(1) continues to follow the reasoning in *Adimi* and the case remains 'one of the most thorough examinations of the scope of article 31 and the protection due'.[6]

This chapter opens in section I with an overview of the facts in *R v Uxbridge Magistrates Court and another ex parte Adimi*, before exploring three themes emerging from the judgment. Section II examines *Adimi* for its interpretation of the scope and terms of Article 31(1). Section III considers the impact of the judgment in the realisation of Article 31 protection into UK domestic law by way

[4] A Aliverti, *Crimes of Mobility: Criminal Law and the Regulation of Immigration* (Routledge, 2013).

[5] On the purpose and interpretation of Art 31, see UNHCR GIP 14 (2024) (n 3); see also C Costello, Y Ioffe and T Buchsell, *Article 31 of the 1951 Convention Relating to the Status of Refugees* (UNHCR Division of International Protection, 2017); GS Goodwin-Gill, 'Article 31 of the 1951 Convention Relating to the Status of Refugees: Non-Penalization, Detention and Protection' in E Feller, V Türk and F Nicholson, *Refugee Protection in International Law: UNHCR's Global Consultations on International Protection* (Cambridge University Press, 2001).

[6] Goodwin-Gill, ibid; UNHCR GIP 14 (2024), ibid.

of a statutory defence. This approach has had significant limitations, including a mismatch in scope between the available defences and the text of Article 31, and as a defence that is poorly understood by both prosecutors and defence solicitors.[7] Section IV considers the legacy of *Adimi* in the context of contemporary migration deterrence policies, particularly in the UK, where post-Brexit refugee law reforms have narrowed the scope of protection from criminal penalties for refugees entering via irregular routes and have even sought to deny such refugees access to the asylum system. In this context, Article 31 is increasingly important in protecting the right to seek and to enjoy asylum and to preserve the integrity of the 1951 Refugee Convention regime.

II. *R v Uxbridge Magistrates Court and Another ex parte Adimi*

Ex parte Adimi joined three cases involving four individuals, each of whom had been prosecuted for false documentation offences and had also claimed protection under the 1951 Refugee Convention.

Chouki Adimi fled Algeria in 1997 and entered the UK at Heathrow airport on a flight from France (having travelled to France from Italy, where he had spent 10 days) using a false Italian passport and identity card. His false documentation was picked up by the immigration officer at entry and Mr Adimi was charged with documentation offences under the Forgery and Counterfeiting Act 1981. Mr Adimi claimed asylum within 24 hours of his initial entry and soon afterwards was recognised as a refugee. His legal representation raised the possibility of applying Article 31 of the Refugee Convention. Nevertheless, the Crown Prosecution Service continued the prosecution against him.

Dylan Sorani was arrested and prosecuted for presenting false documentation when attempting to board a flight from the UK to Canada. He was an Iraqi Kurd from Northern Iraq who fled Iraq after being arrested and tortured by the Iraqi authorities. He travelled to Turkey on 15 June 1997 and then sought to travel onwards for Canada, where he had family members. His route to the UK was not definitively established but his explanation was that he travelled from Istanbul to Heathrow on a false Greek passport on 16 August 1997 and met with an agent at Heathrow airport who furnished him with a second false passport (this time Dutch) to board a second flight on the same day to Canada. He was stopped when attempting to check in to that flight and on 18 August 1997 was charged with and pled guilty to offences under the Forgery and Counterfeiting 1981 Act and the Criminal Attempts Act 1981. He was sentenced to two concurrent sentences of three months' imprisonment. He claimed that he told an immigration officer that he was

[7] G Christie, *Prosecuting the Persecuted in Scotland: Article 31(1) of the Refugee Convention and the Scottish Criminal Justice System* (Scottish Refugee Council, 2016). Y Holiday, E Guild and V Mitsilegas, *The Court of Appeal and the Criminalisation of Refugees* (Criminal Cases Review Commission, 2018).

seeking asylum when he was first arrested, though this was disputed. He made a formal application for asylum after his release from prison on 30 September 1997. His claim remained undetermined at the time of the decision in *Adimi*.

Astrit Kaziu was an Albanian, formerly employed as a bodyguard to the country's President Berisha who left office in July 1997 during a time of political turmoil. Mr Kaziu claimed that he was targeted by the new regime for his political activities against it. Together with his wife, both using false passports, he left Albania for Greece on 18 December 1998 and travelled to England three days later with the intention of travelling to Canada to claim asylum. On 22 December they were arrested and charged with offences under the Forgery and Counterfeiting 1981 Act and the Criminal Attempts Act 1981. These were the same charges that had been issued against Mr Sorani, yet the Kazius received sentences of six months (rather than three). They began an asylum claim in February 1999. It remained undetermined at the time of the decision in *Adimi*.

The applicants sought judicial review of decisions to prosecute and of the failure to stay prosecution for asylum claims to be determined. Sitting as the Divisional Court of the High Court of Justice, it fell to Lord Justice Simon Brown and Justice Newman to determine the application of Article 31 of the Refugee Convention to these cases and any relief due. All applications were granted though no declaratory relief was awarded. Brown LJ considered that the judgment itself should be viewed as the remedy, with insistence that it should be acted on by the executive to ensure the realisation of Article 31 protection in UK domestic law (see further sections III and IV, below).[8]

III. 'Just When Will Article 31 Protect Them?'

> The combined effect of visa requirements and carrier's liability has made it wellnigh impossible for refugees to travel to countries of refuge without false documents. Just when, in these circumstances, will article 31 protect them?[9]

Until *Adimi*, the relevance of non-penalisation obligations under Article 31 of the Refugee Convention had not been considered by any arm of the UK state, whether from the perspective of asylum processing or the criminal justice system. This systemic failure was increasingly anachronistic in the face of new approaches to migration control that sought to shut down irregular migration by creating new offences for both migrants and transport carriers.[10] In his leading judgment, Brown LJ recognised that this context was driving refugees to rely on 'unorthodox means of travel' and thereby making legal violations more likely. He sought

[8] *Adimi* (n 1) per Brown LJ, at [67].
[9] ibid [2].
[10] ibid [10]–[11].

'to stand back from the detail of the individual cases and to look instead at the position in the round' to determine whether and to what extent Article 31 of the 1951 Refugee Convention could provide immunity for such offences. He began by considering the object and purpose of Article 31, providing the much-quoted definition that:

> Self-evidently it was to provide immunity for genuine refuges whose quest for asylum reasonably involved them in breaching the law [...] where the illegal entry or use of false documents or delay can be attributed to a bona fide desire to seek asylum whether here or elsewhere, that conduct should be covered by article 31 [...] That article 31 extends not merely to those ultimately accorded refugee status but also to those claiming asylum in good faith (presumptive refugees) is not in doubt. Nor is it disputed that article 31's protection can apply equally to those using false documents as to those (characteristically the refugees of earlier times) who enter a country clandestinely.[11]

He then considered the terms of Article 31 and the clauses limiting immunity to refugees who

> coming directly from a territory where their life or freedom was threatened in the sense of Article 1, enter or are present in their territory without authorization, provided they present themselves without delay to the authorities and show good cause for their illegal entry or presence.[12]

Quite obviously, the interpretation of these terms is critical to the protection that Article 31 affords in domestic law. Counsel for the Crown (representing the Secretary of State, Director of Public Prosecution and Crown Prosecution Service) argued for a narrow interpretation, asserting that the phrase 'coming directly' required that asylum should be claimed in the first safe country entered. This approach '... allows the refugee no element of choice as to where he should claim asylum. He must claim it where first he may: only considerations of continuing safety would justify impunity for further travel'.[13]

It was further argued that the phrase 'present themselves without delay' requires that an asylum claim must be made immediately at the point of entry to the UK. Brown LJ rejected both arguments, holding that 'coming directly' does not require that a refugee claim asylum in the first country they enter: '... some element of choice is indeed open to refugees [...] merely short-term stopover en route to such sanctuary cannot forfeit the protection of the Article'.

Rather than establish a fixed time threshold, cases should be determined with consideration to three 'touchstones':

> The main touchstones by which exclusion from protection should be judged are the length of stay in the intermediate country, the reasons for delaying there (even a substantial delay in an unsafe third country would be reasonable were the time spent

[11] ibid [15]; repeated in *R v AM and others* [2010] EWCA Crim 2400; *R v Mateta* [2013] EWCA Crim 1372.

[12] Art 31(1) 1951 Refugee Convention.

[13] *Adimi* (n 1) per Brown LJ at [17].

trying to acquire the means of traveling on) and whether or not the refugee sought or found there protection de jure or de facto from the persecution they were fleeing.[14]

The respondents argued that Mr Adimi could not fall within the scope of Article 31 protection, because he had arrived to the UK after transiting through Italy and France (and therefore had not 'come directly') and had pretended to be an Italian citizen on arrival in the UK (and therefore not 'presented himself without delay' to the authorities). These arguments were rejected by Brown LJ, who cited UNHCR Guidelines as supporting authority that asylum seekers may have valid reasons for not declaring themselves to authorities at the border and therefore that: 'If Mr Adimi's intention was to claim asylum within a short time of his arrival [...] then I would not think it right to regard him as having breached this condition'.[15]

Newman J agreed, considering this approach to be consistent with the object and purpose of the 1951 Refugee Convention and sensitive to the flight conditions for refugees:

> The Convention is a living instrument, changing and developing with the times so as to be relevant and to afford meaningful protection to refugees in the conditions in which they currently seek asylum. Apart from the current necessity to use false documents another current reality and advance, occurring since 1951, is the development of a readily accessible and worldwide network of air travel. As a result there is a choice of refuge beyond the first safe territory by land or sea. There have been distinctive and different state responses to requests for asylum. Thus there exists a rational basis for exercising choice where to seek asylum. I am unable to accept that to recognise it is to legitimise forum shopping.[16]

The requirement to 'show good cause for their illegal entry or presence' was less contentious, and it was accepted by all that it would be satisfied 'by a genuine refugee showing that he was reasonably travelling on false papers'.[17]

A. Refugees in Transit

The Divisional Court further held that Mr Sorani and Mr Kaziu were entitled to benefit from Article 31 protection. Both had been charged for offences committed while attempting to leave the UK and it was argued on behalf of the Crown that in such circumstances the applicants could not be considered to have presented themselves without delay (as they had not intended to present themselves at all); furthermore, by not claiming asylum in the UK they also failed to satisfy the requirement of 'coming directly'. The Court disagreed, with Brown LJ concluding that:

> If I am right in saying that refugees are ordinarily entitled to choose where to claim asylum, and that a short-term stopover en route in a country where the traveller's status

[14] ibid [18].
[15] ibid [25].
[16] ibid [60].
[17] ibid [26].

> is in no way regularised, will not break the requisite directness of flight, then it must follow that these applicants would have been entitled to the benefit of article 31 had they reached Canada and made their asylum claims there. If article 31 would have availed them in Canada, then logically its protection cannot be denied to them here merely because they have been apprehended en route [...] both should have been recognised as refugees within the meaning of article 31 and both should have been exempt from penalty under it.[18]

This scenario was later considered by the House of Lords in *R v Asfaw*, where a 3:2 majority upheld the reasoning in *Adimi* that the immunity afforded under Article 31 for 'illegal entry or presence' is not limited to offences of entering or remaining illegally in an intermediate country, but also extends to offences committed when leaving that country to seek asylum elsewhere.[19] This decision was reached from a purposive construction of the Refugee Convention that included close consideration of the terms of Article 31, the *travaux préparatoires* (sections of which were appended to the judgment) and the purpose of the Refugee Convention. In the view of the majority (though with strong dissenting opinions from Lords Rodger and Mance),[20] the drafters' intention was clear: it sought to exclude refugees who had already received protection elsewhere but not to prevent all forms of onward movement. As Lord Bingham explained:

> The single most important point that emerges from a consideration of the travaux préparatoires is that there was universal acceptance that the mere fact that refugees stopped while in transit ought not deprive them of the benefit of the article [...][21]

Brown LJ's interpretation of the scope of Article 31 has been influential in international jurisprudence scholarship and advocacy and his definitions of 'coming directly', 'presenting without delay' and 'showing good cause' for illegal entry are included in the recent UNHCR Guidelines on International Protection for the Interpretation of Article 31 (2024).[22] It is no longer valid law in the UK however, where the scope for judicial discretion was narrowed immediately after the *Adimi* judgment by the adoption of section 31 of the Immigration and Asylum Act 1999 and was reduced further by section 37 of the Nationality and Borders Act (NABA) 2022 (see section IV below). Section 37(4) NABA 2022 excludes offences committed during an attempt to leave the UK from protection from penalties. This is an explicit reversal of the House of Lords decision in *Asfaw* and speaks of a larger struggle in contemporary refugee protection in the UK, which is the attempted narrowing or avoidance of Convention protection via national legislation.

[18] ibid [64].
[19] *Asfaw* (n 3).
[20] Lord Rodger's dissent considered that the words of the treaty text must be paramount. On his reading, 'Refugees who are in a safe country and who want to travel to another country have no more right than anyone else to use criminal means to do so' *Adimi* (n 1) [96], and 'Nothing in the Convention gives refugees the right to choose where to claim asylum' ibid [109].
[21] *Asfaw* (n 3) at [56].
[22] UNHCR GIP 14 (2024) (n 3).

IV. 'An Iceberg of Aggrieved Asylum Seekers': Realising Article 31 Protection

> It must be appreciated that these three cases – grouped together for a single hearing because they raise different facets of a wider problem – represent but the tip of an iceberg of aggrieved asylum seekers.[23]

Adimi is a landmark case in the interpretation of Article 31, but is also important for its consideration of the incorporation of the Refugee Convention into UK domestic law. The UK is a dualist legal system where domestic law has primacy and international obligations are not automatically incorporated. Besides determining the correct interpretation of Article 31, therefore, the Court had to determine the extent to which Refugee Convention obligations were already part of UK law and what would be required to ensure that Article 31 protections were realised.

The incorporation of Refugee Convention obligations had been considered in earlier cases, including *R v SSHD ex p Sivakumaran* and the statement by Lord Keith that, 'The United Kingdom having acceded to the [Refugee] Convention and Protocol, their provisions have for all practical purposes been incorporated into United Kingdom law.'[24] Refugee Convention obligations had been partially incorporated via section 2 of the Asylum and Immigration Appeals Act 1993, providing that 'Nothing in the Immigration Rules shall lay down any practice which would be contrary to the Convention'. The applicants relied on these sources and on the doctrine of legitimate expectation ('that the UK's ratification of the Convention itself created a legitimate expectation that its provisions would be followed') to argue that the Refugee Convention had been fully incorporated in English law.[25]

Newman J was unwilling to extend the reach of either Lord Keith's dicta in *Sivakumaran* or section 2 of the 1993 Act, considering each to apply to a discrete area (provisions for determining refugee status and the Immigration Rules, respectively) neither of which extended to the imposition of penalties in criminal proceedings.[26] He was, however, willing to accept that even in the absence of direct incorporation, refugees had a legitimate expectation that they would benefit from the Convention obligations which the UK has accepted.[27] Brown LJ accepted both arguments, holding that:

> By the time of these applicants' prosecutions, at latest, it seems to me that refugees generally had become entitled to the benefit of Article 31 in accordance with the developing doctrine of legitimate expectations … s.2 of the 1993 Act is by its terms strictly concerned only with the Immigration Rules. Parliament can hardly have intended

[23] *Adimi* (n 1) per Brown LJ at [10].

[24] *R v SSHD, ex parte Sivakumaran* [1988] AC 958 at [990].

[25] *Adimi* (n 1) [54]–[56].

[26] ibid per Newman, J at [76]–[77].

[27] 'Neither the Secretary of State nor the Director of Public Prosecutions advanced argument on this particular topic [legitimate expectation]. In my judgement, if regard and effect is to be paid to Article 31(1) of the Convention it depends principally upon this principle.' Newman, J at [80].

> however, that those entitled to claim asylum under the Rules should nevertheless still be prosecuted in contravention of the Convention.[28]

Brown LJ and Newman J's willingness to accept incorporation of international treaty obligations by legitimate expectation was central to their finding that Article 31 of the 1951 Refugee Convention was applicable law before the Court. Their reasoning was consistent with emerging jurisprudence at the time, and cases cited by Newman J included the Australian case of *Minister for Immigration and Ethnic Affairs v Teoh*[29] and the Court of Appeal case of *R v SSHD ex parte Ahmed and Patel.*[30] However, a doctrine of legitimate expectation has not subsequently been generally accepted for the direct application of international treaty obligations in UK courts. Indeed, Brown LJ would later disavow this element of his opinion in *Adimi* in a subsequent judgment, the Court of Appeal hearing of *R (European Roma Rights) v Prague Airport*:

> I now recognize that the views I expressed in the Divisional Court in [*Adimi*] are to be regarded as at best superficial, and that the conclusion I reached there, with regard to the legitimate expectations of asylum seekers to the benefits of article 31, is suspect.[31]

In *Assange v USA*, the Divisional Court described the acceptance of incorporation by legitimate expectation in *Adimi* as 'tantamount to affording domestic legal force to an unincorporated treaty'.[32] Brown LJ's remarks in the Court of Appeal decision in *Prague Airport* are quoted, with the conclusion: 'We respectfully agree. Adimi is not binding on us. We decline to follow it.'[33]

In *Adimi*, however, both judges accepted that Article 31(1) of the Refugee Convention had been incorporated in UK domestic law. The Court's concern then turned to the question of realising those obligations to 'ensure that Article 31 protection is accorded its proper place in domestic law and practice'. Article 31(1) grants refugees protection from the imposition of penalties for illegal entry or presence and creates an obligation on contracting states not to impose such penalties. As with other elements of the Refugee Convention regime the process for achieving this is not prescribed, raising several questions of implementation. First, is the nature of Article 31 protection a complete immunity from all penalties and proceedings, or a protection that could be exercised by another means (such as a defence or judicial review)? Second, and closely related, which arm of state should

[28] ibid [57].

[29] *Minister for Immigration and Ethnic Affairs v Teoh* [1995] 183 CLR 273.

[30] *R v SSHD ex parte Ahmed and Patel* [1998] INLR 570.

[31] *R (on the application of European Roma Rights Centre) v Immigration Officer, Prague Airport* [2004] QB 811, at [51].

[32] *Assange v USA* [2024] EWHC 700.

[33] ibid [98]–[99]. See also Lord Bingham in *Asfaw* (n 3) at [29]–[30]: 'The British regime for handling applications for asylum has been closely assimilated to the Convention model. But it is also plain (as I think) that the Convention as a whole has never been formally incorporated or given effect in domestic law […] the appellant sought to assert that she had a legitimate expectation that the UK would honour its obligation under article 31 of the Convention. But she cannot, at the relevant time, have had any legitimate expectation of being treated otherwise than in accordance with the 1999 Act'.

have responsibility to ensure compliance with Article 31? Should responsibility rest with the Home Secretary as part of asylum determination, or with the Crown Prosecution Service (CPS) and judicial authorities as part of criminal procedure? Third, what is the timing for determining Article 31 protection and how does this align with or differ from refugee status determination?

Both judges reasoned that primary responsibility for ensuring Article 31 compliance sat more naturally with the Secretary of State than with the CPS and courts, as a matter of asylum and immigration policy rather than a general function of the justice system. While expressing a strong preference for a solution located with the Secretary of State, the judges ultimately declined to insist upon any route, instead requiring the Government 'to give careful consideration as to how they propose now to give effect to article 31'.[34] The approach that was taken was to create a legal defence to prosecution by amending the Immigration and Asylum Bill that was before Parliament at the time of the *Adimi* decision. The resultant section 31 of the Immigration and Asylum Act 1999 provided a defence to a number of specified false document and entry offences:[35]

> s.31(1) It is a defence for a refugee charged with an offence to which this section applies to show that, having come to the United Kingdom directly from a country where his life or freedom was threatened (within the meaning of the Refugee Convention), he—
>
> (a) presented himself to the authorities in the United Kingdom without delay;
> (b) showed good cause for his illegal entry or presence; and
> (c) made a claim for asylum as soon as was reasonably practicable after his arrival in the United Kingdom.

Section 31(1) of the 1999 Act echoes the language of Article 31(1) of the 1951 Refugee Convention, but its scope is qualified by section 31(2). As enacted, this precluded the defence from being used if a refugee stopped in another country before reaching the UK, unless they could show that they could not reasonably be expected to have been granted protection under the Refugee Convention in that country. This was amended by section 37(1) of the NABA 2022, which prevents use of the section 31 defence unless the refugee can show that they could not reasonably be expected to have sought protection in the country in which they stopped.[36] Related defences to false document offences are available under section 2 of the Asylum and Immigration (Treatment of Claimants) Act 2004 (permitting a 'reasonable excuse' defence to the offence of failing to produce an immigration document at an asylum interview) and under section 45 of the Modern Slavery

[34] *Adimi* (n 1) per Brown LJ at [104].

[35] The scope of offences in England, Wales and Northern Ireland include charges under part 1 of the Forgery and Counterfeiting Act 1981 (forgery and connected offences); s 24(a) of the Immigration Act 1971 (use of deception to obtain or seek to obtain leave to enter or remain or to secure avoidance, postponement or revocation of enforcement action); s 26(1)(d) Immigration Act 1971 (falsification of documents), s 4(1) and s 6(1) Identity Documents Act 2010.

[36] Nationality and Borders Act 2022, s 37(5)(a).

Act 2015 (whether an offender might be a victim of modern slavery and may have been forced, coerced or deceived into committing an offence).

These statutory defences offer 'a patchwork of protection' against some but not all immigration offences.[37] The resultant immunity is narrower than envisaged in *Adimi*, failing to provide broad immunity for all applicable offences of irregular entry and failing also to uphold the flexible interpretation of 'coming directly' that was provided in that case. It is also narrower than the terms of the 1951 Refugee Convention. The statutory defences operate against a number of specified offences, whereas the language in Article 31 prohibits 'penalties', a term that is understood to include criminal sanctions but also restrictions on access to economic or social rights (education, work), fines and 'any discriminatory treatment or procedural detriment to the refugee'.[38]

Subsequent cases interpreting section 31 of the 1999 Act have acknowledged the difference in scope with Article 31 of the 1951 Convention and affirmed the primacy of the statutory framing.[39] As Lord Bingham recognised in *Asfaw*, section 31(2) of the 1999 Act 'is not to be found in those terms in article 31(1) [and] has narrowed its scope in comparison with what was contemplated in *Adimi*'.[40] Nevertheless, this is a matter of constitutional law:

> The giving effect in domestic law to international obligations is primarily a matter for the legislature […] that determination having been made, it is the duty of the courts to give effect to it. There can be no free-standing defence, nor can there be any legitimate expectation that one will be provided, where Parliament has chosen in its own words to set out the scope of the defence that is to be available.[41]

Arguably the greatest barrier to the effectiveness of the section 31 defence has been a lack of understanding of its availability from both prosecutors and defence solicitors. A mere five years after the section 31 defence was adopted, a Joint Parliamentary Committee on Human Rights study estimated that as many as 5,000 people may have been wrongfully imprisoned in circumstances where the defence could have been available to them.[42] The Criminal Cases Review Commission, in its role of reviewing possible miscarriages of justice, referred a number of such cases that resulted in the quashing of convictions. The Court of Appeal in *R v Mateta* (considering a set of cases where defence solicitors had failed to instruct their clients on the availability of the section 31 defence) followed *Adimi* and *Asfaw* in holding that the fact that a refugee stopped in a third country in transit was not necessarily fatal to the use of the section 31 defence, and that the requirement that a claim for asylum be made as soon as reasonably practicable did not necessarily

[37] Holiday et al (n 7).

[38] UNHCR GIP 14 (2024) (n 3) para 28. See also Goodwin-Gill (n 5) at 189 and 195.

[39] *R v Navabi* [2005] EWCA Crim 2865; *R v Jaddi (Sina)* [2012] EWCA Crim 2565; *R v H* [2008] EWCA Crim 3117.

[40] *Asfaw* (n 3) [65].

[41] ibid [69].

[42] G Clayton and G Firth, *Immigration & Asylum Law* (Oxford University Press, 2021) at 418.

mean at the earliest possible moment.[43] Again, the scope of this decision has been reduced by the more restrictive interpretation of the section 31 defence that was created in the NABA 2022. In addition, the ability of the Criminal Cases Review Commission to review section 31 cases has itself been restricted by the Court of Appeal decision in *R v YY and Nori*,[44] directing that refugees convicted under offences that might have benefitted from a section 31 defence and were now out of time to appeal their conviction should go directly to the Court of Appeal.[45]

V. 'Article 31 Must Henceforth be Honoured.'

> … I would decline to grant any form of declaratory relief. Rather I would let our judgments speak for themselves, with a view to ensuring that the mistakes of the past are not repeated in future. It must be hoped that these challenges will mark a turning point in the Crown's approach to the prosecution of refugees for travelling on false passports. Article 31 must henceforth be honoured.[46]

One of the features that makes *Adimi* a landmark case is the explicit recognition that it is of broad significance, not solely concerned with the circumstances of the applicants before the Court but also a much larger class of similarly affected persons. The judgment acknowledges that the Court is in the unusual position of addressing a legal lacuna, the boundaries of which will be defined by the Court and must be resolved by the Executive. The tone of the judgment suggests a perception that it has resolved the problem, including what Stevens has described as 'the very evident admonition' to the Government quoted above ('Article 31 must henceforth be honoured').[47]

The short-term response was rapid. As described above, a statutory defence was created within the Asylum and Immigration Act 1999 and accompanied by guidance to raise awareness of its application throughout the criminal justice system and asylum system. Despite the limitations of this approach, it indicated an apparently sincere effort by the Government to give effect to the Divisional Court's decision and to Article 31 of the Refugee Convention. The mid-to-long term assessment is much less positive. Irregular migration has become a political obsession in the UK and many other countries, catalysing extreme legal reforms that criminalise unlawful entrants – including refugees – and directly implicate the application of Article 31. The 'iceberg of aggrieved asylum seekers' that Brown LJ identified in 1999 is now substantially larger and the penalties to which they are subjected are substantially more severe. The applicants in *Adimi* received prison

[43] *Mateta* (n 11); also *R v AM* (n 11) [10], [56].
[44] *R v YY and Nori* [2016] EWCA Crim 18.
[45] Holiday et al (n 7) at 9.
[46] *Adimi* (n 1) per Brown LJ at [67].
[47] D Stevens, 'The Immigration and Asylum Act 1999: A Missed Opportunity' (2001) 64 *MLR* 413 at 426.

sentences of three and six months. Now, immigration offences routinely carry statutory maximum sentences equivalent to those of the most serious violent crimes. The NABA 2022 raised the maximum sentence for 'assisting unlawful immigration or asylum seekers to the UK' to life imprisonment, while knowingly entering the UK without leave has a maximum sentence of four years.[48] Facilitation offences are explicitly excluded from immunity for prosecution, as are offences committed while attempting to leave the UK.[49]

The new provisions have led to grotesquely unfair prosecutions, including the case of Ibrahima Bah, a teenage asylum seeker sentenced to nearly 10 years in prison for crimes of facilitation of entry committed in steering a dinghy from France to the UK.[50] Bah had agreed to pilot the boat as he could not afford to pay smugglers to transport him from France to England. When he saw the boat and the number of passengers he refused on the grounds of safety but was beaten and coerced to depart; circumstances that his defence argued made him a victim of modern slavery rather than a smuggling gangmaster. The dinghy broke apart en route causing the drowning of up to nine people. When the boat fell into trouble, Bah played a heroic role in assisting the rescue of other passengers. He survived, only to face prosecution and a decade of imprisonment.[51] Less than two years after NABA 2022 entered into force, hundreds of people had already faced similar charges under the Act's new facilitation offences.[52] Criminalisation of refugees arriving via irregular routes under facilitation offences ostensibly adopted to tackle smuggling gangs is also a growing concern in European Union (EU) Member States.[53]

A. 'Stop the Boats': Penalties Beyond Prosecution

Increasingly, policies adopted to deter irregular migration are not limited to penalties in the form of criminal prosecutions but seek to deny access to state territory and asylum determination by other means, including first country of asylum, safe third country and inadmissibility regimes. These practices have spread across Global North states in the years since *Adimi* was decided. The EU introduced the concept of 'first country of asylum' through the hierarchy of processing principles under the Dublin arrangements,[54] while Australia pioneered the use of

[48] Nationality and Borders Act (NABA) 2022, ss 40–41.

[49] ibid s 37(5) amending s 31 of the Immigration and Asylum Act 1999.

[50] *Ibrahima Bah v R* [2024] EWCA Crim 1499.

[51] D Taylor, 'Ibrahima Bah was Sentenced to Nine Years for Steering a "Death Trap" Dinghy Across the Channel. Was he Really to Blame? *The Guardian* (12 March 2024); V Taylor, *No Such Thing as Justice Here: The Criminalisation of People Arriving to the UK on Small Boats* (University of Oxford Border Criminologies, 2024).

[52] Taylor, *No Such Thing As Justice Here*, ibid.

[53] E Gordon and H Larsen, 'Sea of Blood': The Intended and Unintended Effects of the Criminalisation of Humanitarian Volunteers Rescuing Migrants in Distress at Sea (2022) 46 *Disasters* 3–26; K Bianchini, *Responses to Sea Migration and the Rule of Law* (Hart Publishing, 2024).

[54] Asylum Management Regulation 2024/1351; Asylum Procedures Regulation 2024/1348.

extraterritorial asylum processing and other extreme measures to deter irregular arrival by sea.[55] Recent measures in the UK have taken both of these approaches to a new level, as a policy agenda to 'stop the boats' of migrants and refugees seeking to enter the UK has culminated in the adoption of the NABA 2022 and Illegal Migration Act 2023.[56]

As noted above, NABA 2022 substantially narrowed protection from criminal penalties for offences of irregular arrival to and exit from the UK.[57] This was an explicit attempt to 'incentivise people to claim asylum in the first safe country they reach, deter irregular travel to the UK and confine the scope of Article 31(1)'s "non-penalisation" provisions', reflecting the position of the UK Government that refugees should claim asylum in the first country entered.[58] Few refugees are able to enter the islands of the UK without first passing through the territory of another state, and the effect of section 37 of NABA 2022 is to exclude almost all refugees who enter or leave the UK from protection under Article 31. This approach was described by UNHCR as a 'fundamental misapplication of Article 31(1)'.[59]

Even more controversially, NABA 2022 created two categories of protection status, with refugees who entered the UK without leave to be defined as 'category 2' and therefore eligible for third country asylum processing.[60] A Migration and Economic Development Partnership was agreed between the UK and Rwanda that would have seen asylum seekers removed from the UK for status determination and protection in Rwanda. The former approach has been put on hold, while the latter was found to be unlawful in the Supreme Court decision in *AAA v SSHD*.[61] However, the judgment in AAA concentrated on non-refoulement obligations,

[55] G Thom, 'Australia's Obligations under Article 31(1) of the Refugees Convention: What are Penalties?' (2006) *Alternative Law Journal* 31(3): 142–64. Thom identifies a range of 'penalties' inherent to the Pacific Solution including transfer to an offshore processing centre; mandatory and indefinite detention of all those removed offshore; a 'markedly inferior' Refugee Status Determination process; leaving refuges on Nauru while resettlement options are considered and hence not leading to a durable solution for refugees; granting Temporary Protection Visas for those who ultimately may be resettled to Australia. He concludes that '[t]hese measures are quite clearly designed to sanction a refugee for their mode of arrival (arriving undocumented by boat) and also have a clear deterrent purpose. The Bill therefore has a decidedly punitive character and would violate Australia's obligations under art 31(1) of the Refugee Convention' (at 164).

[56] UK Government, *New Plan for Immigration: Legal Migration and Border Control Strategy Statement* (2021). The three objectives of the new plan were "to increase the fairness and efficacy of our asylum and immigration system [.] to deter illegal entry into the UK [...] to remove more easily from the UK those with no right to be here."

[57] NABA 2022, s 37.

[58] M Gower, *Article 31 of the Refugee Convention* (House of Commons Library Research Briefing, 2021); UK Parliament, *Nationality and Borders Act Explanatory Notes* (2022) at paras 21, 23, 161; UK Home Office, *Policy Paper: Nationality and Borders Bill: Inadmissibility for those Travelling through or with a Connection to Safe Third Countries* (2021) para 1.

[59] UNHCR, *Updated Observations on the Nationality and Borders Bill* (January 2022) para 236 citing *Adimi* (n 1) *Asfaw* (n 3) and *Mateta* (n 11).

[60] NABA 2022, s 12.

[61] *R (on the application of AAA (Syria) and others) v Secretary of State for the Home Department* [2023] UKSC 42. See also Nikolas Feith Tan, '*R (on the application of AAA and others) v Secretary of*

leaving aside the lines of reasoning that would have explored the potential relevance of Article 31 to such arrangements.[62] Similarly, in *Qurbani*, the Court of Justice of the European Union rejected the opportunity to provide an authoritative interpretation of the application of Article 31 on the basis that it had not been taken over in a piece of EU legislation; reasoning described by Costello and Ioffe as 'unpersuasive'.[63]

Despite such judicial reluctance, clarity on the lawfulness of such arrangements is becoming ever more urgent in light of a proliferation of externalisation agreements including the Italy–Albania agreement and ongoing EU–Libya co-operation. Removal of refugees to a safe third country is not necessarily unlawful where the country complies with legal standards, including access to status determination and Convention rights, and protection from refoulement.[64] Ultimately, however, such arrangements seek to exploit ambiguity in the terms of Article 31 to deter migration and deny access to asylum.[65] Costello and Ioffe argue that to read the 'coming directly' clause as legitimising these practices 'is a profound misinterpretation of article 31, undermining the object and purpose of the Convention'.[66]

Increasingly, the very right to seek asylum is under attack. The Illegal Migration Act 2023 was created 'to prevent and deter unlawful migration, and in particular migration by unsafe and illegal routes, by requiring the removal from the United Kingdom of certain persons who enter or arrive in the United Kingdom in breach of immigration control'.[67] Its provisions denied access to asylum determination in the UK for any refugees who enter without authorisation. This prima facie represents a penalty for unauthorised entry as well as denial of access to asylum, and

State for the Home Department: The Limits of Externalisation and the Failed UK-Rwanda Arrangement' in ch 14 of this volume.

[62] Lack of compliance with Art 31 *was* considered by UNHCR in its comments on the Illegal Migration Act, eg at para 21: 'UNHCR is also concerned that the relocation of asylum seekers from the UK to Rwanda is not in accordance with Article 31(1) of the 1951 Convention. [.]the term 'penalties' should be interpreted broadly, referring to any criminal or administrative measure taken by the State that has a detrimental effect on the refugee or asylum seeker.'

[63] CJEU – C481/13 *Mohammah Ferooz Qurbani* Judgment of 17 July 2014, EU:C:2014:2101; C Costello and Y Ioffe, 'Non-Penalization and Non-Criminalization' in C Costello, M Foster and J McAdam (eds), *The Oxford Handbook of International Refugee Law* (Oxford University Press, 2021) 927.

[64] UNHCR GIP 14 (2024) (n 3) para 16: 'When implemented in line with relevant safeguards and conditions pursuant to international law, the transfer of a refugee or asylum-seeker to an intermediate country in application of a safe third country concept would not be prohibited by Article 31(1).' The UK–Rwanda arrangements were considered by the UK Supreme Court in *AAA v SSHD* (n 50): 'There is, therefore, a clear consensus … the Claimants' article 31 submission merges with their submission on whether Rwanda is a safe third country. If it is a safe third country, decisions taken in exercise of the powers in paragraphs 345A – 345D of the Immigration Rules are not in breach of article 31; if, however, Rwanda is not a safe third country, removal would be both contrary to paragraph 345C of the Immigration Rules and to both article 31 and article 33 of the Refugee Convention' (ibid [125]).

[65] C Saenz Perez, 'The Securitization of Asylum: A Review of UK Asylum Laws Post-Brexit' (2023) 35 *International Journal of Refugee Law* 304–21.

[66] Costello and Ioffe (n 62) at 926.

[67] Illegal Migration Act 2023, s 1(1).

as such directly contravenes Article 31.[68] Curiously, Simon Brown LJ (then retired from the bench and known as Lord Brown of Eaton-Under-Heywood) was a vocal supporter of the Illegal Migration Bill during its passage through Parliament. In a reversal of his views in *Adimi*, and in apparent disregard of Article 31 obligations, he argued that everyone who arrived to the UK by irregular routes should be returned and 'counterpoised' with arrivals from organised resettlement schemes. He considered that this must be explicitly punitive:

> The [Illegal Migration Act] *really does now need to be harshly deterrent to the point of making it a positive disadvantage to arrive unlawfully* […] the boats will continue to come until finally it can be seen not to pay off. (emphasis added).[69]

VI. Conclusion: The Impact of *Adimi*

Adimi is an unusual example of a case that was decided effectively in a legal vacuum, where prior to its decision 'no arm of State had apparently given the least thought to the UK's obligations under Article 31'. Yet it is also an example of a case whose time had come, as a necessary adjudication of the scope and application of the UK's obligations under the 1951 Refugee Convention (and particularly Article 31) in light of increasing prosecutions of refugees for the use of false documents and other offences of irregular entry and exit. Legal recognition of this 'iceberg of aggrieved asylum seekers' was overdue.

The primary legacy of the *Adimi* judgment is in its interpretation of the scope of Article 31, including recognition that refugees have some element of choice as to where they seek asylum; that transiting through another safe country en route to the country of refuge is not fatal to the protection from penalties under Article 31; and that Article 31 protection extends to offences committed in the course of seeking to leave the UK as well as to enter it. This reasoning was subsequently affirmed in apex court decisions such as *Asfaw* and *Mateta*, yet it is the lower court decision in *Adimi* that has had the greatest traction in international scholarship and advocacy, including UNHCR guidance.

However, the long-term impact of the decision is less straightforwardly positive. The generous scope of Article 31 protection as envisaged in *Adimi* was

[68] See UNHCR GIP 14 (n 3) para 5: 'Article 31(1) is a protective clause, not an exclusion clause. It would be inconsistent with the object and purpose of the 1951 Convention, its structure, and its plain language to invoke it to justify denying a person the protection and rights that the 1951 Convention affords'. This adds to earlier UNHCR guidance on irregular movement which stated: 'Under no circumstances, however, can a State, by way of a penalty […] prevent asylum-seekers or refugees who have arrived or are present without authorisation from applying for asylum or accessing an asylum procedure, or impose procedural or other requirements or preconditions which would in practice prevent refugees from applying or accessing such a procedure. This would deny them the right to seek asylum, contrary to the purpose of Article 31(1) and the overall objective and purpose of the 1951 Convention and its 1967 Protocol.' UNHCR *Guidance on Responding to Irregular Onward Movement of Refugees and Asylum-Seekers* (UNHCR, 2019) para 40.

[69] S Brown, 'The Illegal Migration Bill is Essential – but Needs More Work' *The Telegraph* (2 June 2023).

narrowed almost immediately by the terms of its incorporation into UK law via section 31 of the Asylum and Immigration Act 1999 and reduced further by the NABA 2022. Brown LJ himself renounced part of the legal reasoning within the case (his acceptance of incorporation of Convention obligations via 'legitimate expectation') and certainly renounced its spirit in his vigorous support for the Illegal Migration Act 2023.

Thus, the greatest challenge to Article 31 protection is the development of new state practices for the deterrence of irregular migration (and of penalties other than prosecution for refugees who enter via irregular routes). When *Adimi* was heard, state efforts to restrict irregular migration were emerging with the creation of new visa regimes and new offences for both migrants and transport carriers. Over the ensuing years such measures have been accompanied by a panoply of 'crimes of migration' and other tactics of control that characterise all irregular migration as unlawful, even where committed for the purpose of seeking asylum. The 'penalties' imposed on refugees that arrive via irregular routes are wide, varied and increasingly inventive. The result is a punitive climate for asylum seekers and refugees where the centrality of Article 31 to preserving asylum is increasingly apparent, yet the acceptance of its application is increasingly restricted. The time has come for a 'second generation' landmark case on the scope of Article 31, which can confirm its scope and application vis-à-vis such policies.

7

Refugee Rights Adrift: Haitian Interdiction and the Long Term Effects of *Sale v Haitian Centers Council* [1993]

STEPHEN MEILI*

I. Introduction

This chapter examines the seminal United States (US) Supreme Court decision in *Sale v Haitian Centers Council, Inc, et al.*[1] The *Sale* opinion is significant for at least four reasons, each of which will be explored in this chapter. For one, *Sale* was the first apex court decision in the world to consider (and ultimately sanction) a national government's interdiction policy directed even at those migrants who might otherwise satisfy the criteria of a refugee as defined by the 1951 Convention relating to the Status of Refugees (Refugee Convention).[2] As such, the case paved the way for myriad border externalisation policies pursued by countries of refuge over the ensuing decades.

Second, because the dispute in *Sale* resulted from an agreement between the US and Haiti, it is an early example of the increasingly common practice whereby countries of refuge enter into bilateral pacts and other instruments with less resourced states to circumvent their obligations under international refugee law. Indeed, *Sale* can be seen as green-lighting such practices.

Third, *Sale* demonstrates that vague (but nonetheless effective) claims of national security often trump the principle of *non-refoulement*. Indeed, given that *Sale* was decided nearly a decade before the terrorist attacks against the US on 11 September 2001, it shows that the narrative linking migrants with crime and threats to public safety had gained traction well before those attacks and the ever more restrictive migration policies they spawned.

* I am deeply indebted to my Research Assistant, Alex Mysler, for his assistance with research for this chapter, as well as the idea for the title.

[1] *Sale v Haitian Centers Council, Inc, et al* 509 US 155 (1993).

[2] UN General Assembly, 1951 Convention relating to the Status of Refugees (1951 Refugee Convention), United Nations, Treaty Series, 189:137, 28 July 1951.

And finally, *Sale* is a compelling example of the way in which supposedly objective, content-neutral methods of legal analysis like statutory construction and legislative interpretation can nonetheless rob international refugee law of its humanitarian purpose. The majority opinion voices concern about the plight of Haitian refugees, but this surface compassion is undermined by the Court's ultimate decision.

Overall, the political, social, and racial context within which *Sale* arose provides a sobering glimpse at how the decisions in decades-old apex court cases have helped to shape the course of ever-more restrictive national refugee policies in the intervening years.

This chapter proceeds as follows: section II reviews the political, social, and racial context within which *Sale* arose. Section III discusses the key aspects of the lower court and US Supreme Court decisions in *Sale*. Section IV examines the impact of, and scholarly reaction to, *Sale* at the time it was decided. Section V analyses the long term legal and policy impact of *Sale* in the US and other refugee-receiving nations. The chapter concludes with thoughts about why *Sale* is a landmark case. Ultimately, it is argued that *Sale* provided a green light for limitations on the extraterritorial application of the Refugee Convention in a variety of national contexts.

II. Background Context

Though Haitian asylum seekers began arriving in the US as early as 1963, their numbers began to increase dramatically in the late 1970s during the brutal regime of Jean-Claude Duvalier.[3] As a result, on 23 September 1981, the US and Haiti agreed to an interdiction treaty.[4] That treaty allowed the US Coast Guard to intercept vessels engaged in the illegal transport of undocumented immigrants. Haiti pledged that any repatriated citizens would not be punished for their illegal departure. It was the first such interdiction treaty in US history. It is also an early example of exploitative bilateral agreements between countries of the Global North and Global South.[5]

After entering into this agreement with Haiti, then-President Ronald Reagan issued an Executive Order suspending the entry of 'illegal' immigrants from the high seas and ordered the Coast Guard to intercept vessels bringing any people in

[3] SH Legomsky, 'The USA and the Caribbean Interdiction Program' (2006) 18 *International Journal of Refugee Law* 677, 679; US Committee for Refugees and Immigrants, 'A History of Haitian Discrimination by United States Immigration Policy' (September 2021).

[4] *Sale* (n 1) 160.

[5] For a more detailed discussion of such agreements, which often occur between countries with intertwined colonial histories, see Maria O'Sullivan, '*Namah v Pato* [2016]: Constitutional Challenges in Offshore Destination States' in ch 13 of this volume and Nikolas Feith Tan, '*R (on the application of AAA and others) v Secretary of State for the Home Department* [2023]: The Limits of Externalisation and the Failed UK–Rwanda Arrangement' in ch 14 of this volume.

this manner. Reagan issued this Order after characterising 'the continuing illegal migration by sea of large numbers of undocumented aliens into the southeastern United States' as 'a serious national problem detrimental to the interests of the United States'.[6] Such a finding of a national security threat is necessary in order to justify restrictions on entry into the US.[7]

Notably, Reagan's Executive Order also stated that 'no person who is a refugee will be returned [to Haiti] without his [sic] consent'.[8] Pursuant to this Order, the now-defunct Immigration and Naturalization Service (INS) established the following framework for processing asylum claims at sea: 'If the interview suggests that a legitimate claim to refugee status exists, the person involved shall be removed from the interdicted vessel, and his or her passage to the United States shall be arranged'.[9]

For the next 10 years, the US Coast Guard interdicted approximately 25,000 Haitian migrants. The Coast Guard conducted interviews to screen for immigrants who showed credible political refugee status, and transported them to the US to apply for asylum.

Despite this apparent openness toward asylum claims, between 1981 and 1990 the US Government nevertheless returned over 21,000 Haitians to their country of origin, while only six individuals had claims strong enough to justify a full asylum hearing.

The dangers facing Haitians grew even more intense on 30 September 1991, when the first democratically elected president in Haitian history was displaced by a military coup. In the aftermath, hundreds of Haitians were killed, tortured, and/or detained without a warrant and subjected to violence because of their political beliefs. Haitian migration thus expanded dramatically after the coup. In only the six months following October 1991, the US Coast Guard intercepted over 34,000 Haitians on the high seas.[10]

[6] Presidential Proclamation No 4865, 3 CFR 50–51 (1981–1983 Comp). Section §1182(f) of the Immigration and Nationality Act (INA) gives the President unfettered authority to limit the entry of persons into the United States (US) when the President deems such entry would be detrimental to the interests of the US. As the Supreme Court observed, by its terms, §1182(f) 'exudes deference to the President in every clause. It entrusts to the President the decisions whether and when to suspend entry, whose entry to suspend, for how long, and on what conditions. It thus vests the President with ample power to impose entry restrictions in addition to those elsewhere enumerated in the INA.' *Sale* (n 1) at 187.

[7] Presidential Proclamation, ibid. President Trump invoked the same provision in justifying the so-called Muslim-ban that his Administration enacted in early 2017. *Trump v Hawaii* 509 US 155 (1993).

[8] *Sale* (n 1) at 160–61. President Trump has taken the national security justification for immigration restrictions to another level in his second term. In an Executive Order issued commensurate with his inauguration in January 2025, the White House declared 'Enforcing our Nation's immigration laws is critically important to the national security and public safety of the United States. The American people deserve a Federal Government that puts their interests first and a Government that understands its sacred obligation to prioritize the safety, security, and financial and economic well-being of Americans.' *Protecting the American People Against Invasion* (The White House, 20 January 2025).

[9] Legomsky (n 3) at 679.

[10] *Sale* (n 1) at 161–63.

Having difficulty properly processing this flow of migrants, the Coast Guard established temporary facilities in the US naval base in Guantánamo. These facilities had the capacity to hold up to 12,500 people, and by 1992 the facilities were considered overcrowded. Many Haitians attempting to flee to the US did so on unseaworthy vessels, which were overcrowded and presented a serious risk of drowning. Faced with this situation, on 23 May 1992, then-President Bush began repatriating Haitians without providing them the opportunity to establish their qualifications as refugees.[11]

III. Summary of Relevant Court Decisions

A. Lower Court Decisions

The change in policy under the first Bush Administration resulted in a series of legal challenges under both domestic and international law. Claimants generally asserted that the policy violated §243(h)(1) of the Immigration and Nationality Act (INA), which incorporates *non-refoulement* into US domestic law, and Article 33 of the 1951 Refugee Convention.[12] One of these lawsuits was *Sale v Haitian Centers Council*, which reached the US Supreme Court in 1993.

Haitian Centers Council filed the lawsuit in the US District Court for the Eastern District of New York in March 1992, and represented both interdicted Haitians and Haitians detained at Guantánamo. The suit named as defendants the Commissioner of the INS, the Attorney General, the Secretary of State, the Commandant of the Coast Guard, and the Commander of the Guantánamo Naval Base. The complaint alleged that the Coast Guard's screening procedures did not adequately protect Haitians' statutory and treaty rights to apply for refugee status and avoid repatriation to Haiti. It also noted that the coup had created a reign of terror in Haiti, and that over 1,500 Haitians had been killed or subjected to violence because of their political beliefs.

The District Court denied the plaintiffs' request for a temporary restraining order that would have nullified Bush's Executive Order. The Court declared that §

[11] ibid at 164.

[12] ibid at 166–70. §243(h)(1) of the INA states: 'The Attorney General is authorized to withhold deportation of any alien within the United States to any country in which in his opinion the alien would be subject to physical persecution and for such period of time as he deems to be necessary for such reason.' Article 33 of the Refugee Convention states:

> '1. No Contracting State shall expel or return ("refouler") a refugee in any manner whatsoever to the frontiers of territories where his life or freedom would be threatened on account of his race, religion, nationality, membership of a particular social group or political opinion.
> 2. The benefit of the present provision may not, however, be claimed by a refugee whom there are reasonable grounds for regarding as a danger to the security of the country in which he is, or who, having been convicted by a final judgment of a particularly serious crime, constitutes a danger to the community of that country.'

243(h) of the INA was unavailable to migrants in international waters, and that the Refugee Convention's non-self-executing nature made it necessary for a statutory provision to state this ability clearly.

This decision was reversed by the Second Circuit Court of Appeals. The Circuit Court held that the protection afforded by § 243(h) of the INA is not limited to people 'within the United States'.[13] This conclusion was consistent with a broad definition of the term 'alien' and the plain language of § 243(h), especially given that a 1980 amendment had removed the words 'within the United States' from the text. The Circuit Court also determined that the Refugee Convention covered all refugees, regardless of location. The Court claimed this position was supported by the purpose of Article 33 in particular and the Refugee Convention as a whole.

The Second Circuit's ruling was inconsistent with decisions by the Eleventh Circuit and District of Columbia Court of Appeal upholding the Haitian interdiction programme.[14] Attempting to resolve a split among the Courts of Appeal, the Supreme Court granted *certiorari* to consider whether Bush's policy was consistent with US and international law.

B. Supreme Court Decision

The US Supreme Court overturned the Second Circuit Court of Appeals. In short, the Supreme Court found that Acts of Congress (such as the INA) do not generally have application outside US territory, unless explicitly noted. And, in the Court's view, there was no indication of extraterritorial application in the INA. The Supreme Court also held that Article 33 of the Refugee Convention was not applicable in this case.

The Supreme Court's decision began by analysing the text of §243(h)(1) of the INA and its 1980 amendment. The section in question read:

> The Attorney General shall not deport or return any alien (other than an alien described in section 1251(a)(4)(D) of this title) to a country if the Attorney General determines that such alien's life or freedom would be threatened in such country on account of race, religion, nationality, membership in a particular social group, or political opinion.[15]

In analysing this provision, the Court considered whether Congress intended to remove any territorial limitation to its protective scope. It concluded that, without any language affirming the desire for extraterritorial applicability, there was no support for such an alternative (and territorially expansive) purpose. The Court grounded its finding in the lack of Congressional consideration of such an extraordinary change. In the Court's words, 'not a scintilla of evidence' could be found

[13] ibid at 167–68.

[14] *Haitian Refugee Center v Gracey*, 809 F 2d 794 (DC Cir, 1987); *Haitian Refugee Center v Baker*, 949 F 2d 1109 (11th Cir, 1991); *Haitian Refugee Center v Baker*, 953 F 2d 1498 (11th Cir, 1992).

[15] 8 USC §1253(h)(1) (1988 ed, Supp IV).

in the legislative history to support an extraterritorial reach for this section of the INA.[16]

The Supreme Court's discussion of the Refugee Convention was similarly narrow. As mentioned above, this discussion centered on Article 33, which states the following:

> 1. No Contracting State shall expel or return ('refouler') a refugee in any manner whatsoever to the frontiers of territories where his life or freedom would be threatened on account of his race, religion, nationality, membership of a particular social group or political opinion.
> 2. The benefit of the present provision may not, however, be claimed by a refugee whom there are reasonable grounds for regarding as a danger to the security of the country in which he is, or who, having been convicted by a final judgment of a particularly serious crime, constitutes a danger to the community of that country.[17]

In 1968, the US acceded to the 1967 Protocol, but protections from *refoulement* for migrants in exclusion proceedings did not apply in the US until 1980. Before the 1980 amendment to the INA, the Protocol was *not* considered to provide protections to migrants beyond territorial waters. The Supreme Court noted that both the Legislative and Executive branches gave their ratification of the Refugee Convention extensive consideration, and at no point in all published materials did they consider the possibility that the US would assume extraterritorial obligations.[18]

Additionally, the Court stated that if the first paragraph of Article 33 applied on the high seas, no nation could invoke the second paragraph's exception, given that migrants on the high seas are not in any nation. To the Court, this would have created an anomaly in which migrants at sea would be entitled to benefits unavailable to migrants residing in the country. The words 'expel' and 'return' in Article 33.1 would refer to refugees already within the territory of the country, and govern the parties' conduct within their national borders. The Court underlined that though actions like returning migrants to their country of origin might violate the spirit of Article 33, treaties cannot impose uncontemplated extraterritorial obligations on ratifying nations. The object and intent of the treaty were not enough for the Supreme Court to believe that it would limit the President's abilities to interdict migrants beyond the US' territorial seas.

Thus, in an 8–1 decision, the Supreme Court rejected the challenge to President Bush's interdiction policy. The lone dissent came from Justice Blackmun. His dissent focused on non-return being the rule, with the exception of national security needing to be clearly singled out in the treaty.[19] The plain meaning of Article 33, to Blackmun, is that the prohibition on expelling or returning migrants

[16] *Sale* (n 1) at 176–87.
[17] Refugee Convention (n 2) Art 33(1)–(2).
[18] *Sale* (n 1) at 177–78.
[19] ibid at 189.

to unsafe countries applies broadly, even extraterritorially. Blackmun disputed the majority's interpretation of the term 'return', noting that the ordinary meaning of that term is to 'to bring, send, or put (a person or thing) back to or in a former position', which is what the interdiction policy intended to do.

Blackmun also took issue with the majority's reading of the relationship between the two paragraphs of Article 33. He noted that while the signatories were understandably interested in allowing nations to deport criminal non-citizens who have entered their territory (paragraph 2 of Article 33), this did not suggest they intended to permit the apprehension and return of non-criminal aliens who have not entered their territory. His reasoning here was perfectly in line with the signatories' desire for a treaty with extraterritorial reach.

Blackmun's dissent is consistent with most advocates and academics in the field.[20] However, the Supreme Court's majority opinion prevails in the US to this day.

IV. The *Sale* Decision in Contemporaneous Context

The *Sale* decision was one of the US Supreme Court's first decisions on international refugee law in general, and its very first that reviewed US interdiction policy in particular. And because the US is bound by neither regional human rights courts (such as the Inter-American Court on Human Rights) nor human rights treaties that might suggest a more refugee-friendly interpretation of the Refugee Convention, *Sale* had – and continues to have – significant impact both within the US and beyond. Up to that point, all Supreme Court decisions had concerned US policy towards refugee and asylum-seekers who had arrived on US soil and were seeking protection under the US Refugee Act of 1980, which had incorporated into US domestic law both the refugee definition and the principle of *non-refoulement* from the 1951 Refugee Convention.[21] As such, the *Sale* decision is noteworthy for several contemporaneous reasons:

- It reinforced the notion that even though US domestic law on refugees and asylum seekers is based on international law (ie, the 1951 Refugee Convention) the *interpretation* of that law is mostly the province of US legal precedent. Notably, the *Sale* decision includes *no* references to international, regional, or foreign jurisprudence. The decision was based almost entirely on US statutory interpretation.
- It established a rather bright line for the reach of the 1951 Refugee Convention. That is, it has no extraterritorial effect. This principle continues to hold sway under US law.
- It is consistent with a restrictive interpretation toward the Refugee Convention (and its US domestic law analogues) that emerged in the early 1990s. Earlier decisions,

[20] See the discussion in the following section in this chapter.
[21] See *INS v Cardoza-Fonseca*, 480 US 421 (1987); *INS v Elias-Zacharias*, 502 US 478 (1992).

in the 1980s, had been more expansive. For example, in *INS v Cardoza-Fonseca*, the Supreme Court lowered the standard of proof in asylum cases in a dispute involving a Nicaraguan man who claimed persecution by the Sandinista Government.[22] However, in *INS v Elias-Zacharias* (1991), the Supreme Court, perhaps sensing the increase in asylum seekers from northern Central America (mainly countries whom the US had supported during previous guerilla wars), took a restrictive view of the requirements for those seeking protection for reasons of political opinion.[23]

The *Sale* decision was roundly criticised by legal scholars at the time. Writing in the *Harvard International Law Journal*, Harold Hongju Koh (who argued the case at the Supreme Court on behalf of Haitian Centers Council) noted that the decision represented 'a profound disappointment for both human rights advocates and international lawyers'.[24] He characterised the opinion as 'strangely apologetic' and that it condoned 'the Clinton Administration's continuation of the Bush Administration's unprecedented, brutal, and unnecessary violation of human rights'. And in a prescient observation of one of the long-term consequences of the *Sale* decision, Koh noted that it 'continued the Rehnquist Court's disturbing pattern of reflexive deference to presidential power in foreign affairs and hostility toward both aliens and international law'.[25] As any observer of US asylum policy over the subsequent three decades knows, the Supreme Court (regardless of who sits as Chief Justice) has maintained its deference toward the executive in matters of immigration.

Other critics included Andrew Pizor, who termed the decision 'myopic', noting that by refouling all Haitian immigrants without identifying those who are refugees, the US was exposing persecuted Haitians to continued torture, arbitrary detention, and other forms of persecution.[26] He asserted that the 1967 Protocol alone makes

[22] See *INS v Cardoza-Fonseca* (n 21).

[23] See *INS v Elias Zacarias* (n 21).

[24] H Hongju Koh, 'Reflections on Refoulement and Haitian Centers Council' (1994) 35 *Harvard International Law Journal* 1, 1–2.

[25] Koh also made convincing arguments under the law of US statutory interpretation: 'Justice Stevens next argued that Congress in 1980 extended the Refugee Act's protection from "any alien within the United States" to "any alien" with the intent of extending statutory protection only to aliens physically, but not legally, present within the United States. But if Congress meant to protect only aliens "physically present in the United States," why would it not use those exact words, as it did in numerous other places in the statute? The fairest reading of Congress's decision to bar the return of "any alien" is that it meant to address all aliens, wherever located.' ibid at 15.

Koh also noted inconsistencies in the Court's logical reasoning: 'To argue against the application of section 243(h) to aliens stopped on the high seas, Justice Stevens invoked the so-called "presumption against extraterritoriality." But as Justice Blackmun pointed out, that presumption was designed primarily to avoid judicial interpretations of a statute that infringe upon the rights of another sovereign. The presumption should have no force or relevance on the high seas, where no possibility exists for conflicts with other jurisdictions. Nor does it make sense to presume that Congress legislated with exclusively territorial intent when enacting a law governing a distinctively international subject matter-the trans-border movement of refugees-to enforce an international human rights obligation embodied in a multilateral convention. More bizarre, the Court chose to invoke the presumption against extraterritoriality in a case where the executive branch itself cited the statute as the basis for its own extraterritorial authority to act. If, as the Court concluded, the presumption operated to deny the Haitians extraterritorial statutory protection, a fortiori it should also operate to deny the President extraterritorial authority to stop the Haitians in the first place.' ibid at 15–16.

[26] AG Pizor, 'Sale v Haitian Centers Council: The Return of Haitian Refugees Comment' (1994) 17 *Fordham International Law Journal* 1062, 1114.

it possible to extend Article 33 of the Refugee Convention to the high seas. He also noted that the Supreme Court ignored Article 5(1)(a) of the Convention Against Torture, which specifically requires State Parties to establish jurisdiction over acts committed in any territory under its jurisdiction or on board any vessel registered in that country.[27] Pizor also referred to the 'broader ramifications' that *Sale* might have, given that state practice is important in the development of customary international law. Pizor's concerns here were prophetic, as the kind of state practice which constitutes customary international law includes not only relations between states but also how individual states exercise their official functions.[28] Given that, as noted below, *Sale* has been a model for other states' interdiction practices, its continued influence could make it the basis for customary international law on the territorial scope of Article 33.

Sale was also criticised from a legislative history perspective. For example, Maria Luisa Sepulveda noted that before its amendment in 1980, section 243(h)(1) of the INA stated that the Attorney General could withhold the deportation of an alien only if she is 'within the United States'.[29] However, Congress deleted this explicit territorial restriction in the Refugee Act of 1980, which amended the INA to include, among other things, the Refugee Convention's refugee definition and the obligation of *non-refoulement*.[30] Thus, when the Supreme Court issued its decision in *Sale* a little over a decade later, it ignored Congress' clear intent to no longer limit the territorial scope of the Refugee Convention.

Numerous intergovernmental agencies also criticised the *Sale* decision.[31] Indeed, even before the Supreme Court reached its decision, the Organization of American States and its Inter-American Commission on Human Rights (IACHR) determined that the US interdiction programme violated international law.[32] IACHR's conclusion was based, among other things, on the US' inability to prove that the Haitian asylum claimants were provided with fair hearings when they were intercepted in the high seas.[33]

[27] ibid at 1110. See also Convention Against Torture and Other Cruel, Inhuman or Degrading Treatment or Punishment (CAT), 1465 UNTS 85, [1989] ATS 21, UN Doc A/RES/39/46, Art 5(1)(a).

[28] M Wood and O Sender, *Identification of Customary International Law* (Oxford University Press, 2024) 10–11.

[29] ML Sepulveda, 'Barring Extraterritorial Protection for Haitian Refugees Interdicted on the High Seas: Sale v. Haitian Centers' (1994) 44 *Catholic University Law Review* 321, 325–26.

[30] ibid. For other contemporaneous scholarly reactions to the *Sale* decision, see GS Goodwin-Gill, 'The Haitian Refoulement Case: A Comment' (1994) 6 *International Journal of Refugee Law* 103, 103–109, DE Wasitis, 'Sale v. Haitian Centers Council: Closing the Golden Door, Inc' (1993) 27 *Akron Law Review* 237 and RJ Williams, 'Sale v. Haitian Centers Council and its Aftermath: A Problematic Gap in International Immigration Law' (1995) 9 *Temple International and Comparative Law Journal*. 55.

[31] A Fischer-Lescano et al, 'Border Control at Sea: Requirements under International Human Rights and Refugee Law' (2009) 21 *International Journal of Refugee Law* 256, 267.

[32] Organization of American States Press Release, 'OAS Human Rights Committee Calls Clinton Haitian Interdiction Policy a Violation of International Law' (19 March 1993) describing Precautionary Measures taken by the Inter-American Commission.

[33] ibid. Both the Human Rights Committee and the Committee against Torture have stated that the International Covenant on Civil and Political Rights (ICCPR) and the Convention against Torture and Other Cruel, Inhuman or Degrading Treatment or Punishment (CAT), respectively, protect people under the power or control of a state, regardless of territoriality. A Dastyari and D Ghezelbash, 'Asylum

Moreover, the United Nations High Commissioner for Refugees (UNHCR) criticised the Supreme Court for its *Sale* decision and the subsequent policies which were conceived in its wake:

> UNHCR considers the Court's decision a setback to modern international refugee law which has been developing for more than forty years, since the end of World War II. It renders the work of the Office of the High Commissioner in its global refugee protection role more difficult and sets a very unfortunate example.[34]

This critique from UNHCR is noteworthy for a number of reasons. First, given that the US is a major donor to UNHCR, the agency was taking a risk in such a full-throated condemnation of the *Sale* decision and the state policy which it endorsed. Second, it suggests, not without justification, that the US Supreme Court had been a supporter of refugee rights in the past. And third, UNHCR knew that *Sale* was setting a dangerous precedent, one that would be all too easy for other states to follow.

UNHCR discussed its position further in a 2000 note:

> The principle of non-refoulement does not imply any geographical limitation. In UNHCR's understanding, the resulting obligations extend to all government agents acting in an official capacity, within or outside national territory. Given the practice of States to intercept persons at great distance from their own territory, the international refugee protection regime would be rendered ineffective if States' agents abroad were free to act at variance with obligations under international refugee law and human rights law.[35]

UNHCR had filed an amicus brief on behalf of Haitian Centers Council.[36] However, it is not surprising that the Supreme Court ignored it, given the lack of deference that US courts have generally (but not always) shown to UNHCR guidance.[37]

The New York Times also weighed in on the decision, wondering whether:

> this ruling by one of the most influential courts in the world [could] set a tempting precedent, particularly for developing nations? If the United States, with the imprimatur of its highest court, appears to put the protection of its borders above its responsibilities under international law, will others be enticed to follow suit?[38]

at Sea: The Legality of Shipboard Refugee Status Determination Procedures' (2020) 32 *International Journal of Refugee Law* 1 at 7.

[34] 'UN High Commissioner for Refugees Responds to US Supreme Court Decision in *Sale v. Haitian Centres Council*' 32 ILM 1215 (1993). See also Legomsky (n 3) at 692.

[35] United Nations High Commissioner for Refugees (UNHCR), EXCOM., 'Interception of Asylum-Seekers and Refugees: The International Framework and Recommendations for a Comprehensive Approach', Doc EC/50/SC/CRP.17 (9 June 2000) para 23.

[36] See *Sale* (n 1) at 158.

[37] See 'American Courts and the UN High Commissioner for Refugees: A Need for Harmony in the Face of a Refugee Crisis' (2018) 131 *Harvard Law Review* 1399.

[38] D Sontag, 'Reneging on Refuge: The Haitian Precedent' *The New York Times* (27 June 1993) 58, available at www.nytimes.com/1993/06/27/weekinreview/reneging-on-refuge-the-haitian-precedent.html.

While *The New York Times* was for some reason mostly concerned about the impact of *Sale* on 'developing nations', it was nevertheless spot on regarding *Sale*'s 'tempting precedent', given its impact on more resourced states' interdiction policies ever since. Indeed, *Sale* cleared the way for several countries to extend their borders to the high seas in order to prevent refugees from reaching the shore, where they would have stronger protection claims. As a result, many refugee-receiving states have become far more aggressive in intercepting refugees before they have a chance to reach shore and claim protection under the 1951 Refugee Convention. *Sale* emboldened them to do so.

The *Sale* decision also runs counter to other human rights treaties that protect refugees on the high seas. For example, Article 3 of the Convention against Torture and Other Cruel, Inhuman or Degrading Treatment or Punishment (CAT) (which the US ratified in 1994, after the *Sale* decision was announced) disallows states from returning people to places where they might be tortured. CAT contains no geographical limitations. The same is true for the International Covenant on Civil and Political Rights (ICCPR), Articles 6 and 7. Additionally, European states are bound by Article 3 of the European Convention on Human Rights, which reflects the protections provided by CAT. Additionally, interdiction policies are in conflict with International Maritime Organization guidelines, which note that states have an obligation to deliver people rescued at sea 'to a place of safety', which does not include places where their lives are threatened.[39]

Finally, the IACHR rejected the US Government's arguments in support of its interdiction programme in the matter of *Haitian Centre for Human Rights v United States*.[40] In that case, several Haitians interdicted at sea in the early 1990s challenged the Haitian Migrant Interdiction programme on numerous grounds, including the right to seek asylum under Article XXVII of the American Declaration of the Rights and Duties of Man, which guarantees the right to seek asylum. In 1997, several years after the US Supreme Court decision in *Sale*, the Commission ruled that by interdicting and repatriating Haitian refugees to Haiti without providing them a hearing to ascertain whether they qualified as refugees under the Refugee Convention, the US had violated Article XXVII.[41]

In sum, the US Supreme Court's decision in *Sale* was roundly criticised by scholars, advocates, and intergovernmental organisations around the world. But that chorus of rebuke did nothing to blunt its impact. Indeed, as we shall see in the next section of this chapter, *Sale* set the stage for an increasingly narrow interpretation of state obligations toward refugees under both domestic and international that has only intensified with the passage of time.

[39] ibid at 8.

[40] *The Haitian Centre for Human Rights et al v United States*, Case 10.675, Report No 51/96, Inter-Am.C.H.R.,OEA/Ser.L/V/II.95 Doc 7 rev at 550 (1997). March 13, 1997.

[41] ibid at [188]. While the petitioner had alleged a violation of Arts 3 (non-discrimination), 16(1) (access to courts), and 33 (*non-refoulment*) of the Refugee Convention, the Commission did not issue a decision on those claims.

V. *Sale*'s Long Term Influence

The decision in *Sale* justified the continuation of the US interdiction policy. Since 1995, Executive Order 12807 (also known as the Kennebunkport Order, which denotes the location where President Bush issued it) governs the US's basic pre-screening of migrants at sea.[42] Under this framework, the Secretary of Homeland Security has unreviewable discretion to determine which people are not refugees, and thus can be returned.

Another series of violent crises broke out in Haiti in 2004, causing another increase in migrants seeking entry into the US via boat. At the time, President George W Bush instructed the Coast Guard to turn back boats attempting to reach shore, referring to their passengers as 'refugees'.[43] As Stephen Legomsky points out, this was the first time a President referred to the Haitian migrants by boat as refugees, although he nevertheless asserted that they could be returned.[44] Between October 2022 and January 2023, approximately 1,500 Haitians were interdicted at sea. Even as recently as August 2024, 182 Haitians were interdicted near the Turks and Caicos Islands, and promptly returned to the island.[45]

This policy and its relationship to Haitians is notable for its contrast with the policy the US has utilised for Cuban refugees.[46] Cuban refugees who arrive on US territory are generally allowed to remain there through the Cuban Adjustment Act of 1966. However, Cubans interdicted at sea, though they were frequently sent to Guatánamo, were often advised of their right to apply for asylum. This was not the case for interdicted Haitian refugees. The political – and racial – implications of this contrast in policy according to national origin is obvious. Indeed, that interdiction on a grand scale was first initiated against Haitians is another chapter in the long history of the US's racially discriminatory immigration policy.

Since *Sale*, the US Government has attempted to frame the question of interdiction in various ways. Primarily, it has presented the interception of vessels as a partially humanitarian endeavour.[47] The rationale behind this has been that interdiction restricts the actions of human traffickers and deters other migrants from making the voyage to the US through unsafe vessels. Through declarations like the following, the Coast Guard presents itself more as rescuers than regulators of migratory flow:

> 'Hurricane season is an especially dangerous time for unlawful maritime migration,' said Lt. Nicholas Fujimoto, a Coast Guard District Seven enforcement officer. 'The

[42] Dastyari and Ghezelbash (n 33) 17.
[43] Legomsky (n 3) at 682.
[44] ibid.
[45] Coast Guard Seventh District, 'Coast Guard Repatriates 182 Migrants to Haiti' *United States Coast Guard News* (21 August 2024), available at www.news.uscg.mil/Press-Releases/Article/3878831/coast-guard-repatriates-182-migrants-to-haiti/.
[46] Legomsky (n 3) at 684.
[47] ibid at 685.

> Coast Guard is proactively monitoring the maritime approaches to the U.S. and international waters of the Caribbean to prevent the tragic loss of life at sea. Makeshift vessels are unseaworthy and incapable of handling the rougher seas caused by unpredictable weather and tropical storms'.[48]

This comment was presented on the *United States Coast Guard News*, just prior to a press release reminder of the consequences of illegal entrance into the US by sea, including deportation and criminal prosecution upon unlawful re-entry.

The Supreme Court's decision in *Sale* has also influenced judicial opinions and policy beyond the US. Among the myriad 'non-entrée' policies adopted by refugee-receiving nations in recent years, all of which are intended to discourage and prevent asylum seekers from accessing asylum status determinations, interdictions at sea remain extremely popular.[49] The US's continued dependence on the limitation of its *non-refoulement* obligations has clearly made a mark, not only on its own current operations, but also on migratory operations in Australia and the European Union.

Sale's international influence is perhaps best illustrated by Australia's interdiction programme. As Ghezelbash notes, Australia has closely modelled that programme on the US policy approved in *Sale*.[50] That programme started with Operations Sovereign Borders, implemented in 2013, which sought to deter asylum seekers from reaching Australia by sea.[51] For the most part, Australia had historically returned vessels with migrants from Vietnam, Sri Lanka, and Indonesia.[52] Returns to the latter have been especially controversial given that Indonesia is not a signatory of the 1951 Refugee Convention. Furthermore, Australia has not been transparent regarding the details of their screening procedures, especially the right to interpreters or appeal on review.

Since the launch of Operation Sovereign Borders, the success rate of screenings dropped to below one per cent.[53] As in the US, the Australian Department of Home Affairs portrays the policy as a series of rescue missions that benefit the migrant more than the state, as can be observed in their video for the Sovereign Borders webpage.[54]

Sale's influence over judicial support for Australia's interdiction programme is obvious from the decision reached by the Federal Court of Australia in the 2001 case of *Ruddock v Vadarlis*.[55] Like the US Supreme Court, the majority in *Ruddock* gave

[48] Coast Guard Seventh District (n 45).

[49] Legomsky (n 3) at 677–78.

[50] D Ghezelbash, 'Hyper-Legalism and Obfuscation: How States Evade Their International Obligations Towards Refugees' (2020) *The American Journal of Comparative Law* 68(3), 479–516.

[51] Dastyari and Ghezelbash (n 33) at 19; The Nationals for Regional Australia, *The Coalition's Operation Sovereign Borders Policy* (July 2013), available at https://web.archive.org/web/20160303211828/http://lpaweb-static.s3.amazonaws.com/Policies/OperationSovereignBorders_Policy.pdf.

[52] Dastyari and Ghezelbash, ibid at 20.

[53] ibid at 21.

[54] Australian Government, Department of Home Affairs, *Operation Sovereign Borders*, available at https://osb.homeaffairs.gov.au/.

[55] *Ruddock and others v Vadarlis and others* (2001) 115 FCR 229 (Australia).

the executive broad power to intercept and redirect vessels carrying migrants.[56] In both cases, the Court held that executive power was not subject to constraints provided by domestic statutory law, which afforded protections to asylum seekers. They also both indicated that there were no international law norms contrary to the executive power's actions during interdiction.

The influence of *Sale* on Australian jurisprudence was seen even more explicitly in the more recent decision in *CPCF v Minister for Immigration and Border Protection*.[57] In that case, a Sri Lankan national of Tamil ethnicity who feared persecution upon return to that country was on an Indian vessel intercepted by an Australian border protection ship in the Indian Ocean about 16 nautical miles from the Australian territory of Christmas Island. Without providing an opportunity for the plaintiff (and others on the vessel who were similarly situated) to claim asylum, the Australians detained the plaintiff and took him to India. The plaintiffs alleged, among other things, that Australia's actions violated its *non-refoulement* obligations under the 1951 Refugee Convention. In siding with the Australian Government, the Australian High Court (the highest court in the country) cited *Sale*, as well as jurisprudence from Australia and the United Kingdom (UK), for the proposition that the Refugee Convention 'only applied to receiving States in respect of refugees within their territories'.[58]

In Europe, the positions of several states mirrors that espoused by the US and Australia. For example, in 2018, the governments of Austria and Italy proposed the interception of migrant vessels that entered European territorial waters with the subsequent transportation onto state vessels and screening for asylum occurring thereafter.[59] If migrants were found not to be in need of protection, they would be denied entry and promptly returned to their countries of origin.

This interdiction effort within Europe has been part of an overall policy whereby many countries in the region have reneged on their obligations towards migrants. For example, the German Federal Ministry of the Interior has argued that *non-refoulement* obligations are not applicable in the high seas because they are extraterritorial.[60] Moreover, the influence of *Sale* and its progeny can be seen in the policy of the UK, which has drawn on the decision to justify *non-entrée* measures outside the context of maritime interdiction.[61]

However, *Sale's* impact has been blunted somewhat by both the European Court of Human Rights (ECtHR) and the UK Supreme Court. For example, in the case of *Hirsi Jamaa and Others v Italy*, the ECtHR held that Italy violated

[56] ibid; D Ghezelbash, *Refuge Lost. Asylum Law in an Interdependent World* (Cambridge University Press, 2018) at 88–95.

[57] *CPCF v Minister for Immigration and Border Protection* [2015] HCA 1, 28 January 2015, S169/2014.

[58] ibid at 5, fn 10.

[59] Dastyari and Ghezelbash (n 33) at 2.

[60] Fischer-Lescano et al (n 31) at 265.

[61] *Regina v Immigration Officer at Prague Airport and Anor (Respondents) ex parte European Roma Rights Centre & Ors (Appellants)* [2004] UKHL 55 (9 December 2004) at 68, per Lord Hope, see also, Lord Bingham at 17.

European Convention on Human Rights (ECHR) Article 3 (prohibition against torture, inhuman and degrading treatment), Article 4, Protocol 4 (prohibition on collective expulsion) and Article 13 (right to an effective remedy) when an Italian Coastguard vessel intercepted a boat on the high seas and returned the passengers (who were from Eritrea and Somalia) to Libya (from whence the boat had departed) without investigating whether they might have valid asylum claims.[62] Additionally, the European Commission on Human Rights has determined that the ECHR may apply extraterritorially.[63] The language of Article 1 ('Within their jurisdiction') is not considered an express limitation on the territoriality of obligations.[64]

In a similar vein, the UNHCR Executive Committee has regularly emphasised that state mechanisms which do not accurately identify refugees and other migrants who require international protection countervail *non-refoulement* obligations.[65] The ECHR consolidates such obligations in Article 13, which affirms the right to an effective remedy, which has been interpreted to include independent review and legal assistance.[66] UNHCR has also emphasised that assessed individuals have access to proper translation and privacy to ensure the accuracy and legitimacy of such status determinations.[67]

However, regardless of jurisprudence and directives condemning such practices, individual states within Europe, as elsewhere around the world, have proceeded apace with their plans to intercept migrants and redirect them to other nations on the basis of the 'Safe Third Country' doctrine.[68] Indeed, the increased disregard for established norms and rulings within the European framework is, in part, the result of *Sale* and its progeny, as that line of cases has allowed for the argument that a new customary approach to interdiction and *non-refoulement* has formed. The influence of *Sale* in particular can be observed in some policy

[62] *Hirsi Jamaa and Others v Italy* ECLI:CE:ECHR:2012:0223JUD002776509 [169]–[182]. See Elspeth Guild, '*Hirsi Jamaa and Others v Italy* (2012) and the Prohibition on Pushbacks' in ch 8 of this volume for a detailed discussion of the facts, holding, and impact of *Hirsi Jamaa*. *Bankovic and others v Belgium and 16 other states* App no 52207/99 (European Court of Human Rights (ECtHR), 12 December 2001). In that case, the European Court determined that maritime flag sovereignty, effective control over a person, competence and control and functional territorial reference points counted as ways to establish jurisdiction. ibid at 80.

[63] Fischer-Lescano et al (n 31) at 273; European Convention on Human Rights (ECHR) Art 1, Nov 4, 1950, CETS No 213.

[64] However there are clear limits to this approach. In a case decided in June 2025, the ECtHR stressed that acts performed by Contracting States outside their territory, or producing effects outside their territory, could constitute an exercise of jurisdiction within the meaning of Art 1 only in exceptional cases. *SS and Others v Italy (dec.)* – 21660/18, Decision 20.5.2025.

[65] ibid at 11.

[66] ECHR, Art 13.

[67] Dastyari and Ghezelbash (n 33) at 14.

[68] K Appleby, 'How Europe is Slowly Closing Its Doors to Asylum-Seekers' (*Center for Migration Studies*, 30 April 2024), available at https://cmsny.org/how-europe-closing-doors-to-asylum-seekers/; L Semini, 'Italian Ship Transfers 16 Intercepted Migrants to Albania in a First Under their New Migration Plan' (*Associated Press*, 16 October 2024). See also Tan (n 5).

briefs for the European Parliament.[69] Even though the European Parliament states that it is summarising European law, it makes specific reference to *Sale*, and its importance.[70]

VI. Conclusion – Why is *Sale* a Landmark Case?

As this chapter has suggested, *Sale* is a landmark case because of its influence, both nationally and internationally, on the territorial reach of the Refugee Convention. It has inspired both judges and policy-makers in many refugee-receiving nations to sanction the return of refugees on the high seas without any inquiry as to their eligibility for asylum. By thus limiting the applicability of *non-refoulement*, *Sale* has created juridical cover for a range of new mechanisms designed to allow states to deny access to the asylum determination process by those facing harm in their home countries.

Sale has had at least three other long-term influences. First, it has helped foster an appetite among refugee-receiving states for a range of externalisation measures most likely not contemplated in the early 1990s. As pressure on countries of refuge has increased over the ensuing decades, many countries have adopted increasingly creative (and some would say draconian) methods for preventing those fleeing harm from accessing the asylum determination process. For example, bilateral agreements allowing one country to divert asylum seekers to another (such as the UK's now-scrapped Rwanda policy) were based, in part, on the idea that persons intercepted outside the country of refuge were not entitled to seek asylum there.[71] The US's Remain in Mexico programme, under which asylum seekers are required to stay in Mexico while their asylum claims are processed in the US, is another example.

A second influence is the way that *Sale* set a precedent for restrictive domestic court interpretation of international refugee law. The Refugee Convention (and in particular the definition of a refugee and the principle of *non-refoulement*) is one of the few examples where most states have incorporated an international human rights treaty into domestic law (usually through a statute, like the INA, or the national Constitution, or both).[72] Such incorporation gives domestic courts tremendous influence over the way that international law (including international refugee law) is interpreted. In the case of extraterritorial application of the 1951

[69] A Radjenovic, 'Search and Rescue in the Mediterranean' (European Parliamentary Research Service, January 2021).

[70] ibid at 3. Indeed, it does not mention *Ruddock* (n 55), a more recent case with a similar conclusion to *Sale* (n 1).

[71] See also Tan (n 5) for a more detailed discussion of the failed UK–Rwanda Arrangement and the UK Supreme Court decision in *AAA (Syria) and others) v SSHD* [2023] UKSC 42.

[72] See S Meili, *The Constitutionalization of Human Rights Law: Implications for Refugees* (Oxford University Press, 2022).

Refugee Convention, that interpretation has been narrow in several domestic courts, thanks in large part to *Sale* and the decisions it inspired around the world.

Finally, as noted in the Introduction to the chapter, *Sale* was an early indication that apex courts in at least some refugee-receiving states will defer to alleged concerns over national security when determining the rights of asylum seekers in a variety of contexts. Thus, we have seen some national courts uphold barriers to refugee rights when states assert that such barriers are necessitated by national security.[73] *Sale* is another example. The US interdiction policy only arose in response to exaggerated fears of the US being inundated by migrants from Haiti. But once those fears were the [stated] basis for the US policy, it was unlikely that a US domestic court would overturn it.[74]

Will other states continue to look to *Sale* for inspiration? Very likely. For one thing, with the increasingly conservative turn at the US Supreme Court, it is unlikely that *Sale* will ever be overruled. Indeed, given the second Trump Administration's more aggressive pursuit of policies limiting the rights of asylum seekers, that Court may go beyond *Sale* in restricting the extra-territorial reach of the Refugee Convention. Second, with the migration of climate and armed conflict refugees likely to continue their exponential increase, states of refuge will likely concoct ever more restrictive ways to prevent their entry. And third, national security will continue to be invoked as the public policy justification for limiting the scope of the Refugee Convention. Here, too, *Sale* provides cover.

[73] ibid.
[74] See counter examples of this phenomenon in chs 14 and 15 of this volume.

8

Hirsi Jamaa and Others v Italy [2012] and the Prohibition on Pushbacks

ELSPETH GUILD

I. Introduction

The state practice of pushing back aliens to prevent their arrival in a state of destination,[1] has been a challenge for international and European human rights law particularly in the last decades of the twentieth and twenty-first centuries in Europe. The central legal issue regarding pushbacks is the lack of formal procedures within which each individual subject to the action has an opportunity to explain his or her grounds for seeking entry into the state based on individual circumstances. It is only by means of such procedures that individuals can make known to state officials any fears of persecution, torture or other relevant harm which raise the state's absolute duty not to return a person to a place where such a risk exists. The European Court of Human Rights (ECtHR) addressed this issue in its landmark decision *Hirsi Jamaa*[2] published in 2012 where it found pushbacks at sea without any procedure to determine status a violation of the prohibition on *refoulement* and collective expulsion.

The pushback issue has been on the international human rights agenda particularly arising as regards the United States (US) 1980 policy of pushing back to Haiti little boats carrying Haitians towards the US which resulted in the *Sale* judgment of the US Supreme Court discussed elsewhere in this collection.[3] It has also been a core component of Australian border policy developed in the 1980s

[1] Defined by the Office of the United Nations High Commissioner for Human Rights (OHCHR) Special Rapporteur in 2021 as 'an overarching term for all measures, actions or policies that effectively result in the removal of migrants, individually or in groups, without an individualized assessment in line with human rights obligations and due process guarantee'. See www.ohchr.org/en/stories/2021/07/pushbacks-migrants-land-and-sea-must-end-says-un-expert.

[2] *Hirsi Jamaa and Others v Italy* ECLI:CE:ECHR:2012:0223JUD002776509 [169]–[182].

[3] See Stephen Meili, 'Refugee Rights Adrift: Haitian Interdiction and the Long Term Effects of *Sale v Haitian Centers Council* [1993]' in ch 7 in this volume. *Sale v Haitian Centers Council, Inc, et al* 509 US 155 (1993).

and 1990s which has been subject to much academic criticism.[4] The issue of the correct application of maritime law has also been an important issue as regards pushbacks which is discussed elsewhere in this volume.[5]

There are different types of pushbacks, the main ones being those which take place at sea and those at land borders. The most well-known from the US and Australian examples are those which take place at sea. From the European perspective, sea pushback policies began to be developed in the Mediterranean, mainly in Italy, Greece and Spain (where the policies included pushbacks in the Atlantic) in the early 1990s. The purpose of these policies was to seek to avoid responsibility for people seeking to arrive on their shores in small boats (generally to seek asylum though this is rarely discussed in official reports). They became commonplace from the 1990s and these countries have been linked to the development of the EU common visa and border policy.[6] The introduction of mandatory visa policies in the northern Mediterranean countries applicable to nationals of their southern Mediterranean counterparts played a role in the rise of irregular crossings. People who previously were able to travel easily from the south to the north were subject to time consuming, expensive and bureaucratic visas procedures before departure. Pushbacks was one of the answers from the northern Mediterranean countries. As small boat arrivals increased in the 2000s from north Africa to Europe, a political discourse of crisis became ever more vocal in two countries in particular: Greece and Italy.[7] This debate has also been present in Spain but tempered by other political considerations.[8] The language of crisis in the political debate led to the adoption of increasingly coercive measures to prevent arrivals, including pushbacks.[9]

The attraction for policy-makers of sea pushbacks is that they can be carried out in international waters, before the little boats reach the sovereign sea border of the state where state responsibilities traditionally are accepted to commence. The argument is that little boats are pushed back to the country from which they are determined (by state officials carrying out the pushback) to have departed. Thus, such actions allegedly are not inconsistent with international law of the sea as they do not come within the obligations of safe passage in international law of the sea nor do they offend another rule of international law of the sea regarding the duty

[4] S Kneebone, 'Controlling Migration by Sea: The Australian Case' in B Ryan and V Mitsilegas (eds), *Extraterritorial Immigration Control* (Brill Nijhoff, 2010).

[5] See Nikolas Feith Tan, '*R (on the application of AAA and others) v Secretary of State for the Home Department* [2023]: The Limits of Externalisation and the Failed UK-Rwanda Arrangement' in ch 14 of this volume.

[6] T Gammeltoft-Hansen, 'The Perfect Storm: Sovereignty Games and the Law and Politics of Boat Migration' in V Moreno-Lax and and E Papastavridis (eds), *Boat Refugees and Migrants at Sea: A Comprehensive Approach* (Brill Nijhoff, 2017) 60–78; R Barnes, 'The International Law of the Sea and Migration Control' in Ryan and Mitsilegas (n 4) 100–46.

[7] A Triandafyllidou, 'Mediterranean Migrations: Problems and Prospects for Greece and Italy in the Twenty-First Century: PROFILES' (2007) 12(1) *Mediterranean Politics* 77–84.

[8] J Carling, 'Migration Control and Migrant Fatalities at the Spanish-African Borders' (2007) 41(2) *International Migration Review* 316–43.

[9] See also Tan (n 5).

to provide search and rescue within internationally determined state responsibility zones.[10] These arguments have been criticised by academic scholars.[11] It could be said that the existence of international waters which belong to no state are instrumentalised by states carrying out pushbacks to avoid what they consider to be unwanted aliens arriving within their sovereign waters and thus responsibilities.

Another type of pushback takes place at land borders where the rules are somewhat different. Normally there is no territory between states over which no state is exercising state sovereignty.[12] This means that the rules according to which state authorities make decisions on entry or refusal thereof in respect of aliens apply to all aliens crossing the borders. In the European context, however, many states have separate rules regarding those who present themselves at a designated border crossing point and those who cross otherwise.[13] Those who are classified under national law as respecting the rules on border crossing by presenting themselves at a designated place are entitled to present their application to enter the state, have it determined under national or European Union (EU) rules and in the EU context have a non-suspensive right of appeal in the event of a refusal. Those who are found having entered clandestinely over land borders may be subject to less thorough regimes of determination.[14] These can include summary refusals of entry followed by immediate despatch across the border which they have just crossed. The procedural obligations to provide reasons for refusal of entry in writing with information about how to appeal against the decision and where to find assistance to do so are not applied. The effectiveness, of course, is subject to the law and practice of the border control authorities on the other side of the border that may decide that the individual is not admissible to their state and refuse to take charge of them.[15]

Irrespective of how individuals are seeking to cross a border, land or sea, at a border crossing point or not, States Parties to the 1951 Convention relating to the Status of Refugees (1951 Refugee Convention)[16] and other international human rights instruments are prohibited from dispatching them summarily to

[10] E Lauterpacht, 'Freedom of Transit in International Law' (1958) 44 *Transactions of the Grotius Society* 313–56; E Akis Papastavridis, 'Search and Rescue at Sea: Shared Responsibilities in the Mediterranean Sea' in F Ippolito, G Borzoni and F Casolari (eds), *Bilateral Relations in the Mediterranean* (Edward Elgar Publishing, 2020) 229–49.

[11] N Markard, 'The Right to Leave by Sea: Legal Limits on EU Migration Control by Third Countries' (2016) 27(3) *European Journal of International Law* 591–616.

[12] There are exceptions to this rule, see for instance C Grundy-Warr and E Wong Siew Yin, 'Geographies of Displacement: The Karenni and the Shan across the Myanmar-Thailand Border' (2002) 23(1) *Singapore Journal of Tropical Geography* 93–122.

[13] F Lutz, 'The Territorial Scope of Schengen' in F Lutz, *Practical Guide to Schengen Law* (Springer Nature, 2024) 65–85.

[14] G Cornelisse, 'What's Wrong with Schengen? Border Disputes and the Nature of Integration in the Area without Internal Borders' (2014) 51(3) *CMLR*.

[15] F Düvell, 'Paths into Irregularity: The Legal and political construction of irregular migration.' 2011 13(3) *European Journal of Migration and Law* 275–95.

[16] UN General Assembly, 1951 Convention relating to the Status of Refugees, United Nations, Treaty Series, 189:137, 28 July 1951.

some other country (or pushing them back at sea to another country's national waters) if they have indicated that they are seeking asylum. Before any expulsion, officials must carry out procedures to determine whether they will be safe in that other country. The obligation in the 1951 Refugee Convention and increasingly accepted as part of customary international law prohibits *refoulement*, which is the sending of a person to a country where there is a real risk of persecution. The 1951 Refugee Convention is one of many sources of the prohibition on *refoulement* references to which have proliferated in human rights conventions negotiated in the twentieth and twenty-first centuries. International human rights law has extended the prohibition to include return to torture, inhuman or degrading treatment or other irreparable harm.[17] The European Convention on Human Rights (ECHR) as interpreted by the ECtHR also prohibits the sending of individuals to countries where there is a real risk they would be subject to torture, inhuman or degrading treatment or punishment.[18] It also prohibits collective expulsion, a state obligation under the ECHR (Article 4 Protocol 4). This prohibition is absent in an express form in international human rights law though academic literature suggests that it may be a corollary of procedural rights of aliens under Article 13 of the International Covenant on Civil and Political Rights (ICCPR).[19] The corollary rights of fair procedures, remedies and non-discrimination are engaged as soon as a principal right is in question. The protection against collective expulsion is first and foremost a procedural right. In order for an expulsion decision not to be collective, it must be taken on the basis of a full and fair examination of the individual circumstances of each individual. The prohibition on collective expulsion in the ECHR has been the subject of a number of judgments by the ECtHR, setting out what it means. The Court itself has published a guide to its case law on collective expulsions.[20] From the ECtHR's case law, the term 'collective expulsion' is to be understood as 'any measure compelling aliens, as a group, to leave the country, except where such a measure is taken on the basis of a reasonable and objective examination of the particular case of each individual alien of the group'.[21] For an expulsion to be 'collective' in nature, there are no requirements such as a minimum number of

[17] This list includes the *non-refoulement* definition in the 1951 Refugee Convention, the International Covenant on Civil and Political Rights (ICCPR), the Convention against Torture and Other Cruel, Inhuman or Degrading Treatment or Punishment (CAT), Convention on Enforced Disappearance (CED) as well as regional human rights conventions.

[18] M Den Heijer, 'Whose Rights and Which Rights? The Continuing Story of Non-refoulement under the European Convention on Human Rights' (2008) 10(3) *European Journal of Migration and Law* 277–314; H Lambert, 'Protection against Refoulement from Europe: Human Rights Law Comes to the Rescue' (1999) 48(3) *International and Comparative Law Quarterly* 515–44.

[19] See for instance A de Zayas, 'Collective Expulsions: Norms, Jurisprudence, Remedies' (1997) 16(3) *Refugee Survey Quarterly* 149–53 and L Riemer, *The Prohibition of Collective Expulsion in Public International Law* (Freie Universitaet Berlin, 2020).

[20] European Court of Human Rights (ECtHR), 'Guide on Article 4 of Protocol No 4 to the European Convention on Human Rights' (Council of Europe, updated 28 February 2025), available at https://ks.echr.coe.int/documents/d/echr-ks/guide_art_4_protocol_4_eng.

[21] *Khlaifia and Others v Italy* ECLI:CE:ECHR:2016:1215JUD001648312.

persons affected or membership of a particular group.[22] Until the *Hirsi* decision, the prohibition on collective expulsion was generally considered to apply only to aliens who were on the territory of a state, thus not applicable to pushbacks at sea or land borders.

The ECtHR decision in *Hirsi* was revolutionary as regards this approach to state responsibility. The Court considered whether the prohibition applied when the removal took place outside national territory, specifically on the high seas. As neither the text nor the *travaux préparatoires* precluded the extraterritorial application of the provision, the Court considered that the word 'expulsion' should be interpreted 'in the generic meaning, in current use (to drive away from a place)'. The ECtHR followed with an *argumentum a contrario*, if Article 4 Protocol 4 were to apply only to collective expulsions from the national territory of the states,

> a significant component of contemporary migratory patterns would not fall within the ambit of that provision and migrants having taken to the sea, often risking their lives, and not having managed to reach the borders of a State, would not be entitled to an examination of their personal circumstances before being expelled, unlike those travelling by land.[23]

The ECtHR insisted that the special nature of the maritime environment did not make it an area outside the law. Thus, the removal of aliens carried out in the context of interception on the high seas by state authorities in the exercise of their sovereign authority,

> the effect of which is to prevent migrants from reaching the borders of the State or even to push them back to another State, constitutes an exercise of jurisdiction which engages the responsibility of the State in question under Article 4 Protocol 4.[24]

II. The *Hirsi* Facts

It is time to consider the facts of the case. The applicants, 11 Somali and 13 Eritrean nationals, were part of a group of about 200 individuals who left Libya aboard three vessels with the aim of reaching the Italian coast on 6 May 2009. The vessels were 35 nautical miles south of Lampedusa, Italy, which is within the Maltese Search and Rescue Region of responsibility, when they were intercepted by three ships from the Italian Revenue Police and Coastguard. The people on the intercepted vessels were transferred onto Italian military ships and returned to Libya from whence the Italian authorities determined they had departed. The applicants alleged that during that voyage the Italian authorities did not inform them of their real destination and took no steps to identify them. All their personal effects, including documents confirming

[22] *ND and NT v Spain* ECLI:CE:ECHR:2020:0213JUD000867515.
[23] *Hirsi Jamaa* (n 2) [169]–[182].
[24] ibid [182].

their identity, were confiscated by the military personnel. When the ships arrived in Libya the migrants were handed over to the Libyan authorities. According to the applicants' version of events, they objected to being handed over to the Libyan authorities but were forced to leave the Italian ships. The day after the operation the Italian Minister of the Interior held a press conference when he stated that the legal basis of the operation resulted from the entry into force on 4 February 2009 of bilateral agreements concluded with Libya, and represented an important turning point in the fight against clandestine immigration. The same Minister stated in the Italian Senate that between 6 and 10 May 2009 more than 471 irregular migrants had been intercepted on the high seas and transferred to Libya in accordance with those bilateral agreements. According to the Minister, the pushback policy was very effective in combating illegal immigration. According to the Minister of the Interior, the policy discouraged criminal gangs involved in people smuggling and trafficking, helped save lives at sea and substantially reduced landings of irregular migrants along the Italian coast, which had decreased fivefold in May 2009 as compared with May 2008. In the judgment, the ECtHR noted that during the course of 2009, Italy conducted nine operations on the high seas to intercept irregular migrants, in conformity with the bilateral agreements concluded with Libya.

III. The Parties

The applicants and the Italian Government were the main parties. However, the United Nations High Commissioner for Refugees (UNHCR), Human Rights Watch, the Columbia Law School Human Rights Clinic, the AIRE Centre, Amnesty International and the International Federation for Human Rights, acting collectively, were given leave to intervene by the President of the Chamber.[25] The President of the Court also allowed the submission of observations from the Office of the United Nations High Commissioner for Human Rights. Only UNHCR was also given leave to participate in the oral proceedings.

IV. The Applicable Law

The core of any court judgment is the law to which that court has regard in making its decision. According to Article 32, the jurisdiction of the Court extends to all matters concerning the interpretation and application of the ECHR and the Protocols. In the ECHR there is no equivalent to Article 31 Vienna Convention on the Law of Treaties,[26] which sets out the general rules of interpretation, limiting the sources on

[25] Article 36 §2 of the European Convention on Human Rights (ECHR).

[26] United Nations, Vienna Convention on the Law of Treaties, United Nations, Treaty Series, vol 1155, p 331, 23 May 1969, available at www.refworld.org/legal/agreements/un/1969/en/73676.

which the International Court of Justice may rely in its interpretation of a treaty. Thus, while the ECtHR is primarily limited to the interpretation of the Convention and protocols, it is free to take into account other law and material.[27] Thus, the centre of the *Hirsi Jamaa* judgment is the application of Articles 3, 13 and Article 4 Protocol 4 ECHR. But, in order to do so the ECtHR had regard to the 1951 Refugee Convention, Articles 1 and 33 as well as the United Nations Convention on the Law of the Sea (the 'Montego Bay Convention'). Article 89 on the duty to render assistance to any person found at sea in danger of being lost was set out in full.[28] It also considered relevant the 1979 International Convention on Maritime Search and Rescue to clarify the rules of the law of the sea, focusing on the duties of states to assist disembarkation in a place of safety.[29] As regards the claim of the defendant that its actions were in pursuit of the criminal law fight against smuggling of human beings, it considered the UN Protocol against the Smuggling of Migrants by Land, Sea and Air 2000.[30]

As evidence of Council of Europe consensus among European states, it had regard to Resolution 1821 (2011) of the Parliamentary Assembly regarding the arrival, stay and return of unaccompanied minors in Europe.[31] The ECtHR also took into account some EU law, which although outside its jurisdiction nonetheless was considered relevant regarding the legal undertakings of Italy. This included the prohibition on collective expulsion in the EU Charter of Fundamental Rights (Article 19), the 1985 Schengen Agreement which provides for common border controls for EU states and the EU regulation on the law regarding admission of non-EU citizens at the external borders, in particular the provision which excludes those seeking international protection from its scope (Article 3).[32] Additionally, it considered relevant the EU

[27] The ECtHR's regard to the Aarhus Agreement on climate in *Verein Klimaseniorinnen Schweiz and Others v Switzerland* ECLI:CE:ECHR:2024:0409JUD005360020 has led to substantial interest in the sources on which the ECtHR may legitimately rely. See www.ejiltalk.org/klimaseniorinnen-v-switzerland-a-new-era-for-climate-change-protection-or-proceeding-with-the-status-quo/.

[28] UN General Assembly, Convention on the Law of the Sea, 10 December 1982, available at www.refworld.org/legal/agreements/unga/1982/en/40182.

[29] International Maritime Organization (IMO), International Convention on Maritime Search and Rescue (SAR Convention), 1403 UNTS, 27 April 1979, available at www.refworld.org/legal/agreements/imo/1979/en/45159. Sub-paragraph 3.1.9 of the Annex to the SAR Convention: 'Parties shall co-ordinate and co-operate to ensure that masters of ships providing assistance by embarking persons in distress at sea are released from their obligations with minimum further deviation from the ships' [sic] intended voyage, provided that releasing the master of the ship from these obligations does not further endanger the safety of life at sea. The Party responsible for the search and rescue region in which such assistance is rendered shall exercise primary responsibility for ensuring such co-ordination and co-operation occurs, so that survivors assisted are disembarked from the assisting ship and delivered to a place of safety, taking into account the particular circumstances of the case and guidelines developed by the Organization [International Maritime Organization]. In these cases, the relevant Parties shall arrange for such disembarkation to be effected as soon as reasonably practicable.'

[30] UN General Assembly, Protocol against the Smuggling of Migrants by Land, Sea and Air, Supplementing the United Nations Convention against Transnational Organized Crime, 15 November 2000, available at www.refworld.org/legal/agreements/unga/2000/en/53096.

[31] See https://assembly.coe.int/nw/xml/XRef/Xref-XML2HTML-en.asp?fileid=17991.

[32] Regulation (EC) No 562/2006 of the European Parliament and of the Council of 15 March 2006 establishing a Community Code on the rules governing the movement of persons across borders (Schengen Borders Code) [2006] OJ L105/1–32.

Council decision as regards the surveillance of the sea external borders coordinated by the EU external border agency, Frontex.[33]

In accordance with its established practice, the ECtHR also took into account non-legal information relevant to its assessment of the issue before it. Most of this material addressed the human rights situation of asylum seekers and migrants in Libya. The purpose of this evidence was to establish whether the Italian disembarkation of potential asylum seekers there constituted a breach of Article 3 ECHR. These materials included press releases from UNHCR, a letter of 15 July 2009 from the Vice-President of the European Commission, a Report of the Council of Europe's Committee for the Prevention of Torture and Inhuman or Degrading Treatment or Punishment on Italy to Libya returns, a 2009 report by Human Rights Watch on pushbacks in Europe,[34] and a report of a fact finding mission carried out by Amnesty International to Libya from 15 to 23 May 2009. This was the first Amnesty International visit to the country that the Libyan authorities had permitted since 2004. The Court specifically enumerated a number of reports on the basis of which it formed its decision regarding the factual situation.[35] As there were claims of a risk of onward *refoulement* from Libya to the countries of origin, the ECtHR considered documents regarding those countries. The applicants were Somalis and Eritreans, so the Court had regard to material in respect of human rights compliance in those two countries. As regards Somalia, the ECtHR noted that the main international documents were submitted in a previous case which it determined in 2011.[36]

V. Preliminary Issues

The Italian Government challenged the validity of the application in various respects. First, it raised questions regarding the validity of the powers of attorney provided by the applicants' representatives. Secondly, it submitted that the application was inadmissible because domestic remedies had not been exhausted. Both these arguments failed on the facts. Thereafter the Italian Government challenged

[33] Council Decision of 26 April 2010 supplementing the Schengen Borders Code as regards the surveillance of the sea external borders in the context of operational cooperation coordinated by the European Agency for the Management of Operational Cooperation at the External Borders of the Member States of the European Union (2010/252/EU).

[34] Human Rights Watch, 'Pushed Back, Pushed Around: Italy's Forced Return of Boat Migrants and Asylum Seekers, Libya's Mistreatment of Migrants and Asylum Seekers' (2009), available at www.hrw.org/news/2009/09/21/italy/libya-migrants-describe-forced-returns-abuse.

[35] These included: (i) Human Rights Watch, 'Stemming the Flow: Abuses Against Migrants, Asylum Seekers and Refugees' (13 September 2006); (ii) United Nations Human Rights Committee, 'Concluding Observations. Libyan Arab Jamahiriya' (15 November 2007); (iii) Amnesty International, 'Libya – Amnesty International Report 2008' (28 May 2008); (iv) Human Rights Watch, 'Libya: Rights at Risk' (2 September 2008); (v) US Department of State, '2010 Human Rights Report: Libya' (8 April 2010).

[36] *Sufi and Elmi v United Kingdom* App nos 8319/07 and 11449/07 (ECtHR, 28 June 2011) [80]–[195], available at www.refworld.org/jurisprudence/caselaw/echr/2011/en/79664.

the Article 1 jurisdiction of the ECtHR to hear the case. While it acknowledged that the events in question had taken place on board Italian military ships, it denied that the Italian authorities had exercised 'absolute and exclusive control' over the applicants, the test necessary for jurisdiction. The applicants countered that as soon as they had boarded the Italian ships, they had been under the exclusive control of Italy and therefore within the jurisdiction of the ECHR. The third-party interveners considered that, in accordance with the principles of customary international law and the Court's case law, the obligation on states not to return asylum seekers, even 'potential' asylum seekers, and to ensure that they had access to a fair hearing were extraterritorial in their scope.

After a detailed review of its case law, the Court first stressed that the events occurred on the high seas, on board military ships flying the Italian flag. The Italian Government had acknowledged that the Revenue Police and Coastguard ships onto which the applicants were embarked were fully within Italian jurisdiction.[37] The ECtHR considered settled law that by virtue of the relevant provisions of the law of the sea, a vessel sailing on the high seas is subject to the exclusive jurisdiction of the state of the flag it is flying. Thus, it found that the events took place entirely on board ships of the Italian armed forces, the crews of which were composed exclusively of Italian military personnel. In the period between boarding the ships of the Italian armed forces and being handed over to the Libyan authorities, the applicants were under the continuous and exclusive de jure and de facto control of the Italian authorities.[38]

VI. The ECtHR Findings on the Three ECHR Provisions

A. Article 3: The Prohibition on Torture, Inhuman and Degrading Treatment

The applicants contended that they had not been afforded the opportunity to challenge their return to Libya and to request international protection from the Italian authorities; there had been no procedure to identify the intercepted persons and to gather information as to their personal circumstances and that they had asked the Italian military personnel not to disembark them in Libya, from where they had just fled, but rather to take them to Italy. They claimed that they would be subject to torture, inhuman or degrading treatment in Libya and that on the basis of all information publicly available, Italy could not have been unaware of that increasingly worsening situation in Libya regarding the treatment of aliens. This

[37] ibid [76].
[38] ibid [81].

was so even when it signed the bilateral agreements with Libya and carried out the pushback operations in issue. According to the evidence, after return to Libya the applicants in fact did suffer treatment contrary to Article 3 ECHR.

The Italian Government argued that the applicants were transferred to Libya in accordance with bilateral agreements between the countries which were a response to increasing migratory flows between Africa and Europe and had been signed in a spirit of cooperation between two countries engaged in combating clandestine immigration.[39] It argued that Libya was a safe host country for asylum seekers notwithstanding that it was not a signatory to the 1951 Refugee Convention. The interveners argued that in accordance with the principle of *pacta sunt servanda*, a state could not evade its obligations under the ECHR by relying on commitments arising out of bilateral or multilateral agreements concerning the fight against clandestine immigration. In its judgment, the ECtHR frequently cited the arguments made by UNHCR to establish the facts and the law in preference over the other intervenors.

In its assessment, the ECtHR acknowledged the difficulties which states face when seeking to crack down on irregular entry but it held that having regard to the absolute character of the rights secured by Article 3, a state is not absolved of its obligations under that provision by the fight against smuggling. Protection against the treatment prohibited by Article 3 imposes on states the obligation not to remove any person who, in the receiving country, would run the real risk of being subjected to such treatment.[40] In light of the evidence produced, the Court held that there was such a risk and that the Italian Government could not have been ignorant of it. Thus, the ECtHR considered that, by transferring the applicants to Libya, the Italian authorities, in full knowledge of the facts, exposed them to treatment proscribed by the Convention and thereby committed a breach of Article 3.[41]

B. Article 4 Protocol 4: The Prohibition on Collective Expulsion

As regards this ground, the Italian Government argued that Article 4 Protocol 4 was not applicable. The guarantee provided by the provision came into play only in the event of the expulsion of persons on the territory of a state or who had crossed the national border illegally. Hence the measures taken on the ships were refusals to authorise entry into national territory rather than expulsion.[42] The applicants submitted that an evolutive approach should lead the Court to recognise the applicability of Article 4 Protocol 4 on the basis of a functional and

[39] ibid [93].
[40] ibid [122].
[41] ibid [137].
[42] ibid [160].

teleological interpretation of the provision.[43] Only this approach would render the provision practical and effective rather than theoretical and illusory. The intervenors supported the applicants' arguments as consistent with international law.

After reviewing its case law, the Court found that that was the first time it was called upon to examine whether Article 4 Protocol 4 applies to a case involving the removal of aliens to a third state carried out outside national territory. It held that the transfer of the applicants to Libya constituted a 'collective expulsion of aliens' within the meaning of the provision at issue. Relying on the Vienna Convention on the Law of Treaties, the Court found that the ordinary meaning to be given to the terms in their context and in the light of the object and purpose of the provision from which they are taken required such an interpretation.[44] Although the notion of expulsion was clearly principally territorial, where a state had, exceptionally, exercised its jurisdiction outside its national territory, the exercise of extraterritorial jurisdiction by that state could take the form of collective expulsion. Pushbacks to another state constitute an exercise of jurisdiction which engages the responsibility of the state in question under Article 4 Protocol 4.[45] The transfer of the applicants to Libya was carried out without any form of examination of each applicant's individual situation. The ECtHR found that the action constituted collective expulsion as no individual procedure was conducted within which the applicants could present their personal circumstances. It found that the removal of the applicants was of a collective nature, in breach of Article 4 Protocol 4 and accordingly, there was a violation of that Article.[46]

C. Article 13: The Right to an Effective Remedy

The general rule regarding access to an effective remedy under Article 13 is that it must guarantee the availability at national level of a remedy to enforce the substance of the Convention rights in whatever form they may happen to be secured. It must be effective in practice as well as in law. While the determining authority does not necessarily have to be judicial if it is not, its powers and the guarantees must be considered to determine whether it is effective. This means it must be independent and provide rigorous scrutiny and it must have the power to suspend the implementation of the measure at issue. A remedy, as regards an Article 3 expulsion complaint, does not meet the requirements if it does not have suspensive effect. As the complainants in the *Hirsi Jamaa* case had no access to a procedure even to identify themselves and thereafter for an assessment of their personal circumstances before they were returned to Libya (including the fact that there were

[43] ibid [162].
[44] ibid [171].
[45] ibid [169]–[182].
[46] ibid [185].

neither interpreters nor legal advisers available and they had no information on where they were being taken), the Court found a violation of Article 13.[47]

VII. The Relevance of Agreements with Third Countries

On 29 December 2007, Italy and Libya signed a bilateral cooperation agreement in Tripoli to combat clandestine immigration. On the same date the two countries signed an Additional Protocol setting out the operational and technical arrangements for implementing the agreement. The Italian Government relied on the provisions of the agreement to contend that the Libyan authorities were responsible for the treatment of the applicants. The Court found that Italy could not evade its own responsibility by relying on the bilateral agreements. It stated that even if those agreements made express provision for the return to Libya of migrants intercepted on the high seas, the state's ECHR responsibilities continued even after entering into other treaty commitments subsequently. It did not accept that the presence of a UNHCR office in Tripoli changed this responsibility, not least as it was never recognised in any way by the Libyan Government and could not guarantee any kind of protection in Libya. It found that the Italian authorities knew or should have known that, as irregular migrants, the applicants would be exposed in Libya to treatment contrary to Article 3.[48] Further, as far as the entitlement to ECHR protection was concerned, the Court found that numbers do not matter, the fact that a large number of irregular immigrants in Libya found themselves in the same situation as the applicants does not make the risk concerned any less individual where it is sufficiently real and probable.[49]

VIII. Academic Analysis

The judgment elicited a substantial amount of academic comment. Nascimbene welcomed the judgment as a step towards the limitation of the national doctrine of state sovereignty in the face of human rights violations.[50] Moreno-Lax, writing in 2012, considered that the impact of the decision was enormous not least at it placed all pushbacks into the category of unlawful acts clarifying states' obligations under the ECHR in the light of the law of the sea.[51] Guiffre, the same year, focused more centrally on the issue of extraterritoriality and the importance of

[47] ibid [207].
[48] ibid [131].
[49] ibid [136].
[50] B Nascimbene, 'The "Push-back Policy" Struck Down Without Appeal? The European Court of Human Rights in Hirsi Jamaa and Others v. Italy' (2012) 12 *Instituto Affari Internazionali*.
[51] V Moreno-Lax, 'Hirsi Jamaa and Others v Italy or the Strasbourg Court versus extraterritorial migration control?' (2012) 12(3) *Human Rights Law Review* 574–98.

the ECtHR's move to block efforts by states to avoid their responsibilities by acting outside their sovereign territory and with the cover of a bilateral agreement. She also highlighted the possibility left open by the ECtHR of the value of diplomatic assurances which in theory might have been obtained from the Libyan authorities by their Italian counterparts promising to treat the complainants in a manner consistent with the ECHR (which of course does not apply to a non-party such as Libya).[52] Papanicolopulu, in 2017, focused on the importance of political changes both in Italy and Libya neither of which augured well for the safety of persons in the position of the claimants. Further, she addressed the question of responsibility where the authorities do not take physical control of the persons but merely facilitate their interception by the authorities of another country (for instance the Libyan coastguard).[53] This, in fact has become a common practice which is currently being challenged as regards the sharing of EUROSUR[54] geolocalisation data on small boats with the Libyan authorities for the purposes of intervention.[55] While the academic analysis following the judgment welcomed the approach of the Court, it also foresaw challenges for the future.

IX. After *Hirsi Jamaa*

Two judgments which followed *Hirsi Jamaa* raise problems regarding the consistency of the prohibition on collective expulsion. The first one in 2016 again regarded sea border interception where the Italian authorities rescued and landed in Italy persons seeking asylum only to return them under a bilateral agreement with their country of origin (Tunisia) without an individual determination of their asylum claims.[56] In this case the Italian authorities held the applicants in detention (hence an Article 5 liberty claim was successful) and issued pro forma refusals without an interview before expelling the applicants to their country of origin. While the ECtHR found violations of Articles 5, 3 and 13, it did not find a violation of Article 4 Protocol 4. Instead, it found that although the applicants had stated that although they were subject to identification there was no individual assessment of their personal circumstances. On the evidence of several healthcare professionals, interpreters and cultural mediators that they facilitated communication between the migrants and the Italian authorities, the ECtHR found that there had been

[52] M Giuffré, 'Watered-Down Rights on the High Seas: Hirsi Jamaa and Others v Italy' (2012) 61(3) *International and Comparative Law Quarterly*.

[53] Irini Papanicolopulu, 'Hirsi Jamaa v. Italy. Application No. 27765/09' (2013) 107(2) *American Journal of International Law* 417–23.

[54] European Border Surveillance system (EUROSUR) is a framework for information exchange and cooperation between Member States and Frontex to improve situational awareness and increase reaction capability at the external borders.

[55] See https://digitalfreedomfund.org/unlawful-surveillance-and-data-sharing-of-asylum-seekers-by-the-european-border-and-coast-guard-agency/.

[56] *Khlaifia* (n 21).

a sufficient individualisation of the procedure. It also found that the applicants had the opportunity to raise their *refoulement* concerns during the identification procedure. The Court found that Article 4 Protocol 4 does not guarantee the right to an individual interview in all circumstances. The procedural requirement may be satisfied where the individual has a genuine and effective possibility to raise arguments in respect of their expulsion, which are examined appropriately. As Mauro argues, this was a step away from the judgment in *Hirsi Jamaa* and one which would weaken the case law generally.[57]

The second case was *ND & NT v Spain*, decided in 2017 regarding the land border at the Spanish enclave of Melilla and Morocco.[58] A group of persons rushed the highly securitised fence between Moroccan and Spanish territory in Melilla. They were repulsed with no consideration of the reasons why they were seeking to enter Spain, a practice known as 'hot returns'. They claimed they had been subject to a collective expulsion but the ECtHR disagreed. While the Grand Chamber reiterated its position in *Hirsi Jamaa* and stated its support for the findings in the earlier case, on the facts it found no breach of Article 4 Protocol 4 because the applicants had caused their own collective expulsion by their culpable conduct because they did not go through regular border procedures (which on the evidence produced the ECtHR held was possible).[59]

The key feature which differentiated *Hirsi Jamaa* and *ND & NT* seems to be the lack of an immediate *refoulement* risk. While the ECtHR held in *Hirsi Jamaa* that the risk of treatment contrary to Article 3 (torture, inhuman or degrading treatment) was evident if the applicants were sent to Libya, it did not find in *ND & NT* such a risk in Morocco, or at least not an immediate risk. Instead, it found that the applicants had the opportunity to make an application within Morocco to the Spanish authorities to obtain a visa to travel but they chose rather to rush the fences. Thus the protection of Article 4 Protocol 4 was not available to them. Some academic commentators see this as a deconstruction of the *Hirsi* judgment.[60]

In a Chamber judgment in 2024,[61] the ECtHR came to a nuanced position between *Hirsi Jamaa* and *ND & NT* as regards a group of Syrian applicants who had been pushed back from Cyprus towards Lebanon without consideration of

[57] M Rosaria Mauro, 'A Step Back in the Protection of Migrants' Rights: The Grand Chamber's Judgment in Khlaifia v. Italy' (2017) 26(1) *The Italian Yearbook of International Law Online* 287–317, available at https://doi.org/10.1163/22116133-90000167a.

[58] *ND and NT* (n 22).

[59] C Gortázar Rotaeche and N Ferré Trad, 'A Cold Shower for Spain–Hot Returns from Melilla to Morocco: ND and NT v Spain ECtHR, 3 October 2017' (2017) *European Migration Law*. N Markard, 'A Hole of Unclear Dimension: Reading ND and NT v Spain' (*EU Immigration and Asylum Law and Policy*, 1 April 2020), available at https://eumigrationlawblog.eu/a-hole-of-unclear-dimensions-reading-nd-and-nt-v-spain/.

[60] L Alonso Sanz, 'Deconstructing Hirsi: The Return of Hot Returns: ECtHR 13 February 2020, Nos. 8675/15 and 8697/15, ND and NT v Spain' (2021) 17(2) *European Constitutional Law Review* 335–52; A Pijnenburg, 'Is ND and NT v. Spain the new Hirsi?' (Tilburg University, 2027); L Leboeuf and J Carlier, 'The Prohibition of Collective Expulsion as an Individualisation Requirement' (2020) *Law and Judicial Dialogue on the Return of Irregular Migrants from the European Union* 467.

[61] *MA & ZR v Cyprus* ECLI:CE:ECHR:2024:1008JUD003909020.

their asylum claims. It was accepted that the Lebanese authorities were not actively carrying out treatment against Syrians which would constitute a breach of Article 3 ECHR. However, the dire conditions in the refugee camps and the rapid deterioration of living standards, coupled with the complete lack of any alternative for the Syrians in Lebanon constituted a situation which violated Article 3 norms and thus meant that the pushbacks breached Article 4 Protocol 4. The judgment is being appealed to the Grand Chamber. Also pending before the Grand Chamber are a number of cases of pushbacks from Poland, Lithuania and Estonia to Belarus across a land border which was heard on 12 February 2025.

The *Hirsi Jamaa* decision changed the political and legal landscape of Europe. In April 2022, the executive director of Frontex, Fabrice Leggeri, resigned from his post at the EU external border agency as a result of allegations of his personal involvement in pushbacks of asylum seekers carried out by the agency during his mandate.[62] The pressure on Leggeri was in no small part the result of the judgment which held that these actions in which Frontex had allegedly been complicit constituted violation of the ECHR.

The lasting legacy of the *Hirsi Jamaa* judgment is the firm prohibition of pushbacks where there is a risk of treatment contrary to Article 3 ECHR in the destination country including a real risk of onward *refoulement*. Whenever a state is engaging in summary refusal (at the border or within the jurisdiction) and immediate expulsion it must ensure that there is no risk in the destination country of torture, inhuman or degrading treatment or onward *refoulement* to such a place. This means examining not only state practices but also the conditions of life for the individuals to be sent back and whether they violate the prohibition. Article 4 Protocol 4, coupled with Article 3 ECHR constitute the basis of the duty on states to provide fair and effective procedures for anyone within their jurisdiction, including at the border or on the high seas, who claims asylum.

European states have reacted to this clarification of the ECHR in a variety of ways, generally covered by the term 'externalisation'. The first such move has been the rather brutal 'pullbacks' conducted by the Libyan authorities, mainly at the instigation of Italy with Frontex possibly participating. Under this initiative, the Libyan coastguard has in recent years commenced operations to catch small boats in international waters and drag them back to Libya from where they had departed.[63] The next response has been more nuanced agreements or arrangements adopted by European states with third countries, to prevent people who might be 'unwanted' migrant arrivals to the region from leaving bordering countries.[64] An example of

[62] See https://schengen.news/head-of-frontex-resigns-following-reports-of-migrant-pushbacks/; E Guild (ed), *Monitoring Border Violence in the EU: Frontex in Focus* (Taylor & Francis, 2023).

[63] A Pijnenburg, 'From Italian Pushbacks to Libyan Pullbacks: Is Hirsi 2.0 in the Making in Strasbourg?' (2018) *European Journal of Migration and Law* 20.4, 396–426.

[64] P García Andrade, 'EU External Competences in the Field of Migration: How to Act Externally when Thinking Internally' (2018) 55 *CMLR* 1, 157–200.

this was the EU–Turkey Deal of 2016.[65] More recently, Italy has been experimenting with a programme whereby people appearing to be heading towards Italy in small boats are intercepted in international waters and taken to an Italian-run detention centre in Albania for processing of their cases, including asylum claims with potential expulsion in the event of rejection.[66] The UK sought a similar deal with Rwanda to send people seeking international protection there for the processing of their asylum claims, but under the exclusive authority of the Rwandan authorities. This project was abandoned following a successful judicial challenge and a change of government in 2024.[67] At the time of writing, the European Commission is reviewing its rules regarding the safe third country (STC) concept and preparing a European list of safe countries of origin for those seeking international protection.[68] Unfortunately, though positive in its immediate impact, efforts by a number of European states to avoid the full effect of the judgment in *Hirsi Jamaa* regarding fair procedures for those seeking international protection are likely to continue throughout this decade at least.

[65] MH Zoeteweij and O Turhan, 'Above the Law-Beneath Contempt: The End of the EU-Turkey Deal' (2017) *Swiss Review of International and European Law* 27–151.

[66] A De Leo and E Celoria, 'The Italy–Albania Protocol: A New Model of Border-Shifting within the EU and its Compatibility with Union Law' (2024) *Maastricht Journal of European and Comparative Law* 31.5, 595–618.

[67] K Ritchie, 'The *Rwanda Case*: Testing the Limits of Judicial Competence' (2024) *Judicial Review* 29(2), 91–106. See also Tan (n 5).

[68] N Lonta, 'EU Migration Chief Confirms Acceleration of Safe Third Country Review and Origin List' (*Euractiv*, 5 March 2025), available at www.euractiv.com/section/politics/news/eu-migration-chief-confirms-acceleration-of-safe-third-country-review-and-origin-list/.

9

MSS v Belgium and Greece [2011]: The Interplay between *Non-Refoulement* and Refugee Protection

EVANGELIA (LILIAN) TSOURDI* AND PAUL McDONOUGH**

I. Introduction

MSS v Belgium and Greece[1] is a landmark case for two reasons. First, the European Court of Human Rights (ECtHR) reaffirmed the absolute nature of the *non-refoulement* principle within the European Union's (EU) regional cooperation framework on asylum, which foresees transfers of asylum seekers between EU Member States based on responsibility allocation arrangements. Second, the Court established, for the first time, that extreme socioeconomic deprivation of asylum seekers constitutes a violation of the prohibition of torture, inhuman or degrading treatment or punishment. As analysed in this chapter, both pronouncements had far reaching implications for refugee protection in the EU, and more widely.

This contribution first outlines the legal and policy context against which the *MSS* case evolved (section II). It analyses the significance of the principle of *non-refoulement* within a regional inter-state cooperation framework on refugee protection, the EU's Common European Asylum System (CEAS) (section III). It then explores how the prohibition of torture, inhuman, and degrading treatment or punishment links with socioeconomic rights of asylum seekers (section IV).

II. The Legal and Policy Context of the *MSS* Case

MSS rests at the intersection of EU asylum law, Council of Europe regional human rights law, and international refugee law. This section first provides the context

* This research was supported by a European Research Council Starting Grant (Soft Enforcement of EU Migration Law- SoftEn, PI: Lilian Tsourdi), Grant Agreement 101165167.

** My contribution was funded by the ERC-2022-STG Gatekeepers to International Refugee Law? – The Role of Courts in Shaping Access to Asylum (ACCESS), Grant No. 101078683.

[1] *MSS v Belgium and Greece* [GC] App no 30696/09 (ECtHR, 21 January 2011) (hereinafter *MSS*).

necessary to support an analysis of the interactions among these sources of law, then outlines the main facts of the *MSS* case.

A. The CEAS, its Interrelation with International Refugee Law, and the ECtHR

The CEAS aims to guide the EU Member States towards a harmonised implementation of the 1951 Convention relating to the Status of Refugees (1951 Refugee Convention).[2] In addition to their obligations under the Convention and the CEAS, Member States are bound by international and European human rights treaties.[3] Rights and freedoms such as the right to liberty and security,[4] and the prohibition of torture, inhuman and degrading treatment,[5] as well as principles such as the primacy of the best interests of the child,[6] although not specifically addressed to refugees or persons seeking international protection, have an impact on their treatment and establish a series of entitlements and guarantees.

The CEAS operates under EU law, supervised by the Court of Justice (CJEU). The Dublin Regulation,[7] the CEAS legal instrument whose operation led to the *MSS* case, determines which state should take responsibility for an asylum applicant, so that each application is assessed, once, by one Member State. It applies a hierarchy of criteria,[8] to identify the Member State 'primarily "responsible" for the person's presence in the EU', which in practice usually means the '[s]tate of first

[2] UN General Assembly, 1951 Convention relating to the Status of Refugees, United Nations, Treaty Series, 189:137, 28 July 1951. The Convention recognises rights progressively, as the refugee becomes more closely connected to the host state. Rights attach to refugees under the host state's jurisdiction; on its territory; lawfully present in its territory; lawfully staying; and durably resident. J Hathaway, *The Rights of Refugees Under International Law* (Cambridge University Press, 2005) 174–75.

[3] Of particular relevance are the International Covenant on Civil and Political Rights, 16 December 1966, United Nations, Treaty Series, vol 999, 171 (entry into force 23 March 1976) (ICCPR); Convention for the Protection of Human Rights and Fundamental Freedoms, 4 November 1950, 005 CETS 1 as amended by Protocol 14, 13 May 2004, 194 CETS 1 (entry into force 3 September 1953) (ECHR); and the Convention on the Rights of the Child, 20 November 1989, United Nations, Treaty Series, vol 1577, 3 (entry into force 2 September 1990) (CRC).

[4] See, eg, Art 9 ICCPR and Art 5 ECHR.

[5] See, eg, Art 7 ICCPR and Art 3 ECHR.

[6] See Art 3 CRC.

[7] Regulation (EU) 604/2013 of the European Parliament and of the Council of 26 June 2013 establishing the criteria and mechanisms for determining the Member State responsible for examining an application for international protection lodged in one of the Member States by a third-country national or a stateless person (recast) [2013] OJ L180/31 (hereinafter Dublin Regulation 2013). At the time of *MSS* the predecessor 2003 Dublin Regulation was in effect, Council Regulation (EC) No 343/2003. This chapter references the equivalent provisions from the current 2013 regulation to those in front of the *MSS* Court.

[8] Dublin Regulation 2013, ibid ch III. After some exceptional rules to protect the rights of children and family unity, the criteria ascertain first whether the applicant has recently held a residence permit or visa for a Member State (Art 12); then irregular entry or stay in the EU (Art 13); whether another Member State has granted visa-free entry (Art 14); and applications made in an airport's international transit area (Art 15).

irregular entry to the EU'.[9] If an asylum seeker is in another Member State than the one designated as responsible, that state may transfer them to the responsible state (a 'Dublin transfer').[10] Member States may 'abstain from a transfer for any other reason, including on humanitarian and compassionate grounds'.[11]

Under the Reception Conditions Directive,[12] another CEAS legislative instrument, Member States are responsible to 'provide an adequate standard of living for [asylum] applicants, which guarantees their subsistence and protects their physical and mental health'.[13] This is grounded in international refugee law and the fact that refugee status is declarative.[14] The Directive implements this,[15] harmonising material reception conditions, the practical support and socioeconomic rights Member States owe to asylum seekers while their claim is being determined.[16] Harmonisation of reception conditions was seen as an important step in limiting incentives or objective needs for asylum seekers to move between Member States.[17]

All EU Member States are also members of the Council of Europe, and parties to the European Convention on Human Rights (ECHR), the treaty that is the cornerstone of the Council of Europe system. Unusually among international treaties, the ECHR provides standing for individuals to claim against states for violations.[18] The ECtHR has jurisdiction to interpret the ECHR, and to pronounce on such claims. The ECHR neither regulates the situation of refugees directly, nor does it provide a right to asylum. Nevertheless, it contains several asylum-relevant rights.[19] The most notable here is the prohibition of torture, inhuman, or degrading treatment or punishment (Article 3), which the ECtHR interprets as incorporating a *non-refoulement* rule.

[9] E Tsourdi and C Costello, 'The Evolution of EU Law on Refugees and Asylum' in P Craig and G de Búrca (eds), *The Evolution of EU Law: Third Edition* (Oxford University Press, 2021) 793–823, 805.

[10] Dublin Regulation 2013 (n 7) ch V.

[11] ibid ch IV.

[12] Directive 2013/33/EU of the European Parliament and of the Council of 26 June 2013 laying down standards for the reception of applicants for international protection (recast) [2013] OJ L180/96 (hereinafter Reception Conditions Directive 2013).

[13] ibid Art 17(2).

[14] See, eg, Department of International Protection (DIP), *Handbook on Procedures and Criteria for Determining Refugee Status Under the 1951 Convention and the 1967 Protocol relating to the Status of Refugees*, HCR/IP/4/Eng/REV. 1 Re-edited (UNHCR 1979, 1992) para 28.

[15] See Reception Conditions Directive 2013 (n 12), and Directive (EU) 2024/1346 of the European Parliament and of the Council of 14 May 2024 laying down standards for the reception of applicants for international protection (recast) [2024] OJ L2024/1346 (hereinafter Reception Conditions Directive 2024). The latter was under transposition at the time of writing.

[16] See *Council of the European Union, The Stockholm Programme – An Open and Secure Europe Serving and Protecting the Citizens*, Doc 17024/09, 2009, at para 6.2.

[17] E Tsourdi, 'EU Reception Conditions: A Dignified Standard of Living for Asylum Seekers?' in V Chetail, P De Bruycker and F Maiani (eds), *Reforming the Common European Asylum System: The New European Refugee Law* (Brill, 2016) 271–316, 272–73.

[18] ECHR, Art 34.

[19] See also analysis in E Tsourdi, 'Regional Refugee Regimes – Europe' in C Costello, M Foster, and J McAdam (eds), *Oxford Handbook of International Refugee Law* (Oxford University Press, 2021) 352–69, 362–64.

The ECtHR cannot supervise Member States' application of EU law, but it can adjudicate claims of state violations of the ECHR. To decide *MSS*, the Court also had to take cognisance of international law, in the form of the 1951 Refugee Convention, and the CEAS. In previous cases concerning Dublin transfers, the ECtHR had seemingly allowed Member States to rely on the presumption that their counterpart Member States would uphold their obligations toward asylum seekers under EU and international law. However in *MSS*, the Court confronted a scenario where two Member States acting under the colour of EU law (the Dublin Regulation) had caused an asylum applicant to face conditions that might amount to violations of Article 3 ECHR, and potential deportation to face a real risk of further Article 3 violations.

B. Main Facts and Arguments of the Case

In February 2009, MSS, an Afghan national without identity documents, applied for asylum in Belgium.[20] A 'hit' in the EU asylum database, Eurodac, showed that the Member State of first entry to the EU was Greece,[21] thus the Belgian Aliens Office ordered him to be transferred back there based on the Dublin Regulation.[22] With his appeal to the Asylum Appeals Board pending, MSS applied to the ECtHR for relief, and for an interim order to suspend the transfer.[23] The ECtHR declined to issue interim measures.[24] MSS was transferred on 15 June 2009.[25] While his ECtHR case proceeded, MSS lived destitute in Greece without progressing his asylum claim there. In a January 2011 Grand Chamber judgment, the ECtHR ruled that Belgium and Greece had violated the ECHR's prohibition against torture, or inhuman or degrading treatment or punishment, both in the socioeconomic conditions MSS endured in Greece, and in exposing him to a risk of onward *refoulement*, as well as the right to an effective remedy against those violations.

At the time of *MSS*, the leading ECtHR cases concerning Article 3 *non-refoulement* and the Dublin system were the admissibility decisions *TI v the United Kingdom*,[26] where the ECtHR stated that the Dublin system did not obviate the need to verify that a transfer would not result in *refoulement*, and *KRS v the United Kingdom*,[27] which allowed a transfer to proceed under the presumption that Greece would abide by its international human rights obligations. In *KRS*, the ECtHR considered itself bound 'in the absence of proof to the contrary' to

[20] *MSS* (n 1) [11].
[21] ibid [12].
[22] ibid [17].
[23] ibid [34]. Under Rule 39 of the Rules of Court in the ECHR, the ECtHR may issue interim measures 'in cases of imminent risk of irreparable harm to a Convention right'. Rule 39(1).
[24] ibid [32].
[25] ibid [33].
[26] *TI v the United Kingdom* App no 43844/98 (ECtHR, 7 March 2000) (*TI*).
[27] *KRS v the United Kingdom* App no 32733/08 (ECtHR, 2 December 2008) (*KRS*).

assume that Greece complied with its CEAS obligations and 'with Article 3 of the Convention'.[28] In *MSS*, the Court instead highlighted that Member States retain their obligation not to expel anyone, even to an EU Member State, if there are 'substantial grounds … for believing' they would thereby face a real risk of 'treatment contrary to Article 3'.[29]

The Court ruled that by leaving him to live on the streets with no means of subsistence, Greece had subjected MSS to socioeconomic deprivation rising to such a level as to violate Article 3 ECHR,[30] and that shortcomings in Greece's asylum system as it applied to him created a risk of *refoulement* in the form of his potential expulsion from the EU.[31] The Court pointed to the by then amply available information regarding conditions facing asylum seekers in Greece, and to a 2009 letter from UNHCR to Belgium's Government warning about conditions in Greece and asking for a suspension of transfers there.[32] Belgium, according to the Court, had a duty to consider these risks before asking Greece to accept its transfer of MSS.[33] The ECtHR dismissed the argument that it had previously refused to order the transfer's suspension, reminding that interim measures are made urgently and with incomplete information, and do not 'prejudge' the case.[34]

According to the Court, notwithstanding general assurances given by the Greek Government, Belgium should have known a transfer to Greece risked violating Article 3.[35] The Court also refuted the argument that the Dublin system compelled Belgium to rely on the 'presumption of equivalent protection' by another Member State, as the Dublin Regulation clearly afforded Belgium the discretion to forego a transfer.[36] Ultimately, the Court ruled that Greece had violated Article 3 via the detention conditions and living conditions MSS experienced there and that Belgium had violated Article 3 by returning him to those conditions, and to a risk of onward *refoulement*. It further held that Belgium and Greece had each violated Article 13 of the ECHR in conjunction with Article 3: Belgium by carrying out the Dublin transfer and Greece in the *refoulement* risk created by a deficient asylum procedure, and both by failing to provide access to an effective remedy.[37]

The rest of this chapter will explore the role of *MSS* in developing the international understanding of *non-refoulement*, and the relationships between vulnerability, socioeconomic rights, and the prohibition on inhuman or degrading treatment.

[28] *MSS* (n 1) [343].
[29] ibid [342].
[30] ibid [263].
[31] ibid [313]–[315].
[32] ibid [349].
[33] ibid [352] (possibility that Greece would not assess the asylum claim), [366] (living conditions for asylum seekers in Greece were well known to the Belgian authorities).
[34] ibid [355].
[35] ibid [354].
[36] ibid [339].
[37] See ibid [394] (the parties apparently agreed that MSS had no chance of a successful appeal in Belgium).

III. Beyond 'Blind' Mutual Trust: *Non-Refoulement* and Intra-EU Transfers of Asylum Seekers

The facts of *MSS* engaged *non-refoulement* rules of at least three legal instruments: the 1951 Refugee Convention, the EU's Qualification Directive,[38] and by virtue of the ECtHR's longstanding jurisprudence, the ECHR. One lesson of *MSS* is that *non-refoulement* imposes the same obligations on states, regardless of whether a state is participating in a collective protection regime such as the CEAS. Any claim of a *refoulement* risk requires rigorous scrutiny, backed up by a meaningfully effective remedy with suspensive effect, and an assessment of the individual's circumstances. By subtly reframing a Dublin transfer as a potential first link in a *refoulement* chain, the Court asserted the priority of the ECHR's protections.

A. Dublin Transfers and their Link with *Non-Refoulement* According to Article 3 ECHR

In the earlier landmark *Soering* case, the ECtHR underlined that Contracting States may remove individuals to states where ECHR safeguards are not fully met,[39] with two exceptions. First, because of the absolute and non-derogable nature of Article 3 of the ECHR, individuals may not be sent to countries where they face real risks of being subjected to inhuman or degrading treatment or punishment.[40] Given the reasoning in *Soering*, this prohibition also applies to violations of other non-derogable rights.[41] Second, the ECHR 'might exceptionally' prohibit extradition if there is a risk the individual would face a 'flagrant denial of justice' in the receiving state.[42] Given that it was the ECtHR that adjudicated *MSS*, that Court could engage only with these standards, even though the case concerned EU Member States and the operation of the EU asylum acquis.

[38] Council Directive 2004/83/EC of 29 April 2004 on minimum standards for the qualification and status of third country nationals or stateless persons as refugees or as persons who otherwise need international protection and the content of the protection granted [2004] OJ L304/12.

[39] *Soering v United Kingdom* App no 14038/88 (ECtHR, 07 July 1989) [86].

[40] ibid at [88]. An important body of case law has developed around the absolute nature of *non-refoulement*; see, eg, *Vilvarajah and others v United Kingdom* App nos 13163/87; 13164/87; 13165/87; 13447/87; 13448/87 (ECtHR, 30 October 1991); *Chahal v United Kingdom* App no 22414/93 (ECtHR, 15 November 1996); *Saadi v Italy* App no 37201/06 (ECtHR, 28 February 2008).

[41] K Wouters, *International Legal Standards for the Protection from Refoulement* (Intersentia, 2009) 345. See, eg, *Bader and Kanbor v Sweden* App no 13284/04 (ECtHR, 8 November 2005) [42] where the ECtHR concluded that the applicant's deportation to Syria would violate Arts 2 and 3 ECHR.

[42] *Soering* (n 39) [113]. See, eg, *Einhorn v France* App no 71555/01 (admissibility) (ECtHR, 16 October 2001); *Al-Moayad v Germany* App no 35865/03 (admissibility) (ECtHR, 20 February 2007); *Othman (Abu Qatada) v United Kingdom* App no 813909; M Puechavy, 'L'extradition et les risques de violation des articles 3 et 6 de la Convention par ricochet' (2002) 51 *Revue trimestrielle des droits de l'homme* 729.

A core issue in *MSS* was whether, following a Dublin transfer to Greece, the applicant might be again expelled, to face a real risk of treatment in violation of article 3 ECHR. The Court's main explicit *non-refoulement* concern was whether Belgium's transfer of MSS to Greece put him at risk of expulsion from Greece (and hence from the EU) without having the merits of his asylum claim assessed. From the Court's point of view, an administrative transfer under the Dublin regulation could become the first link in a chain of *refoulement*, if the receiving Member State could not or would not provide access to a robust asylum procedure.

The claims MSS raised in his asylum application implicated both a fear of persecution in the sense of the 1951 Refugee Convention (and by extension the CEAS), and a risk of death or ill treatment contrary to Article 2 or 3 of the ECHR. The ECtHR readily identified a prima facie risk of such treatment if he were returned: MSS had worked as an interpreter for foreign military forces in Afghanistan, which given the security situation at the time could lead 'to reprisals at the hands of the anti-government forces'.[43] However, the Court deferred a full, individuated investigation into the risk to the Greek asylum authorities, limiting its own inquiry to 'whether effective guarantees exist in the present case to protect the applicant against arbitrary removal directly or indirectly to his country of origin'.[44]

To the ECtHR as a regional human rights court, it is immaterial which state provides guarantees against removal to a risk of ill-treatment, so long as they are provided. The *non-refoulement* inquiry in *MSS* thus turned on an assessment of whether either Belgium or Greece had provided an opportunity for full examination of the asylum claim. Article 13 ECHR provides a right to an 'effective remedy before a national authority' against violations of the ECHR.[45] National authorities must give claims of 'substantial grounds for fearing a real risk of treatment contrary to Article 3' close scrutiny; a prompt response; and automatic suspensive effect (that is, the person may not be deported before the case or appeal is decided).[46] Greece's failure to provide access to an asylum procedure would violate this right, as would a lack of a way for MSS to contest the Dublin transfer from Belgium to Greece. While MSS was in Greece, the obligation to provide an effective remedy lay on Greece, but when he relocated to Belgium so, arguably, did the obligation. Belgium could only decline to examine the applicant's claim itself if it would be examined in Greece – otherwise Belgium could become the first link in a chain of *refoulement* leading to a real risk of an Article 3 violation.

The ECtHR emphasised that its remit does not cover the 1951 Refugee Convention or asylum determination, but rather, provides a safeguard against arbitrary *refoulement*.[47] Regarding Greece, many international reports had

[43] *MSS* (n 1) [295]–[96].
[44] ibid [298].
[45] See ibid [288] ('The effect of Article 13 is thus to require the provision of a domestic remedy to deal with the substance of an "arguable complaint" under the Convention and to grant appropriate relief').
[46] ibid [293].
[47] ibid [286]–[87].

indicated 'the asylum procedure is marked by such major structural deficiencies that asylum-seekers have very little chance of having their applications and their complaints under the Convention seriously examined'.[48] Claims eventually considered on their merits faced near certain rejection, with decisions often 'drafted in a stereotyped manner without any details of the reasons for the decision'.[49] Appeals were similarly difficult to present and unlikely to succeed.[50] In light of this evidence of the general situation, the Court readily accepted MSS's description of the challenges he had faced in trying to have his claim evaluated,[51] and found that a transfer to Greece could result in *refoulement* to Afghanistan.[52] In this sense, the risk of violation of Article 3 flowed through the absence of an effective remedy in Greece. This led the ECtHR to find Greece had violated Article 13 in conjunction with Article 3.

In light of this risk of *refoulement* from Greece, the ECtHR considered whether Belgium had a duty under Article 3 to refrain from transferring MSS to Greece. The Court found that the risk he would not have his claim fully heard in Greece was significant and known to the asylum authorities in Belgium, which had violated Article 3 by carrying out the transfer. Before it could reach this conclusion, however, the Court had to consider whether mutual participation in a regional asylum regime under EU law – the CEAS – enabled Member States to presume their counterparts would implement their human rights and asylum obligations. This presumption of mutual trust was argued in two forms.

First, the Court dismissed the assertion that the 'principle of inter-State confidence', enunciated in its earlier *Bosphorus* decision, required Belgium to carry out the Dublin transfer.[53] *Bosphorus* established that the ECHR does not prevent states from transferring some sovereign powers to international organisations such as the EU, if those organisations protect fundamental rights equivalently to the Convention, but that states remain responsible for their discretionary acts.[54] A transfer is discretionary, because the Dublin Regulation's sovereignty clause allowed Belgium to derogate from the responsibility determination criteria and not initiate a transfer if it considered that Greece 'was not fulfilling its obligations under the [ECHR]'.[55]

Second, the earlier ECtHR/Dublin case *KRS* had arguably recognised a principle of mutual trust between Member States within the Dublin system. In

[48] ibid [300]. The challenges included insufficient information available to asylum seekers about the procedures; access to or communication with the responsible authorities; shortages of interpreters and legal aid; shortcomings in asylum staff training; and lengthy delays. ibid [301].

[49] ibid [302].

[50] ibid [316]–[20].

[51] ibid [313].

[52] ibid [314]–[15]. For asylum seekers in general in Greece, a risk of *refoulement* before their claims and appeals are heard 'be it indirectly, to Turkey, or to the country of origin, is a constant concern'. ibid [192]–[93].

[53] ibid [330].

[54] ibid [338].

[55] ibid [340].

MSS, the Court clarified that any such presumption is rebuttable, and that the basic rules of *TI* and *KRS* remain.[56] The key question was 'whether the Belgian authorities should have regarded as rebutted the presumption that the Greek authorities would respect their international obligations in asylum matters'.[57] By the time of *MSS*, 'the general situation [in Greece] was known to the Belgian authorities'.[58] Assurances by the Greek authorities were pro forma and did not specifically refer to MSS, or to the practical application of asylum legislation.[59] Had the Belgian authorities 'verif[ied] how the Greek authorities applied their legislation on asylum in practice ... they would have seen ... that the risks the applicant faced were real and individual enough to fall within the scope of Article 3'.[60] In these circumstances, Belgium should have examined the asylum application itself.[61] Transfer to Greece violated Article 3 because it created a (chain) *refoulement* risk.

Having established a risk of *refoulement* via Greece, the Court examined whether the Belgian asylum process offered MSS a realistic chance to challenge the Dublin transfer (and to remain in Belgium pending its outcome). An appeal to the Belgian Asylum Appeals Board would lack suspensive effect, falling short of the ECtHR's threshold for an effective remedy.[62] An alternative 'extremely urgent procedure' could suspend the transfer for 72 hours while the Board decided,[63] but that procedure 'reduces the rights of the defence and the examination of the case to a minimum'.[64] This would clash with the Court's longstanding view 'that any complaint that expulsion to another country will expose an individual to treatment prohibited by Article 3 of the Convention requires close and rigorous scrutiny'.[65] Finally, Belgian case law placing the burdens of proof on the appellant, particularly to demonstrate that concrete harm already incurred, left no chance of an appeal succeeding.[66] The Court found that Belgium had violated Article 13 in conjunction

[56] The presumption was implicit in the *TI* rule that states applying the Dublin regulation must 'make sure that the intermediary country's asylum procedure affords sufficient guarantees' against removal without an assessment of the risks of an Art 3 violation (*MSS* (n 1) [342]), and the *KRS* Court's conditioning its applicability on absence of proof before the Court, showing that Greece could not protect the claimant if transferred (*MSS*, ibid [343]).

[57] ibid [345].

[58] ibid [354].

[59] ibid.

[60] ibid [359] (citing *Saadi v Italy* (n 40) [132] for the proposition that the fact that many other persons are 'in the same situation as the applicant does not make the risk concerned any less individual where it is sufficiently real and probable').

[61] *MSS*, ibid [358] ('at the time of the applicant's expulsion the Belgian authorities knew or ought to have known that he had no guarantee that his asylum application would be seriously examined by the Greek authorities. They also had the means of refusing to transfer him').

[62] ibid [386].

[63] ibid.

[64] ibid [389].

[65] ibid [387].

[66] The Court reminded that 'while the effectiveness of a remedy does not depend on the certainty of a favourable outcome for the applicant, the lack of any prospect of obtaining adequate redress raises an issue under Article 13'. ibid [394] (citing *Kudła v Poland* App no 30210/96 (ECtHR, 26 October 2000)).

with Article 3 by failing to provide MSS with an effective remedy against the decision to transfer him to Greece.

With *MSS*, the ECtHR either clarified or modified the doctrine of *non-refoulement* that flows from Article 3 ECHR. The Court (re)asserted the primacy of Article 3 *non-refoulement* over international or supranational administrative cooperative frameworks such as the CEAS or the Dublin Regulation, emphasising that mutual trust between states must yield to evidence of a protection risk. The judgment also put Member States on notice that whether or not a person expresses a fear of *refoulement*, states are presumed to be aware of widely known dangers, or dangers they have been warned about.[67]

B. The End of 'Blind' Mutual Trust and the Evolving Significance of Systemic Deficiencies in EU Asylum Law

In *MSS*, the ECtHR reaffirmed that the principle of *non-refoulement* applies even to transfers of asylum applicants between Member States cooperating under EU law. In the Court's framing, the principle of mutual trust under EU law that the Dublin system rests on must yield to a risk of *refoulement*, and the states involved in a transfer share responsibility for protection against extra-EU *refoulement*. The first state in a potential chain (the state that would initiate a Dublin transfer) must assume protection responsibilities, if the next state in the chain (the responsible state per the Dublin criteria) might not fully assess the risk of the next transfer.

Although *MSS* was a decision of the ECtHR, the Court's reasoning is also relevant in the EU context. The EU asylum policy's legal basis explicitly refers to an obligation to comply with the principle of *non-refoulement*, the 1951 Refugee Convention, and 'other relevant treaties'.[68] Similarly to the ECHR, Article 4 of the EU Charter of Fundamental Rights (EUCFR) prohibits torture or inhuman or degrading treatment or punishment,[69] and Article 19 forbids removal, expulsion, or extradition to 'a State where there is a serious risk [of] the death penalty, torture or other inhuman or degrading treatment or punishment'.[70]

At the EU level, the case initially seemed to lead to a divergence of human rights standards via a 'systemic breach' criterion developed from the case law of the ECtHR. In *NS/ME*,[71] the CJEU mostly followed the *MSS* reasoning, clarifying

[67] ibid [346].

[68] See Treaty on the Functioning of the European Union [2012] OJ 326/47, Art 78(1).

[69] See EU Charter, Art 4.

[70] See ibid Art 19(2). Guild notes that Art 19 appears to be *lex specialis* to the general prohibition in Art 4, although the Court of Justice of the European Union (CJEU) nevertheless applied Art 4 in respect to removals from one Member State to another. E Guild, 'Article 19-Protection in the Event of Removal' in S Peers, T Hervey, J Kenner and E Ward, *The EU Charter of Fundamental Rights: A Commentary* (Hart Publishing, 2021) 575 referring to EU Charter, Art 52(3) and CJEU, Joined Cases C-411/10 and C-493/10 *NS and ME* ECLI:EU:C:2011:865.

[71] *NS and ME*, ibid 611.

that EU law precludes a Dublin transfer when there are 'substantial grounds for believing that the asylum seeker would be subject to inhuman or degrading treatment'. However, the CJEU also adopted 'systemic deficiency' as an element in assessing the compatibility of a Dublin transfer with fundamental rights. The CJEU again endorsed this approach in Opinion 2/13 on possible EU accession to the ECHR, citing the fundamental importance of mutual trust in the EU legal order, especially in the area of freedom, security, and justice (which includes the CEAS).[72] Thus, while apparently endorsing the *MSS* approach, the CJEU seemed to treat 'systemic breaches' as a threshold: Dublin returns were obligatory, unless there were systemic breaches of CEAS rules leading to a risk of violating Article 4 EUCFR (equivalent to Article 3 ECHR).[73]

The systemic deficiencies concept carries the potential to fracture the absolute prohibition of *refoulement*. For instance, in *Abdullahi*, the CJEU ruled that asylum seekers could only challenge Dublin deportations by 'pleading systemic deficiencies in the asylum procedure and in the conditions for the reception of applicants for asylum' amounting to a violation of Article 4 EUCFR.[74] The EU's recast Dublin Regulation, adopted in 2013, added further potential for conflated interpretations, prohibiting transfers where there 'are systemic flaws in the asylum procedure and in the reception conditions for applicants in that Member State, resulting in a risk of inhuman or degrading treatment'.[75] While this provision in itself does not require systemic deficiencies in order to rebut the presumption of safety in an EU state, the incorporation in legislation of language pointing to a particular factual situation and type of breach fuelled legal arguments in that direction.

In 2014, the ECtHR Grand Chamber in *Tarakhel* implicitly rejected systemic breaches, making no reference to such a test as being part of its established case law.[76] It also effectively rejected the need to demonstrate systemic breaches in the specific case, asserting that the source of the risk does not alter the level of protection guaranteed by the Convention or the obligations of the state ordering the person's removal.[77] The CJEU partially resolved this discord in *CK*, rejecting systemic deficiencies as the *sole reason* to substantiate a real risk of inhuman or degrading treatment in the framework of Dublin transfers.[78] The CJEU affirmed

[72] See C-2/13, *Opinion 2/13 on the Accession of the EU to the European Convention for the Protection of Human Rights and Fundamental Freedoms* ECLI:EU: C:2014:2454 [191]–[95]; B de Witte and Š Imamovic, 'Opinion 2/13 on Accession to the ECHR: Defending the EU Legal Order against a Foreign Human Rights Court' (2015) 40 *European Law Review* 683, 701–703; L Halleskov Storgaard, 'EU Law Autonomy versus European Fundamental Rights Protection – On Opinion 2/13 on EU Accession to the ECHR' (2015) 15 *Human Rights Law Review* 485, 507–10.

[73] *NS/ME* (n 71) [94].

[74] Case C-394/12 *Abdullahi v Bundesasylamt* ECLI:EU:C:2013:473 [60]. For a cogent critique, see M Hennessy, *The Dublin System and the Right to an Effective Remedy–The case of C-394/12 Abdullahi* (ECRE, 2013), available at www.asylumlawdatabase.eu/en/journal/dublin-system-and-right-effective-remedy--case-c-39412-abdullahi.

[75] Dublin Regulation 2013 (n 7) Art 3(2).

[76] *Tarakhel* App no 29217/12 (ECtHR, 04 November 2014) at [93]–[99].

[77] ibid [100]–[105].

[78] Case C-578/16 *CK and Others v Republika Slovenija* ECLI:EU:C:2017:127.

that for asylum seekers whose state of health is particularly serious, the transfer would *in itself* entail a real risk of inhuman or degrading treatment, irrespective of the quality of reception and care in the Member State of transfer.[79] Referring to the absolute nature of the prohibition of torture, inhuman or degrading treatment or punishment, the CJEU also highlighted that the introduction of a 'systemic deficiencies' clause in the Dublin Regulation did not exclude other exceptional grounds for halting transfers.[80]

In two further cases, *Jawo* and *Ibrahim*,[81] the CJEU clarified that the absolute nature of *non-refoulement* makes it immaterial whether the risk would occur during the transfer, in the asylum process, or upon recognition. Consequently, no differentiation could be made based on the procedural stage, ie, between asylum seekers or recognised international protection beneficiaries. In *Jawo*, the CJEU further held that deficiencies 'may be systematic or generalised, or […] may affect *certain groups of people*' (emphasis added),[82] in essence 'individualising' the criterion.

These interpretations render the systemic deficiencies criterion more compatible with the absolute prohibition of *refoulement*. However, a more principled approach would have been the abandonment of the criterion, in favour of an individualised assessment of both the circumstances of the applicant (including specific sources of vulnerability such as minority, or particular health challenges) in relation to the situation in the Member State of transfer (such as systemic deficiencies in the provision of material reception conditions). This individualised assessment would be due where there is an alleged real risk of inhuman or degrading treatment or punishment, or of violations of other rights involving a *non-refoulement* component.

The risks of the 'systemic deficiencies' criterion became evident in two more recent CJEU cases. In *Ministero dell'Interno*, the CJEU held that differences in the judicial practice of assessment of asylum claims between Member States did not warrant a halt of a Dublin transfer,[83] since they involved neither systemic deficiencies in the national asylum system, nor the specific vulnerability of an applicant. Yet, persistently differentiated interpretations of the refugee and subsidiary protection (a complementary status of protection under EU law) definitions could lead to similarly situated applicants finding themselves returnable in one Member State while they would benefit from international protection in another. Next, the *X* case concerned returns to Poland, where the applicant alleged pushback practices

[79] ibid [73].

[80] ibid [91]–[94].

[81] Case C-163/17 *Jawo v Bundesrepublik Deutschland* ECLI:EU:C:2019:218; Case C-318/17 *Ibrahim et al v Bundesrepublik Deutschland & Bundesrepublik Deutschland v Magamadov* ECLI:EU:C:2019:219; see also M Den Heijer, 'Transferring a Refugee to Homelessness in another Member State: Jawo and Ibrahim' (2020) 57 *Common Market Law Review* 539.

[82] *Jawo*, ibid [90].

[83] Joined Cases C 228/21, C 254/21, C 297/21, C 315/21 and C 328/21 *Ministero dell'Interno* ECLI:EU:C:2023:934 [130]–[142].

between Poland and Belarus. The CJEU held that the 'systemic deficiencies' criterion contains two cumulative conditions: i) a pattern of 'systemic flaws' and ii) their capacity to result in a risk, for the person concerned, of treatment contrary to the prohibition of torture, inhuman, or degrading treatment which the Court seemed to connect exclusively with extreme material poverty.[84] Thus, by focusing on the 'systemic deficiencies' criterion the Court failed to engage with the risk of indirect *refoulement* via pushbacks.

In conclusion, the CJEU only partially adopted into EU law the main legal conclusions of *MSS*. The CJEU eventually accepted that specific vulnerabilities of the applicant could be an additional basis for halting Dublin transfers, and somewhat relativised the systemic deficiencies criterion by considering that they could affect only specific groups. However, the CJEU has not definitively abandoned the systemic deficiencies criterion in favour of an individualised assessment of personal circumstances. Thus, it has not yet taken the opportunity to buttress *non-refoulement* as an international principle that forms a core part of EU law.

IV. Socioeconomic Deprivation of Asylum Seekers as Torture, Inhuman or Degrading Treatment

The ECtHR has long grappled with the contours of Article 3 ECHR, which prohibits torture and inhuman or degrading treatment or punishment, and in particular to assess whether the situation of individuals who are living in, or are to be returned to, destitution or extreme poverty could fall within its scope.[85] Although the Court has explicitly stated that the Convention does not guarantee as such socioeconomic rights,[86] it has also said that an interpretation of the Convention may extend into the sphere of social and economic rights.[87] More recently, the Court noted that it cannot exclude that situations of serious deprivation or want would be incompatible with human dignity.[88]

In *MSS*, the ECtHR asserted that asylum seekers on the whole are 'a particularly underprivileged and vulnerable population group in need of special protection'.[89]

[84] Case C-392/22 *X* ECLI:EU:C:2024:195 [57]–[65].

[85] An extensive analysis of the relevant pre-*MSS* case law of the Court goes beyond the scope of this contribution. However, see: C O'Cinneide, 'A Modest Proposal: Destitution, State Responsibility and the European Convention on Human Rights' (2008) *European Human Rights Law Review* 583; M Hesselman, 'Sharing International Responsibility for Poor Migrants? An Analysis of Extra-territorial Socio-Economic Human Rights Law' (2013) 25 *European Journal of Social Security* 187; K Wouters, *International Legal Standards for the Protection from Refoulement* (Intersentia, 2009).

[86] See *Pancenko v Latvia* App no 40772/98 (ECtHR, 28 October 1999).

[87] *Airey v Ireland* App no 6289/73 (ECtHR, 9 October 1979) at [26]. See also I Leijten, 'Defining the Scope of Economic and Social Guarantees in the Case Law of the ECtHR' in E Brems and J Gerards (eds), *Shaping Rights in the ECHR: The role of the European Court of Human Rights in Determining the Scope of Human Rights* (Cambridge University Press, 2014) 109.

[88] *Budina v Russia* App no 45603.05 (ECtHR, 18 June 2009) (admissibility).

[89] *MSS* (n 1) [251].

Following this pronouncement on vulnerability, the Court considered the situation of MSS, an asylum seeker who, due to state inaction, '[f]ound himself for several months, living in the street, with no resources or access to sanitary facilities, and without any means of providing for his essential needs'.[90] He experienced an 'ever-present fear of being attacked and robbed'[91] and a 'total lack of any likelihood of his situation improving'.[92] As a result, the applicant was 'the victim of humiliating treatment showing a lack of respect for his dignity'[93] severe enough to violate Article 3 of the ECHR.

In reaching this conclusion, the Court emphasised that Greece had enacted national legislation transposing the Reception Conditions Directive, creating positive obligations towards asylum seekers.[94] Vedsted-Hansen has convincingly argued that this reasoning is in line with the Court's general method of interpretation, according to which various international standards suggesting European consensus on a matter can provide an interpretative basis if the scope and extent of ECHR obligations seem unclear or in need of reconsideration.[95] Further authors considered this element crucial and critiqued the Court, arguing that reliance on vulnerability would tie the scope of Article 3 to the legality of the applicant's migration status.[96]

These pronouncements make *MSS* a landmark case in terms of viewing socioeconomic deprivation as a fundamental rights violation.[97] Ensuring socioeconomic rights of asylum seekers through human rights mechanisms, however, also carries risks. The Court's approach risked fragmenting human rights obligations towards asylum seekers between EU Member States and other Council of Europe members. It also carries the risk of exceptionalism, creating an extremely high threshold for proclaiming a violation of Article 3 based on socioeconomic deprivation. From the perspective of international refugee law, ascertaining states' obligations towards asylum seekers through mechanisms geared to protect human rights, which cannot directly engage with the 1951 Refugee Convention standards, risks diminishing the importance of that Convention and its protection mandate. This section outlines the impact of the *MSS* case, and comments on the extent to which such risks have materialised.

[90] ibid [263].

[91] ibid [254].

[92] ibid.

[93] ibid [263].

[94] See ibid [250].

[95] See J Vedsted-Hansen, 'Reception Conditions as Human Rights: Pan-European Standard or Systemic Deficiencies' in V Chetail, P De Bruycker and F Maiani (eds), *Reforming the Common European Asylum System: The New European Refugee Law* (Brill, 2016) 317–52, 328.

[96] S Da Lomba, 'Vulnerability, Irregular Migrants' Health-Related Rights and the European Court of Human Rights' (2014) 21 *European Journal of Health Law* 339–64, 358; L Lavrysen, 'European Asylum Law and the ECHR: An Uneasy Coexistence' (2012) 4 *Goettingen Journal of International Law* 217–62, 250.

[97] See also, I Leijten, *Core Socio-Economic Rights and the European Court of Human Rights* (Cambridge University Press, 2017) 49–52.

Since the *MSS* decision, asylum seekers have continued to raise judicial challenges linked to socioeconomic deprivation, mostly by arguing that they have particular vulnerabilities. However, states have tried to overcome vulnerability arguments via securing diplomatic assurances that individual asylum seekers will be guaranteed access to appropriate reception facilities.[98]

More broadly, the element of exclusive control of the state over the individual, whether due to deprivation of liberty, other institutionalisation, or restrictions attached to migration status, seems to be emerging as a key prerequisite for a finding of a rights violation on the basis of socioeconomic deprivation.[99] Slingenberg has conceptualised this line of ECtHR case law through the concept of freedom as non-domination, as developed in (neo)republican theory,[100] arguing that the Court is only willing to protect against situations of destitution if there is evidence of individuals being dominated by the state.[101]

In the migration field, this means that the ECtHR engages with an applicant's formal migration status. For example, in *Hunde*, the Court rejected as inadmissible the application of a failed asylum seeker squatting in an indoor park in the Netherlands and facing severe destitution, noting that:

> the applicant was a failed asylum-seeker at the material time, the uncertainty he found himself in was inherently different from M.S.S. in that it was not linked to the Netherlands authorities' assessment of his asylum request.[102]

Rules under the EU's New Pact on Migration and Asylum legislative package, in force at the time of writing but not yet applicable, even contemplate planned destitution of asylum seekers as a coercive means of migration management. For example, asylum seekers who undertake secondary movements will face penalties in respect of asylum procedures and reception conditions.[103] The compatibility of these provisions with EU fundamental rights, and with CJEU case law, is dubious.[104] According

[98] See, eg, *Ali and ors v Switzerland & Italy* App no 30474/14 (ECtHR, October 27 2016); *AME v Netherlands* App no 51428/10 (ECtHR, January 13 2015); *FH v Greece* App no 78456/11 (ECtHR, 31 July 2014); *Amadou v Greece* App no 37991/11 (ECtHR, 4 February 2016).

[99] For a panorama of the Court's case law on vulnerability in relation to ill-treatment, see C Heri, *Responsive Human Rights: Vulnerability, Ill Treatment and the ECHR* (Hart Publishing, 2021) 31–120.

[100] L Slingenberg, 'The Right Not to be Dominated: The Case Law of the European Court of Human Rights on Migrants' Destitution' (2019) 19 *Human Rights Law Review* 291–314.

[101] ibid.

[102] *Hunde v Netherlands* App no 17931/16 (ECtHR, 5 July 2016) [56].

[103] See respectively, Regulation (EU) 2024/1348 of the European Parliament and of the Council of 14 May 2024 establishing a common procedure for international protection in the Union and repealing Directive 2013/32/EU, [2024] OJ L2024/1348 (Asylum Procedures Regulation) Art 41(1)(f) in combination with Regulation (EU) 2024/1351 of the European Parliament and of the Council of 14 May 2024 on asylum and migration management, amending Regulations (EU) 2021/1147 and (EU) 2021/1060 and repealing Regulation (EU) No 604/2013 (Asylum and Migration Management Regulation) Art 36(3) for procedural sanctions, as well as Asylum and Migration Management Regulation (EU) 2024/1351, Art 18 in combination with the Reception Conditions Directive 2024 (n 12) Art 21 for sanctions pertaining to reception conditions.

[104] C-79/13 *Saciri* EU:C:2014:103 [48]; *Jawo* (n 81) [92]; C-233/18 *Haqbin*, ECLI:EU:C:2019:956 [47]. See also E Tsourdi, 'Asylum Reception Conditions Directive 2013/33/EU' in D Thym and K Hailbronner (eds),

to the CJEU, complete withdrawal of reception conditions that would render asylum seekers destitute would contravene the principle of human dignity and the prohibition of inhuman and degrading treatment, which are absolute rights that admit no limitation or derogation. Only limitations of reception conditions would be possible, while asylum seekers' basic needs (eg housing and subsistence) must be ensured. Pronouncements of international treaty bodies and regional committees on economic, social, and cultural rights also adopt such argumentation.[105]

Scholars have critiqued the ECtHR approach through different lenses. Tsourdi and Costello argued that insisting on individualised assessment when there is clear evidence of generalised deficiencies or systemic flaws in socioeconomic conditions or asylum procedures puts too high a burden on applicants, while at the same time rendering the concept of systemic breach empty.[106] Morris,[107] Heri,[108] and Kagiaros[109] have argued that the ECtHR's approach leads to an incomplete view of vulnerability which permits unequal treatment of claimants facing the same level of deprivation. In addition, Peroni and Timmer identified that the Court's approach can reinforce vulnerability by essentialising, stigmatising, victimising, and paternalising certain groups.[110]

Scholars have proposed different legal solutions and normative perspectives to overcome the limitations of the ECtHR's case law. Morris argues that the political theory of care can transform the Court's vulnerability analysis while empowering the care receiver.[111] Heri advances a departure from the vulnerable/non-vulnerable binary by constructing vulnerability as a spectrum and engaging with both an applicant's vulnerability and resilience through a multi-tiered test.[112] This echoes the ideas of Baumgärtel on the principle of 'migratory vulnerability', which moves away from a group-based approach to a notion of vulnerability as situational and

EU Immigration and Asylum Law: Article-by-Article Commentary (Beck/Hart Publishing, 2022) 1540–1638, 1617–18. The Pact provisions are at the very least contradictory. Article 18(1) of the Asylum and Migration Management Regulation (n 103) enshrines both that asylum seekers are only entitled to reception conditions in the responsible Member State, and that the provision is 'without prejudice to the need to ensure a standard of living in accordance with Union law, including the Charter, and international obligations'.

[105] See for analysis J Wessels, 'Planned Destitution as a Policy Tool to Control Migration in the EU: Socio-Economic Deprivation and International Human Rights Law' (*EU Migration and Asylum Law and Policy*, 17 May 2023), available at https://eumigrationlawblog.eu/planned-destitution-as-a-policy-tool-to-control-migration-in-the-eu-socio-economic-deprivation-and-international-human-rights-law/.

[106] E Tsourdi and C Costello, '"Systemic Violations" in EU Asylum Law: Cover or Catalyst?' (2023) 24 *German Law Journal* 982–94, 985–88.

[107] K Morris, 'Vulnerability, Care Ethics and the Protection of Socioeconomic Rights via Article 3 ECHR' (2023) 23 *Human Rights Law Review* 1–18, 4.

[108] Heri (n 99) 88.

[109] D Kagiaros, 'Vulnerability as a Path to a "Social Minimum"? An Analysis of ECtHR Jurisprudence' in T Kotkas, I Leijten and F Pennings (eds), *Specifying and Securing A Social Minimum in the Battle Against Poverty* (Hart Publishing, 2019) 245–60, 245–47.

[110] See L Peroni and A Timmer, 'Vulnerable Groups: The Promise of an Emerging Concept in European Human Rights Convention Law' (2013) 11(4) *International Journal of Constitutional Law* 1056.

[111] Morris (n 107) 13–17.

[112] Heri (n 99) 225–27.

socially induced.[113] On this basis, Baumgärtel and Ganty explore the potential of the ECHR's non-discrimination provision, Article 14, to address discrimination based on migratory vulnerability.[114] Finally, Ferolla Vallandro do Valle recognises an autonomous basis for *non-refoulement* obligations in treaty provisions on economic, social and cultural rights.[115] We consider that a principled approach would be to centre protection on an inviolable minimum socioeconomic core inherent in the prohibition of torture, inhuman or degrading treatment, regardless of migration status.

V. Conclusion

The impact of *MSS v Belgium and Greece* is far reaching, extending to international refugee law, EU asylum law, international and regional (Council of Europe) human rights law, as well as EU constitutional and fundamental rights law. The case solidified the *non-refoulement* principle in two seminal ways. First, it reaffirmed that regional cooperation, even in a highly integrated regulatory environment such as the EU, cannot entail 'blind' mutual trust arrangements among states that do not take into account the actual situation on the ground in relation to fundamental rights. Next, it was the first case where the ECtHR held that extreme socioeconomic deprivation could amount to a violation of the prohibition of torture, inhuman, or degrading treatment or punishment. Thus, knowingly returning asylum applicants to where they would face a real risk of such socioeconomic deprivation would constitute unlawful *refoulement*.

Nevertheless, the *MSS* case also leaves many questions unanswered and has led to subsequent case law that has been critiqued from various angles. The early discrepancy that seemed to occur between the ECtHR and CJEU with the emergence of a 'systemic deficiencies' threshold to contest intra-EU transfers of asylum seekers was only partially resolved. By prioritising the functioning of the principle of mutual trust among Member States over the absolute prohibition of *refoulement*, the CJEU's approach could lead to risks of *refoulement*, for example indirect *refoulement* due to variances in national asylum procedures or divergent interpretations of the refugee and subsidiary protection definitions.

Additional problem areas have also emerged through the ECtHR's selective use of the concept of vulnerability in linking socioeconomic deprivation to the prohibition of torture, inhuman, or degrading treatment or punishment. By insisting

[113] M Baumgärtel, 'Facing the Challenge of Migratory Vulnerability in the European Court of Human Rights' (2020) 38 *Netherlands Quarterly of Human Rights* 12–29.

[114] M Baumgärtel and S Ganty, 'On the Basis of Migratory Vulnerability: Augmenting Article 14 of the European Convention on Human Rights in the Context of Migration' (2024) *International Journal of Law in Context* 92–112.

[115] M Ferolla Vallandro do Valle, 'Fleeing Deprivation: Deducing Non-Refoulement Obligations from Economic, Social and Cultural Rights' (2024) 36 *International Journal of Refugee Law* 353–76.

on the element of exclusive control of the state over the individual, the ECtHR has generated differing standards in relation to similarly situated claimants. Moreover, by hinging on the applicant's migration status, the Court risks premising fundamental rights violations on malleable administrative rules. This approach carries numerous risks in an era where planned destitution is envisaged as a migration management technique.

10

Kituo Cha Sheria and Others v The Attorney General [2013]: Betwixt Executive Opposition and Judicial Affirmation of Refugee Rights

SAMUEL BERHANU WOLDEMARIAM*

I. The Judiciary and the Protection of Refugee Rights in Kenya

Kituo Cha Sheria and Others v The Attorney General[1] (hereinafter *Kituo Cha Sheria*) is a landmark refugee judgment from the High Court of Kenya where the judiciary applied human rights protections of the Kenyan Constitution and international law to courageously assert the protections that refugees and asylum seekers are owed. The case unfolded as a challenge against a government directive that sought to close urban centres for the processing of asylum claims and proposed to relocate all refugees and asylum seekers hosted in urban centres to refugee camps.[2] This attempt to force all refugees living in urban areas to relocate to camps, or to permanently close refugee camps, would not be the last such in Kenya.[3] However, *Kituo Cha Sheria* is the first of cases where, amidst a political turmoil and the rising rhetoric of securitisation of refugee protection, the judiciary stood as a

* The author wishes to extend his appreciation to the editors for the feedback provided on earlier drafts, for organising an excellent workshop discussing the landmark cases and for the excellent support provided throughout the process of getting this publication ready.

[1] *Kituo Cha Sheria and Others v The Attorney General* (*Kituo Cha Sheria*) [2013] eKLR (High Court of Kenya).

[2] The Government directive was published in the *Daily Nation* on 18 December 2012. See Order of DS Majanja in *Kituo Cha Sheria v The Attorney General* (High Court (Kenya), Petition 19 of 2013, 23 January 2013.

[3] The Government has for example threatened to close refugee camps in 2016, 2019 and 2022. H Misigo Amatsimbi, 'Refugee Protection in Kenya' (2024) 16 *Journal of Policy and Development Studies* 245, 254; C Wanjiku Kihato, 'Securitization is (Normal) Politics: Epistemological Insights from Kenya's Forced Migration and Security Experience' (2025) 13(2) *Migration Studies* 1, 1–2.

moderating force against the political scapegoating of refugees and asylum seekers by the executive.

In this regard, *Kituo Cha Sheria* introduced a turn to refugee rights in Kenya's refugee protection policy by ensuring that rights guaranteed for Kenyan citizens were also extended to refugees. The traditional approach to refugee protection considered refugees and asylum-seekers as outsiders whose presence in Kenyan territory was temporary and their circumstance was deserving of sympathy. This was particularly true for the pre-1990 period where the number of refugees and asylum-seekers was low and the country had a relatively liberal approach towards their protection.[4] However, a policy shift came in the early 1990s following the rise in the number of refugees and asylum seekers, making their growing presence in the country suspect.[5] This led to a perception of refugees as national security risks and a turn to encampment as the primary policy response; narratives and policies that have shaped refugee protection in Kenya since the early 1990s.[6] This was the pre-*Kituo Cha Sheria* policy environment, where refugees were accommodated in large refugee camps, such as the Dadaab camp that hosts more than 400,000 refugees and asylum seekers. Following the 2011 intervention of Kenyan forces in Somalia, the country became a target for attacks from *Al-Shabaab*.[7] This further heightened the scepticism against Somali refugees, their association with terrorism, and a renewed securitised approach towards them.[8]

However, Kenya is host to a diverse set of refugee populations mainly from East and Central Africa. As of December 2024, Kenya hosted 823,926 refugees and asylum seekers.[9] Of these, 604,263 were refugees while 219,663 were asylum seekers.[10] In terms of country of origin, refugees and asylum seekers from Somalia make up 54 per cent of the total, followed by South Sudanese refugees who make up 24.5 per cent.[11] As per the report, 44 per cent of refugees and asylum seekers reside in the *Dadaab* refugee camp, 40 per cent in *Kakuma* and 16 per cent in urban areas.[12]

[4] K Hargrave, I Mosel and A Leach, 'Public Narratives and Attitudes towards Refugees and other Migrants: Kenya Country Profile' (ODI, 2020) 7, available at https://media.odi.org/documents/kenya_migration_country_profile_final.pdf.

[5] ibid 8.

[6] N Omata, 'Refugee Livelihoods: A Comparative Analysis of Nairobi and Kakuma Camp in Kenya' (2021) 45 *Disasters* 865, 869; Refugee Consortium of Kenya, *Myths and Truths: The Facts about Refugee Self-Sufficiency and Economic Contribution in Nairobi* (Refugee Consortium of Kenya, 2015) 4; L Juma, 'Protection of Rights of Urban Refugees in Kenya: Revisiting Kituo Cha Sheria v The Attorney General' (2018) 33 *Southern African Public Law* 1, 4; R Jaji, 'Historical Complexities and Transformations of Refugee Policies in Kenya and Tanzania' (2022) 69 *Africa Today* 88, 99.

[7] J Lind, P Mutahi and M Oosterom, '"Killing a Mosquito with a Hammer": Al-Shabaab Violence and State Security Responses in Kenya' (2017) 5 *Peacebuilding* 118, 118.

[8] See generally, L Freeman, 'They're All Terrorists: The Securitisation of Asylum in Kenya' (2019) 2 *Extremisms in Africa* 92–123.

[9] Operational Data Portal, 'Refugees and Asylum-Seekers in Kenya' (United Nations High Commissioner for Refugees (UNHCR), 2024), available at https://data.unhcr.org/en/country/ken.

[10] ibid.

[11] ibid.

[12] ibid.

While *Kituo Cha Sheria* was focused on challenging a specific government directive, it nevertheless raised fundamental questions of law that were relevant to situating Kenya's obligations as a host country in the proper perspective of the national Constitution and regional and international law rules pertaining to the protection and assistance of refugees and asylumseekers. In this respect, the case challenged the *status quo* and its foundations, such as the policy of encampment[13] and the hitherto unquestioned power of the executive branch of the Government in refugee policy-making.[14] It also strategically promoted a human rights-based approach to protection and refugee policy-making. However, *Kituo Cha Sheria* was just the start of the move towards overturning narratives and approaches built over decades.

The judgment in *Kituo Cha Sheria* did not bring about immediate overriding changes to the entire system of refugee protection. On the contrary, it prompted government effort to ramp up the securitisation narrative. These government actions formed the subject of further strategic litigations.[15] However, what it succeeded in doing was unsettling the *status quo* and promoting an alternative human rights-based approach that the judiciary, refugees, human rights advocates, non-governmental organisations (NGOs) and international organisations can hold onto to continue their advocacy for change.

With the adoption of the Refugees Act,[16] there is now a more favourable environment for refugee protection in Kenya. Inter alia, the Refugee Act has solidified 'refugee self-reliance',[17] expanded 'socioeconomic rights and opportunities for refugees',[18] and toned down encampment 'as the centrepiece of Kenya's refugee policy'.[19] Kenya was selected as one of the 15 original roll-out countries for the Comprehensive Refugee Response Framework (CRRF) and the adoption of the Refugee Act was partly prompted by pledges to implement the CRRF. The CRRF forms part of the Global Compact on Refugees and serves as a framework to guide responses to large-scale movements, promote international co-operation, and enhance responsibility-sharing.

It is important to also acknowledge Kenya's contribution to refugee protection. As one of the largest refugee hosting countries in Africa, Kenya has and continues

[13] Misigo Amatsimbi (n 3) 247.

[14] See, eg, how the treatment of Somalia refugees in Kenya is marked by violence, arbitrary policy enforcements, and harmful discourse perpetrated by government actors: Freeman (n 8).

[15] See, eg, *Coalition for Reform and Democracy (CORD) & 2 others v Republic of Kenya & 10 others* eKLR (High Court of Kenya): finding the limitation of the number of refugees in Kenya under s 48 of the Security Laws (Amendment) Act unconstitutional; *Kenya National Commission on Human Rights & Kituo Cha Sheria v The Attorney General & others* eKLR: finding unconstitutional the decision of the Government to close the Dadaab refugee camp and repatriate all refugees in the camp to the frontiers of their country.

[16] The Refugees Act, Kenya Gazette Supplement No 210 (Acts No 10), 2021 (Kenya).

[17] E Maloba and S Merve Is, *Refugee Policy in the Horn of Africa: What Can Development Partners Learn from Kenya's Polict Change?* (Florence School of Transnational Governance, 2024) 5.

[18] G Ogutu, 'Between Integration and Separation: The Impact of Legal and Policy Restrictions on Refugees in Kenya' (2024) 1 *Legal Empowerment Journal* 65, 69.

[19] M Jacobi and R Jaji, *Refugee Policy and Selective Implementation of the Comprehensive Refugee Response Framework in Kenya* (German Institute of Development and Sustainability (IDOS), 2022) 3.

to serve as a destination for many displaced persons who flee from internal and inter-state conflicts to seek sanctuary in its relative political stability.[20] While the country's refugee policy has gone through several cycles of liberalisation and restriction[21] and much needs to be improved in fully achieving its protection responsibility, Kenya continues to shoulder significant regional and international responsibility as a refugee host country.

In the following section, I will provide a summary of the *Kituo Cha Sheria* decision followed by a discussion of the contemporaneous and subsequent reception of the decision in Kenya and outside. I will then outline the features that distinguish *Kituo Cha Sheria* as a landmark refugee judgment. These include the judicial readiness shown to interpret and apply the relevant law without undue deference to the executive, the robust application of human rights principles, the role of strategic litigation and the authoritative voice of the United Nations High Commissioner for Refugees (UNHCR).

II. Summary of Case and Decision

Kituo Cha Sheria and Others v Attorney General was a consolidated petition from *Kituo Cha Sheria*, an NGO, and seven refugees who lived in urban areas in Kenya. The petitioners' action challenged a government Directive issued in December 2012 that sought to 'stop reception, registration and close down all registration centres in urban areas with immediate effect'.[22] The Directive communicated the Government's intention to move all refugees residing in urban areas to refugee camps and asked refugees from Somalia to report to *Dadaab* refugee camps and others to report to *Kakuma* refugee camps. The Government devised a 'quick impact project' to be 'carried out through a Rapid Results Initiative in 100 days'.[23] It also established an inter-ministerial committee, headed by the Department of Refugee Affairs, to 'oversee and guide the relocation process'.[24]

The petitioners challenged the government Directive on several grounds, including its constitutionality and compliance with Kenya's Refugee Act,[25] the 1969 Organisation of African Unity Convention Governing the Specific

[20] Amatsimbi (n 3) 246; E Mogire, 'Refugee Realities: Refugee Rights versus State Security in Kenya and Tanzania' (2009) 26 *Transformation* 15, 16.

[21] As noted earlier, the pre-1990 refugee policy in Kenya is often described as being welcoming owing to the small number of refugees that the country hosted. However, several episodes of mass influx of forcibly displaced persons in the early 1990s triggered a more restrictive response. Mogire, ibid 16; J Milner, 'A History of Asylum in Kenya and Tanzania: Understanding the Drivers of Domestic Refugee Policy' (2019) 15 *Monde(s)* 69, 73.

[22] *Kituo Cha Sheria* (n 1). The government Directive was published in the *Daily Nation* on 18 December 2012. Order of DS Majanja in *Kituo Cha Sheria v The Attorney General* (n 2).

[23] ibid 5.

[24] ibid 4.

[25] The relevant act at the time was the Refugees Act of 2006.

Aspects of Refugee Problems in Africa (OAU Refugee Convention),[26] and 1951 United Nations Convention relating to the Status of Refugees (1951 Refugee Convention).[27] On the question of constitutionality, the petitioners argued that the Directive violated the requirements under Article 47 of the Constitution for administrative actions to be made in an 'expeditious, efficient, lawful, reasonable and procedurally fair' manner.[28] The petitioners also alleged that the Directive violated the right of refugees and asylum seekers to dignity, movement, a fair administrative action and the prohibition against arbitrary and discriminatory actions under Articles 28, 39, 47 and 27 respectively.

One of the main contentions of the petitioners related to the blanket nature of the Directive. The Directive sought to relocate *all* refugees living in urban areas irrespective of their individual circumstances and conditions. The respondent argued that the Directive complied with statutory authority and was issued 'in the interest of promoting the welfare and protection of asylum seekers and refugees'.[29] The respondent also argued that urban registration of refugees and asylum seekers was a provisional arrangement and that it had no basis in the Refugee Act of 2006.[30] On the contrary, the respondent argued, the Refugee Act envisions an encampment policy and the application of sections 16, 17(f) and 25(f) of the Act 'presupposes that all refugees and asylum seekers shall ordinarily reside in gazetted refugee camps'.[31] The respondent further argued that the Department of Refugee Affairs had the legal mandate to implement the Directive and that it had, though 'unnecessary', consulted with stakeholders out of courtesy.[32] The respondent therefore requested the Court to dismiss the petition.

The High Court started its analysis by outlining the constitutional provisions implicated in the case, the relevance of international law to the case and the importance of a purposive approach to the interpretation of the relevant constitutional provisions.[33] The Court framed the following two issues for determination:

- Whether the petitioners have established violation of their rights and fundamental freedoms or rights and fundamental freedoms of refugees; and
- If so, whether such violation can be justified under Article 24 of the Constitution.

The Court approached the first issue through an evaluation of whether the government Directive violated the provisions of the Constitution and the law. The assessment began with an evaluation of the freedom of movement of refugees and

[26] Assembly of Heads of State and Government, Organization of African Unity Convention Governing the Specific Aspects of Refugee Problems in Africa (1969).

[27] UN General Assembly, 1951 Convention relating to the Status of Refugees (1951 Refugee Convention), United Nations, Treaty Series, 189:137, 28 July 1951.

[28] *Kituo Cha Sheria* (n 1) 6.

[29] ibid 11.

[30] ibid.

[31] ibid 12.

[32] ibid.

[33] ibid 13–15.

the policy of encampment under Kenyan law. After reviewing the Constitution and relevant international instruments, including the 1951 Refugee Convention, the OAU Refugee Convention, and the International Covenant on Civil and Political Rights (ICCPR), the Court concluded that Article 39 of the Constitution neither 'expressly limit[s] the right of refugees to move within Kenya' nor 'prohibit refugees from residing anywhere in Kenya'.[34]

With respect to the respondent's argument that section 17(f) of the Refugee Act requires all refugees and asylum seekers to ordinarily reside in camps, the Court noted that the said section merely enumerates the responsibilities of a refugee camp officer and 'does not require that all refugees and asylum seekers to ordinarily reside in camps nor does it preclude the State from providing refugee services in urban centres'.[35] The Court also noted that the 'closure of registration centres in urban centres has deleterious effects of the rights and fundamental of urban refugees'.[36]

The Court then scrutinised the government Directive based on the right to fair administrative action. While the Court conceded that the Commissioner of Refugees (a post within the Kenyan Government administration) has the legal mandate to make administrative decisions, it also noted that such decisions need to comply with the right to expeditious, efficient, lawful, reasonable and procedurally fair administrative action as stipulated under Article 47 of the Constitution.[37] The Court noted that the government Directive was 'a blanket directive' that had the effect of 'taking away accrued or acquired rights without due process of the law', and was therefore inconsistent with the Refugee Act and international law.[38] The Court found that the Directive was indiscriminate in its application and that the failure to consider the individual circumstances of refugees rendered it 'arbitrary and discriminative'.[39] Moreover, the Court noted the impact that the Directive would have on a range of rights, such as the right to work and the security of the person.

The Court then assessed the Directive's compliance with the right to dignity as enshrined under Article 28 of the Constitution and in international human rights law. While the Constitution does not provide a definition of dignity, courts have analysed that the right to dignity has a 'foundational constitutional value'[40] and 'constitutes the basis and the inspiration for the recognition that is given to other more specific protections that are afforded by the Bill of Rights'.[41] With regard to the proposed implementation of the Directive, the Court noted that it would uproot refugees and asylum seekers from their homes, family, work and neighbourhood. In finding that

[34] ibid 24.
[35] ibid 25.
[36] ibid.
[37] ibid 26.
[38] ibid 27.
[39] ibid.
[40] *MWK & another v Attorney General & 4 others* [2017] KEHC 1496 (KLR).
[41] *Kituo Cha Sheria* (n 1) 28.

the Directive violated the right to dignity of refugees and asylum seekers, the Court concurred with the petitioner's argument that the impacts of the Directive need:

> to be understood against the backdrop of appreciating the vulnerability of refugees and the suffering they have endured, the trauma and insecurity associated with persecution and flight, the need and struggle to be independent and the need to provide for themselves and their families and the struggle to establish normalcy in a foreign [country].[42]

The Court next evaluated whether the Directive breached the *non-refoulement* obligation under Article 18 of the Refugee Act and international law. The Court noted that the principle of *non-refoulement* is a 'cornerstone of refugee protection and has gained the status of international customary law' and that by virtue of Article 2(5) of the Constitution, forms part of the law of Kenya.[43] Section 18 of the Refugee Act also provides for the application of the principle. The Court also cited Article 33(1) of the 1951 Refugee Convention, Article 13 of the ICCPR and Article 3 of the Convention Against Torture and Other Cruel, Inhuman or Degrading Treatment or Punishment as international instruments that forbid *refoulement*.

An official government letter dated 16 January 2013 had previously stated that: 'The Government intends to move all refugees residing in Urban areas to the *Daadab* and *Kakuma* Refugee Camps and ultimately to their home countries after necessary arrangements are put in place.'[44]

The Court noted that the proposed manner of 'implementation of the overall policy of relocation and encampment … may violate the State international refugee protection obligations'.[45] The Court further noted that the 'aggressive pursuit of such a policy may have the effect of constructively repatriating urban refugees back to the countries from which they had fled'.[46] The Court concluded that the Directive violated the principle of *non-refoulement*.

Having concluded that the Directive was unreasonable, and violated the rights of refugees including freedom of movement, the right to dignity and the principle of *non-refoulement*, the Court then proceeded to inquire whether the Directive could be justified as a legitimate limitation of rights under Article 24 of the Constitution.[47]

[42] ibid 29.
[43] ibid 30.
[44] ibid 31.
[45] ibid.
[46] ibid.
[47] Article 24(1) of the Constitution states:

> (1) A right or fundamental freedom in the Bill of Rights shall not be limited except by law, and then only to the extent that the limitation is reasonable and justifiable in an open and democratic society based on human dignity, equality and freedom, taking into account all relevant factors, including—
>
> (a) the nature of the right or fundamental freedom;
> (b) the importance of the purpose of the limitation;
> (c) the nature and extent of the limitation;
> (d) the need to ensure that the enjoyment of rights and fundamental freedoms by any individual does not prejudice the rights and fundamental freedoms of others; and
> (e) the relation between the limitation and its purpose and whether there are less restrictive means to achieve the purpose.

Under Article 24 of the Constitution, the state bears the burden of proving that the limitation of rights is justified. In this respect, the Government stated that the Directive was issued 'in the interest of promoting the welfare and protection of asylum [seekers] and refugees'.[48] However, no evidence was supplied in support of this alleged rationale of the Directive. Upon review of official letters from the relevant government bodies and the proposed manner of implementation of the Directive, the Court concluded that national security was 'the rationale for the policy of relocation and encampment' rather than this stated aim.[49]

The Court acknowledged that national security could be a valid rationale for limiting rights. However, to meet the standard of constitutionality, the Government needed to 'demonstrate that in the circumstances, such as the present case, a specific person's presence or activity in the urban areas is causing danger to the country and that his or her encampment would alleviate the menace'.[50]

The Court further stated that 'tarring a group of person[s] known as refugees with a broad brush of criminality' was not enough to justify a policy that was also disproportionate in the suffering that it would occasion compared to the goal it sought to achieve.[51] The Court applied strict scrutiny requiring the Government to demonstrate 'a real connection' between the refugees sought to be relocated or repatriated and the danger to national security and to show how the proposed measures would 'alleviate the insecurity'.[52]

The Court finally quashed the government Directive, having concluded that:

> the Government Directive is a threat to the petitioners' fundamental rights and freedoms including the freedom of movement, right to dignity and infringes on the right to fair and administrative action and is a threat to the *non-refoulement* principle incorporated by section 18 of the *Refugees Act, 2006*. It is [*sic*] also violates the State responsibility to persons in a vulnerable situations. I have also concluded that the policy intended to be implemented by the Government Directive cannot be justified under Article 24.[53]

III. Decision in Contemporaneous and Subsequent Context

As profound as the *Kituo Cha Sheria* decision was, the contemporaneous reception of the case was gloomy, having received little to no attention among refugee scholars,

[48] *Kituo Cha Sheria* (n 1) 36.

[49] ibid 37.

[50] ibid 38–39.

[51] ibid 39.

[52] ibid. The level of scrutiny the Court applied is akin to the strict scrutiny standard adopted by the Supreme Court of the United States where 'governmental action is not presumed to be constitutional, and will not be upheld by the Court unless shown to be necessarily related to a compelling state interest.': JM Shaman, 'Cracks in the Structure: The Coming Breakdown of the Levels of Scrutiny' (1984) 45 *Ohio State Law Journal* 161.

[53] *Kituo Cha Sheria* (n 1) 42.

institutions and advocates at the time of the decision. The few that noticed it took the decision with mixed feelings, considering it as 'a major step forward in protecting a refugee's right to freedom of movement and the right to work'[54] while anticipating severe difficulties in its practical implementation. In its *amicus curiae* brief, the UNHCR indicated that even before its official implementation, the Directive had resulted in harm, suffering and abuse of protection.[55] Human Rights Watch and scholars made similar observations.[56] Despite the uncertainties, by enjoining the Government from implementing the Directive while the case was pending and ultimately quashing it, the decision brought a measure of relief to the refugees and asylum seekers that stood to be impacted by its implementation. This stopped enforcement bodies from forcibly deporting refugees and asylum seekers to camps. However, this legal victory was short lived and prompted further governmental action and litigation.

In this regard, three significant developments are worth highlighting in the aftermath of the *Kituo Cha Sheria* decision. The first, and perhaps a more profound event relates to the decision of the High Court in *Samow Mumin Mohamed & 9 others v Cabinet Secretary Ministry of Interior Security and Co-Ordination & 2 others* (*Samow*).[57] The *Samow* decision is important for several reasons as it relates to the *Kituo Cha Sheria* decision. First, the subject matter of the litigation involved almost identical issues. The Kenyan Government issued a Directive on 17 March 2014 that designated a list of areas as refugee camps.[58] This was followed by a press release on 26 March 2014 from the Cabinet Secretary for Interior and Coordination of National Government on Refugees and National Security Issues that directed 'all refugees residing outside the designated refugee camps of Kakuma and Dadaab … to return to their respective camps with immediate effect'.[59] The press release cited 'emerging security challenges in … urban centres and the need to streamline the management of refugees' as the reason for the Directive. The press release further announced the closure of refugee registration centres in urban areas; requested Kenyans 'to report to the police any refugee and or illegal immigrants found outside the designated refugee camps'; and deployed 500 police officers to ramp up security in Nairobi, Mombasa and other urban centres.[60]

Second, the petitioners raised similar arguments as in *Kituo Cha Sheria* pertaining to the constitutionality of the Directive, its impact on the human rights of

[54] A Wirth, C Defilippis and J Therkelsen, *Taking the Movement from Theory to Practice* (Asylum Access and the Refugee Work Rights Coalition, 2014) 30.

[55] UNHCR, *Kituo Cha Sheria and Others v. The Attorney General* (2013) 7.

[56] '"You Are All Terrorists": Kenyan Police Abuse of Refugees in Nairobi' (*Human Rights Watch*, 2013), available at www.hrw.org/report/2013/05/29/you-are-all-terrorists/kenyan-police-abuse-refugees-nairobi; Juma (n 6) 10.

[57] *Samow Mumin Mohamed & 9 others v Cabinet Secretary Ministry of Interior Security and Co-Ordination & 2 others (Samow)* [2014] eKLR (High Court of Kenya).

[58] Designation of Areas As Refugee Camps, *Gazette Notice* (2014), available at https://new.kenyalaw.org/akn/ke/officialGazette/2014-03-28/39/eng@2014-03-28; B Frouws, *Behind Bars: The Detention of Migrants in and from the East & Horn of Africa* (Regional Mixed Migratino Secretariat, 2015) 61, 61–62.

[59] *Samow* (n 57) 2.

[60] ibid 2–3.

refugees and asylumseekers and its violation of international law.[61] The petitioners also explicitly mentioned that the implementation of the Directive was contrary to the ruling in *Kituo Cha Sheria*. Third, the same judge that decided in *Kituo Cha Sheria*, judge David Majanja, was presiding over the *Samow* decision.

However, in a stark change of direction, the High Court ultimately rejected the petition primarily on procedural grounds. The Court stated that the petitioners had failed to plead their case 'with such precision as regards the right violated' and therefore failed to establish a violation of their rights under the Constitution.[62] The Court also ruled that the government Directive in question did not 'violate the petitioners' rights and fundamental freedoms'.[63] Lastly, the Court ruled that the designation of areas to serve as refugee camps was not unconstitutional.[64] Unlike in the *Kituo Cha Sheria* decision, the Court did not rebuke the Government for the sweeping blanket rhetoric of securitisation against refugees.[65] The *Samow* decision left the the *Kituo Cha Sheria* decision on shaky legal grounds and created uncertainties.

Considering the similarities between the two cases and the decision-maker, the different result reached in *Samow* has left scholars divided, some suggesting that 'the reasons for the decision in *Samow Mumin Mohamed* include some technical and procedural matters that have little to do with rights per se',[66] while others argue that 'the change in judicial decision on the freedom of movement of refugees is a result of the process of securitisation orchestrated by the national government'.[67] However, irrespective of the justifications as to why the outcomes were so different, the dismissal of the *Samow* case left thousands of refugees and asylumseekers living in urban areas exposed to arbitrary executive actions.

The second post-*Kituo Cha Sheria* development relates to the Attorney General's appeal of the *Kituo Cha Sheria* decision. This appeal was pending during the litigation in the *Samow* case, and the final decision came in 2017. In a decisive vindication of and reaffirmation of the rights of refugees and asylum seekers, the Court of Appeal reviewed the High Court's decision in *Kituo Cha Sheria* and upheld it entirely. The appellate decision provided a rigorous and enhanced application and analysis of the human rights of refugees and asylum

[61] ibid 3–4.

[62] ibid 5, 8.

[63] ibid 8.

[64] ibid.

[65] The Court's very decision to strike the case may have itself been impacted by the high rhetoric of securitisation. A Maina, 'Securitization of Kenya's Asylum Space: Origin and Legal Analysis of the Encampment Policy' in J Dragsbaek Schmidt, L Kimathi and M Omondi Owiso (eds), *Refugees and Forced Migration in the Horn and Eastern Africa: Trends, Challenges and Opportunities* (Springer, 2019) 89.

[66] Juma (n 6) 2. See also, R Doya Nanima, 'An Evaluation of Kenya's Parallel Legal Regime on Refugees, and the Courts' Guarantee of their Rights' (2017) 21(1) *Law, Democracy & Development* 42, 62: arguing that the 'divergent views [between *Kituo Cha Sheria* and *Samow*] indicate that, first, it is the duty of the court to adjudicate cases that raise issues of constitutional rights. Secondly, an individual has an obligation to state his or her claim with precision'.

[67] Maina (n 65) 89.

seekers. More significantly, by upholding the *Kituo Cha Sheria* judgment, it clarified the legal uncertainty created by the High Court's refusal to hear the *Samow* petitions.

The last significant development in the post-*Kituo Cha Sheria* period, albeit a more recent one, is the policy changes introduced through the enactment of the Refugee Act of 2021. In a significant shift of policy direction, the Act focuses on promoting local integration as opposed to encampment or repatriation. This change has not occurred in a vacuum. The bold stance of the judiciary in *Kituo Cha Sheria* in countering the dehumanising narrative against refugees and asylum seekers and asserting their constitutional and human rights has played a role in gradually introducing favourable policy changes. This leads us to the next section where I will explore the several features that distinguish the *Kituo Cha Sheria* decision as a landmark decision in international refugee protection.

IV. Landmark Features of *Kituo Cha Sheria*

There are several reasons that distinguish *Kituo Cha Sheria* as a landmark case. This section highlights some of these reasons, starting with the judicial readiness to objectively adjudicate the case. This judicial readiness paved the way for effective procedural interventions and robust substantive analysis that asserted the rights of refugees and asylum seekers. The procedural interventions included the grant of interim measures enjoining the Government from enforcing the Directive and admitting the UNHCR and *Katiba* Institute, an NGO working to promote constitutionalism in Kenya, as *amici curiae*. The substantive analysis of the Court also promoted a human rights-based approach that critically scrutinised government action through the interpretation of the Constitution, national law, and regional and international law obligations.

A. Judicial Readiness

The very first sentence of *Kituo Cha Sheria* frames the issue in the case as one that concerns 'the nature and extent of the rights and fundamental freedoms of refugees residing in urban areas in Kenya'.[68] Amidst high political rhetoric on the security risks that refugees pose to Kenyan society, such a bold framing of the issue demonstrated the readiness of the High Court to affirm the state of the law on the rights and fundamental freedoms of refugees. One of the ways through which judicial readiness was demonstrated was through procedural orders. One of the procedural victories that the plaintiffs had in *Kituo Cha Sheria* was securing an interim order from the High Court enjoining the Government from implementing

[68] *Kituo Cha Sheria* (n 1) 1.

the Directive and relocating the refugees to camps.[69] The Court also granted leave to the UNHCR and *Katiba* Institute to appear before it as *amicus curiae*, providing a further avenue for a broader analysis on the legal issues involved in the case.

This judicial readiness is significant considering the myriads of structural issues surrounding judicial independence in Africa generally, and in Kenya specifically.[70] The judiciary is often accused of being subservient to the other branches of the Government, especially the executive, and lacking independence.[71] Not only was the judgment strong on the merits, it was also strong in asserting the independence of the judiciary and its constitutional power to review executive actions and quash them when they are found to be unconstitutional.

B. Human Rights-Based Approach

As noted earlier, the seven petitioners in the case were individual refugees who resided in different urban areas in Kenya. The Court carefully considered and outlined the personal, family, social, health and other relevant circumstances of the seven petitioners at length, noting that doing so was 'necessary in making determinations'.[72] This was a significant move considering the fact that refugees are often used as scapegoats and pawns in national and international political spaces.[73] The Court strategically used the individual circumstances of the refugees to demonstrate the failure of the blanket Directive.

The Court achieved this by ensuring access to fair trial, putting the rights of refugees in focus and, importantly, the onus of proving the legality of the Directive on the Government. The personalised approach to the situation of the seven refugees named in the case, instead of using a generic reference to 'refugees' or 'asylum seekers', served the important function of making the individuals visible as against the powerful narrative the Government was espousing. It also enabled the Court to reach the inductive conclusion that what does not apply to the seven individuals, most probably does not apply to the many thousands of refugees who stood to be impacted by the Directive.

Accordingly, the Court made a progressive interpretation and application of domestic and international law to protect the rights of refugees. Justice Mayanja's interpretation of Article 24 of the Constitution on the limitation of rights is, for

[69] Order of DS Majanja, *Kituo Cha Sheria v The Attorney General* (n 2).

[70] See generally, C Manga Fombad, 'The Struggle to Defend the Independence of the Judiciary in Africa' in S Shetreet, H Chodosh and E Helland (eds), *Challenged Justice: In Pursuit of Judicial Independence* (Brill, 2021); M Mutua, 'Justice Under Siege: The Rule of Law and Judicial Subservience in Kenya' (2001) 23 *Human Rights Quarterly* 96.

[71] L Okpaluba Juma, Chuks, 'Judicial Intervention in Kenya's Constitutional Review Process' (2012) 11 *Washington University Global Studies Law Review* 287, 364; Mutua (n 70) 109.

[72] *Kituo Cha Sheria* (n 1) 7.

[73] R Salih, 'From Bare Lives to Political Agents: Palestinian Refugees as Avant-Garde' (2013) 32 *Refugee Survey Quarterly* 66, 70, 85; N Hirt, *Eritrean Refugees: The Pawns of European Interests* (GIGA German Institute of Global and Area Studies, 2016).

example, noted for its correct analysis compared to other cases that glibly glossed over the provision, stating that the limitation of rights simply 'means rights are not absolute'.[74] The Court also rejected the Government's contention that Article 17(f) of the 2006 Refugees Act 'presupposes that all refugees and asylum seekers shall ordinarily reside in gazetted refugee camps' and 'reflects an encampment policy'.[75] The Court noted that the said provision merely set out the 'responsibilities of a refugee camp officer' and did not 'require that all refugees and asylum seekers to ordinarily reside in camps nor does it preclude the State from providing refugee services in urban centre'.[76]

C. Strategic Litigation

The other landmark feature of *Kituo Cha Sheria* is the successful deployment of strategic litigation. As non-citizens, refugees and asylum seekers are generally excluded from full participation in the political life of a state. They are often neglected and sidelined from policy and decision-making procedures and not offered consultation even on matters that affect them.[77] In *Kituo Cha Sheria*, the Government even described consultation with stakeholders as being 'unnecessary' and that any consultation that was done 'was done out of courtesy'.[78] This lack of agency in the political system of the host-state renders refugees and asylum seekers passive objects of the law, as opposed to subjects with rights and duties. The *actio popularis* that *Kituo Cha Sheria*, an NGO, initiated and pleaded on behalf of refugees and asylum seekers filled the gap in agency in this particular case.[79]

This is crucial for several reasons. First, refugees and asylum seekers face many challenges in a host country, such as lack of the financial resources to bring their own individual claims, unfamiliarity with the legal environment and lack of professional and social connections to help bring their claims.[80] The public interest actions brought by NGOs alleviates some of these burdens. It provides enhanced legal representation and ensures that refugees and asylum seekers receive proper

[74] J Cottrell Ghai, 'The Bill of Rights and County Governments: Emerging Jurisprudence from the Courts' in CM Bosire and W Gikonyo (eds), *Animating Devolution in Kenya: The Role of the Judiciary* (International Development Law Organization (IDLO), 2015) 188, 188–89.

[75] *Kituo Cha Sheria* (n 1).

[76] ibid 25. However, note that the same Court declares in *Samow* that the *Kituo Cha Sheria* 'decision did not affect the existence of refugee camps which are provided for under the law'. *Samow* (n 57) [23].

[77] U Ramazani, *Building Meaningful Refugee Participation into Protection Policymaking* (Migration Policy Institute, 2023) 1, 1.

[78] *Kituo Cha Sheria* (n 1) 12.

[79] S Berhanu Woldemariam and M Pacifique, 'Securitisation of Refugee Protection: The Judiciary's Role in the Protection of the Rights of Refugees: Attorney General v. Kituo Cha Sheria & 7 others' (2024) 43 *Refugee Survey Quarterly* 169, 181; A Wirth, 'Reflections from the Encampment Decision in the High Court of Kenya' (2014) 48 *Forced Migration Review* 80–82, 81, available at www.fmreview.org/faith/wirth.

[80] Juma (n 6) 2: noting that cases 'relating to the flagrant abuse of refugee rights rarely reach the courts' and that part of the reason is inability to 'find access to the courts'.

legal advice. Second, the involvement of NGOs *internalises* the litigation and gives a local voice to those who are considered 'foreigners' or 'outsiders'. This is key to ensure that the executive branch of the Government does not take advantage of the fact that refugees and asylum seekers are non-citizens. The local representation of refugees and asylum seekers provides the opportunity to scrutinise the accountability and responsibility of the executive in its decision-making towards non-citizens.

D. UNHCR's *Amicus Curiae*

Another landmark feature in *Kituo Cha Sheria* relates to UNHCR's *amicus* brief and oral submission, which the Court granted a leave to and made part of its analysis and determination.[81] The *amicus* brief focused on matters of law relevant to the interpretation and application of the 1951 Refuge Convention, its additional protocol and the 1969 OAU Refugee Convention. In this regard, the UNHCR argued that the implementation of the Directive was likely 'to affect the institution of asylum in Kenya and interfere with rights recognized under' the above instruments.[82] The UNHCR made progressive arguments noting that the proposed *en masse* encampment 'may be viewed as being punitive and amount to a breach of a State's obligations in international law, in particular Article 31 of the 1951 Convention'.[83]

With respect to the *non-refoulement* obligation, UNHCR's brief noted that the obligation is 'the cornerstone of international refugee protection' and extends to 'repatriation, removal, expulsion, deportation, extradition, rejection at the frontier or non-admission, or induced return'.[84] The UNHCR noted that this obligation protects refugees who have been recognised through an individual status determination or on a *prima facie* basis, as well as those who are seeking asylum but have not yet had their status determined.[85] Accordingly, the UNHCR argued that the proposal in the government Directive to repatriate Somali refugees and others would amount to *refoulement*.[86]

While the UNHCR acknowledged the national security exceptions under Article 33(2) of the 1951 Refugee Convention with respect to the prohibition of

[81] *Kituo Cha Sheria* (n 1) 13.

[82] UNHCR, *Kituo Cha Sheria and Others v. The Attorney General* (n 55) 9. For a comprehensive analysis on the role of the UNHCR in the development of international refugee law, see generally GS Goodwin-Gill, 'The Office of the United Nations High Commissioner for Refugees and the Sources of International Refugee Law' (2020) 69 *International and Comparative Law Quarterly* 1.

[83] UNHCR, *Kituo Cha Sheria and Others v. The Attorney General* (n 55) 9. Article 31 of the 1951 Refugee Convention (n 27) prohibits the imposition of penalties against refugees on account of their illegal entry or presence and the application of restrictions to their movements unless it is necessary and temporary till their status is regularised.

[84] ibid 10.

[85] ibid.

[86] ibid.

refoulement, it also outlined the procedural and substantive safeguards that have to be met before a state could return a person. First, such actions must follow 'a decision reached in accordance with due process of law' where the concerned refugee is provided the opportunity to submit evidence, appeal and be represented in the proceedings before a competent authority.[87] Second, there needs to be 'compelling reasons of national security' to justify the return and the person affected needs to 'have a reasonable period within which to seek legal admission to another country'.[88] Third, any proposed action to return refugees needs to follow an individualised procedure where determinations are made based on the assessment of individual cases as opposed to a collective expulsion.[89] Where these conditions are not met, any repatriation needs to be carried out on a voluntary basis or upon the cessation of refugee status.[90]

UNHCR's brief also affirmed the freedom of movement and choice of residence of refugees and asylum seekers as enshrined in Article 26 of the 1951 Refugee Convention. The UNHCR again emphasised the need for individual decisions in this respect, and that any restriction on the freedom of movement must be proportionate, non-discriminatory and avoid collective enforcement against groups of individuals.[91] The Court's decision was ultimately in line with the arguments espoused under UNHCR's brief.

V. Conclusion

The impact of the *Kituo Cha Sheria* decision continues to reverberate in Kenya's refugee policy-making space. While the decision had minimal immediate impact in driving tangible change, considering that it did not halt the Government from issuing and enforcing similar directives, its gradual influence is more profound. The High Court's decision, and its ultimate confirmation by the Court of Appeals in 2017 on appeal, shifted the national discourse on the rights of refugees and asylum seekers by demanding that the Government act within the scope of the national Constitution as well as international law obligations when issuing and enforcing refugee policies.

Beyond Kenya, the *Kituo Cha Sheria* decision also makes a profound contribution to regional and international refugee law. The comprehensive analysis the Court applied in respect of scrutinising refugee policies that are designed to impact refugees and asylum seekers *en masse* establishes a leading jurisprudence. The Kenyan High Court closely scrutinised the government Directive for its administrative soundness, compliance with the human rights enshrined

[87] ibid 12.
[88] ibid.
[89] ibid 11, 13.
[90] ibid 13.
[91] ibid 15–16.

in the Kenyan Constitution, and adherence to international legal obligations as contained under the relevant refugee and human rights instruments. The Court's analysis of whether the Directive could be justified as a legitimate limitation of rights under Article 24 of the Constitution was also insightful and strong. This approach required the Government to demonstrate a compelling national interest in taking such action and demonstrate the action taken was specifically tailored to achieving the desired objective.

However, despite the profound nature of the decision, its acceptance by scholars was slow and still insufficient. As a landmark case, it is positive that this case has received attention from some leading scholars of refugee law outside Africa, but there is much more work to do in terms of acknowledging and engaging with the decision widely.[92] This partly speaks to the neglect of human rights jurisprudence from institutions in the Global South.[93] African scholars have been leading the way in providing a more detailed examination of the decision.[94] Breaking the barrier that inhibits African jurisprudence from making it to the international stage is a challenge that faces all scholars, African and non-Africans alike.

Overall, the *Kituo Cha Sheria* decision has demonstrated the importance of the role of the judiciary in protecting the rights of vulnerable groups against undue encroachment by the other branches of the Government. It also demonstrated that the voice of the judiciary may not echo as loud as that of the executive, but that it definitely outlasts it. That is the very reason we are now seeing favourable legislative changes in Kenya, especially the Refugee Act of 2021, in respect of the protection of refugees and asylum seekers. This legislative change may not be the end of the quagmire for refugees, but it is a step in the right direction.

[92] For examples of the few Western scholars who discussed the case, see C D'Orsi, '"We Cannot Manage This Plight Alone Anymore": analysing the Kenyan Threats to Forcibly Repatriate All Somali Refugees from Dadaab Camp' in J Dragsbaek Schmidt, L Kimathi and M Omondi Owiso (eds), *Refugees and Forced Migration in the Horn and Eastern Africa: Trends, Challenges and Opportunities* (Springer International, 2019) 260: highlighting *Kituo Cha Sheria's* reversal of the restrictions pertaining to refugees living outside of designated camps; JC Hathaway, *The Rights of Refugees under International Law* (Cambridge University Press, 2021) 302, 529: highlighting the analysis of *Kituo Cha Sheria* in respect of national security and the circumstances under which it can lead to suspension of refugee rights; M Sharpe, *The Regional Law of Refugee Protection in Africa* (Oxford University Press, 2018) 72, 102: highlighting the Kenyan High Court's application and interpretation of the Kenyan Refugee Act and the Refugee Convention in respect of *non-refoulement* and the freedom of movement. See generally also K Ogg, *Protection from Refuge: From Refugee Rights to Migration Management* (Cambridge University Press, 2022).

[93] For a detailed take on this, see R Murray, 'International Human Rights: Neglect of Perspectives from African Institutions' (2006) 55 *International and Comparative Law Quarterly* 193.

[94] For examples of African scholars who highlighted or examined the case, see Maina (n 65): discussing the High Court's interpretation of the freedom of movement in *Kituo Cha Sheria* and how the decision was impacted by later decisions; D Tladi, *Peremptory Norms of General International Law (Jus Cogens): Disquisitions and Disputations* (Brill, 2021) 286: highlighting *Kituo Cha Sheria* as one of the 'limited and isolated' cases involving violation of the principle of *non-refoulement*.

PART C

Future Directions in Refugee Protection

11

Protection from Conflict: *Sufi and Elmi v UK* [2011]

CHRISTEL QUERTON

I. Introduction

Violence in situations of armed conflict is the main cause of forced displacement in the world today.[1] Although most persons fleeing armed conflicts have valid claims for protection under the 1951 Refugee Convention,[2] many host states continue to deny them refugee status.[3] This is due to the many misconceptions surrounding the relevance of the 1951 Refugee Convention in tackling the particular circumstances of their flight and whether its 'individualistic' refugee definition[4] encompasses conflict refugees.[5]

This is best illustrated by the United Nations High Commissioner for Refugees' (UNHCR) Handbook on Procedures and Criteria for Determining Refugee Status, which treated persons fleeing wars as 'special cases'. UNHCR's position was that 'persons compelled to leave their country of origin as a result of international or national armed conflicts are not normally considered refugees under the 1951 Refugee Convention or 1967 Protocol'.[6] The Agency's position, together with states' restrictive

[1] C (Kees) Wouters, 'Conflict Refugees' in C Costello, M Foster and J McAdam (eds), *The Oxford Handbook of International Refugee Law* (Oxford University Press, 2021) 815; see also United Nations High Commissioner for Refugees (UNHCR), 'A Year of Turmoil: Conflicts, Crises and Displacement in 2024' (26 December 2024), available at www.unhcr.org/uk/news/stories/year-turmoil-conflicts-crises-and-displacement-2024.

[2] UN General Assembly, 1951 Convention relating to the Status of Refugees, United Nations, Treaty Series, 189:137, 28 July 1951 (1951 Refugee Convention).

[3] C Querton, *Conflict Refugees: European Union Law and Practice* (Cambridge University Press, 2023).

[4] A refugee is defined in Art 1A(2) 1951 Refugee Convention as a person who 'owing to a well-founded fear of being persecuted for reasons of race, religion, nationality, membership of a particular social group or political opinion, is outside the country of his nationality and is unable or, owing to such fear, is unwilling to avail himself of the protection of that country; or who, not having a nationality and being outside the country of his former habitual residence as a result of such events, is unable or, owing to such fear, is unwilling to return to it'.

[5] Querton (n 3) 4.

[6] UNHCR, *Handbook and Guidelines on Procedures and Criteria for Determining Refugee Status under the 1951 Convention and the 1967 Protocol relating to the Status of Refugees*, UN doc HCR/IP/4/Eng/Rev.3 (1979, reissued 2011) para 34.

interpretation of the 1951 Refugee Convention in the 1970s, led to many jurisdictions requiring persons fleeing armed conflicts to demonstrate a risk over and above the rest of the population.[7] It was only in 2016 that UNHCR issued International Protection Guidelines on claims for refugee status related to situations of armed conflict and violence, asserting that

> the majority of [armed conflict and violence] situations engender political, religious, ethnic, social, or gender persecution. The 1951 Convention relating to the Status of Refugees and/or its 1967 Protocol (1951 Refugee Convention) is directly applicable to civilians displaced by situations of armed conflict and violence.

Accordingly, when the European Court of Human Rights (ECtHR) issued the *Sufi and Elmi v the United Kingdom* judgment in 2011,[8] it provided a substantial contribution to international protection by strengthening an essential complementary mechanism for the protection of persons fleeing widespread violence in conflicts who tended to be refused refugee protection.

International human rights law has developed as a complementary protection mechanism for those who may not be recognised as refugees but who nonetheless face a real risk of serious harm on return to their country of origin.[9] Further, human rights law is an essential source of protection for those in the 43 UN Member States that have not ratified the 1951 Refugee Convention.[10] International human rights law has extended the principle of *non-refoulement* beyond international refugee law, to prohibit the removal of persons to territories where they face a real risk of being arbitrarily deprived of their life, or subjected to the death penalty, torture, or cruel, inhuman, or degrading treatment or punishment.[11] Over time, international human rights norms have played an essential role in strengthening international protection frameworks and influencing state practice. This contribution explores the landmark judgment of *Sufi and Elmi*. It was described as a leading case by former ECtHR judge, Ledi Bianku,[12] and it has had wide implications for the protection of persons from return to situations of widespread violence in countries experiencing armed conflicts, such as Somalia.[13]

[7] Querton (n 3) 4–5.

[8] *Sufi and Elmi v the United Kingdom* (*Sufi and Elmi*) (2012) 54 EHRR 9.

[9] J McAdam, *Complementary Protection in International Refugee Law* (Oxford University Press, 2007). Refugees might also have been excluded from protection under the various exclusion provisions, 1951 Refugee Convention (n 2) Arts 1D, 1F, 32(1) and 33(2).

[10] V Chetail, 'Moving Towards an Integrated Approach of Refugee Law and Human Rights Law' in Costello, Foster and McAdam (n 1) 203.

[11] M-T Gil-Bazo, 'Refugee Protection under International Human Rights Law: From Non Refoulement to Residence and Citizenship' (2015) 34(1) *Refugee Survey Quarterly* 11; J McAdam, 'Complementary Protection' in Costello, Foster and McAdam (n 1) 661.

[12] L Bianku, 'Roundtable Discussion with the IARLJ, the CJEU and the ECtHR on Leading Asylum Cases' (2013) 25(2) *International Journal of Refugee Law* 382, 385–86.

[13] It is noteworthy that the gender dimension of risk on return to situations of armed conflict was not the subject of consideration by the European Court of Human Rights (ECtHR) because of the individual characteristics of the applicants. The ECtHR later assessed the general treatment of women

In *Sufi and Elmi*, the ECtHR unanimously concluded that if the United Kingdom (UK) deported Mr Sufi and Mr Elmi to Mogadishu, the capital of Somalia, this would amount to a breach of Article 3 of the European Convention on Human Rights (ECHR),[14] which prohibits torture, inhuman or degrading treatment or punishment. The ECtHR found that Mr Sufi and Mr Elmi were at risk of ill-treatment, in relation to: (i) the level of violence in Mogadishu,[15] (ii) relocation to or travel through regions controlled by Al-Shabaab in the rest of Somalia,[16] and (iii) the humanitarian conditions in camps for displaced people.[17] The ECtHR considered that the violence in Mogadishu was of such a level of intensity that anyone, except possibly those who were exceptionally well-connected to 'powerful actors', would be at risk of ill-treatment contrary to Article 3 ECHR.[18]

Clearly, the judgment was going to have a significant immediate impact on the protection claims of most Somali nationals within the 47 Member States of the Council of Europe. Although it could be argued that the outcome of the case was very fact-specific, as it was based on extensive evidence of the dire humanitarian circumstances in Somalia in 2011,[19] the influence of the judgment continues to be felt in the assessment of protection claims by persons fleeing armed conflicts to this day.

Following the Introduction, this chapter provides a summary of the case and the judgment of the ECtHR. It then discusses two themes arising from this landmark judgment. Firstly, the chapter discusses generalised risk on return to situations of armed conflict and the assessment of violence levels, concluding that *Sufi and Elmi* was groundbreaking at the time but that the indicators of violence adopted by the ECtHR have had mixed results for protection from conflict to date. Secondly, the chapter reviews the ECtHR's consideration of potential bars to removal on the basis of dire humanitarian conditions in the country of origin, which for the first time were assessed as part of an internal relocation assessment. The chapter concludes that the true potential of the judgment is yet to be fully realised, most likely in cases concerning removal to situations of dire socioeconomic conditions, including those resulting from the effects of disasters and climate change.

in Somalia in *RH v Sweden* (2018) 67 EHRR 22, although the ECtHR's approach to non-state actors of protection has been criticised, see C Querton, 'Non-State Actors of Protection and the Sliding Scale of Protection for Refugee Women' (2022) 41(3) *Refugee Survey Quarterly* 444.

[14] Convention for the Protection of Human Rights and Fundamental Freedoms (European Convention on Human Rights, as amended) (ECHR).

[15] *Sufi and Elmi* (n 8) [248].

[16] ibid [277].

[17] ibid [291]–[92]. For critique, see M Bossuyt, 'Is the European Court of Human Rights on a Slippery Slope?' in S Flogaitis, T Zwart and J Fraser (eds), *The European Court of Human Rights and its Discontents: Turning Criticism into Strength* (Edward Elgar, 2013) 31–32.

[18] *Sufi and Elmi* (n 8) [250].

[19] Judicial authorities in different regions have also considered indirect *refoulement* to Somalia, see, eg, the Kenyan High Court judgment in Samuel Berhanu Woldemariam, '*Kituo Cha Sheria and Others v The Attorney General* [2013]: Betwixt Executive Opposition and Judicial Affirmation of Refugee Rights' in ch 10 of this volume.

II. Summary of the Case and Decision

The case of *Sufi and Elmi* concerned two Somali nationals whom the UK Government sought to deport to Somalia, when the country was experiencing an armed conflict between the Transitional Federal Government (TFG) and Al-Shabaab, a jihadist organisation with links to Al-Qaida.[20]

Mr Abdisamad Adow Sufi entered the UK in 2003 where he sought asylum. He claimed that he had a well-founded fear of persecution on account of being a member of the Reer-Hamar, a minority sub-clan in Somalia. His asylum and human rights claims were dismissed due to adverse credibility findings in 2005. He was later convicted for offences such as burglary, threats to kill and theft. In July 2006, the Secretary of State for the Home Department (SSHD) issued an intention to issue a deportation order because the offences were serious and to protect the public from serious crime. His appeal against the decision was refused in September 2006 and a deportation order was signed.

Mr Abdiaziz Ibrahim Elmi had been given six months leave to enter the UK in 1988 to join his father who worked for the Somali Embassy in London. Following his father's death in 1989, Mr Elmi filed an asylum claim as he had a well-founded fear of being persecuted in Somalia on account of his father's former position as a high-ranking officer in the army during the Barré regime and because of the civil war in Somalia. He was granted refugee status followed by Indefinite Leave to Remain in the UK. He was later convicted of serious offences including handling stolen goods, robbery, possessing an imitation firearm while committing an offence, theft, and supplying class A drugs. In 2006, the SSHD decided to issue a deportation order as he constituted a danger to the community. He submitted that he had made efforts to address his drug addiction, but the SSHD considered he had failed to demonstrate he did not constitute such a danger and there was no risk of death or serious harm on return because he was a member of the Isaaq, a majority clan in Somalia. His appeal against the decision failed and a deportation order was signed in 2007.

In their applications to the ECtHR, Mr Sufi and Mr Elmi claimed that their removal to Somalia would breach Article 2 (the right to life), Article 3 (the prohibition of torture or inhuman or degrading treatment or punishment) and Article 8 (the right to private and family life) ECHR. Considering the similar factual and legal backgrounds, the Court joined the cases and examined the complaints under Article 3 ECHR only. Three main findings were made in this case, relating to the risk of experiencing treatment contrary to Article 3 ECHR (i) on return to Mogadishu due to the general situation of violence, (ii) when relocating to southern and central Somalia (outside Mogadishu) on account of the human rights violations committed by Al-Shabaab in the regions under their control, and (iii) whilst living in camps for the displaced as a result of the dire humanitarian conditions.

[20] For more information about the origins of Al-Shabaab, see H Maruf and D Joseph, *Inside Al-Shabaab: The Secret History of Al-Qaeda's Most Powerful Ally* (Indiana University Press, 2018).

Firstly, the Court concluded that 'the violence in Mogadishu is of such a level of intensity that anyone in the city, except possibly those who are exceptionally well-connected to "powerful actors", would be at real risk of treatment prohibited by Article 3 of the Convention'.[21] Secondly, the Court found that there may have been areas of southern and central Somalia where the level of violence was not such to place any returnees at risk of treatment contrary to Article 3 ECHR, however, any relocation to such an area would only be possible if the returnee had close family connections in that location.[22] Moreover:

> a returnee with no recent experience of living in Somalia would be at real risk of being subjected to treatment proscribed by Article 3 in an al-Shabaab controlled area. Accordingly, if a returnee's home area is in an al-Shabaab controlled area, or if it could not be reached without travelling through an al-Shabaab controlled area, the Court does not consider that he could relocate within Somalia without being exposed to a real risk of Article 3 ill-treatment.[23]

Finally, the Court established that 'any returnee forced to seek refuge in [the Afgooye Corridor or the Dadaab camp] would be at real risk of Article 3 ill-treatment on account of the dire humanitarian conditions'.[24]

The *Sufi and Elmi* judgment was expected to have an instantaneous impact across Europe, having been identified as a lead case by the ECtHR in order to determine issues of law and facts, namely what was the general risk for returnees in Somalia and how the level of violence should be assessed. The judgment would determine the protection claims of Mr Sufi and Mr Elmi but also the large number of displaced persons from Somalia across Europe with similar claims.[25] Accordingly, the judgment was met very positively by the refugee sector. Indeed, the European Legal Network on Asylum (ELENA) decided to dedicate its next Advanced Course on the topic of Generalised Violence, Armed Conflict and the Need for International Protection in May 2012 where the (then) recent case was discussed at length for its implication for future practice. With the passage of time, it is now possible to evaluate the decision in subsequent and current context and broadly, the implications and consequences for international refugee law and international protection.

III. Implications and Consequences for International Refugee Law and International Protection

Two issues arising from the judgment are now discussed in more depth. The first theme is generalised risk in situations of armed conflict and assessing levels of violence. The second topic is internal relocation and humanitarian conditions.

[21] *Sufi and Elmi* (n 8) [250].
[22] ibid [271], [294].
[23] ibid [277].
[24] ibid [292].
[25] H Storey, 'Briefing Note for Participants' (2013) 25(2) *International Journal of Refugee Law* 328.

A. Generalised Risk in Situations of Armed Conflict and Assessing Levels of Violence

Significantly the ECtHR dispelled any remaining doubt as to whether a person at risk of serious harm arising from 'a mere situation of general instability' could come within the protective scope of Article 3 ECHR in expulsion cases.[26] Indeed, in the earlier case of *Vilvarajah v the United Kingdom*, the Court seemed to indicate that a person was required to show that they were in a worse position than the generality of other members of their community.[27] In *NA v the United Kingdom*, the Court clarified that an applicant was not expected to show the existence of special distinguishing features if in the country of return there was a level of general violence of sufficient intensity to create a real risk that anyone present would experience treatment contrary to Article 3 ECHR.[28] Yet, the Court was also at pains to indicate that not every situation of general violence would give rise to such a risk, and only in the most extreme cases of general violence would the test be satisfied.[29] This set the bar very high and was considered as having introduced a test of exceptionality. By June 2011, when *Sufi and Elmi* was promulgated, the Court had never found on the facts that such a situation existed.[30]

In *Sufi and Elmi*, for the first time, the Court also provided guidance on how to assess the level of violence in situations of armed conflict. It did so by endorsing the approach of the UK Asylum and Immigration Tribunal (UKAIT) in the case of *AM and AM (Somalia)*, which was a Country Guidance determination concerned with the return of asylum seekers to Somalia.[31] The ECtHR endorsed the criteria identified by the Tribunal as follows,

> first, whether the parties to the conflict were either employing methods and tactics of warfare which increased the risk of civilian casualties or directly targeting civilians; secondly, whether the use of such methods and/or tactics was widespread among the parties to the conflict; thirdly, whether the fighting was localised or widespread; and finally, the number of civilians killed, injured and displaced as a result of the fighting.[32]

The ECtHR highlighted that those criteria were not exhaustive, nonetheless they formed an 'appropriate yardstick by which to assess the level of violence' in Mogadishu and in future cases.[33]

[26] *Sufi and Elmi* (n 8) [217].

[27] *Vilvarajah and Others v the United Kingdom* (1991) 14 EHRR 248 [111]; Although Vedsted-Hansen has argued the absolute nature of Art 3 ECHR meant the ECtHR in *Vilvarajah and Others* never instituted a requirement of special distinguishing features, J Vedsted-Hansen, 'European Non-Refoulement Revisited' (2010) 55 *Scandinavian Studies in Law* 269, 276.

[28] *NA v the United Kingdom* (2009) 48 EHRR 15 [114].

[29] ibid [115].

[30] C (Kees) Wouters, 'Protecting People Fleeing Conflict and Generalized Violence: UNHCR's Perspective' in *Joint Council of Europe/UNHCR Colloquium on the Role of Regional Human Rights Courts in Interpreting and Enforcing Legal Standards for the Protection of Forcibly Displaced Persons* (16 June 2011) 68, available at www.refworld.org/reference/confdoc/unhcr/2011/en/84024.

[31] *AM and AM (armed conflict: risk categories) Somalia CG* [2008] UKAIT 00091 (27 January 2009).

[32] *Sufi and Elmi* (n 8) [241].

[33] ibid [241].

The question of how to determine protection claims based on widespread violence has long been the subject of debate in academic and policy circles.[34] Debates were centred on exploring different legal frameworks, particularly international humanitarian law (IHL), as an aid to interpretation of complementary protection mechanisms in Europe.[35] UNHCR consultations confirmed there were varied views on the issue.[36] The *Sufi and Elmi* case was thus decided at a time of conflicting views and unsettled doctrine. By endorsing the indiscriminate violence factors set out in *AM and AM (Somalia)*, the ECtHR positioned itself within that debate. Yet, the real impact of *Sufi and Elmi* has remained unrecognised by many. Although the ECtHR endorsed the IHL approach adopted by the UKAIT, the ECtHR failed to explicitly address the question of whether IHL is a relevant framework for understanding violence in armed conflict and to give reasons for using it to determine conflict-related protection claims. The ECtHR might possibly have failed to appreciate this itself.

When *AM and AM (Somalia)* was decided in October 2008, the UKAIT relied on the norms of IHL to interpret European Union (EU) subsidiary protection provisions in Article 15(c) of the Qualification Directive for those at risk of a 'serious and individual threat to a civilian's life or person by reason of indiscriminate violence in situations of international or internal armed conflict'.[37] The indicators of (1) the methods and tactics of warfare which increase the risk to civilians or which directly target civilians, (2) whether the use of such methods and/or tactics is widespread, (3) whether the fighting is localised or widespread, and (4) the number of

[34] See, eg, J Magnusson, 'A Question of Definition – The Concept of Internal Armed Conflict in the Swedish Aliens Act' (2008) 10 *European Journal of Migration and Law* 381; H Lambert and T Farrell, 'The Changing Character of Armed Conflict and the Implications for Refugee Protection Jurisprudence' (2010) 22 *International Journal of Refugee Law* 237; P Tiedemann, 'Subsidiary Protection and the Function of Article 15(c) of the Qualification Directive' (2012) 31 *Refugee Survey Quarterly* 123; H Lambert, 'The Next Frontier: Expanding Protection in Europe for Victims of Armed Conflict and Indiscriminate Violence' (2013) 25 *International Journal of Refugee Law* 207.

[35] See, eg, the various contributions in DJ Cantor and J-F Durieux (eds), *Refuge from Inhumanity? War Refugees and International Humanitarian Law* (Brill Nijhoff, 2014); R (Ruvi) Ziegler, 'International Humanitarian Law and Refugee Protection' in Costello, Foster and McAdam (n 1) 226–28.

[36] UNHCR, *Summary Conclusions on International Protection of Persons Fleeing Armed Conflict and Other Situations of Violence; Roundtable 13 and 14 September 2012, Cape Town, South Africa* (UNHCR, 2012) para 10.

[37] Council Directive 2004/83/EC of 29 April 2004 on minimum standards for the qualification and status of third country nationals or stateless persons as refugees or as persons who otherwise need international protection and the content of the protection granted [2004] OJ L304/12; it was replaced by Directive 2011/95/EU of the European Parliament and of the Council of 13 December 2011 on standards for the qualification of third-country nationals or stateless persons as beneficiaries of international protection, for a uniform status for refugees or for persons eligible for subsidiary protection, and for the content of the protection granted (recast) [2011] OJ L337/9 (Qualification Directive). On 14 May 2024, Regulation (EU) 2024/1347 of the European Parliament and of the Council on standards for the qualification of third-country nationals or stateless persons as beneficiaries of international protection, for a uniform status for refugees or for persons eligible for subsidiary protection and for the content of the protection granted [2024] OJ L2024/1347 (Qualification Regulation) was adopted. It will repeal the recast Qualification Directive by 2026. However, the subsidiary protection provisions were not amended in the recast Directive or the Regulation.

civilians killed, injured or displaced draw on the principle of distinction in IHL which places an obligation on parties to the conflict not to directly target civilians and ensure that any civilian casualties are proportional to the lawful military objective sought.[38] Using this concept of violence to determine the risk of serious harm on return to situations of armed conflict under the ECHR is problematic. Indeed, under IHL some loss of life may be lawful, where civilians are not directly targeted or where loss of life is proportionate to the military benefit, whereas this cannot be permitted under Article 3 ECHR. By analogy with Bauloz' commentary on Article 15(c) Qualification Directive, using an IHL-inspired concept of violence would exclude from the risk assessment violence that is directed at military targets, violence whose impact on civilians is proportionate and violence which is exercised by persons without any nexus to the armed conflict.[39] The purpose of IHL norms is to ensure military attacks are lawful, whereas the assessment of a risk of ill-treatment contrary to Article 3 ECHR includes the consideration of all forms of violence. Broadly, assessing risk on return by drawing on IHL norms imports limitations to what violence should be considered in the risk assessment and fails to reflect the nature of contemporary armed conflicts, which increasingly blurs the boundaries between conflict-related and criminal violence.[40] Indeed, the Court of Appeal later departed from the IHL approach endorsed in *AM and AM (Somalia)*.[41] Moreover, the ECtHR position in this respect is at odds with the later judgment of the Court of Justice of the European Union (CJEU) which strongly distanced itself from IHL as the relevant framework for interpretation of subsidiary protection mechanisms in the EU.[42]

Nonetheless, following *Sufi and Elmi*, the ECtHR continues to apply IHL indicators to evaluate levels of violence, for example to determine whether there is a real risk to returnees from Syria.[43] Moreover, the factors have been adopted by various courts and institutions. Importantly, the European Union Agency for Asylum (EUAA) explicitly draws on the *Sufi and Elmi* criteria as 'indicators of indiscriminate violence' for all its country of origin information (COI) reports on the security situation of countries experiencing armed conflict and widespread violence.[44] The EUAA's use of the *Sufi and Elmi* indicators has wide implications as

[38] See more detailed discussion in C Querton, 'Country Guidance, Country of Origin Information, and the International Protection Needs of Persons Fleeing Armed Conflicts' (2023) 42(2) *Refugee Survey Quarterly* 204, 235–38.

[39] C Bauloz, 'The (Mis)Use of International Humanitarian Law under Article 15(c) of the EU Qualification Directive' in Cantor and Durieux (n 35) 252–53.

[40] See more detailed discussion in C Querton, 'Protection from Indiscriminate Violence in Armed Conflict: The Scope of Subsidiary Protection in the European Union' (2025) 37(1) *International Journal of Refugee Law* 36–59.

[41] *QD (Iraq) v Secretary of State for the Home Department* [2009] EWCA Civ 620, [2011] WLR 689 [18].

[42] Case C–285/12 *Diakité v Commissaire Général aux Réfugiés et aux Apatrides* [2014] 1 WLR 2477.

[43] *LM and Others v Russia*, App nos 40081/14, 40088/14 and 40127/14 (ECtHR, 15 October 2015) [123]–[24]; *SK v Russia* App no 52722/15 (ECtHR, 15 February 2017) [61]–[62].

[44] Querton (n 38) 234–35.

EU Member States now have to 'take into account the [Agency's] common analysis and guidance notes when examining applications for international protection, without prejudice to their competence to decide on individual applications for international protection'[45] in order to promote convergence in the determination of protection claims.[46] EU Member States, including their administrative and judicial authorities, are thus increasingly relying on the EUAA's assessment of country conditions, including levels of indiscriminate violence. Whereas this may lead to positive outcomes for persons in need of international protection where the EUAA's position is that a group of persons should be granted refugee protection, such as women from Afghanistan for example,[47] reliance on a restricted understanding of violence in conflict is likely to lead to reduced refugee and subsidiary protection rates in the EU. According to the EUAA's current Country Guidance, there are no areas in Afghanistan, Iraq, Nigeria and Somalia currently assessed to reach such an exceptionally high level of violence that 'mere presence' on the territory would be considered sufficient in order to establish a real risk of serious harm under Article 15(c) Qualification Directive.[48] Only five governorates in Syria have been determined to meet the threshold of indiscriminate violence.[49] Wider factors have been recommended for inclusion in the assessment of violence in armed conflicts, including population displacement, state failure, threats to human dignity resulting from starvation and destruction of critical infrastructure and services,[50] armed groups' strategies, and fighting parties' spheres of control.[51] The suggestions here draw from different scholarly fields such as human security and security studies. Despite the complementarity between international human rights law and IHL,[52] the assessment of violence levels should be a factual, rather than a legal, question for asylum decision-makers.

Overall, *Sufi and Elmi* represented a watershed moment in establishing that the ECHR could be deployed to prevent the removal of persons due to a general situation of violence without distinguishing characteristics or circumstances, that

[45] Article 11 (3) Regulation (EU) 2021/2303 of the European Parliament and of the Council of 15 Dec. 2021 on the European Union Agency for Asylum and repealing Regulation (EU) No 439/2010 [2021] OJ L468/1 (EUAA Regulation).

[46] ibid Art 11(1).

[47] See, eg, the modified refugee status determination process adopted in Denmark in order to facilitate the protection of women from Afghanistan following the EUAA's Afghanistan Country Guidance report dated 25 January 2023, Flygtningenævnet, 'Flygtningenævnet Giver Asyl til Kvinder og Piger fra Afghanistan' (30 January 2023), available at https://fln.dk/da/Nyheder/Nyhedsarkiv/2023/30012023.

[48] EUAA, 'Country Guidance: Afghanistan' (May 2024) 116, available at https://euaa.europa.eu/country-guidance-afghanistan-2024; EUAA, 'Country Guidance: Iraq' (November 2024) 73, available at https://euaa.europa.eu/country-guidance-iraq-2024; EUAA, 'Country Guidance: Nigeria' (October 2021) 111, available at https://euaa.europa.eu/country-guidance-nigeria-2021; EUAA, 'Country Guidance: Somalia' (August 2023) 51, available at https://euaa.europa.eu/country-guidance-somalia-2023.

[49] EUAA, 'Country Guidance: Syria' (April 2024) 121, available at https://euaa.europa.eu/country-guidance-syria-2024.

[50] Lambert and Farrell (n 34).

[51] Querton (n 38) 241.

[52] *Georgia v Russia (II)* (2021) 73 EHRR 6.

certain country conditions (such as Somalia at the time) were capable of reaching such severity to meet what had been considered an almost insurmountable threshold, and for providing guidance on how to determine future cases but with mixed results for international protection.

B. Humanitarian Conditions, Internal Relocation and Encampment

Sufi and Elmi was the first time a Court accepted that widespread violence exercised by parties to an armed conflict could cause a severe deterioration of humanitarian conditions which should be taken into account in expulsion cases under Article 3 ECHR. In *Sufi and Elmi*, this finding was adopted in the context of considering whether the applicants could internally relocate to other areas of Somalia (because they were at risk of widespread violence in Mogadishu) where they would have no option but to live in a camp for the displaced. But the ECtHR's approach is relevant for cases regarding return to poor humanitarian conditions whether these arise in the home area or an area of relocation.

The assessment of whether it is reasonable to expect a person to internally relocate in the country of origin is particularly relevant in the context of refugee status determination. Internal relocation[53] is the description of a factual situation whereby a person may be refused refugee protection if there is a safe place within the country where they can relocate.[54] The ECtHR explored whether the returnees, who were at risk in their area of origin, could reasonably be expected to relocate to camps for the displaced in Somalia and in Kenya. The ECtHR considered that camp conditions, including overcrowding, limited access to shelter, water and sanitation facilities, and exposure to violent crime, exploitation, abuse and forcible recruitment may cumulatively amount to inhuman or degrading treatment.[55] It concluded that the humanitarian conditions in camps for displaced Somalis were so dire that a Contracting State would be in breach of Article 3 ECHR for expelling them. This was a landmark holistic assessment of conditions on return conducted by the ECtHR, which benefited many Somali nationals as the level of violence was only 'exceptionally high' in Mogadishu and thus, many states relied on the principle of internal relocation to refuse international protection. The judgment is also of wider relevance for encampment as a refugee reception policy, adopted by most states in certain regions such as Southern Africa.[56] Janmyr notes that following

[53] Sometimes described as the internal protection alternative or internal flight alternative.

[54] B Ní Ghraínne, 'The Internal Protection Alternative' in Costello, Foster and McAdam (n 1) 695.

[55] *Sufi and Elmi* (n 8) [291]; M Janmyr, 'Spaces of Legal Ambiguity: Refugee Camps and Humanitarian Power' (2016) 7(3) *Humanity* 413, 421; B Ní Ghráinne, 'Complementary Protection and Encampment' (2021) 21(1) *Human Rights Law Review* 54, 67.

[56] N Maple, *Refugee Reception in Southern Africa: National and Local Policies in Zambia and South Africa* (University of London Press, 2024) 1.

Sufi and Elmi, scholars and activists started questioning the legality of long-term encampment.[57]

The judgment was groundbreaking in the choice of legal test adopted to determine whether dire socioeconomic conditions in the country of origin would amount to ill-treatment contrary to Article 3 ECHR. Prior to this case, the ECtHR had established a threshold test in relation to the obligation of Contracting States not to return a foreign national to their country of origin for medical reasons. In this earlier case, the ECtHR had first envisaged the possibility of Contracting States being compelled not to return a person to their country of origin, where to do so would have serious consequences for them, such as dying in distressing circumstances due to the withdrawal of care, support and treatment.[58] In the following case of *N v the United Kingdom* however, the ECtHR considered that a significant reduction in life expectancy due to lack of medical treatment would not be sufficient by itself to breach Article 3 ECHR and the humanitarian circumstances would need to be compelling.[59] This would arise 'only in a very exceptional case',[60] a threshold which Stoyanova describes as equivalent to a risk of imminent death.[61]

In *Sufi and Elmi*, the ECtHR departed from the high threshold established in these Article 3 ECHR socioeconomic conditions expulsion cases, because the humanitarian conditions in Somalia were the result of the direct and indirect actions of parties to the armed conflict.[62] Instead, the ECtHR determined that a lower threshold, first set out in *MSS v Belgium and Greece* 'which requires it to have regard to an applicant's ability to cater for his most basic needs, such as food, hygiene and shelter, his vulnerability to ill-treatment and the prospect of his situation improving within a reasonable time-frame', would be applicable.[63] Although the *N v UK* test would continue to apply 'where the problems facing the applicant would be largely as a result of inadequate social provisions through a want of resources',[64] *Sufi and Elmi* constituted a major development in the case law regarding expulsion of foreign nationals to countries experiencing 'man-made' poor socioeconomic conditions, in which case a less exacting standard should be applied.

A holistic assessment of risk on return that considers dire humanitarian conditions predominantly caused by parties to conflicts is a significant development that promotes effective protection, particularly where conflict and violence have not spread

[57] Janmyr (n 55) 419.

[58] *D v UK* (1997) 24 EHRR 423.

[59] *N v United Kingdom* [GC] App no 26565/05 (ECtHR, 27 May 2008) [42].

[60] ibid.

[61] V Stoyanova, 'How Exceptional Must "Very Exceptional" Be? *Non-Refoulement*, Socio-Economic Deprivation, and *Paposhvili v Belgium*' (2017) 29 *International Journal of Refugee Law* 580.

[62] *Sufi and Elmi* (n 8) [282].

[63] ibid [283]; *MSS v Belgium and Greece* [GC] App no 30696/09 (ECtHR, 21 January 2011) [254]. See Evangelia (Lilian) Tsourdi and Paul McDonough, '*MSS v Belgium and Greece* [2011]: The Interplay between *Non-Refoulement* and Refugee Protection' in ch 9 of this volume for a detailed analysis.

[64] *SHH v UK* (2013) 57 EHRR 18 [92].

to every area in the country of origin. In this sense, *Sufi and Elmi* acts as an important safeguard against the tide of international protection refusals based on an internal relocation alternative. The number of countries considering the suitability of internal relocation is likely to increase in Europe from 2026, since the EU Qualification Regulation will mandate EU Member States to examine this alternative.[65] The *Sufi and Elmi* principles and standards regarding internal relocation in the context of armed conflict will therefore continue to guide practice in this area.

Whether this approach will extend protection to those fleeing armed conflicts in countries where the displaced tend to relocate to urban areas rather than camps remains to be seen, particularly as those residing in camps rather than cities are more dependent on humanitarian aid, which is often weaponised by parties to conflicts. Most internally displaced persons currently live in urban areas outside camp settings.[66] Decision-makers often find that relocation by able-bodied young men to larger urban centres that are not experiencing excessive levels of violence, such as Kabul or Baghdad, is not unreasonable or 'unduly harsh' and therefore not contrary to Article 3 ECHR.[67] Nonetheless, as the CJEU declined to determine whether a humanitarian situation caused by parties to a conflict must be taken into account when determining a person's entitlement for subsidiary protection in EU law, the ECtHR's inclusion of such humanitarian conditions in the assessment of risk on return under the ECHR is vital.[68]

Nonetheless, *Sufi and Elmi* has been criticised for maintaining the source of harm test in expulsion cases which consider dire socioeconomic and humanitarian conditions in the country of removal as a potential bar to removal, when the ECtHR noted that

> if the dire humanitarian conditions in Somalia were solely or even predominantly attributable to poverty or to the State's lack of resources to deal with a naturally occurring phenomenon, such as a drought, the test in [*N v UK*] may well have been considered to be the appropriate one.[69]

Ní Ghráinne argues it would be difficult to show that the acts or omissions of the parties to the conflict are the predominant cause of the serious harm (even in Sudan) and thus Article 3 ECHR is unlikely to be breached on return to camp

[65] Qualification Regulation (n 37) Art 8. European Council on Refugees and Exiles, *ECRE Comments on the Commission Proposal for a Qualification Regulation* COM(2016) 466 (November 2016) 7, available at www.asylumlawdatabase.eu/sites/www.asylumlawdatabase.eu/files/aldfiles/ECRE%20Comments%20QR.pdf.

[66] D Regasa, A Godesso and I Lietaert, 'Living on the Margins: The Socio-spatial Representation of Urban Internally Displaced Persons in Ethiopia' (2023) 47(3) *International Journal of Urban and Regional Research* 369.

[67] In the case of Kabul, see, eg, *AS (Safety of Kabul) Afghanistan CG* [2020] UKUT 00130(IAC) [253(iii)]; in the case of Baghdad, see, eg, *SMO & KSP (Civil status documentation; article 15) Iraq CG* [2022] UKUT 00110 (IAC) [144(25)].

[68] Case C-125/22, *X, Y, their six minor children v Staatssecretaris van Justitie en Veiligheid*, EU:C:2023:843 [75]–[83].

[69] *Sufi and Elmi* (n 8) [282].

conditions.[70] Other scholars however have pointed to the human aspects of climate change-induced disasters, suggesting that the lower threshold may apply to claims based on a risk of ill-treatment resulting from disasters and climate change.[71] More optimistically, Burson argues in this volume that the ECtHR's approach to *non-refoulement* in socioeconomic/humanitarian conditions cases is the most expansive practice globally.[72] In any event, what *Sufi and Elmi* calls for, is further exploration of the links between armed conflict and environmental degradation.[73] This would contribute to this judgment's full potential by expanding the range of cases where the lower threshold under Article 3 ECHR would apply, thereby enhancing international protection from returns to dire socioeconomic and humanitarian conditions, including those resulting from conflict or climate and disaster-related displacement.

IV. Conclusion

Some domestic courts have treated the case of *Sufi and Elmi* as a landmark case for its determination of facts, namely determining risk on return to Somalia based on evidence before the ECtHR at the time. In 2011, the evidence demonstrated that violence in Mogadishu was of such high intensity that anyone present on the territory would face a real risk of ill-treatment[74] and the humanitarian conditions in Somalia were primarily attributed to the direct and indirect actions of the parties to the conflict. By 2014, the Upper Tribunal in the UK, for example, concluded that this was no longer the case as the situation on the ground had improved significantly.[75] The ECtHR itself considered that the situation of widespread violence had improved in later cases.[76] Undoubtedly, this was an historic case on the facts. Although the ECtHR had already established the principle that there may be a real risk of ill-treatment contrary to Article 3 ECHR simply by virtue of being present on a territory due to exceptional levels of violence in the case of *NA v UK*, this was the first time the factual circumstances were such that the high threshold was met.

[70] Ní Ghráinne (n 55).

[71] See, eg, M Scott, 'Natural Disasters, Climate Change and Non-Refoulement: What Scope for Resisting Expulsion under Articles 3 and 8 of the European Convention on Human Rights?' (2014) 26 *International Journal of Refugee Law* 404; M Scott, 'Finding Agency in Adversity: Applying the Refugee Convention in the Context of Disasters and Climate Change' (2016) 35(4) *Refugee Survey Quarterly* 26, 28.

[72] See Bruce Burson, '*Ioane Teitiota v New Zealand* [2020]: Meeting the Challenge of Climate Change through International Protection Law' in ch 15 of this volume.

[73] C Scissa, 'Environmental Crimes and Forced Migration: An Overlooked Nexus' (2024) 24(66) *Istituto Affari Internazionali* (IAI) Commentaries.

[74] Except possibly for those who were exceptionally well-connected to powerful actors.

[75] *MOJ & Ors (Return to Mogadishu) (Rev 1) (CG)* [2014] UKUT 442 (IAC) (3 October 2014).

[76] *KAB v Sweden* [2014] Imm AR 371; *RH v Sweden* (n 13); For a critique of the ECtHR's assessment of the facts in this later case law, see Ní Ghráinne (n 55) 68–69.

Since then however, the ECtHR has never found that levels of violence are so high as to create a general risk of serious harm engaging Article 3 ECHR,[77] except possibly for two cases concerning Syria considered below.[78] Instead, the ECtHR has been more amenable to considering risk on return to situations of widespread violence for groups of persons defined as particularly vulnerable on account of personal characteristics such as religion, race, age or sex.[79] Only the cases concerning return to Syria could potentially be read as extending to all returnees, although the ECtHR emphasised the applicants' particular characteristics which increased the risk, namely being men of military drafting age.[80] The ECtHR's focus on individual circumstances increasing the risk of serious harm, even where violence in armed conflicts is widespread, reifies the impression of exceptionality for Article 3 ECHR to apply. Hence, the ECtHR's case law since *Sufi and Elmi* has confirmed that the threshold would be met 'only in the most extreme cases of general violence'.[81] Yet, the principles developed by the ECtHR in *Sufi and Elmi* have much wider legal implications for international refugee law and practice. Those implications, as we have seen, have been both positive and negative.

As noted above, refugee claims from persons fleeing conflicts have often been treated with a degree of exceptionalism, leading UNHCR to adopt Guidelines on Armed Conflict and Violence.[82] However, in the absence of published evidence that the Guidelines have improved state practice and refugee protection globally, it is fair to assume that *Sufi and Elmi* continues to play an important role in the determination of conflict-related international protection needs in Europe.

Yet in certain respects, the *Sufi and Elmi* legacy is one which has contributed to restrictive policy and practice relating to complementary forms of protection in the EU, in particular subsidiary protection under Article 15(c) of the EU Qualification Directive. This is because the assessment of indiscriminate violence

[77] Iraq: *SA v Sweden* App no 66523/10 (ECtHR, 27 June 2013) [47]; *JK and Others v Sweden* App no 59166/12 (ECtHR, 23 August 2016) [110]. Afghanistan: *Husseini v Sweden*, App no 10611/09 (ECtHR, 13 October 2011) [84]; *H and B v the United Kingdom* App nos 70073/10 and 44539/11 (ECtHR, 9 April 2013) [93]; *AGR v Netherlands* App no 13442/08 (ECtHR, 12 January 2016) [59]. Sudan: *Mohammed v Austria* App no 2283/12 (ECtHR, 6 June 2013) [109]; *AA v Switzerland* App no 58802/12 (ECtHR, 7 January 2014) [39].

[78] *LM and Others v Russia* (n 43); *SK v Russia* (n 43).

[79] See, eg, *RH v Sweden* (n 13) (single women with no male network in Mogadishu, Somalia: violation); *LM and Others v Russia* (n 43) (young Syrian and Palestinian men in Aleppo and Damascus, Syria: violation); *SK v Russia* (n 43) (man at risk of drafting in Damascus, Syria: violation); *JK and Others v Sweden* (n 77) (family perceived as collaborating with international forces in Iraq: violation); *ASN and others v the Netherlands* App nos 68377/17 and 530/18 (ECtHR, 25 February 2020) (Sikhs in Afghanistan: no violation); *SA v The Netherlands* App no 49773/15 (ECtHR, 2 June 2020): (non-Arabs in Darfur, Sudan: no violation).

[80] *LM and Others v Russia* (n 43) [123]–[24]; *SK v Russia* (n 43) [61]–[62].

[81] *LM and Others v Russia* (n 43) [119].

[82] UNHCR, *Guidelines on International Protection No. 12: Claims for refugee status related to situations of armed conflict and violence under Article 1A(2) of the 1951 Convention and/or 1967 Protocol relating to the Status of Refugees and the regional refugee definitions* (2 December 2016) UN Doc HCR/GIP/16/12.

by EU Member States continues to draw on principles of IHL norms,[83] partly due to the endorsement of the *Sufi and Elmi* 'indicators' of indiscriminate violence by the EUAA.[84] The absence of long-lasting improvements in the protection of conflict refugees stands in stark contrast to the optimism with which the judgment was initially received in the field, casting doubt on the positive impact of this case.

The true potential of the *Sufi and Elmi* judgment is yet to be fully realised and will likely materialise in claims related to dire humanitarian and socioeconomic conditions, whether resulting from armed conflicts or not.[85] *Sufi and Elmi* extended consideration of removal to armed conflict situations to include humanitarian conditions partly caused by parties to conflicts, thereby limiting the use of an internal relocation alternative as a basis to refuse international protection claims. Moreover, parallels have been drawn with dire humanitarian conditions caused by man-made disasters and climate change. As argued in this chapter, further investigation into the links between the actions of warring parties in armed conflicts and environmental degradation may enhance *Sufi and Elmi*'s true potential. If so, the principles developed by the ECtHR would continue to expand the boundaries of protection for persons fleeing serious harm *en masse*.

[83] Querton (n 40).
[84] Querton (n 38).
[85] See Burson (n 72).

12

Pacheco Tineo Family v Bolivia [2013]: Human Rights and Procedural Guarantees for Refugees in the Americas

LILIANA LYRA JUBILUT, CAMILA MARQUES GILBERTO AND FLÁVIA OLIVEIRA RIBEIRO

I. Introduction

Refugee protection in the Americas takes place in a complex and diverse context, with significant regional and national differences, from the countries themselves (in terms for instance of language, history, culture, levels of development and economic and political structures[1]) to their policies and perspectives on migration and displacement.[2] Despite this, a common thread can be found in the work of the Inter-American Human Rights System (IAHRS), which has been engaged with the protection of refugees and other migrants within a human rights framework since the 1990s.[3]

Central to this advocacy is the landmark 2013 decision of the Inter-American Court of Human Rights (IACtHR) in the *Pacheco Tineo* case.[4] This decision not

[1] For example, F Piovesan, LL Jubilut and MM Casagrande, 'The 1951 Convention and the Americas: Regional Developments' in A Zimmermann and others (eds), *Commentary on the 1951 Convention Relating to the Status of Refugees and its 1967 Protocol* (Oxford University Press, 2024) 262; LL Jubilut, MV Espinoza and G Mezzanotti, 'Refugee Protection in Latin America: Logics, Regimes and Challenges' in LL Jubilut, MV Espinoza and G Mezzanotti (eds), *Latin America and Refugee Protection: Regimes, Logics, and Challenges* (Berghahn Books, 2021) 1–28.

[2] LL Jubilut and RO Lopes, 'Forced Migration and Latin America – Peculiarities of a Peculiar Region in Refugee Protection' (2018) *Archiv des Völkerrechts* 56, 2.

[3] LL Jubilut, MM Casagrande and ACC Kosiak, 'Tendências na atuação da Corte Interamericana de Direitos Humanos sobre proteção a pessoas refugiadas e demais migrantes' in AMD Lopes, FP Paredes and RB Lazarte (eds), *Tendências jurisprudenciais da Corte Interamericana de Direitos Humanos* (Livraria do Advogado, 2020) 130.

[4] Inter-American Court of Human Rights (IACtHR), *Pacheco Tineo Family v Bolivia: Call to a Public Hearing* (19 February 2013), available at jurisprudencia.corteidh.or.cr/en/vid/883975926; IACtHR, *Pacheco Tineo Family v Bolivia: Preliminary Objections, Merits, Reparations and Costs* (25 November 2013) Series C No 272, available at jurisprudencia.corteidh.or.cr/en/vid/883975323; IACtHR, *Pacheco Tineo Family v Bolivia: Reimbursement of the Victims' Legal Assistance Fund* (26 January 2015), available at

only reinforced the crucial link between refugee protection and human rights,[5] and, thus, enhanced the protection architecture in the region, but also established essential procedural guarantees for refugees (and other migrants). Moreover, it set a precedent for how the region should approach the right to asylum[6] and refugee rights,[7] including the protection of refugee children.

This chapter seeks to explore the implications of the *Pacheco Tineo* case within the broader context of international human rights law (IHRL) and international refugee law (IRL) and aims to showcase how this landmark decision has shaped the field of refugee law in the Americas. To this end, it will: (i) describe the legal and institutional background, outlining the foundations of refugee protection in the Americas (section II), (ii) present key aspects of the *Pacheco Tineo* case, detailing the facts, the proceedings before the Inter-American Commission and the IACtHR, and the Court's decision (section III), (iii) examine the substantive and procedural legacy for refugee (and other migrants) protection standards, as well as its relevance to child protection (section IV), and (iv) situate the case within the broader jurisprudence of the IAHRS, analysing subsequent decisions that have further shaped the protection of refugees and other migrants in the Americas (section V).

II. The Normative and Institutional Contexts of the Case

A. Right to Asylum

In the Americas, the right to asylum has developed within a complex legal framework, with Latin America standing out for its strong tradition of political asylum[8] and of expanding the humanitarian space.[9] Unlike many other parts of

jurisprudencia.corteidh.or.cr/en/vid/883974830; IACtHR, *Pacheco Tineo Family v Bolivia: Monitoring Compliance with Judgment* (17 April 2015), available at jurisprudencia.corteidh.or.cr/en/vid/883975191.

[5] *Pacheco Tineo Family v Bolivia* (n 4) [129], [132].

[6] It is relevant to note that the IACtHR sentence uses the phrase 'right to asylum' whereas other instruments (such as the summary of the American Declaration of the Rights and Duties of Man use 'right of asylum'). As this chapter tackles the *Pacheco Tineo* case it will follow the Court's wording. *American Declaration of the Rights and Duties of Man* (Bogotá, 2 May 1948), available at www.oas.org/en/iachr/mandate/Basics/american-declaration-rights-duties-of-man.pdf.

[7] *Pacheco Tineo Family v Bolivia* (n 4) [137], [139].

[8] LL Jubilut, 'Refugee Law and Protection in Brazil: A Model in South America?' (2006) *Journal of Refugee Studies* 19, 1; JC Murillo González, 'El derecho de asilo y la protección de refugiados en el continente americano' in *La protección internacional de refugiados en las Américas* (ACNUR, 2011); JH Fischel de Andrade, 'Forced Migration in South America' in E Fiddian-Qasmiyeh and others (eds), *The Oxford Handbook of Refugee and Forced Migration Studies* (Oxford University Press, 2014); MM Casagrande, 'Refugee Protection and the Inter-American Court of Human Rights' in LL Jubilut, MV Espinoza and G Mezzanotti, *Latin America and Refugee Protection: Regimes, Logics and Challenges* (Berghahn, 2021) 154.

[9] Jubilut, Espinoza and Mezzanotti (n 1).

the world, where (political) asylum and refuge are considered synonymous,[10] Latin America distinguishes the two normatively and operationally.[11]

Although both political asylum and refuge aim to provide humanitarian protection,[12] they have distinct legal histories and characteristics in Latin America.[13] Political asylum has a longer and deeply rooted tradition in the region, grounded in both customary and conventional law.[14] It is typically granted to individuals persecuted on political grounds, whether through territorial or diplomatic asylum, and is generally understood as a discretionary decision by the host state.[15] Political asylum in Latin America is based on a plethora of treaties since the nineteenth century.[16] In international jurisprudence, the International Court of Justice (ICJ) articulated the parameters of a regional custom of political asylum in Latin America[17] in the case of *Haya de la Torre (Colombia v Peru)*,[18] which revolved around diplomatic asylum.

Refuge, on the other hand, is implemented through refugee status as developed under international law.[19] It is considered a right, declaratory in nature, and becomes obligatory when certain legal criteria are met.[20] These include, as per the 1951 Refugee Convention and its 1967 Protocol, extraterritoriality, a well-founded fear of persecution, on the grounds of political opinion, race, religion, nationality, or membership of a particular social group,[21] as well as the expanded refugee definition provided by the 1984 Cartagena Declaration, which encompasses those fleeing generalised violence, massive human rights violations, and other circumstances seriously disturbing public order.[22]

[10] LL Jubilut, MM Casagrande and RO Lopes, 'A Convenção Americana sobre Direitos Humanos e o Direito de Asilo na América Latina' in AA, Jr. F Piovesan and PM Danese (eds), *50 anos da Convenção Americana de Direitos Humanos: O Sistema Interamericano: legado, impacto e perspectivas* (Editora Jus Podivm, 2020) 447.

[11] ibid.

[12] Jubilut (n 8) 28; LL Jubilut, *O Direito Internacional dos Refugiados* (São Paulo, Editora Método 2007) 50.

[13] Jubilut, Espinoza and Mezzanotti (n 1).

[14] Jubilut (n 8) 28.

[15] ibid.

[16] For example Tratado de Direito Internacional Penal (Montevidéu, 23 January 1889); Convenção sobre Asilo (Havana, 20 February 1928) (VI Conferência Pan-americana); Convenção sobre Asilo Político (Montevidéu, 26 December 1933) (VII Conferência Internacional Americana); American Declaration of the Rights and Duties of Man (n 6); Convenção sobre Asilo Diplomático (Caracas, 28 March 1954) (X Conferência Interamericana).

[17] Jubilut (n 12).

[18] ICJ, *Asylum Case (Colombia v Peru)* (20 November 1950) ICJ Reports 266.

[19] Jubilut, Casagrande and Lopes (n 10).

[20] Jubilut (n 8).

[21] The criteria also include the need for protection and being deserving of it (ie not subjected to exclusion clauses). United Nations High Commissioner for Refugees (UNHCR), '1951 Refugee Convention and 1967 Protocol relating to the Status of Refugees' (1951), available at www.unhcr.org/sites/default/files/2025-02/1951-refugee-convention-1967-protocol.pdf.

[22] Cartagena Declaration, 3rd conclusion. Organisation of American States (OAS), Cartagena Declaration on Refugees (1984), available at www.oas.org/dil/1984_cartagena_declaration_on_refugees.pdf.

In relation to refuge, it is relevant to note that the Americas have been engaged with the contemporary refugee protection regime from the beginning, with some countries (Brazil, Canada, Colombia, the United States, and Venezuela) taking part in the *travaux préparatoires* of the 1951 Convention,[23] most adhering to it and/or the 1967 Protocol (30 states to the former and 28 to the latter),[24] and the majority positively engaging with the most recent documents, such as the 2018 Global Compact on Refugees.[25]

In broader terms, and encompassing both political asylum and refuge, there is the application of the right to asylum in the region, both in its internationally recognised manner (Article 14 of the 1948 Universal Declaration of Human Rights (UDHR)) and in regional norms, the first of which, in fact, pre-dates the universal norm: Article 27 of American Declaration of the Rights and Duties of Man (ADHR), which states that 'Every person has the right, in case of pursuit not resulting from ordinary crimes, to seek and receive asylum in foreign territory, in accordance with the laws of each country and with international agreements'. The right was reaffirmed in the 1969 American Convention on Human Rights (ACHR), whose Article 22(7) states: 'Every person has the right to seek and be granted asylum in a foreign territory, in accordance with the legislation of the state and international conventions, in the event he is being pursued for political offense related common crimes'.

From their wording one sees that the two regional norms affirm both the right to seek (as in the UDHR) and to *receive/to be granted* asylum,[26] thus expanding the normative context of protection under this right in the Americas.

The relevance of the right to asylum in refugee protection was highlighted in the IACtHR Advisory Opinion 25 (OC-25/18),[27] issued in 2018, and dealing with the nature of the right to asylum, in which the Court further strengthened the recognition of asylum as a human right,[28] thus reinforcing the link between IRL and IHRL.

B. Refuge and Human Rights in the Protection of Refugees in the Americas

This intrinsic connection between IRL and IHRL is found in the concept of integral protection, meaning the assurance of all rights a person is entitled to due to being a human being (human rights) and of all rights resulting from the specific

[23] Piovesan, Jubilut and Casagrande (n 1) 260.

[24] ibid 265.

[25] ibid 271, 282.

[26] Jubilut, Casagrande and Lopes (n 10) 448.

[27] IACtHR, *Advisory Opinion OC-25/18* (30 May 2018) Series A No 25, available at www.corteidh.or.cr/docs/opiniones/seriea_25_ing.pdf.

[28] ibid [112], [132]. The IACtHR recognised refuge and territorial asylum as human rights but not diplomatic asylum. ibid [124], [61], [156], [157].

status of being a refugee.[29] The pursuit of integral protection for refugees in the Americas has sources in both hard and soft law.

The principle of *non-refoulement* for instance is mandated by the ACHR (Article 22(8)),[30] ensuring that individuals are not to be returned to areas where their life or freedom may be at risk.[31] This formula is the basis for the concept of persecution (with the addition of threats to security)[32] in the 1984 Cartagena Declaration on Refugees, which also expands the concept of a refugee beyond the 1951 Refugee Convention definition to include criteria that address the specific conditions of forced migration in Latin America, such as fleeing from threats to life, safety, or freedom due to widespread violence or massive human rights violations.[33]

This regional approach, integrating human rights into refugee protection, is a defining feature of the IAHRS. By addressing forced migration through a human rights lens, the IAHRS provides a broader and more inclusive framework for refugee protection – one that goes beyond the 1951 Refugee Convention and other regional or national approaches, by explicitly recognising the right to seek and receive/be granted asylum and the principle of *non-refoulement* as human rights obligations. This framework has significantly influenced legal standards and shaped national practices throughout the region,[34] and is a key trend in the IAHRS dealing with refugee protection cases, such as the *Pacheco Tineo*.

C. The IAHRS

The IAHRS operates within the framework of the Organisation of American States (OAS), and applies to the Americas as a whole. The IAHRS is a central stakeholder in the protection of human rights, through two main bodies: the Inter-American Commission on Human Rights (IACmHR) and the IACtHR.[35] Through its actions, the IAHRS has significantly framed both national practices and regional norms related to the protection of refugees and asylum seekers,[36] influencing the interpretation and implementation of the right to asylum and refugee rights in the Americas.[37]

[29] LL Jubilut and SMO Apolinário, 'A população refugiada no Brasil: em busca da proteção integral' (2008) *Universitas Relações Internacionais*, Brasília 6, 2.

[30] American Convention on Human Rights (ACHR) (Pact of San José, Costa Rica) (San José, 22 November 1969), available at www.oas.org/dil/treaties_b-32_american_convention_on_human_rights.pdf.

[31] Jubilut, Casagrande and Lopes (n 10) 442.

[32] Cartagena Declaration on Refugees (Cartagena, 22 November 1984) 3rd Conclusion, available at www.oas.org/dil/1984_cartagena_declaration_on_refugees.pdf; Jubilut, Casagrande and Lopes (n 10) 452.

[33] Jubilut, Casagrande and Lopes (n 10).

[34] ibid 453.

[35] ibid 457.

[36] ibid; Jubilut, Casagrande and Kosiak (n 3) 130.

[37] For example IACtHR, *Advisory Opinion OC-16/99* (1 October 1999) Series A No 16, available at www.corteidh.or.cr/docs/opiniones/seriea_16_ing.pdf; IACtHR, *Advisory Opinion OC-18/03* (17 September 2003) Series A No 18, available at www.corteidh.or.cr/docs/opiniones/seriea_18_ing.pdf.

The IAHRS has clarified rights' content and reinforced the broader human rights-based approach of the system, as well as positioned itself and its organs as key actors in shaping migration policy and refugee protection in the region.[38]

In addition to advisory opinions,[39] the IACtHR has issued a number of landmark judgments[40] that illustrate its continuing commitment to addressing the human rights of refugees and other migrants in a variety of circumstances, such as forced displacement,[41] violations of the right to nationality,[42] migrants' rights[43] and protection.[44]

In parallel, the IACmHR has also been active in developing standards for refugee and other migrants' protection in the region. Three key documents from the IACmHR underscore this commitment: 1) the 2015 'Human Rights of Migrants, Refugees, Stateless Persons, Victims of Trafficking, and Internally Displaced Persons: Norms and Standards of the Inter-American Human Rights System',[45] 2) Resolution 2/18 on the Forced Migration of Venezuelans,[46] and 3) the 2019 'Inter-American Principles on the Human Rights of All Migrants, Refugees, Stateless Persons, and Victims of Trafficking in Persons',[47] formalised by Resolution 4/19.[48]

[38] ibid. Referring to both opinions: OC-16/99 on due process rights of migrants in deportation or detention cases; and OC-18/03 on the protection of labour rights of migrant workers, including those in an undocumented situation.

[39] eg. IACtHR, *Advisory Opinion OC-16/99* (n 37), *Advisory Opinion OC-18/03* (n 37), and *Advisory OC-25/18* (n 27).

[40] These cases include judgments relating to (i) forced displacement involving Colombia, eg *Mapiripán Massacre v Colombia* (15 September 2005); *Pueblo Bello Massacre v Colombia* (31 January 2006); *Ituango Massacres v Colombia* (1 July 2006); *Afro-descendant Communities Displaced from the Cacarica River Basin (Operation Genesis) v Colombia* (20 November 2013); *Yarce and Others v Colombia* (22 November 2016); *Omeara Carrascal and Others v Colombia* (21 November 2018), (ii) violations of the right to nationality, eg *Yean and Bosico Children v Dominican Republic* (8 September 2005); *Expelled Dominicans and Haitians v Dominican Republic* (28 August 2014), (iii) rights of migrants, eg *Vélez Loor v Panama* (23 November 2010), and (iv) the protection of individuals in a refugee or migrant context, eg *Roche Azaña and Others v Nicaragua* (3 June 2020). During the COVID-19 pandemic, the IACtHR adopted urgent measures to address the increased vulnerability of migrant populations, in three provisional measures in *Vélez Loor v Panama* (26 May 2020, 29 July 2020 and 24 June 2021). All documents are available at www.corteidh.or.cr.

[41] With several cases mainly against Colombia, from 2005 to 2018.

[42] Mainly against the Dominican Republic from 2006 to 2014.

[43] For example, *Case of Vélez Loor v Panama: Preliminary Objections, Merits, Reparations and Costs* (23 November 2010) Series C No 218, available at www.corteidh.or.cr/docs/casos/articulos/seriec_218_ing.pdf.

[44] For example, *Case of Roche Azaña and Others v Nicaragua: Merits and Reparations* (3 June 2020) Series C No 403, available at www.corteidh.or.cr/docs/casos/articulos/seriec_403_ing.pdf.

[45] Inter-American Commission on Human Rights (IACmHR), *Human Rights of Migrants, Refugees, Stateless Persons, Victims of Trafficking, and Internally Displaced Persons: Norms and Standards of the Inter-American Human Rights System* (2015), available at www.oas.org/en/iachr/reports/pdfs/human-mobility.pdf.

[46] IACmHR, *Resolution 2/18 on the Forced Migration of Venezuelans* (2 March 2018), available at www.oas.org/en/iachr/decisions/pdf/Resolution-2-18-en.pdf.

[47] IACmHR, *Inter-American Principles on the Human Rights of All Migrants, Refugees, Stateless Persons, and Victims of Trafficking in Persons (Resolution 4/19)* (7 December 2019), available at www.oas.org/en/iachr/decisions/pdf/Resolution-4-19-en.pdf.

[48] For example IACmHR, *Pandemic and Human Rights in the Americas (Resolution 1/2020)* (10 April 2020); IACmHR, *Due Process in Procedures for the Determination of Refugee Status and Statelessness and the Granting of Complementary Protection* (2020), available at www.oas.org/en/iachr/

By ensuring that refugees are entitled more broadly to human rights, the IACtHR has promoted a more comprehensive and humane approach to (integral) protection in the Americas. The *Pacheco Tineo* case provides a foundation for the further development of the rights of refugees and other migrants in the region and remains a reference point for this rights-based approach within the IAHRS.

III. The *Pacheco Tineo* Case of the Inter-American Human Rights System[49]

A. The Facts

The case of the *Pacheco Tineo Family v Bolivia*, albeit being decided in 2013, focused on events that took place between 19 and 24 February 2001. In fact, the family's situation dates back almost a decade earlier, reflecting the political and social complexities of the time in Peru.

According to the case documents,[50] in the early 1990s, Rumaldo Juan Pacheco Osco and his wife, Fredesvinda Tineo Godos, were accused and imprisoned in Peru for alleged involvement in terrorist activities. In 1992, while they were serving their sentences, a riot broke out in the prison where they were being held, triggered by prisoner transfer procedures. In this episode, later assessed as the *Miguel Castro-Castro Prison v Peru* case,[51] which was submitted to the IAHRS[52] to determine the responsibility of the Peruvian state, the inmates, including Mr and Mrs Pacheco Tineo, suffered serious human rights violations as a result of the excessive use of force by prison officials.

In 1994, the couple were found not guilty of terrorism and released. At the end of 1995, however, they decided to leave Peru after learning that new arrest warrants had been issued following annulment of their trial. The family, consisting of the couple and their two daughters, Frida Edith and Juana Guadalupe, sought refuge in Bolivia, where they were recognised as refugees by the Bolivian authorities in November 1996.[53]

reports/pdfs/DueProcess-EN.pdf; IACmHR, *IACHR Calls on States in the Americas to Adopt Migration and Border Management Policies that Incorporate a Human Rights Approach (Press Release No 82)* (7 April 2021); IACmHR, *IACHR Urges States to Protect Migrants in Recovery Efforts Following the COVID-19 Pandemic (Press Release No 345)* (22 December 2021); IACmHR, *Protection of Haitians in Human Mobility: Inter-American Solidarity (Resolution 2/2021)* (20 October 2021).

[49] *Pacheco Tineo Family v Bolivia* (n 4). This section is developed based on the facts narrated in [65]–[113] of the case.

[50] ibid.

[51] IACtHR, *Case of Miguel Castro-Castro Prison v Peru: Merits, Reparations and Costs* (25 November 2006) Series C No 160, [5], [344], available at www.corteidh.or.cr/docs/casos/articulos/seriec_160_ing.pdf.

[52] IACmHR, *Inmates of Miguel Castro-Castro Prison (Peru)*, Report No 53/99, Case 11.015 (13 April 1999), available at cidh.oas.org/annualrep/2000sp/CapituloIII/Admisible/Peru11.015.htm.

[53] *Pacheco Tineo Family v Bolivia* (n 4) [68].

In 1998, Mr Pacheco Tineo signed a repatriation statement.[54] However, the family did not return to Peru. Instead, the family went to Chile, where they again applied for and were recognised as refugees in August 1998.[55] During their stay in Chile, their third child, Juan Ricardo, was born and acquired Chilean nationality. In February 2001, they decided to travel to Peru to update their academic and professional information and to assess the possibility of returning permanently to their country of origin.

In Peru, after consulting their lawyer, they were informed that the arrest warrants issued in 1995 were still in force, exposing them to considerable risk. Faced with this situation, they decided to return to Chile via Bolivia. On 19 February 2001, upon entering Bolivian territory, they were detained by migration authorities for lack of proper documentation. The family explained their situation and asked for permission to continue their journey to Chile.

The Bolivian authorities, wishing to avoid possible diplomatic issues with Chile, prevented them from travelling there, claiming that they could not travel to a third country given their irregular entry into Bolivia. Mrs Pacheco Tineo was arrested and released only after a *habeas corpus* had been granted. Faced with this situation, Mr Pacheco Tineo submitted a new application for recognition of refugee status, based on the fact that they had previously been recognised as such in Bolivia.

The Bolivian National Committee for Refugees (CONARE) summarily rejected the application and decided not to analyse it, not granting the Pacheco Tineo family any hearings. One of the reasons for the rejection was the repatriation declaration signed by the couple in 1998, which CONARE interpreted as a tacit renunciation of refugee status, on the understanding that the reasons for the first refugee status application had ceased to exist and that there was no basis for a new application.

Following this rejection, on 24 February 2001, the Bolivian migration authorities (SENAMIG) expelled the family to Peru, their country of origin, without formally notifying them of CONARE's decision or giving them the opportunity to appeal.[56] The family's forced return to Peru exposed them once again to the risks they had originally fled. Upon their arrival in Peru, Mr and Mrs Pacheco Tineo were detained for four months, confirming the concrete threat they faced and highlighting their extreme vulnerability.[57]

In 2002, the family submitted the case to the IACmHR, which accepted it in 2004. The legal questions concerned whether Bolivia had violated the ACHR, in particular:

- the obligation to respect rights (Article 1(1)),
- the right to humane treatment (Article 5),

[54] ibid [69]. The voluntary repatriation statement later became a key element in Bolivia's rejection of the family's new asylum application, as the authorities interpreted it as a declaration of cessation of refugee status (ibid [175]). However, the Court did not examine whether the family's decision to return had been entirely voluntary, a factor that could have led to a 'forced repatriation' (ibid [176]).

[55] ibid [72].

[56] ibid [93]–[113].

[57] ibid.

- the right to personal liberty (Article 7),
- the right to a fair trial/judicial guarantees (Article 8),[58]
- the right to the family (Article 17(1)),
- the rights of the child (Article 19), and
- freedom of movement and residence (Article 22, which includes the right to seek and to be granted asylum (Article 22(7)), and the principle of *non-refoulement* (Article 22(8)).[59]

B. The Position of the IACmHR

Following the admission of the case seven years earlier (ie 2004), in October 2011, the IACmHR issued a Merits Report (No 136/11)[60] in which it concluded that the family had experienced violation of the following rights:[61]

- the obligation to respect rights (Article 1(1)),
- the right to mental and moral integrity (Article 5(1)),
- the right to a fair trial (Article 8),
- the obligation to provide special protection to children (Article 19),
- the right to seek asylum (Article 22(7)),
- the principle of *non-return* (Article 22(8)), and
- the right to judicial protection (Article 25).[62]

Hence, the IACmHR recognised the majority of violations claimed by the Pacheco Tineo family, as the general right or in their ACHR specifications, with the exceptions of the violations of the right to personal liberty and the right to family.

Recommendations for monetary and non-monetary reparations were made to the Bolivian State. Due to the lack of compliance and the absence of a response from Bolivia to the recommendations, the IACmHR referred the case to the IACtHR on 21 February 2012.

[58] The right in the ACHR is the right to a fair trial but in the case it is often referred to as the right to judicial guarantees.

[59] IACmHR, *Petition 301/02, Pacheco Tineo Family (Bolivia), Admissibility Report No 53/04* (13 October 2004), available at https://cidh.org/annualrep/2004eng/Bolivia.301.02eng.htm.

[60] IACmHR, *Case 12.474, Pacheco Tineo Family (Bolivia), Merits Report No 136/11* (31 October 2011), available at www.oas.org/en/iachr/decisions/court/12474FondoEn.doc; eg IACtHR, *Pacheco Tineo Family v Bolivia* (n 4) [2], [3].

[61] The rights are listed with the formula found in the IACmHR decision, and therefore sometimes do not mirror the wording of the ACHR. They are listed in the order in which they appear in the ACHR and not in the IACmHR decision.

[62] IACmHR, *Case 12.474, Pacheco Tineo Family (Bolivia), Merits Report No 136/11* (n 59).

C. The Position of the IACtHR

The IACtHR formally accepted the case and opened the proceedings on 29 March 2012 with the appointment of Inter-American Public Defenders.[63] Both parties were notified and given the opportunity to submit written pleadings, motions, and evidence. During the proceedings, the Court received *amicus curiae* briefs, and also heard expert testimony from the United Nations High Commissioner for Refugees (UNHCR), which had been invited to intervene in its capacity as the body mandated to monitor the application of IRL instruments.[64] In its submissions, UNHCR provided legal guidance on two key issues: the incorporation of core principles of international protection, in particular asylum and *non-refoulement*, into the regional normative framework of the Americas; and the need to uphold due process and judicial guarantees, as established in Articles 8 and 25 of the ACHR, in refugee status determination procedures.

A public hearing was held on 19–20 March 2013, when testimony, evidence and oral arguments were presented. The IACtHR delivered its judgment on 25 November 2013.

i. *The Ruling of the IACtHR*

In its reasoning, the IACtHR advanced a normative convergence between IRL and IHRL[65] to ensure the maximum protection of the individuals. The Court concluded that Bolivia had violated fundamental principles and norms of IRL, as well as several rights guaranteed by the ACHR:[66]

- the obligation to respect rights (Article 1(1)),
- the right to mental and moral integrity (Article 5(1)),
- the right to judicial guarantees (Article 8),
- the right to be heard with due guarantees in an administrative proceeding (Article 8(1)),
- the right to protection of the family (Article 17),
- the right to protection of children (Article 19),
- the right to seek and to be granted asylum (Article 22(7)),
- the principle of *non-refoulement* (Article 22(8)), and

[63] *Pacheco Tineo Family v Bolivia* (n 4) [4].

[64] UNHCR, *UNHCR's Expert Witness Testimony before the Inter-American Court of Human Rights, Hearing in the Case of Pacheco Tineo v Bolivia, Case 12.474* (19 March 2013), available at www.refworld.org/jurisprudence/amicus/unhcr/2013/en/96289.

[65] For example, *Pacheco Tineo Family v Bolivia* (n 4) [142].

[66] The rights are listed with the formula found in the IACtHR decision, and therefore sometimes do not mirror the wording of the ACHR. They are listed in the order in which they appear in the ACHR and not in the IACtHR decision.

- the right to judicial protection (Article 25).[67]

The IACtHR thus recognised most of the same violations as the IACmHR, changing the wording of some of them (such as the right to asylum and the principle of *non-refoulement*) and detailing others (such as the rights related to a fair trial). The Court, however, also found a violation of the right to protection of the family, as initially claimed by the Pacheco Tineo family.

The international responsibility of the Bolivian state arose from the actions and omissions of its SENAMIG and CONARE officials, who had failed to comply with international obligations.[68]

The IACtHR identified a number of reparation measures to address the harm suffered by the Pacheco Tineo family as a result of violations of the ACHR.[69] With regard to restitution, the IACtHR considered its judgment itself to be a reparative measure and did not grant additional restitution, noting that there was no evidence regarding the alleged withholding of family documents.[70] With regard to rehabilitation, while the IACtHR recognised the psychological damage suffered by the family, it did not establish a direct causal link to the responsibility of the Bolivian state, which led to no specific rehabilitation orders.[71] As a form of satisfaction, Bolivia was required to publish a summary of the judgment in its official gazette, a national newspaper and on a government website for one year.[72] To prevent future violations, the IACtHR ordered Bolivia to provide ongoing human rights training to immigration officials who interact with migrants, in line with international standards.[73]

On 17 April 2015, the IACtHR decided by resolution to close and archive the case, recognising that Bolivia had complied with all the reparations ordered in the judgment.

IV. The Substantive and Procedural Legacy of the *Pacheco Tineo* Case: A Landmark of IRL

The *Pacheco Tineo* case is emblematic for being the first in which the IACtHR specifically addressed refugee-related issues, establishing important precedents for the protection of refugees in the Americas. The case reaffirmed the need for states to fully implement their international obligations, both at the normative and practical levels, thus resulting in the establishment of both substantive and procedural

[67] *Pacheco Tineo Family v Bolivia* (n 4) [198], [199], [208], [229].
[68] ibid [247].
[69] ibid s VIII.
[70] ibid.
[71] ibid.
[72] ibid.
[73] ibid.

guarantees for refugee protection in the Americas. The former focusing on the content and concept of the right to asylum and refugee status, as well as the link between IRL and IHRL; the latter addressing proper refugee status determination, which is the focus of a transversal analysis in the establishment of procedural guarantees by the IACtHR.

Moreover, in the *Pacheco Tineo* case the IACtHR was able to highlight the enhanced vulnerability of forced migrants, including refugees, and to determine measures of protection for refugee children. These three areas (substantive and procedural guarantees and refugee children's protection) can be understood to be significant legacies of the Court's ruling.

A. Substantive Guarantees

The determination of substantive guarantees in the *Pacheco Tineo* case directly dialogues with the previously mentioned issues of the contexts of refugee protection in the Americas. In this sense, the IACtHR recognised the interaction between the UDHR and the 1951 Refugee Convention in light of an interpretative evolution of the right to asylum and refuge, stating that:

> (…) the institution of asylum, which is a direct emanation of the right to seek and enjoy asylum enshrined in paragraph 1 of Article 14 of the Universal Declaration of Human Rights, is one of the most fundamental mechanisms for the international protection of refugees.[74]

Making this interaction explicit is beneficial to both fields, as it allows interpretative advances in both. This trend is observed in the jurisprudence of international courts, which employ human rights principles in defining refugee status. This is apparent in the *Pacheco Tineo* case with the IACtHR's consideration of both refugee law norms (mainly drawn from the 1951 Refugee Convention)[75] and human rights law norms (such as the ACHR).[76] Considering the *corpus juris* represented by the 1951 Convention, the 1967 Protocol and the 1984 Cartagena Declaration, the IACtHR analysed the evolution of the right to seek and receive/to be granted asylum, the legal definition of a refugee and the principle of *non-refoulement*.[77]

The IACtHR considered that the international and regional refugee protection *corpus juris* shows that once a state has recognised refugee status, protection extends beyond the borders of that state,[78] as failing this might lead to violations of *non-refoulement*. This means that other states in which the person concerned enters must take this status into account when adopting any migratory-related

[74] ibid [139].
[75] ibid [145].
[76] ibid [143].
[77] ibid [141], [143]–[60].
[78] ibid [150].

measure in respect of that person and, consequently, guarantee a duty of special care in the verification of that status and in the measures that they may adopt.[79] In the *Pacheco Tineo* case, despite the fact that the family informed authorities of their recognised refugee status in Chile and their well-founded fear of persecution in Peru, they were expelled from Bolivia to Peru. Because of this the IACtHR found violations of Article 22(7) and 22(8) of the ACHR, which provides for the right to seek asylum and protection against *refoulement*.[80]

The IACtHR decision in the *Pacheco Tineo* case thus confirms substantive guarantees of refugee protection, specifically in terms of the legal definition of a refugee, the right to seek and to be granted asylum, and the principle of *non-refoulement*. However, it can be seen that the main focus of the IACtHR in the *Pacheco Tineo* case, in line with a trend in all of its case law on migration,[81] is on procedural guarantees.

B. Procedural Guarantees

Procedural guarantees have emerged as essential instruments for the realisation of the recognised material rights of refugees, especially in light of an increase in the number of refugee status applications, the lack of political will towards (forced) migrants and restrictive policies. In light of this, the creation of universal standards for procedures becomes crucial.

The IACtHR's articulation of procedural standards in the *Pacheco Tineo* case is one of the most significant contributions of this judgment. The Court reinforced the general obligation to allow access to adequate international protection through fair asylum procedures[82] and confirmed that the enshrinement of individual rights in Article 8 (right to a fair trial) and Article 25 (right to judicial protection) of the ACHR imposes specific procedural obligations on states.[83]

The IACtHR held that the legal guarantees[84] applicable in criminal proceedings, in particular the right to a fair trial, must be extended to situations that may lead to the expulsion of a migrant.[85] This means that the state has an obligation to ensure

[79] ibid.

[80] ibid [139]. The IACtHR also determined that *non-refoulement* applies irrespectively of one's legal or migratory status (ibid [152]).

[81] There are five specific trends in the IACtHR engagement with migration and displacement issues: 1) an increase in its activity, 2) the enhancement of refugees and other migrants' protection and a greater dialogue between IHRL and IRL, 3) reaffirmation of human rights principles in migration and displacement, 4) non-linear decisions, with some advancing and others limiting protection, and 5) the advancement of procedural guarantees. Jubilut, Casagrande and Kosiak (n 3) 144–46.

[82] *Pacheco Tineo Family v Bolivia* (n 4) [153].

[83] ibid [156], [160]–[219], [236].

[84] ACHR (n 30) Art 8(2).

[85] FT Burson and DJ Cantor, 'Introduction: Interpreting the Refugee Definition via Human Rights Standards' in FT Burson and DJ Cantor (eds), *Human Rights and the Refugee Definition: Comparative Legal Practice and Theory* (Brill Nijhoff, 2016) 1; IACtHR, *Pacheco Tineo Family v Bolivia* (n 4) [159].

that any decision that may significantly affect an individual's rights is taken in accordance with fair and just procedures.

In addition, the IACtHR defined specific obligations for states in dealing with asylum claims, based on the guarantees contained in the ACHR and drawing on UNHCR guidelines, which the Court has considered to be an integral part of IRL.[86]

Among the obligations[87] highlighted by the IACtHR are:

a) Facilities for the applicant: States must ensure the necessary facilities, including the services of a competent interpreter and, where appropriate, access to legal assistance and representation. Clear instructions on the procedure must be provided in a language they understand. Contacting a UNHCR representative if necessary must be allowed.
b) Objective analysis of the claim: The application must be objectively examined by a competent and clearly identified authority within the relevant procedure, including a personal interview with the applicant.
c) Reasons for decisions: Decisions taken by competent authorities must be duly reasoned and in writing, allowing the applicant to understand the reasons for the decision.
d) Protection of confidentiality: At all stages of the asylum procedure, the protection of the applicant's personal data and the principle of confidentiality must be respected.
e) Right of appeal: If the applicant is denied refugee status, they must be informed of the possibilities for appeal within the current system and be given a reasonable time to do so.
f) Suspensive effect of appeal: The appeal must have a suspensive effect, allowing the applicant to remain in the country pending a final decision by the competent authority, unless the application is manifestly unfounded.[88]

The decision in the *Pacheco Tineo* case reaffirms the applicability of procedural guarantees established in previous advisory opinions, in particular OC-16/99 and OC-18/03.[89] These include (i) the right to consular assistance, (ii) the need to achieve material equality with nationals through due process, (iii) the right to a full defence,[90] and (iv) the obligations of states to ensure that the fundamental rights of migrants are respected, regardless of their migration status.[91]

The IACtHR went beyond the analysis of the rights of refugees and enumerated relevant aspects of the rights of migrants, such as (i) labour rights of migrant workers, including those in an undocumented situation, respecting the principles of equality

[86] Burson and Cantor, ibid.

[87] *Pacheco Tineo Family v Bolivia* (n 4) [159].

[88] These protections are grounded in the rights to due process and judicial protection under the ACHR (n 30) Art 8(1), 25(1) and set forth in *Pacheco Tineo Family v Bolivia* (n 4) [159].

[89] See n 37 above.

[90] IACtHR, *Cuadernillo de Jurisprudencia de la Corte Interamericana de Derechos Humanos No. 2: Migrantes.*

[91] *Pacheco Tineo Family v Bolivia* (n 4) [228].

and non-discrimination, (ii) migration policies having an inherent link with IHRL protection instruments, (iii) horizontal obligations[92] – encompassing both states and individuals – aimed at ensuring freedoms and guarantees to all persons under the jurisdiction of states, without privileges or discrimination, and (iv) the principles of equality before the law and non-discrimination as *jus cogens* norms, upon which all legal foundations of national and international public order are based[93] and which permeate the entire legal system and impose on states the obligation to ensure their effectiveness.[94]

In the *Pacheco Tineo* case, the IACtHR emphasised that the refugee status determination procedure must always take into account the potential vulnerability of the migrant in the face of arbitrary state decisions,[95] which has an ideological dimension and occurs in a historical context specific to each state, and is perpetuated by *de jure* situations (legal inequality between nationals and migrants) and *de facto* situations (structural inequalities).[96]

From all of these, one sees that the IACtHR has been assertive, both conceptually and procedurally. By emphasising the inseparability of substantive and procedural guarantees, the IACtHR reinforced the idea that the effective protection of refugees depends both on the formal recognition of their rights and on the existence of procedural mechanisms that allow for the concrete implementation of these rights. Without adequate procedures, substantive protections risk becoming ineffective.

Effective procedures require that any additional vulnerabilities are taken into account in any given case. In the *Pacheco Tineo* case, this meant a concern by the IACtHR with the protection of refugee children.

C. Protection of Refugee Children

As the *Pacheco Tineo* case involved three children and their rights, the IACtHR reaffirmed the international obligation of states to provide special protection for children in addition to the general rights guaranteed by the ACHR.[97]

The principle of the *best interests of the child* was central to the IACtHR's reasoning which reaffirmed that this principle must be rigorously applied in all decisions affecting children in order to ensure their full development.[98]

The judgment explicitly referred to Article 19 of the ACHR, which provides for special protection of children and guarantees them the rights recognised in other applicable international instruments. In this sense, the Court referred to

[92] A Beduschi, 'The Contribution of the Inter-American Court of Human Rights to the Protection of Migrants' Rights' (2020) *Refugee Survey Quarterly* 39, 55.
[93] IACtHR, *Advisory Opinion OC-18/03* (n 37) [101].
[94] *Pacheco Tineo Family v Bolivia* (n 4) [129]–[30].
[95] Burson and Cantor (n 84).
[96] IACtHR, *Advisory Opinion OC-18/03* (n 37) [112].
[97] *Pacheco Tineo Family v Bolivia* (n 4) [216].
[98] ibid [218].

Articles 12 and 22 of the Convention on the Rights of the Child.[99] These provisions establish the right of children to be heard in judicial and administrative proceedings affecting them and the obligation of states to provide special protection and humanitarian assistance to refugee children.[100]

The IACtHR identified two key procedural errors in Bolivia's handling of the case, both related to the fact that the children were not given the opportunity to be heard.[101] First, the procedural error occurred during the asylum application process, when the children were not given the opportunity to be heard.[102] Second, the authorities disregarded the children's individual rights in the expulsion proceedings by treating them merely as dependents of their parents rather than as subjects of the law with their own legal status.[103] The Court found that there was no evidence that SENAMIG's expulsion decisions even remotely considered the best interests of the children,[104] based on the principle of *non-refoulement* and the principle of family unity enshrined in Article 17 of the ACHR.[105]

The IACtHR also emphasised that states must avoid arbitrary or unnecessary separation of children from their families and should exhaust all possible measures to preserve family unity in migration proceedings.[106]

Ultimately, the Court found Bolivia responsible for violating the right to the protection of the child and the family, as recognised in Articles 19 and 17, respectively, of the ACHR.[107] By failing to assess the children's situation independently of their parents and disregarding their need for protection, Bolivia failed to fulfil its obligations under the ACHR and the Convention on the Rights of the Child and to consider the specific needs and legal protection of children.

The *Pacheco Tineo* case can therefore be considered a landmark for its substantive, procedural and child protection aspects. Its influence extends to subsequent decisions by the IACtHR, thus assisting in the development and deepening of refugees' protection in the region.

V. Other Cases of the Inter-American System in the Post-*Pacheco Tineo* Era

Since the *Pacheco Tineo* case in 2013, the IACtHR has remained active in consolidating its jurisprudence on refugees and other migrants. Although no specific refugee cases

[99] ibid [219].
[100] ibid.
[101] ibid [222].
[102] ibid [223], [225].
[103] ibid [228].
[104] ibid.
[105] ibid.
[106] ibid [226], [227].
[107] ibid [229].

have been decided by the IACtHR since then, various advisory opinions and related decisions were adopted which are relevant for the rights of refugees and migrants more broadly.

The emphasis on recognising the vulnerability of migrants was further developed in Advisory Opinion OC-21/14,[108] in which the IACtHR consolidated its understanding of the increased vulnerability of migrant children,[109] emphasising that states must guarantee the principles of *non-refoulement* and the *best interests of the child*,[110] and that detention measures for migrant children should be avoided.[111]

Advisory Opinion OC-25/18 reaffirmed the right to seek and to be granted asylum as a fundamental human right within the IAHRS[112] and emphasised that the principle of *non-refoulement* is *jus cogens*.[113] Moreover, OC-25/18 underlined the need for fair and efficient procedures for refugee status determination, in line with the procedural guarantees set out in the *Pacheco Tineo* case.[114] In this regard, the IACtHR stressed that states must ensure that asylum procedures are accessible, adequate and adapted to the needs of persons in vulnerable situations, including women, children, persons with disabilities and victims of persecution based on gender or sexual orientation.[115]

The jurisprudence following *Pacheco Tineo* demonstrates that the IACtHR has continued to develop and strengthen the protection of refugees and other migrants in these key areas,[116] showing that the legacy of the *Pacheco Tineo* case remains influential in the jurisprudence of the IACtHR, serving as a reference point for consolidating substantive and procedural guarantees in favour of refugees and other migrants.

[108] Advisory Opinion OC-21/14 was requested by Argentina, Brazil, Paraguay, and Uruguay. The states asked the Court to pronounce on the types of procedures that should be adopted to identify migrant children. They also inquired about the guarantees of due process in procedures involving children; whether children should be detained in such procedures when accompanied by their parents or when travelling unaccompanied; the scope and content of the principle of *non-refoulement*; and how to protect a child's right not to be separated from their parents in the context of deportation. IACtHR, *Advisory Opinion OC-21/14* (19 August 2014) Series A No 21, available at www.corteidh.or.cr/docs/opiniones/seriea_21_eng.pdf.

[109] Beduschi (n 90) 59.

[110] IACtHR, *Advisory Opinion OC-21/14* (n 106) [69], [103]–[107].

[111] ibid [144].

[112] IACtHR, *Advisory Opinion OC-25/18* (n 27) [61]–[163].

[113] ibid [194]–[99].

[114] ibid [99].

[115] On the issue of gender and sexual orientation, see, eg, IACtHR, *Advisory Opinion OC-24/17* (24 November 2017) Series A No 24, available at www.corteidh.or.cr/docs/opiniones/seriea_24_eng.pdf; IACtHR, *Advisory Opinion OC-25/18* (n 27) [61]–[163].

[116] This development occurred in other topics, for example *Expelled Dominicans and Haitians v Dominican Republic* (28 August 2014) Series C No 282; *Wong Ho Wing v Peru* (30 June 2015) Series C No 297; *Vélez Loor v Panama* (n 43).

VI. Conclusion

The *Pacheco Tineo* case is a landmark decision from the IAHRS not only for its emphasis on substantive principles (reinforcing multiple aspects of refugee protection in the Americas including the long tradition of the right to asylum, the respect for refugee status, and the connection between IRL and IHRL), establishing essential procedural guarantees, and highlighting the protection of refugee and migrant children, but also due to its continued role in influencing refugee protection at a regional level.

The emphasis in the decision on due process and the need for effective access to fair asylum procedures reflects a broader recognition that substantive rights cannot be fully realised without robust procedural safeguards. The integration of IHRL with refugee protection not only enhances the safeguards available to individuals fleeing persecution but also serves to promote a more humane and equitable approach to migration. As IAHRS jurisprudence continues to evolve, the legacy of the *Pacheco Tineo* case serves as a fundamental reference point to guide on-going efforts to strengthen the integral protection of refugees and other migrants and ensure full respect for all their rights.

13

Namah v Pato [2016]: Constitutional Challenges in Offshore Destination States

MARIA O'SULLIVAN

I. Introduction

Externalisation of refugee protection via the use of offshore processing and extra-territorial detention of asylum seekers poses significant challenges for strategic litigation. Such regimes split the allocation of legal responsibilities across different jurisdictions, rendering accountability mechanisms for the treatment of asylum seekers unclear and contested. Often, asylum seekers seeking to challenge the legality of their transfer and detention in a destination state are constrained in their ability to seek redress because the sending state is able to avoid legal responsibility for the treatment of those asylum seekers in a third country. This means that utilising international refugee law and human rights law to protect the rights of transferred asylum seekers can face significant obstacles.

This is clearly illustrated by the use of litigation to challenge the operation of Australia's offshore asylum regime. This system, which permits Australian authorities to transfer 'unauthorised' asylum seekers to 'regional processing centres' in the Pacific for processing and detention, currently operates in Nauru and operated in Papua New Guinea (PNG) from 2012–2021.[1] One aspect of the offshore processing regime which operated in PNG was that asylum seekers transferred by Australia to PNG were held in detention on the Manus Island Processing Centre

[1] 'Regional processing' or 'offshore processing' within the Australian context is the system by which legislatively designated 'unauthorized maritime arrivals' (persons who attempt to arrive to Australia by boat), are transferred by Australian authorities to an offshore Regional Processing Centre for processing, detention and resettlement. Note that Australia terminated its regional processing contract with Papua New Guinea (PNG) in 2021 and PNG is no longer utilised as an offshore processing/detention centre: see Minister for Home Affairs, 'Joint Media Release with the Hon. Westly Nukundj MP – Finalisation of the Regional Resettlement Arrangement' (06 October 2021), available at minister.homeaffairs.gov.au/KarenAndrews/Pages/finalisation-of-the-regional-resettlement-arrangement.aspx.

('Manus Island'). The operation of this 'processing centre' as a closed centre raised human rights concerns, including the right to liberty.[2]

Despite Australia's offshore processing centre in PNG being widely criticised by various United Nation (UN) bodies, civil society and academics over the last two decades,[3] it has been extremely difficult for asylum seekers to challenge the operation of this regime. Numerous legal challenges within Australia were instigated in an attempt to overturn the Australian legislative and constitutional underpinning of the offshore detention regime. However, whilst a class action based in tort (negligence and false imprisonment) was successful, none of these cases were successful in dismantling the legal underpinnings of the offshore system.[4]

Against this background, the 2016 decision of the Supreme Court of PNG in *Namah v Pato*[5] represents a significant judgment in the context of accountability and oversight of offshore processing regimes and the related detention of asylum seekers in those extra-territorial centres. In this case, the PNG Supreme Court, in a unanimous decision of five judges, held that detention of refugees and asylum seekers in the Australian-funded centres in that country was unconstitutional under the right to liberty set out in the PNG Constitution.[6] Importantly, the Court order sought to bind Australia as well as PNG, ordering (inter alia) that both the Australian and PNG governments 'take all steps necessary to cease and prevent the continued unconstitutional and illegal detention of the asylum seekers or transferees … on Manus Island'.[7]

This decision represents a landmark case for international refugee law as it represents an example of the utility of seeking redress in an offshore *destination* state (PNG) rather than the *sending* state (Australia).[8] It also highlights the importance of utilising the constitutional provisions of that destination state to protect the rights of asylum seekers and the importance of an independent judiciary in upholding those constitutional provisions.[9]

[2] See discussion in section III.

[3] See discussion in A Dastyari and M O'Sullivan, 'Not for Export: The Failure of Australia's Extraterritorial Processing Regime in Papua New Guinea and the Decision of the PNG Supreme Court in Namah' (2016) 42(2) *Monash University Law Review* 308, 311–13.

[4] See, eg, *Plaintiff S156-2013 v Minister for Immigration and Border Protection* (2014) 254 CLR 28, challenging the legality of offshore detention in PNG. See also *Plaintiff M68/2015 v Minister for Immigration and Border Protection* (2016) 257 CLR 42, challenging the legality of offshore detention on Nauru. A number of class actions based in tort were successful, but these have not been directed at the lawfulness of the legal foundation of the system, see discussion in text associated with nn 67–69.

[5] *Namah v Pato* [2016] PGSC 13 (PNG Supreme Court).

[6] *Constitution of the Independent State of Papua New Guinea* (Papua New Guinea), came into effect 16 September 1975 (PNG Constitution) s 42; *Namah* (n 5).

[7] *Namah* (n 5) 28 [74].

[8] The common approach in strategic litigation relating to externalisation is to bring a case in the sending state, see for instance the challenge to the United Kingdom (UK)-Rwandan arrangement before the UK Supreme Court, discussed in Nikolas Feith Tan, '*R (on the application of AAA and others) v Secretary of State for the Home Department* [2023]: The Limits of Externalisation and the Failed UK-Rwanda Arrangement' in ch 14 of this volume.

[9] Similar legal dynamics can be observed in the litigation before the High Court of Kenya in *Kituo Cha Sheria and Others v Attorney-General*, discussed in Samuel Woldemariam, '*Kituo Cha Sheria and*

To analyse the significance of this decision, I begin in section II by setting out the context in which the decision operates. Here I discuss the legal and political context of offshore processing and detention, followed by a brief discussion of the international context, with a focus on the role of the UN High Commissioner for Refugees (UNHCR). I then utilise this context to discuss the findings of the PNG Supreme Court in more detail in section III, followed by an examination of its contemporaneous and contemporary significance in sections IV and V. In concluding, I discuss the significance of the decision more broadly for international refugee law in section VI. Issues discussed include the place of human rights and constitutional provisions in the development of international refugee law, judicial citations of jurisprudence from the Global South and the allocation of legal responsibility in offshore processing and detention regimes.

II. The Legal, Political and International Context of *Namah v Pato*

A. The Legal Context of Offshore Processing and Detention in PNG

Australia established a system of offshore processing in the Asia-Pacific from 2001 onwards via bilateral agreements with two key developing nations in the region: Nauru and PNG.[10] Offshore processing by Australia has been undertaken in two phases: the first from 2001–2008 and then from 2012 onwards.[11] It is the latter phase which is the focus of discussion in this chapter.

The legal framework for the transfer of asylum seekers from Australia to PNG is comprised of legislative authorisation under the Australian Migration Act and a number of bilateral agreements between the two countries. In 2012, PNG was designated as a 'regional processing country' pursuant to the Australian Migration Act[12] and a set of bilateral agreements were signed to underpin the transfer of asylum

Others v Attorney-General [2013]: Betwixt Executive Opposition and Judicial Affirmation of Refugee Rights', in ch 10 of this volume.

[10] A fuller history of the establishment of the Pacific Solution can be found in G Holly, 'Challenges to Australia's Offshore Detention Regime and the Limits of Strategic Tort Litigation' (2020) 21 *German Law Journal* 549, 551–53; and Dastyari and O'Sullivan (n 3) at 314–16.

[11] The existence of the two phases is due to the dismantling of the first phase of offshore processing by a newly-elected Labour government in 2008. It was reinstated by a different Labour government in 2012, see discussion in M Gleeson and N Yacoub, 'Cruel, Costly and Ineffective: The Failure of Offshore Processing in Australia' (*Kaldor Centre for International Refugee Law Policy Brief*, August 2021) 11, 2–4, available at www.kaldorcentre.unsw.edu.au/sites/kaldorcentre.unsw.edu.au/files/Policy_Brief_11_Offshore_Processing.pdf.

[12] Minister for Immigration and Citizenship (Cth), *Instrument of Designation of the Independent State of Papua New Guinea as a Regional Processing Country under Subsection 198AB(1) of the Migration Act 1958*, F2012L02003, 9 October 2012.

seekers to PNG in 2012[13] and 2013.[14] In this chapter, I focus on the 2013 documents: the 'Regional Resettlement Arrangement'[15] and Memorandum of Understanding ('2013 MOU')[16] as the relevant agreements in force between Australia and PNG at the time of the Supreme Court decision in *Namah*.

Two provisions in these bilateral agreements are particularly relevant to the discussion in this chapter. First, clause 5 of the 2013 MOU provides that: 'The Government of Papua New Guinea will conduct all activities in respect of this MOU in accordance with its Constitution and all relevant domestic laws'.[17] This was central to the litigation in *Namah v Pato* as the PNG Constitution includes a number of human rights protections, specifically, the right to liberty. Relevantly, all transferees were subject to deprivation of liberty in a closed detention centre during this period.[18]

Second, the 2013 Regional Resettlement Arrangement states that '[t]he regional processing centre will be managed and administered by Papua New Guinea under Papua New Guinea law, with support from Australia'.[19] As I have noted earlier, one of the obstacles faced by asylum seekers wishing to challenge offshore processing and detention arrangements is the obfuscation of legal responsibility for the treatment of transferees. This has meant that challenges under Australian law have been extremely difficult to successfully undertake because, although the designation of PNG as a 'regional processing country' is made under *Australian* law, the management and operation of the offshore centres is stated in the bilateral agreements to be a matter of *PNG* law.

[13] *Memorandum of Understanding Between the Republic of Nauru and the Commonwealth of Australia, Relating to the Transfer to and Assessment of Persons in Nauru, and Related Issues* (Intergovernmental Agreement, 29 August 2012); Independent State of Papua New Guinea and Commonwealth of Australia, *Memorandum of Understanding between the Government of the Independent State of Papua New Guinea and the Government of Australia, Relating to the Transfer to and Assessment of Persons in Papua New Guinea, and Related Issues* (Intergovernmental Agreement, 8 September 2012).

[14] Independent State of Papua New Guinea and Commonwealth of Australia, *Regional Resettlement Arrangement between Australia and Papua New Guinea* (Intergovernmental Agreement, 19 July 2013) ('2013 RRA'); Independent State of Papua New Guinea and Commonwealth of Australia, *Memorandum of Understanding between the Government of the Independent State of Papua New Guinea and the Government of Australia, Relating to the Transfer to, and Assessment and Settlement in, Papua New Guinea of Certain Persons, and Related Issues* (Intergovernmental Agreement, 6 August 2013) ('2013 MOU').

[15] 2013 RRA (n 14).

[16] 2013 MOU (n 14).

[17] A similar provision exists in cl 4 of the 2013 MOU requiring Australia to conduct all activities in respect of the MOU in accordance with the Australian Constitution and relevant municipal laws.

[18] See UN High Commissioner for Refugees (UNHCR): 'UNHCR considers that, at present, all transferees at the Centre are subject to deprivation of liberty in a closed place which amounts to "detention" under international law': UNHCR, 'Regional Representation in Canberra, UNHCR Mission to Manus Island, Papua New Guinea, Mission Report' (15–17 January 2013) 12, para 51, available athttps://webarchive.archive.unhcr.org/20230518102136/https://www.refworld.org/docid/5139ab872.html.

[19] 2013 RRA (n 14) cl 4.

B. The Political Context of Offshore Processing and Detention in PNG

An important historical aspect of the PNG decision in *Namah* is that PNG was formerly a protectorate of Australia: PNG was administered by Australia from 1905 to 1975, with the administration role ceasing in 1975 when PNG gained independence.[20] The PNG Constitution, the instrument at the heart of the litigation in *Namah*, came into effect in 1975.[21]

This political history is important for understanding the decision in *Namah v Pato* for a number of reasons. First, although Australia has ceased to be the formal administrator of PNG, it still seeks to wield power over its former protectorate. Foreign aid from Australia to PNG is significant and this has allowed Australia to exert considerable influence over successive PNG governments in relation to the acceptance of offshore processing agreements.[22] Thus, the bilateral agreements between Australia and PNG and the decision in *Namah v Pato* must be considered against the context of power and international relations between the Global North and Global South. Indeed, some commentators have suggested that Australia's offshore processing arrangements are a form of neo-colonialism. As Nethery and Lea state:

> When we survey refugee externalisation policies around the world, it is striking that many are forged upon old colonial relationships. Australia's two partners in its offshore processing policy, Nauru and Papua New Guinea (PNG) are its two former colonies. Similar histories lie beneath externalisation arrangements between the EU and its member states in North Africa, such as Libya.[23]

I will discuss the theme of power and post-colonialism later in this chapter when discussing the broader significance of the decision.

The second implication of Australia's colonial link to PNG is that Australian judges can be appointed to the PNG Supreme Court. This is significant in relation to *Namah v Pato* as one of the two judges who gave reasons for their decisions was an Australian judge (Justice Higgins). As Pacific judiciary expert, Anna Dziedzic has

[20] Section 4 of the Papua New Guinea Independence Act 1975 (Cth) states that Australia withdraws all sovereign rights over PNG.

[21] PNG Constitution (n 6). For a discussion of the drafting of the PNG Constitution, see J Goldring, *The Constitution of Papua New Guinea: A Study in Legal Nationalism* (Law Book Co, 1978).

[22] See discussion in L Button and S Evans, 'At What Cost? The Human, Economic and Strategic Cost of Australia's Asylum Seeker Policies and the Alternative' (Save the Children Australia and UNICEF Australia, 2016) 58–60, available at apo.org.au/node/270056.

[23] A Nethery and J Lea, 'Australia's Offshore Processing Arrangements: A Form of Neo-Colonialism?' (Comparative Network on Refugee Externalisation Policies (CONREP) Blog, 17 June 2020), available at arts.unimelb.edu.au/school-of-social-and-political-sciences/our-research/comparative-network-on-refugee-externalisation-policies/blog/australias-offshore-processing-arrangements-a-form-of-neo-colonialism.

noted, '[t]he practice of appointing foreign judges to a state's highest court is unusual in global practice, but prevalent in the Pacific region'.[24]

In addition to the implications of PNG's colonial history, more contemporary political developments in PNG in the lead up to the Court decision in *Namah v Pato* are relevant. As noted above, the acceptance of the terms of the offshore processing agreements between Australia and PNG were significantly influenced by the power relationship between the two countries and the foreign aid which often came with such agreements. However, in early 2016, the detention centre in PNG became politically controversial within the PNG Government. The detention centre was called a 'problem' by the PNG Prime Minister who stated that it 'has done a lot more damage … than anything else' to the reputation of PNG.[25] The PNG Prime Minister also declared that the Centre would at some stage have to be closed.[26]

C. The International Context – The Role of UNHCR

In examining the context of *Namah*, another factor is the influence of UNHCR guidance and commentary in the development of jurisprudence. UNHCR and other bodies raised concerns about the detention of asylum seekers and refugees in PNG on numerous occasions leading up to the decision in *Namah*.[27] Of these reports, the findings of two UNHCR Monitoring Visits to PNG in 2013 are of significance. In both of those reports, UNHCR found that:

> The current PNG policy and practice of detaining all asylum-seekers at the closed Centre, on a mandatory and indefinite basis without an assessment as to the necessity and proportionality of the purpose of such detention in the individual case, and without being brought promptly before a judicial or other independent authority amounts to arbitrary detention that is inconsistent with international human rights law.[28]

These public comments of UNHCR are relevant to the significance of the decision in *Namah* for two primary reasons. First, the Australian Government largely ignored the findings of UNHCR, with the Government repeatedly denying the

[24] A Dziedzic, 'Right to Liberty, Unconstitutional Constitutional Amendments, and Foreign Judges in PNG' (IACL-IADC Blog, 31 May 2016), available at blog-iacl-aidc.org/2016-posts/2016/5/31/analysis-right-to-liberty-unconstitutional-constitutional-amendments-and-foreign-judges-in-png.

[25] P O'Neill, 'Westpac Address at the National Press Club' (Speech delivered at the National Press Club, Canberra, 3 March 2016).

[26] ibid.

[27] See, eg, UNHCR, Regional Representation in Canberra, UNHCR Mission to Manus Island, Papua New Guinea, Mission Report (15–17 January 2013), available at www.refworld.org/docid/5139ab872.html; UNHCR, Regional Representation in Canberra, UNHCR Monitoring Visit to Manus Island, Papua New Guinea, Mission Report (11–13 June 2013), available at www.refworld.org/reference/countryrep/unhcr/2013/en/94304.

[28] UNHCR Monitoring Visit June 2013, ibid, 1, The same finding was made in UNHCR's January 2013 Monitoring report, ibid 1.

existence of harms or their responsibility for any international law violations.[29] Second, the findings of UNHCR on the Manus detention centre were cited by the PNG Supreme Court in its decision,[30] which underlines the importance of the UNHCR's commentary in jurisprudence.[31]

I will now turn to discuss the decision of the PNG Supreme Court in *Namah v Pato*.

III. Summary of the Case and Decision

A. The Legislative and Constitutional Provisions and Litigation

The provision which was central to *Namah v Pato* is section 42 of the PNG Constitution.[32] This provides that '[n]o person shall be deprived of his personal liberty', except in defined, limited circumstances.[33] This constitutional provision also sets out eight exceptions to this right. Relevantly, section 42(1)(g) sets out an exception which relates to the entry of persons into PNG. It provides that one of the exceptions to the right to liberty is where this is:

> for the purpose of preventing the unlawful entry of a person into Papua New Guinea, or for the purpose of effecting the expulsion, extradition or other lawful removal of a person from Papua New Guinea, or the taking of proceedings for any of those purposes.

There are two points to note about section 42 of the PNG Constitution. First, the fact that section 42(1)(g) refers to 'unlawful entry' was pivotal to the Supreme Court case as the agreed facts demonstrated that Australian 'transferees' were brought to PNG as *lawful* entrants. Therefore, the applicant argued that, utilising the words of section 42 in conjunction with the detention provisions of the PNG Migration Act, the asylum seekers did not come within the scope of the exception in section 42(1)(g).

Second, the PNG Constitution was amended in 2014 to take account of Australia's interests in the offshore processing regime and in an attempt to forestall

[29] See discussion in J Barnes, 'Suffering to Save Lives: Torture, Cruelty, and Moral Disengagement in Australia's Offshore Detention Centres' (2002) 35(4) *Journal of Refugee Studies* 1508. For instance, Barnes states that Australia used international law to 'disavow its responsibilities' (at 1518).

[30] Discussed in section III below.

[31] On the issue of UNHCR's role in interpretation of the law by courts, see GS Goodwin-Gill, 'The Search for the One, True Meaning …', in GS Goodwin-Gill and H Lambert (eds), *The Limits of Transnational Law: Refugee Law, Policy Harmonization and Judicial Dialogue in the European Union* (Cambridge University Press, 2010) 204–41, especially at 218 onwards.

[32] PNG Constitution (n 6) s 42.

[33] ibid. The listing exceptions include criminal offences, quarantine breaches and guardianship matters.

the Supreme Court litigation which had just been commenced in *Namah*.[34] Thus, from 2014 onwards, section 42(1)(ga) of the PNG Constitution provided that deprivation of liberty is permitted 'for the purposes of holding a foreign national under arrangements made by Papua New Guinea with another country or with an international organisation that the Minister responsible for immigration matters, in his absolute discretion, approves'.

Before discussing the decision in *Namah v Pato*, it is important to understand how the litigation was lodged – which legal issues were able to be argued by the plaintiffs and why others were not raised. First, whilst PNG is a signatory to the 1951 Refugee Convention,[35] UNHCR considered that there was no adequate domestic legal framework to implement PNG's responsibilities under the 1951 Refugee Convention at the time of this case.[36] In particular, there were no provisions in PNG law which incorporated the provisions of the 1951 Refugee Convention.[37] Hence, the focus of the litigation was on human rights arguments utilising the national constitution.

Second, an interesting political aspect is that the lead plaintiff was Belden Norman Namah, the then leader of the opposition in PNG. Mr Namah was granted standing in the litigation in 2014.[38] This illustrates the importance of utilising various avenues for redress in relation to offshore detention, and also the need for liberal standing rules which allow for representative complaints (individuals or groups acting as litigation representatives in the public interest). The importance of access to litigation for asylum seekers is also highlighted in chapter 10 of this volume where Samuel Woldemariam analyses the judgment of the High Court of Kenya in *Kituo Cha Sheria and Others v Attorney General*.[39] Woldemariam notes that the plaintiff in the first petition[40] in that case – Kituo Cha Sheria – was a non-governmental organisation (NGO) which was able to initiate and plead an *actio popularis* on behalf of refugees and asylum seekers affected by the decision in question. As Woldemariam quite rightly notes, public interest actions brought by NGOs are important for a number of reasons, particularly because they can alleviate some of the challenges that refugees and asylum seekers may face in a host country, such as lack of financial resources to bring their own individual claims,

[34] Constitutional Amendment (No 37) (Citizenship) Law 2014 (PNG).

[35] UN General Assembly, 1951 Convention relating to the Status of Refugees, United Nations, Treaty Series, 189:137, 28 July 1951. PNG acceded to the 1951 Refugee Convention and its 1967 Protocol in 1986. It made seven reservations in signing the Convention – these are discussed in *Namah* (n 5) 25 [67].

[36] UNHCR Mission to Manus Island, January 2013 (n 27) 9, para 36.

[37] This has been recognised by UNHCR, ibid 9, para 36.

[38] See discussion in 'PNG Judges Surprised at Lack of Challenge to Manus Island Detention Centre' (*ABC News*, 4 February 2014), available at www.abc.net.au/news/2014-02-04/an-png-manus-transparency-international/5236528.

[39] *Kituo Cha Sheria and Others v Attorney General* (2013) eKLR 1.

[40] The case was heard as a consolidated petition comprised of the first petition by Kituo Cha Sheria and the second petition comprised of seven refugees who resided in different urban areas in Kenya.

unfamiliarity with the legal environment and lack of professional and social connections to help bring their claims.

B. The Court's Decision

The PNG Supreme Court in *Namah v Pato*, in a unanimous decision of five judges, held that detention of refugees and asylum seekers in the Australian-funded centres in that country was unconstitutional under the right to liberty set out in the PNG Constitution.[41] The Court ordered, inter alia, that both the Australian and PNG governments 'take all steps necessary to cease and prevent the continued unconstitutional and illegal detention of the asylum seekers or transferees … on Manus Island'.[42]

The Supreme Court found the detention of asylum seekers and recognised refugees in the processing centres was unconstitutional for a number of reasons. First, it interpreted the migration exception to the right to liberty in section 42(1)(g) of the PNG Constitution as only available against persons who have entered or remain in the country without a valid entry permit.[43] The Court found that 'the asylum seekers had no intention of entering and remaining in PNG' (rather, their intended destination was Australia).[44] It held that they did not enter PNG and did not remain there of their own accord but were forcibly transferred and detained on Manus Island by the PNG and Australian governments.[45]

The Court also found the 2014 amendment to the PNG Constitution passed to forestall the litigation in the matter (see discussion above) was invalid. It held that the PNG Government had failed to demonstrate that the amendment was 'reasonably justifiable in a democratic society having a proper respect for the rights and dignity of mankind' having regard to section 38 of the PNG Constitution.[46]

Significantly the Court considered international material in reaching this conclusion.[47] This material included UNHCR Detention Guidelines and a UNHCR monitoring report on the Manus Island processing centre published in 2013.[48] The Court held that the Manus Detention Centre did not meet the UNHCR Detention Guidelines[49] and cited the criticisms of the Manus centre in the 2013 UNHCR

[41] *Namah* (n 5) (per Salika DCJ, Sakora, Kandakasi, Sawong and Higgins JJ). Their Honours were in general agreement as to the conclusions and reasoning in the decision, with Kandakasi and Higgins JJ writing individual reasons.

[42] *Namah* (n 5) 28 [74].

[43] ibid 15 [38]. In doing so, the Court read s 42(1)(g) of the Constitution in light of the detention provisions in s 13 of the PNG Migration Act.

[44] ibid 15 [39].

[45] ibid 15–16 [38]–[39].

[46] ibid 21 [54].

[47] Note that the Court is explicitly permitted to do this pursuant to s 39 of the PNG Constitution.

[48] Discussed above at section II.C.

[49] *Namah* (n 5) 24–25 [66].

Monitoring Report.[50] This Report had criticised the Manus Island facilities for its lack of 'basic conditions and standards', 'the closed detention setting and the lack of freedom of movement', and 'the absence of an appropriate legal framework and capacitated system to assess refugee claims'. Thus, the Court found that:

> [t]reating those required to remain in the relocation centre as prisoners irrespective of their circumstances or their status save only as asylum seekers, is to offend against their rights and freedoms as guaranteed by the various conventions on human rights at international law and under the *PNG Constitution*.[51]

In concluding that the 2014 amendment was invalid, the Court specifically stated that '[t]he human rights and dignity of the detainees or the asylum seekers which are guaranteed by the relevant provisions of the *Constitution* need to be respected'.[52] This is a significant finding as it categorises asylum seekers as holders of human rights under the PNG Constitution.

It is important to note that the Supreme Court did not simply focus on the *fact* of detention in rendering the detention unconstitutional, it also considered the *conditions* of detention to be relevant. This is reflected in the findings of Justice Kandakasi who considered the *manner* in which the asylum seekers were treated at the Manus Island Centre:

> The detention *and the way in which the asylum seekers are treated at the Manus Island Relocation or Processing Centre* in so far as they affect their other constitutional rights and freedoms such as the right to freedom under s 32 of the Constitution are unconstitutional and are also ultra vires the powers available under the Migration Act (emphasis added).[53]

The judgment of Justice Higgins also noted that an additional consideration was whether 'the *conditions* of detention are such as to damage the rights and dignity of the detainees or, worse, causes physical or mental suffering' (emphasis added).[54] This is important as the PNG Manus detention centre had been criticised by a number of international organisations and civil society groups for overcrowding and poor conditions and lack of safety for the detainees.[55]

It is also of significant interest that both leading judgments of the PNG Court mentioned the responsibility of Australia in that act of detention. For instance, Justice Kandakasi stated that '[i]t was the joint efforts of the Australian and PNG

[50] ibid 25 [68].

[51] ibid 24–25 [66]–[69], citing UNHCR, *Guidelines on the Applicable Criteria and Standards Relating to the Detention of Asylum Seekers and Alternatives to Detention* (2012) and the 1951 Refugee Convention.

[52] ibid 21 [56].

[53] ibid 27 [74].

[54] ibid 34 [118].

[55] See, eg, Amnesty International, *This is Breaking People: Human Rights Violations at Australia's Asylum Seeker Processing Centre on Manus Island, Papua New Guinea* (December 2013); Senate Legal and Constitutional Affairs References Committee, Parliament of Australia, *Incident at the Manus Island Detention Centre from 16 February to 18 February 2014* (2014).

governments that has seen the asylum seekers brought into PNG and kept at the MIPC against their will'.[56] His Honour also held that '[t]he First Respondent and the Second Respondent with the assistance of the Australian government are responsible for all of the decisions and actions that have led to the transfer and detention of asylum seekers or transferees'.[57]

IV. Decision in Contemporaneous Context

A. Compliance with the PNG Supreme Court Orders – Closure of the Detention Centre

One feature of the decision in *Namah* was the complex and protracted nature of its implementation by PNG and Australia (reflecting the complex and intertwined nature of the responsibility of those two countries for the asylum seekers affected by the decision). Immediately following the decision of the Court, PNG Prime Minister Peter O'Neill stated that the PNG executive would comply with the Court order and would close the detention facility.[58] PNG authorities also informed the UN Human Rights Council that it would comply with the Court ruling.[59] However, Australia was recalcitrant – the Australian Government failed to endorse the PNG Government's decision to close the centre and, instead, attempted to persuade PNG to 'work around' the Supreme Court decision.[60] Specifically, the then Australian Minister for Immigration argued that the Court decision was not binding on Australia and the asylum seekers and refugees in the centre were solely PNG's responsibility.[61]

Eventually, the Australian Government and PNG did officially confirm their intention to close the Manus Island detention facility, some four months later, on 17 August 2016. Following this, it is significant in terms of the rule of law that the PNG Supreme Court saw it necessary to reiterate its call for the closure of the facility and to state that any refugee status determination of the men on the island would need to be completed by the end of October 2016. The PNG Supreme Court

[56] *Namah* (n 5) 15–16 [39].

[57] ibid 27 [73].

[58] S Anderson, 'Manus Island Detention Centre to Be Shut, Papua New Guinea Prime Minister Peter O'Neill Says' (*ABC News*, 28 April 2016), available at www.abc.net.au/news/2016-04-27/png-pm-oneill-to-shut-manus-island-detention-centre/7364414.

[59] UN Human Rights Council, 'Papua New Guinea Review – 25th Session of Universal Periodic Review', discussed in B Doherty, 'Papua New Guinea Tells UN It Accepts Court Decision on Manus Island Illegality' *The Guardian* (7 May 2016), available at www.theguardian.com/australia-news/2016/may/07/papua-new-guinea-tells-un-it-accepts-court-decision-on-manus-island-illegality.

[60] F Keany and L Yaxley, 'Manus Island Detention: PNG Responsible for Asylum Seekers, Peter Dutton Says' (*ABC News*, 29 April 2016), available at www.abc.net.au/news/2016-04-28/png-responsible-for-manus-island-asylum-seeker-dutton-says/7369032.

[61] ibid.

also confirmed its position that both Australia and PNG were jointly responsible for complying with the Court's ruling on the closure of the detention centre.[62]

Ultimately, Australia announced that it intended to withdraw from Manus Island entirely on 31 October 2017 and the Manus detention centre was formally closed on that day. However, Australia claimed that the transferred persons were the sole responsibility of PNG from this point and thus detainees were transferred to transit accommodation centres elsewhere in PNG rather than transferred back to Australia. This caused diplomatic tensions between the two governments, with the then Attorney-General of PNG, Davis Steven, expressing public criticism of the Australian stance. He stated that the PNG Government was 'not going to allow a situation where Australia has withdrawn and leaves behind all these international fugitives who they expect us to carry on our steam'.[63] Australia's behaviour in closing down the operation of the Manus Island Centre was also criticised by the UN Human Rights Committee.[64] As of 2018, 589 refugees remained in PNG without a durable solution.[65] These problems with implementation continued into 2019, with the PNG Prime Minister calling on Australia to act urgently to remove the remaining refugees from the island.[66] Thus, one could question whether the decision resulted in a substantial improvement of the conditions of the detained asylum seekers.

B. Basis for Further Litigation

The findings in the *Namah* decision also contributed to a successful class action – a tort claim for compensation for negligence and false imprisonment – approved by the Victorian Supreme Court in Australia in 2017.[67] This class action was lodged

[62] 'Both Australia and PNG Responsible for Manus – Court' (*Radio New Zealand*, 23 August 2016), available at www.radionz.co.nz/international/pacific-news/311614/both-australia-and-png-responsible-for-manus-court.

[63] E Tlozek, 'PNG Tells Australia it Can't Shut Manus Island Detention Centre and Leave Asylum Seekers Behind' (*ABC News*, 25 August 2017), available at www.abc.net.au/news/2017-08-25/png-says-australia-cant-shut-down-manus-island-detention-centre/8844082.

[64] See UN Human Rights Committee, *Concluding Observations on the Sixth Periodic Report of Australia*, CCPR/C/AUS/CO/6, 1 December 2017, para 35(c): 'The closure of the Manus Island regional processing centre on 31 October 2017 without adequate arrangements for long-term viable relocation solutions for all the refugees and asylum seekers who were transferred there by the State party.'

[65] See NF Tan, 'The Manus Island Regional Processing Centre: A Legal Taxonomy' (2018) 20 *European Journal of Migration and Law* 427, 437.

[66] P Mercer, 'Papua New Guinea Demands Australia Remove Refugees' (*VOA*, 19 July 2019), available at www.voanews.com/a/east-asia-pacific_papua-new-guinea-demands-australia-remove-refugees/6172205.html.

[67] *Kamasaee v Commonwealth of Australia & Ors*, S CI 2014 6770 *Kamasaee v Commonwealth of Australia & Ors (Approval of settlement)* [2017] VSC 537. The class action was instigated in 2014 and the plaintiff sought leave to amend his statement of claim in April 2016 to include a claim for damages for false imprisonment following the decision in *Namah* – see discussion in *Kamasaee v Commonwealth of Australia & Ors (No 10) (Issues for trial ruling)* [2017] VSC 272 [7] where the decision in *Namah* is specifically referred to. Note that another class action was instigated shortly following the decision in *Namah* but was discontinued and relodged: *Plaintiffs S99-2014 v Minister for Immigration and Border Protection (Cth) & Ors* [2016] HCATrans 125 (31 May 2016).

by 1,923 asylum seekers[68] who had been detained at the Manus Island detention centre between 2012 and 2016. The plaintiffs claimed that they had been falsely imprisoned, that the Australian Government and its contractors had a duty of care to asylum seekers and that this duty had been breached through deaths, systemic sexual and physical abuse, and inadequate medical treatment/neglect.[69] In 2017, the Australian Court made orders for a $70 million settlement of this action. This was a highly-publicised decision in Australian media and served to have a chilling effect on the operation of the offshore processing regime (in addition to achieving some justice for affected asylum seekers).

V. Decision in Subsequent and Current Context

A. Wider Implications in the Asia-Pacific Region (for Offshore Processing)

The landmark decision in *Namah* had significant practical implications for off-shored refugees in PNG as it led to the dismantling of the Manus Island detention centre and was able to be utilised as a basis for compensation for false imprisonment. However, it did not affect the constitutionality or broader legality of the basis for offshore processing in Australia. This is demonstrated by the Australian High Court case of *Plaintiff S195/2016* where the Court was asked to consider the consequences of *Namah* for the legality of the regional processing designation made under Australian legislation.[70] Specifically, the Australian High Court was asked to adjudicate upon whether the designation of PNG as a regional processing country in 2012 was beyond the power conferred by s 198AB(1) of the Migration Act 1958 (Cth) by reason of the decision in *Namah*.

The plaintiff's case before the High Court raised a novel argument as it sought to link the validity of action taken under Australian law with the validity of those actions in another country, that is, PNG. The plaintiff in *S195* argued that Australia had joint responsibility with PNG for the detention of refugees: that Australia had agreed with PNG's detention of the asylum seekers and had then undertaken a major part in that detention.[71] The plaintiff noted that the Administrative Arrangements entered into by PNG and Australia clearly provided for detention: transferees to be directed by the Minister to reside at the centre and were allowed

[68] Of these, 1,690 asylum seekers were part of the eventual settlement to registered members of the class action: see Supreme Court of Victoria, 'Manus Island Detention Centre Class Action' (24 November 2017), available at www.supremecourt.vic.gov.au/news/manus-island-detention-centre-class-action-0#_ftn1.

[69] *Kamasaee v Commonwealth of Australia & Ors*, S CI 2014 6770 (n 67).

[70] *Plaintiff S195/2016 v Minister for Immigration and Border Protection* [2017] HCA 31.

[71] See the plaintiff's submissions in *Plaintiff S195/2016*, available at www.hcourt.gov.au/sites/default/files/assets/cases/s195-2016/Plf-S195-2016_Plfs.pdf (Plaintiff's Submissions); and www.hcourt.gov.au/sites/default/files/assets/cases/s195-2016/Plf-S195-2016_Reply.pdf (Plaintiff's Reply).

to leave only under escort for approved activities. The plaintiffs argued that the PNG Supreme Court judgment in *Namah* was relevant as it established that the detention was unconstitutional under PNG law, therefore the Memorandum of Understanding arrangements were unlawful.

Despite these arguments, and the references to Australian responsibility for the detention centre by the PNG Supreme Court in *Namah*, the High Court of Australia did not accept the plaintiff's arguments. In particular, the High Court stated that the plaintiff had misunderstood the decision in *Namah*.[72] The High Court emphasised that the PNG Supreme Court held that the treatment of detainees at the centre contravened provisions of the PNG Constitution but did *not* invalidate the various memoranda or arrangements entered into between Australian and PNG. That is, there was no finding in *Namah* that those bilaterial arrangements contravened any provision of the PNG Constitution.[73] Indeed, the High Court in *S195* described the plaintiff's propositions about the interaction between Australian law and that of PNG as 'novel and sweeping'.[74] As Thomas Spijkerboer notes:

> In Plaintiff S195/2016, while the High Court of Australia does cite the PNG Supreme Court's injunction, it does not deign to respond. It does not even reject the injunction by mentioning the doctrine of state immunity, and in effect ignores the injunction.[75]

Thus, the High Court decision in this case reflects that the PNG decision in *Namah* had no legal implications for the constitutional and legislative underpinnings of the offshore processing regime operated under the authority of Australian law.

The Australian High Court's decision can be explained by the fact that the Court is constrained by the clear provisions of the Migration Act which permit the transfer and detention of refugees in PNG, even though that may be contrary to international law or the Constitution of PNG.[76] However, it does illustrate a weakness in utilising litigation in a destination state in offshore processing regimes, as such litigation may not legally result in a broader dismantling of the regime in the sending state (in this case, Australia). As noted above, the decision in *Namah* did

[72] *Plaintiff S195/2016* (n 70) [22]: 'Both of the plaintiff's propositions appear, in any event, to proceed on a misunderstanding of the Namah Decision'.

[73] ibid [25].

[74] ibid [19]: 'as a basis on which to invalidate all of the impugned actions, the plaintiff advanced the novel and sweeping proposition that the Constitution denies to the Commonwealth any legislative or executive power to authorise or take part in activity in another country which is unlawful according to the domestic law of that country'.

[75] T Spijkerboer, 'Coloniality and Case Law on the Australian Asylum Offshoring Scheme' (2022) *International Journal of Migration and Border Studies*, VU University Amsterdam Legal Studies Paper Series, available at https://ssrn.com/abstract=4138437 (no page numbers).

[76] M O'Sullivan, 'The Legality of Manus Island Detention under Australian Law – The High Court Decides in Plaintiff S195' (*Castan Centre for Human Rights Law*, 17 August 2017), available at https://castancentre.com/2017/08/17/the-legality-of-manus-island-detention-under-australian-law-the-high-court-decides-in-plaintiff-s195/.

eventually lead to the closure of the Manus Detention Centre in PNG. However, the offshore processing centre in Nauru remains operational to this day.

Despite, this, it has been able to be utilised as a cautionary tale by civil society and academics in response to other proposals for offshore processing regimes based on the 'Australian model', which I will now turn to discuss.

B. Wider Implications for Use in Challenging Other Offshore Processing Regimes

Arguably, the decision in *Namah* has implications for offshore processing regimes which are being replicated or inspired by the Australian offshore processing model. The influence of the 'Australian model' internationally is illustrated by its significance in the development of the United Kingdom (UK)–Rwandan deal. For instance, the Australian model was referred to a number of times in the debates in the UK Parliament, with one member of the House of Lords noting that:

> For 10 years now, Australia has been operating an outsourcing policy of the kind to which the UK aspires. We should therefore follow the Australian example, which is now operating successfully and is supported by both parties.[77]

In the light of this, a number of Australian academics released public statements and publications persuasively arguing against the wisdom of such 'copying'.[78] In this context, I made a submission to the UK House of Commons inquiry into the Nationality and Borders Bill in which I specifically utilised the litigation in *Namah* as illustrating 'the legal confusion and complexities which arose in relation to the detention of asylum seekers on Manus Island in Papua New Guinea'.[79] I also submitted that the PNG Supreme Court's finding in *Namah* as to the unlawfulness of the detention centre and the aftermath demonstrated 'the legal and political failure of the extraterritorial detention and processing regime in PNG'[80] and concluded that the UK should not emulate the Australian offshore processing regime as a result. This demonstrates that the *Namah* decision allowed academics to highlight the legal complexities and weaknesses of offshore processing regimes to other countries.

[77] Safety of Rwanda (Asylum and Immigration) Bill Volume 836: debated on Monday 12 February 2024 Lord Horam, Column 38–39.

[78] See discussion in Gleeson and Yacoub (n 11) 3; M Matera, T Tubakovic and P Murray, 'Is Australia a Model for the UK? A Critical Assessment of Parallels of Cruelty in Refugee Externalization Policies' (2023) 36(2) *Journal of Refugee Studies* 271, 273–78.

[79] UK House of Commons, Written evidence submitted by Associate Professor Maria O'Sullivan, Deputy Director, Castan Centre for Human Rights Law, Faculty of Law, Monash University, Australia (NBB32) Nationality and Borders Bill (19th October 2021), available at https://publications.parliament.uk/pa/cm5802/cmpublic/NationalityBorders/memo/NBB32.htm.

[80] ibid.

VI. Why this is a Landmark Case/Implications and Consequences for International Refugee Law and Refugee Protection

The landmark decision discussed in this chapter – the 2016 decision of the PNG Supreme Court in *Namah v Pato* – was an important part of the dismantling of the offshore processing agreement between Australia and PNG in that it led to the closure of the Manus Island Detention Centre. It also reflects some interesting trends and aspects of international refugee law and protection.

A. The Significance of Case Law from the Global South

Historically, litigation to protect the rights of refugees has predominantly been focused on the 1951 Refugee Convention and the European Convention on Human Rights. The decision in *Namah* is significant in this regard as it represents the findings of a court in the Global South using constitutional provisions which were interpreted in a way which ultimately served to protect the human rights of asylum seekers. Similar observations can be made about the decision of the High Court of Kenya in *Kituo Cha Sheria and Others v Attorney General*[81] which is discussed in chapter 10 in this volume.[82]

Refugee law scholar Nik Tan has commented on this aspect of *Namah v Pato*, and noted in 2018 that:

> *Namah v Pato* represents an important defence of the right to liberty in the context of extraterritorial asylum processing. Moreover, the decision comes from a somewhat surprising source: rather than the courts of the destination State, or a human rights treaty body, it is the partner country's judiciary that provides protection of refugee rights. The decision from the Supreme Court was unexpected due to refugee lawyers' preoccupation with destination State responsibility, too often overlooking partner State responsibility and corollary avenues for accountability.[83]

Thus, the decision in *Namah* has two implications for the utilising of litigation in the Global South. First, it illustrates the importance of a focus on domestic adjudication and remedies in those countries. Second, the need more generally for a broad range of redress mechanisms to be utilised in relation to offshore processing regimes (given their jurisdictional complexity and extra-territorial effect). As Tan and Gammeltoft-Hansen have also noted:

> As migration control is enacted extraterritorially or in concert, involving cooperation between multiple states, private actors, and international organizations, the choice of

[81] *Kituo Cha Sheria and Others* (n 39).

[82] The case involved several constitutional rights, including the right to expeditious, efficient, lawful, reasonable and procedurally fair administrative action and the right to dignity in the Nigerian Constitution.

[83] Tan (n 65) 443 [citations omitted].

> forum through which to pursue accountability for human rights violations becomes particularly important.[84]

The one rider to this is that *Namah* has not been judicially-cited in any significant way in jurisprudence in the Global North. The failure of many courts in Europe, the United States and Canada to engage with the jurisprudence of countries such as PNG is a matter which should be addressed as it illustrates the problems with the over-influence of European law on the development of international refugee law and international human rights law. As Thomas Spijkerboer has quite rightly noted, '[c]omparative law scholarship will gain in relevance if it takes sources from the global South seriously as sources of international migration law'.[85]

B. The Pushback of a Colonised State against the Coloniser

The role of the PNG judiciary in *Namah* also speaks to the role of local judiciaries in destination states in constraining political agreements with powerful states. Thus, it could be said that the decision in *Namah* represents an act by a colonised state (PNG) to pushback on the power and influence by its former coloniser (Australia). As I noted earlier in this chapter, the substantial economic and political power exercised by Australia in the Asia-Pacific region and its status as a former protector/coloniser of a number of countries (including Nauru and PNG) have resulted in an unequal power relationship in the formation of offshore processing arrangements in the region. As Azadeh Dastyari and myself argued in 2016:

> The bilateral agreements finalised with these countries for extraterritorial processing and detention represent a highly asymmetrical, hierarchical relationship where a wealthy, industrialised nation is seeking to outsource its protection obligations to developing nations. The use of aid is a significant leverage and a means of Australia being able to exercise considerable political and legal influence in PNG and Nauru.[86]

In this context, the action by the PNG Supreme Court in handing down the decision in *Namah* reflects the significant power which can be wielded by an independent judiciary in providing a level of accountability in this area. This is important as some offshore processing agreements have been established as non-binding arrangements in an attempt to prevent accountability. As the 2013 UNHCR Guidance Note on bilateral and/or multilateral transfer arrangements of asylum seekers notes:

> An arrangement between States for the transfer of asylum-seekers is best governed by a *legally binding instrument, challengeable and enforceable in a court of law* by the affected

[84] NF Tan and T Gammeltoft-Hansen, 'A Topographical Approach to Accountability for Human Rights Violations in Migration Control' (2020) 21 *German Law Journal* 335, 346–47.
[85] Spijkerboer (n 75) (no page numbers).
[86] Dastyari and O'Sullivan (n 3) 308–38.

> asylum-seekers. The arrangement would need to clearly stipulate the rights and obligations of each State and the rights and duties of asylum-seekers (emphasis added).[87]

The importance of the judiciary being empowered to undertake such a role is enhanced in the context of a colonial or post-colonial relationship such as existed between Australia and PNG. Indeed, Thomas Spijkerboer, who has written specifically on the influence of colonial concepts and ideologies in the case law concerning Australia's offshore processing system, has stated that the PNG Supreme Court engaged in 'tactical resistance' in handing down the judgment in *Namah*.[88] Nethery and Lea also argue that in *Namah*, the PNG judiciary 'asserted PNG policy sovereignty'.[89] They state: 'This fissure in the neo-colonial narrative sets the case of PNG apart from other states of externalisation, such as Nauru and Libya, in which judiciaries have had less power or inclination to pushback against their wealthy patrons.'[90]

The discussion in this chapter therefore reflects that the decision of the PNG Supreme Court in *Namah* is laudable and represents a significant judgment in refugee law and protection. It represents a landmark case for international refugee law as it provides an example of the utility of strategic litigation in an offshore *destination* state and highlights the importance of utilising the constitutional provisions of that destination state to protect the rights of asylum seekers. It is hoped that this example demonstrates the depth and richness of jurisprudence which exists in countries outside the Global North, that such cases will be cited more widely by courts and academics and, thus, more influential in the development of international refugee law.

[87] UNHCR, *Guidance Note on Bilateral and/or Multilateral Transfer Arrangements of Asylum-Seekers* (2013), available at www.refworld.org/policy/legalguidance/unhcr/2013/en/16943.
[88] Spijkerboer (n 75) (no page numbers).
[89] Nethery and Lea (n 23).
[90] ibid.

14

R (on the Application of AAA and Others) v Secretary of State for the Home Department [2023]: The Limits of Externalisation and the Failed UK–Rwanda Arrangement

NIKOLAS FEITH TAN

I. Introduction

On 13 April 2022, the United Kingdom (UK) and Rwanda signed a non-binding agreement for the transfer of asylum seekers reaching the UK irregularly to Rwanda, following a screening procedure by UK authorities.[1] Upon arrival, Rwandan authorities would assume responsibility for the asylum procedure. Asylum seekers found to be refugees were to be offered protection in Rwanda, while those not in need of protection would be returned or provided with leave to remain in Rwanda. Under the arrangement, the UK paid the Rwandan Government £140 million, despite the agreement never being implemented. In July 2024, the new UK Government cancelled the arrangement.[2]

On 15 November 2023, before the arrangement could be operationalised, the UK Supreme Court invalidated the agreement in *R (on the Application of AAA and Others) v Secretary of State for the Home Department* ('*AAA*') due to inadequacies in the Rwandan asylum system, holding that there existed 'substantial grounds for believing that there is a real risk that asylum claims will not be determined properly, and that asylum seekers will in consequence be at risk of being returned directly or indirectly to their country of origin.'[3]

[1] Memorandum of Understanding between the Government of the United Kingdom of Great Britain and Northern Ireland and the Government of the Republic of Rwanda for the Provision of an Asylum Partnership Arrangement signed 13 April 2022 in Kigali.

[2] S Francis, 'Starmer Confirms Rwanda Deportation Plan "Dead"' (*BBC*, 7 July 2024), available at www.bbc.com/news/articles/cz9dn8erg3zo.

[3] *R (on the Application of AAA and Others) v Secretary of State for the Home Department* [2023] UKSC 42 (hereafter '*AAA*') [105].

Despite its recency, *AAA* is a landmark judgment given its critical role in ending the Rwanda scheme, as well as furthering our understanding of the limits imposed by international law on externalisation policies. The Court's narrow but principled judgment reiterated to the UK Government, and other states, the grave and manifold obligations required by the principle of *non-refoulement* as a matter of international refugee law and international human rights law, as expressed through domestic guarantees. *AAA* thus played a key role in stepping back the UK's asylum policy from the abyss of a bad faith and unlawful externalisation of asylum responsibility to a distant country that risked becoming a corrosive precedent for future externalisation approaches.

The UK–Rwanda arrangement was one in a line of co-operative arrangements that seek to shift asylum responsibility from destination states to partner countries, often in the Global South.[4] These arrangements include the Unites States' (US) extraterritorial processing of asylum seekers intercepted at sea in Guantanamo Bay,[5] Australian-led attempts at third country processing and protection in Nauru and Papua New Guinea,[6] Israel's secret transfer of Eritrean and Sudanese asylum seekers to Rwanda and Uganda[7] and the short-lived US–Guatemala Asylum Cooperation Arrangement for the transfer of asylum seekers reaching the US southern border to Guatemala.[8] Most recently, in November 2023, Italy and Albania concluded a protocol for the transfer of persons rescued by Italian vessels in the Mediterranean Sea to Albania for asylum processing.[9]

The preamble to the 1951 Convention relating to the Status of Refugees ('1951 Refugee Convention') acknowledges the need for international co-operation in respect to hosting refugees, providing that 'the grant of asylum may place unduly heavy burdens on certain countries' and that a satisfactory solution of the humanitarian challenges posed by refugees 'cannot therefore be achieved without international cooperation.'[10] During the negotiations on the 1951 Refugee Convention, the UN Secretary General proposed inclusion of an article obliging states to relieve the burden assumed by initial reception countries which have

[4] See, eg, M Foster, 'The Implications of the Failed "Malaysian Solution": The Australian High Court and Refugee Responsibility Sharing at International Law' (2012) 13 *Melbourne Journal of International Law* 395.

[5] A Dastyari, *United States Migrant Interdiction and the Detention of Refugees in Guantánamo Bay* (Cambridge University Press, 2015).

[6] M Gleeson and N Yacoub, 'Cruel, Costly and Ineffective: the Failure of Offshore Processing in Australia' (*Kaldor Centre for International Refugee Law Policy Brief*, August 2021) 11. See further M O'Sullivan, '*Namah v Pato* [2016]: Constitutional Challenges in Offshore Destination States' in ch 13 of this volume.

[7] S Bar-Tuvia, 'Australian and Israeli Agreements for the Permanent Transfer of Refugees: Stretching Further the (Il)legality and (Im)morality of Western Externalization Policies' (2018) 30 *International Journal of Refugee Law* 1.

[8] Agreement Between the Government of the United States of America and the Republic of Guatemala on Cooperation Regarding the Examination of Protection Claims (26 July 2019).

[9] Protocol between the Government of the Republic of Italy and the Council of Ministers of the Republic of Albania for the Strengthening of Cooperation in Migration Matters (2023).

[10] UN General Assembly, 1951 Convention relating to the Status of Refugees, United Nations, Treaty Series, 189:137, 28 July 1951 ('Refugee Convention') preamble.

afforded asylum to refugees by agreeing to receive a certain number of refugees in their territory.[11] This article was not included in the operative part of the Refugee Convention, since many states did not wish to be bound by an explicit duty to co-operate in asylum matters. Furthermore, according to the preamble, co-operative arrangements must be consistent with the 'widest possible exercise of the fundamental rights and freedoms' of refugees.

Most recently, the 2018 Global Compact on Refugees provides a framework for 'more equitable and predictable responsibility sharing' though the Compact is silent on key questions of access to territory, access to asylum procedures and co-operation modalities.[12] While the Compact is an explicitly non-binding instrument, paragraph 5 reiterates that the Compact is 'grounded in the international refugee protection regime, centred on the cardinal principle of *non-refoulement*, and at the core of which is the 1951 Refugee Convention and its 1967 Protocol', as well as various regional protection instruments.[13]

Notwithstanding these calls for responsibility sharing, states in the Global North have increasingly used the language of co-operation to craft arrangements to shift, rather than share, asylum responsibilities to other countries, often in the Global South. This despite the status quo that low and middle-income countries presently host 75 per cent of the world's refugees.[14] Existing arrangements are generally for the purpose of deterring and deflecting asylum seekers rather than providing for genuine responsibility sharing for refugees.[15] As such, the UK–Rwanda arrangement should be understood as a form of externalisation, defined as policies and practices that externalise asylum processing and refugee protection functions to third states.[16] The United Nations High Commissioner for Refugees (UNHCR) has defined the term as 'measures preventing asylum-seekers from entering safe territory and claiming international protection, or transfers of asylum-seekers and refugees to other countries without sufficient safeguards'.[17]

This chapter provides an analysis of the UK–Rwanda arrangement, assessing its normative and policy implications on international refugee law and policy and the impact of the judgment of the UK Supreme Court. The chapter proceeds in four sections. First, the chapter describes the arc of the UK–Rwanda arrangement, from the policy development of the UK Government to the critical intervention of the UK Supreme Court in *AAA*. Second, the chapter lays out the contributions of the *AAA* decision with respect to the UK's *non-refoulement* obligations,

[11] Global Compact on Refugees (United Nations, 2018) para 3.

[12] S Als and others, *Externalization and the UN Global Compact on Refugees: Unsafety as Ripple Effect* (ASILE policy brief, 2022).

[13] Global Compact on Refugees (n 11) para 5.

[14] United Nations High Commissioner for Refugees (UNHCR), 'Global Trends: Forced Displacement in 2023' (2024) 2.

[15] NF Tan, *Transnational Asylum: Toward a Principled Framework* (Routledge, 2025).

[16] Refugee Law Initiative, 'Declaration on Externalisation and Asylum' (2022) 34 *International Journal of Refugee Law* 114. See further D Cantor and others, 'Externalisation, Access to Territorial Asylum, and International Law' (2022) 34 *International Journal of Refugee Law* 120.

[17] UNHCR, *UNHCR Note on the "Externalization" of International Protection* (28 May 2021).

unanswered questions on the safe third country concept and the form, monitoring and role of UNHCR in the UK–Rwanda arrangement. Third, the chapter situates the UK–Rwanda arrangement alongside other attempts at externalisation. Finally, the chapter explores the implications of the *AAA* judgment and the UK–Rwanda arrangement. Despite its non-operationalisation, the arrangement has significant implications for the future of refugee protection, including the normalisation of such externalisation arrangements and adaptation of co-operative practices.

II. Setting the Scene: The Rise and Fall of the UK–Rwanda Arrangement

The 2022 UK–Rwanda Migration and Economic Development Partnership (MEDP) allowed the UK Government to transfer responsibility for the asylum process and subsequent protection to Rwanda.[18] Under the MEDP, asylum seekers reaching the UK irregularly were subject to transfer to Rwanda, following a screening procedure by UK authorities. Upon arrival, Rwandan authorities would assume responsibility for the asylum procedure. Asylum seekers found to be refugees were to be offered protection in Rwanda, while those not in need of protection were to be returned or provided with leave to remain in Rwanda. This section sets out the policy development of the MEDP as the context in which *AAA* was decided.

The origins of the MEDP can be traced to March 2021, when then-Prime Minister Boris Johnston announced a 'comprehensive reform' of the UK asylum system, including the possibility of extraterritorial processing of asylum claims, through a policy document entitled 'New Plan for Immigration'.[19] The Plan included a reference to developing 'the capacity for offshore asylum processing – in line with our international obligations'.[20] The MEDP clearly reflected the logic of Australia's regional processing arrangements in the Pacific, with a focus on deterring irregular maritime arrivals and shifting responsibility for asylum processing and refugee protection to poorer states.[21]

A significant increase in unauthorised arrivals via small boat across the English Channel drove the creation of the MEDP. In 2018, for example, 218 people arrived via small boat across the Channel. This figure has increased significantly in recent years, peaking at 45,774 arrivals in 2022, with 29,437 arrivals in 2023 and 36,816

[18] Memorandum of Understanding (n 1); NF Tan, 'Externalisation of Asylum in Europe: Unpacking the UK-Rwanda Asylum Partnership Agreement' (*EU Immigration and Asylum Law and Policy*, 17 May 2022), available at www.ein.org.uk/blog/externalisation-asylum-europe-unpacking-uk-rwanda-asylum-partnership-agreement.

[19] UK Government, *'New Plan for Immigration' Policy Statement* (24 March 2021).

[20] ibid 19.

[21] M Gleeson, 'Protection Deficit: The Failure of Australia's Offshore Processing Arrangements to Guarantee "Protection Elsewhere" in the Pacific' (2019) 31(4) *International Journal of Refugee Law* 415.

in 2024.[22] The 'small boats issue' has become highly visible, dominating the front pages of British newspapers in recent years. Furthermore, since Brexit, the UK has lacked a legal or practical mechanism to readmit asylum seekers to France, given its withdrawal from the European Union's Dublin Regulation.[23]

Amidst the febrile environment around the small boats issue, in April 2022, the UK Parliament passed the Nationality and Borders Act which, along with existing Immigration Rules and legislation, provided a legal basis for the removal of asylum seekers to a third country for the purposes of asylum processing. On 14 April 2022, then-Prime Minister Boris Johnston announced the signing of the MEDP.[24]

On 14 June 2022, a flurry of last-minute judicial interventions blocked the first flight from London to Kigali. Originally, around 130 asylum seekers were scheduled for transfer, but by the day of the flight around 10 people were on board. A rule-39 interim measures injunction from the European Court of Human Rights (ECtHR) stopped the flight taking off.[25]

In July 2023, the UK Parliament passed the Illegal Migration Act, which sought to require the Home Office to remove nearly all asylum seekers who arrived in the UK irregularly. The Act required that asylum seekers be returned to their home country, 'or another safe third country, such as Rwanda' without the possibility of subsequent re-entry to the UK.

On 15 November 2023, the arrangement was found to be unlawful by the UK Supreme Court in *AAA*.[26] On 5 December 2023, in response to the decision in *AAA*, the UK Government signed a treaty with Rwanda that included various safeguards for asylum seekers, including an assurance that they would not be expelled from Rwanda if their asylum claims were rejected.[27]

On 6 December 2023, the UK Government introduced the Safety of Rwanda Act, which declared Rwanda a safe country as a matter of British law in response to the decision in *AAA*. The bill further sought to curtail the power of the judiciary to review removal decisions, raising constitutional questions about the power of the

[22] 'How Many People Cross the Channel in Small Boats?' (*BBC*, 12 August 2025), available at www.bbc.com/news/uk-53699511.

[23] Regulation (EU) 604/2013 of the European Parliament and of the Council of 26 June 2013 establishing the criteria and mechanisms for determining the Member State responsible for examining an application for international protection lodged in one of the Member States by a third-country national or a stateless person (recast) [2013] OJ L180/31.

[24] The legal basis for transfer to Rwanda was found in the UK's existing Immigration Rules (Rules 345A–345C) in combination with sch 3 of the 1971 Nationality, Immigration and Asylum Act (paras 3–5), as well as cl 30 of the Nationality and Borders Act passed in 2022 to support the operation of the Migration and Economic Development Partnership (MEDP). M Gower, P Butchard and CJ McKinney, 'The UK-Rwanda Migration and Economic Development Partnership' (UK House of Commons Library, 29 May 2024) 6.

[25] *NSK v United Kingdom* App no 28774/22 (ECtHR, 14 June 2022).

[26] *AAA* (n 3) [28].

[27] Agreement between the Government of the United Kingdom of Great Britain and Northern Ireland and the Government of the Republic of Rwanda for the provision of an asylum partnership to strengthen shared international commitments on the protection of refugees and migrants (5 December 2023).

executive vis-à-vis the judiciary.[28] Ultimately, however, the UK–Rwanda arrangement was terminated by the new UK Labour Government in July 2024 without a single forced transfer taking place.[29]

III. International Law and Externalisation: The Contributions of *AAA*

A. Overview of the Litigation

Critical to the failure of the UK–Rwanda Arrangement was the UK Supreme Court's decision in *AAA*, which invalidated the Arrangement on the basis that there were 'substantial grounds for believing that there is a real risk that asylum claims will not be determined properly, and that asylum seekers will in consequence be at risk of being returned directly or indirectly to their country of origin'.[30] The *AAA* decision also furthers our understanding of the limits imposed by international law on externalisation policies.

The applicants were a group of 10 asylum seekers from Iran, Iraq, Sudan, Syria and Vietnam, who travelled to the UK irregularly in small boats or, in one case, by lorry. The UK Secretary of State, acting under the Immigration Rules, decided their asylum claims were inadmissible in the UK and, instead, ordered their removal to Rwanda between May and July 2022 on the basis that Rwanda was a safe third country.[31]

AAA originated in the UK High Court which, in December 2022, ruled in favour of the Government, determining that the MEDP was lawful.[32] In June 2023, the Court of Appeal overturned that judgment in a 2–1 majority, deeming that Rwanda was not a safe third country and the policy was unlawful.[33] The Supreme Court unanimously upheld that majority decision of the Court of Appeal, finding that deficiencies within the Rwandan asylum system gave rise to a real risk of ill-treatment in contravention of the UK's *non-refoulement* obligations. The following section analyses selected key parts of the judgment, notably the scope of the UK's *non-refoulement* obligation, the legality of safe third country arrangements and formal and operational aspects of the UK–Rwanda arrangement.

[28] S Singer, 'Why the Safety of Rwanda Bill Should be Concerning For Us All' (*Refugee Law Initiative blog*, 15 December 2023), available at https://rli.blogs.sas.ac.uk/2023/12/15/why-the-safety-of-rwanda-bill-should-be-concerning-for-us-all/.

[29] Francis (n 2).

[30] *AAA* (n 3) [105].

[31] ibid [13].

[32] *R ((AAA) Syria and Ors) v Secretary of State for the Home Department* [2022] EWHC 3230 (Admin).

[33] *R ((AAA) Syria and Ors) v Secretary of State for the Home Department* [2023] EWCA Civ 745.

B. Substantive and Procedural Aspects of the *Non-Refoulement* Obligation

The decision in *AAA* is based 'on narrowest and most solid of grounds'[34] – that of *non-refoulement*. The Court's starting point is a contemporary recounting of the centrality of the principle to international refugee and human rights law, ranging across Article 33(1) of the 1951 Refugee Convention, Article 3 of the Convention Against Torture, Article 7 of the International Covenant on Civil and Political Rights (ICCPR) and Article 3 of the European Convention on Human Rights (ECHR), as well as potentially customary international law. The Court goes on to explain how these international law obligations are expressed in a range of domestic law instruments, including the UK Human Rights Act.[35]

Absent from the Court's analysis is the corollary of the *non-refoulement* question: whether the UK's international obligations give rise to a positive duty to hear AAA's asylum claim. This question was dismissed by the Court of Appeal and did not go before the Supreme Court.[36] On the one hand, this narrow approach may be read as a restrictive interpretation of international refugee law, on the other hand the Court's silence on this question may be read as pragmatic neutrality as the arguments put forward in *AAA* turned on safety in Rwanda rather than the territorial asylum obligations on the part of the UK.[37]

The Court goes on to set out its reasons for supporting the Court of Appeal's decision that removal to Rwanda would amount to a real risk of *refoulement*, in which Lord Underhill concluded that 'the Rwandan asylum system for refugee status determination was not, as at the relevant date, reliably fair and effective'.[38] The Supreme Court highlighted the general human rights situation in Rwanda; several concerns around the adequacy of Rwanda's asylum system in practice; and the relevance of a previous transfer arrangement between Israel and Rwanda, operational between 2013 and 2018. In so doing, the Supreme Court identifies in Rwanda a 'practice of refoulement',[39] a failure on the part of Rwandan authorities to understand the substantive requirements of the *non-refoulement* prohibition[40] and that Rwanda's failure to meet obligations it had assumed in the arrangement with

[34] C Briddick and C Costello, 'Supreme Judgecraft: Non-Refoulement and the End of the UK-Rwanda "Deal"?' (*Verfassungsblog*, 20 November 2023), available at https://verfassungsblog.de/supreme-judgecraft/.

[35] *AAA* (n 3) [27]–[33].

[36] *AAA* (Court of Appeal) (n 33) [300]–[21].

[37] According to Briddick and Costello therefore, 'to those concerned with legality of different kinds of arrangements for responsibility sharing or shifting, the judgement offers a silence that neither precludes nor permits'. Briddick and Costello (n 34). See also N Palmer, 'AAA and Others (2023-4): Judging Rwanda' (*Border Criminologies*, 24 November 2023), available at https://blogs.law.ox.ac.uk/border-criminologies-blog/blog-post/2023/11/aaa-and-others-2023-4-judging-rwanda.

[38] *AAA* (Court of Appeal) (n 33) [263].

[39] *AAA* (n 3) [87].

[40] ibid [91].

Israel was relevant to the forward-looking risk assessment under the MEDP.[41] The Court thus concluded:

> As matters stand, the evidence establishes substantial grounds for believing that there is a real risk that asylum claims will not be determined properly, and that asylum seekers will in consequence be at risk of being returned directly or indirectly to their country of origin. In that event, genuine refugees will face a real risk of ill-treatment in circumstances where they should not have been returned at all.[42]

Ultimately, the cumulative effect of these failings were held to amount to a real risk of *refoulement*, including based on evidence that certain asylum seeker profiles, including nationals of Syria, Yemen and Afghanistan, are routinely rejected in the Rwandan system, despite relatively high recognition rates in the UK.[43] The specific risk of *refoulement* under the MEDP thus arises not in Rwanda itself but due to inadequacies in the Rwandan asylum procedure that amount to a real risk of indirect *refoulement*, whereby refugees transferred by the UK would be rejected and face forced return to their country of origin.[44] In so doing, the Court in *AAA* adds to the rich jurisprudence on the principle of *non-refoulement* developed by both the ECtHR[45] and domestic courts.[46]

The Court further acknowledges that 'it may be the principle of *non-refoulement* also forms part of customary international law', indicating support for the widely-held scholarly view.[47] However, the Court stops short of explicitly declaring the customary status of the principle. This is significant within the UK political debate, which has included repeated calls from politicians to withdraw from the ECHR and, more recently, from the 1951 Refugee Convention. The Supreme Court notes: 'The significance of non-refoulment being a principle of customary international law is that it is consequently binding upon all states in international law, regardless of whether they are party to any treaties which give it effect.'[48] In other words, the

[41] ibid [100].
[42] ibid [105].
[43] ibid [85].
[44] ibid [94].
[45] See, among others, *Soering v United Kingdom* App no 14038/88 (ECtHR, 7 July 1989); *MSS v Belgium and Greece* App no 30696/09 (ECtHR [GC], 21 January 2011); and *Hirsi Jamaa and Others v Italy* App no 27765/09 (ECtHR, 23 February 2012). On *MSS*, see Evangelia (Lilian) Tsourdi and Paul McDonough, '*MSS v Belgium and Greece* [2011]: The Interplay between *Non-Refoulement* and Refugee Protection' in ch 9 in this volume. On the *Hirsi* decision, see Elspeth Guild, '*Hirsi Jamaa and others v Italy* [2012] and the Prohibition on Pushbacks' in ch 8 in this volume.
[46] See, eg, *R v Secretary of State for the Home Department, Ex parte Adan* [2001] 2 AC 477; and *Plaintiff M70/2011 v Minister for Immigration and Citizenship; and Plaintiff M106 of 2011 v Minister for Immigration and Citizenship* [2011] HCA 32 (High Court of Australia). On the scope of the obligation more broadly, see C Wouters, *International Legal Standards for the Protection from Refoulement* (Intersentia, 2009).
[47] *AAA* (n 3) [25]. See, eg, E Lauterpacht and D Bethlehem, 'The Scope and Content of the Principle of Non-Refoulement: Opinion' in E Feller, V Türk and F Nicholson (eds), *Refugee Protection in International Law: UNHCR's Global Consultations on International Protection* (Cambridge University Press, 2003); C Costello and M Foster, 'Non-Refoulement as Custom and Jus Cogens? Putting the Prohibition to the Test' in M den Heijer and H van der Wilt (eds), *Netherlands Yearbook of International Law 2015: Jus Cogens: Quo Vadis?* (TMC Asser Press, 2016).
[48] *AAA* (n 3) [25].

Court sounds a warning to the UK Government that the *non-refoulement* obligation may be of such international legal weight that it binds the UK irrespective of accession to treaties containing its terms.

Finally, the Supreme Court makes a pointed critique of the High Court in reiterating the role of national judiciaries in assessing the existence of a risk of *refoulement*, highlighting the erroneous approach of the lower court in paying undue deference to the expertise of the executive in finding that Rwanda was safe for asylum seekers. The Supreme Court, drawing on case law from the ECtHR, reiterated that judiciaries are bound to make their own assessment of a risk of *refoulement* based on the 'evidence as a whole and to reach its own conclusion'.[49] In its original decision, the High Court had essentially limited itself to the evidence of the UK Government to the exclusion of UNHCR evidence on the operation of the Rwandan asylum system.[50]

C. Unanswered Questions on Safe Third Country Arrangements

The legal mechanism at the core of the MEDP was the safe third country concept. While the 1951 Refugee Convention is silent on the possibility of safe third country arrangements, states have entered into bilateral and multilateral agreements employing the concept for decades, with prominent examples including the EU Dublin Regulation,[51] US–Canada Safe Third Country Agreement and the short-lived EU–Turkey Statement.[52] In general, safe third country arrangements are considered internationally lawful where a range of standards are met, including that the third state will admit the person; provide fair and efficient asylum procedures and a right to remain for the duration of these processes; accord persons found to be refugees standards of treatment commensurate with the 1951 Convention and international human rights standards; and grant refugees lawful stay in the country.[53]

[49] ibid [55].

[50] ibid [51].

[51] Regulation (EU) 604/2013 of the European Parliament and of the Council of 26 June 2013 establishing the criteria and mechanisms for determining the Member State responsible for examining an application for international protection lodged in one of the Member States by a third-country national or a stateless person (recast) [2013] OJ L180/31.

[52] For an overview of the safe third country concept and international refugee law, see M Foster, 'Responsibility Sharing or Shifting? "Safe" Third Countries and International Law' (2008) 25 *Refuge* 64; M-T Gil-Bazo, 'The Safe Third Country Concept in International Agreements on Refugee Protection Assessing State Practice' (2015) 33 *Netherlands Quarterly of Human Rights* 42; E Karageorgiou, L Feline Freier and K Ogg, 'The Evolution of Safe Third Country Law and Practice' in C Costello et al (eds), *The Oxford Handbook of International Refugee Law* (Oxford University Press, 2021); and Cantor and others (n 16) 141–43.

[53] UNHCR, 'Legal Considerations Regarding Access to Protection and a Connection between the Refugee and the Third Country in the Context of Return or Transfer to Safe Third Countries' (April 2018) para 4. See also UNHCR, 'International Agreements for the Transfer of Refugees and Asylum-seekers' (August 2025).

The UK–Rwanda arrangement, however, represented a significant distortion of the safe third country concept. While all the arrangements noted above operate on the basis that the asylum seeker could have found protection in a previous state of transit or residence, the UK–Rwanda regime sought to transfer people to a state with which they had *no prior connection*. While there is no international legal obligation requiring a connection between the asylum seeker and a third country, UNHCR has emphasised the need for a meaningful link or connection that 'would make it reasonable and sustainable for a person to seek asylum in another state'.[54]

The MEDP was also notable in its focus on deterrence, with its express focus on both deterring irregular arrivals to the UK and shifting responsibility for hearing asylum claims and affording protection to Rwanda. According to Briddick and Costello, therefore, the 'explicit purpose of the UK's scheme [was] to *evade* responsibility, potentially contrary to the object and purpose of the Refugee Convention'.[55]

As noted above, while EU law limits the application of the safe third country concept to applicants with a connection to the third state, the UK Supreme Court in *AAA* noted that paragraph 345C of the Immigration Rules allowed the safe third country concept to be deployed where the applicant was previously present in a third country to which they have a connection, or *any other safe third country which may agree to their entry* (emphasis added).[56]

The *AAA* judgment with respect to safe third country arrangements raises more questions than it answers.[57] First, the decision leaves in place the Court of Appeal's positive finding on the lawfulness of delegating the UK's asylum responsibilities to safe third countries, thus leaving ajar the possibility of future externalisation arrangements, including to countries with which the asylum seeker has no previous connection.[58] Indeed, the judgment specifically notes that within the Rwandan asylum system the 'structural changes and capacity-building needed to eliminate [the risk of *non-refoulement*] may be delivered in future'.[59] As a result, according to Palmer, the 'core legal outcome is that so-called "safe third country agreements" are now a firm part of the UK asylum landscape'.[60]

Second, the judgment, in confining itself to deficiencies in the Rwandan asylum system, would seem to overlook broader questions relevant to the inquiry as to whether Rwanda amounts to a safe third country. In the seminal case of *Plaintiff M70*, for example, the Australian High Court struck down a putative agreement between Australia and Malaysia for the transfer of asylum seekers, including on the basis that the arrangement did not provide legal guarantees that refugees

[54] ibid para 6.
[55] Briddick and Costello (n 34).
[56] *AAA* (n 3) [123]. See also ibid.
[57] According to Briddick and Costello (n 34), with respect to 'the legality of different kinds of arrangements for responsibility sharing or shifting, the judgement offers a silence that neither precludes nor permits'.
[58] Palmer (n 37).
[59] *AAA* (n 3) [105].
[60] Palmer (n 37).

would be afforded the suite of rights catalogued in Articles 2–34 of the 1951 Refugee Convention.[61] Unlike Rwanda, Malaysia is not a party to the Convention and has no national asylum system. In that case, the Australian High Court found that the third country must provide refugees with treatment at least as favourable as nationals with respect to employment, education and religious freedom, well beyond the scope of the *non-refoulement* obligation.[62]

Third, and related, the judgment is silent on the humanitarian principles underlying the 1951 Refugee Convention in connection to the UK–Rwanda arrangement. Rather than drawing on the object and purpose of the Convention and the duty to interpret treaty obligations in good faith, the judgment is narrowly focused on technical deficiencies in the Rwandan asylum system. This approach raises questions of whether the UK–Rwanda arrangement would have been internationally lawful had the Rwandan asylum system satisfied the UK's *non-refoulement* obligations. Experts have argued that, as a matter of international law, states may only externalise their asylum functions to another state where this is done for good faith reasons – for example in the context of mass influx or as part of a regional responsibility sharing arrangement.[63]

D. Form, Monitoring and Role of UNHCR in the UK–Rwanda Arrangement

Finally, *AAA* provides some important guidelines on the form, monitoring and role of UNHCR with respect to the UK–Rwanda Arrangement and future externalisation arrangements. With respect to form, the MEDP included an explicit provision providing that the arrangement 'does not create or confer any right on any individual, nor shall compliance with this Arrangement be justiciable in any court of law by third-parties or individuals' (para 2.2). While the UK and Rwandan governments converted the MEDP to treaty form following the *AAA* decision, on the basis that a treaty would provide 'firmer guarantee that refugees will not be removed from Rwanda in breach of the agreement',[64] there is nothing in the judgment to suggest that the non-binding nature of the MEDP was decisive to the outcome. Instead, the Court's judgment is focused on practical realities on the ground rather than the assurances of the Rwandan Government.[65] While the Court in *AAA* was clearly concerned with the capacity of the Rwandan asylum

[61] *Plaintiff M70/2011* (n 46); Foster (n 4). See further T Wood and J McAdam, 'Australian Asylum Policy all at Sea: An analysis of Plaintiff M70/2011 v Minister for Immigration and Citizenship and the Australia–Malaysia Arrangement' (2012) 61 *ICLQ* 274.

[62] Foster (n 4).

[63] Refugee Law Initiative (n 16) para 25.

[64] M Gower, P Butchard and CJ McKinney, 'The UK-Rwanda Migration and Economic Development Partnership' (UK House of Commons Library, 29 May 2024) 24.

[65] V Mitsilegas, 'The Supreme Court Rules the UK-Rwanda Policy Unlawful' (*EU Immigration and Asylum Law and Policy*, 21 November 2023), available at www.liverpool.ac.uk/law-and-social-justice/blog/UK-Rwanda-Policy-Ruled-Unlawful/.

system to deliver on its obligations under the non-binding MEDP, it also made clear that the 'structural changes and capacity-building required' would take time and could not be wished into reality by the conversion of the arrangement into treaty form.[66]

With respect to monitoring, the MEDP provided for an independent Monitoring Committee with a mandate to monitor 'entire relocation process' encompassing the four phases outlined above (para 15). The Monitoring Committee had wide access to both individuals and facilities under the arrangement, though the Committee lacked express powers to request the return of individuals to the UK or to suspend transfers to Rwanda where breaches of international law were uncovered.[67] While the Court in *AAA* acknowledged the importance of this function, it found that the mere existence of a monitoring mechanism is insufficient to render a third country safe, noting that 'detection of failures in the asylum system by means of monitoring, however effective it may be, will not prevent those failures from occurring in the first place'.[68]

Moreover, *AAA* made crucial contributions on the role of UNHCR and, specifically, the UN refugee agency's evidence, in evaluating externalisation arrangements. While the High Court found that UNHCR's evidence 'carried no special weight', the Supreme Court judgment emphasised the internationally enshrined role of the agency to supervise the interpretation and application of the 1951 Refugee Convention, with reference to Article 35 of the Convention.[69] UNHCR played a key role in advocating against the UK–Rwanda arrangement, as early as May 2021 urging the UK to 'refrain from adopting policies or laws that could in practice minimise and shift asylum and protection obligations either through an overly broad and blanket use of safe country concepts, or offshoring asylum processing'.[70] In the more narrow confines of the *AAA* litigation, UNHCR provided expert evidence on the operation of the Rwandan asylum system relied upon by the Supreme Court, which concluded that the 'particular importance of the should have been attached to the evidence of UNHCR in the present case'. This dual role points to the critical function of the agency in advocating against unlawful externalisation policies as guardian of the 1951 Refugee Convention.[71]

IV. Situating the UK–Rwanda Arrangement and the Decision in *AAA*

The fundamental questions of international refugee law and policy raised by the *AAA* litigation – notably the idea of externalising asylum processing and/or

[66] *AAA* (n 3) [105].
[67] Tan (n 18).
[68] *AAA* (n 3) [105].
[69] ibid [65].
[70] UNHCR, 'UNHCR Observations on the New Plan for Immigration policy statement of the Government of the United Kingdom' (May 2021) para 17.
[71] UNHCR (n 17).

protection to another state – are not new. Destination states have been proposing and, in some cases, implementing such approaches since as early as 1986.[72] In 2003, the UK put forward its 'New Vision for Refugees'[73] proposing extraterritorial processing as a way of decreasing the number of asylum applications in the EU territory.[74] In 2009, France and Italy suggested partnerships with countries of origin and of transit to find 'innovative solutions for access to asylum procedures', including by taking people back to Libya to process their claims extraterritorially.[75] This discussion was reignited after the boat tragedy of Lampedusa in October 2013, when hundreds of people lost their lives trying to reach the EU.[76] Once more, the Italian prime minister called for the establishment of refugee camps in Libya,[77] and the German interior minister suggested the implementation of 'welcome centers' in North African countries.[78]

Since 2015, Europe is again experiencing a proliferation of proposals and practice for extraterritorial processing modalities. In 2017, French President Emmanuel Macron called for the establishment of asylum 'hotspots' in North Africa as an extension of the EU hotspot approach, which contained asylum seekers in Greek and Italian points of entry.[79] Discussions of extraterritorial processing were revived once again in 2018, via a UNHCR–International Organization for Migration proposal for 'regional disembarkation arrangements', under which individuals rescued at sea while trying to reach Europe would be transferred to non-EU third states where their asylum claims would be processed.[80] The proposal was considered by the European Council but not taken up.

In June 2021, Denmark's parliament passed L226, a legislative amendment inserting a new paragraph in the Aliens Act allowing for the transfer of asylum seekers to a third country outside the EU for the purposes of both asylum processing and protection of refugees in the third country.[81] Transfers must take place

[72] P Mathew and T Harley, *Refugees, Regionalism and Responsibility* (Edward Elgar, 2016) 115.

[73] UK Home Office, 'A New Vision for Refugees' (7 March 2003).

[74] A Betts, 'The International Relations of the "New" Extraterritorial Approaches to Refugee Protection: Explaining the Policy Initiatives of the UK Government and UNHCR' (2004) 22(1) *Refuge* 58.

[75] Council of the European Union, 'Migration Situation in the Mediterranean: Establishing a Partnership with Migrants' Countries of Origin and of Transit, Enhancing Member States' Joint Maritime Operations and Finding Innovative Solutions for Access to Asylum Procedures' 13205/09 (Brussels, 11 September 2009).

[76] UNHCR, 'UNHCR Shocked by Boat Tragedy Off Lampedusa' (Press Release, 3 October 2015).

[77] ANSAMed, 'Italian Premier Renzi Calls for UN Refugee Camps in Libya' (*ANSAMed News*, 20 May 2014).

[78] T Kleditzsh, 'Die haben gelernt zu töten: Interview with Thomas de Maizière' (*Die Freie Presse*, 27 November 2014).

[79] BBC News, 'EU Migrant Crisis: France Plans Asylum "Hotspots" in Libya' (*BBC News*, 27 July 2017). The hotspot approach was a Union–Member State hybrid method for registering, identifying, and filtering new arrivals into asylum and return procedures. See Danish Refugee Council, *Fundamental Rights and the EU Hotspot Approach* (Danish Refugee Council, 2017).

[80] European Council, 'Non-Paper on Regional Disembarkation Arrangements' (2018).

[81] L 226 Forslag til lov om ændring af udlændingeloven og hjemrejseloven (Indførelse af mulighed for overførsel af asylansøgere til asylsagsbehandling og eventuel efterfølgende beskyttelse i tredjelande), Lovforslag som vedtaget, 3 June 2021.

under an international agreement between Denmark and the third country and that asylum seekers are to be transferred 'unless it would be in breach of Denmark's international obligations'. While the Danish Government has referred to negotiations with a handful of countries, notably Rwanda, no concrete agreement is currently in place.[82] Instead, since elections in November 2022, Denmark has sought to craft a multilateral, EU-based solution to the challenges of irregular migration, rather than seeking a bilateral arrangement with a third state.

Most recently, in November 2023, Italy and Albania concluded a non-binding protocol for the transfer of persons from a list of safe countries of origin rescued by Italian vessels in the Mediterranean Sea to Albania for asylum processing.[83] The agreement only governs search and rescue operations in international waters, outside the scope of EU law. The Protocol provides that Italy will have exclusive jurisdiction and control over certain 'areas' in Albania where Italy will construct facilities to receive disembarked people with asylum and return procedures carried out by Italian authorities (Article 3). Italy is responsible for almost all activities under the Protocol, including all financial costs, carrying out border and return procedures in the areas (Article 4(3)), health care inside the areas and transferring persons out of Albania following border and return procedures (Article 9(1)). No reference is made to solutions for those found to require international protection, though it is clear that Italy retains responsibility for removing persons from Albania following asylum/return procedures (Article 9(1)). The Protocol is limited to 3,000 persons present in Albania at any one time (Article 4) and the agreement runs for five years. To date, the operation of the Protocol has been prevented by a series of rulings from Italian domestic courts on the use of the safe country of origin concept.[84]

A key obstacle to the operation of these proposals in the EU context is the connection requirement under the safe third country concept under EU secondary law.[85] At present, both the Asylum Procedures Directive (APD)[86] and the Asylum Procedures Regulation (APR),[87] which will replace the APD from June 2026, require the existence of a connection between the third receiving country and the asylum applicant present in the EU that would make it reasonable for the individual to seek asylum there. With Brexit, the UK became unencumbered by

[82] NF Tan, 'Visions of the Realistic? Denmark's Legal Basis for Extraterritorial Asylum' (2022) 91(1) *Nordic Journal of International Law* 172.

[83] Protocol between the Government of the Republic of Italy and the Council of Ministers of the Republic of Albania for the Strengthening of Cooperation in Migration Matters (2023).

[84] A Amante and P Chiriatti, 'Italy Court again Blocks Migrant Detentions in Albania, in Blow to Meloni' (*Reuters*, 1 February 2025), available at www.reuters.com/world/europe/italy-court-again-blocks-migrant-detentions-albania-blow-meloni-2025-01-31/.

[85] The safe third country concept is a legal mechanism for an inadmissibility finding on the basis that a person 'could have or can find protection in a third state', generally under an agreement between the relevant states. UNHCR, 'Legal Considerations' (n 53) para 4.

[86] Directive 2013/32/EU of the European Parliament and of the Council of 26 June 2013 on common procedures for granting and withdrawing international protection (recast) [2013] OJ L180/60.

[87] Regulation (EU) 2024/1348 of the European Parliament and of the Council of 14 May 2024 establishing a common procedure for international protection in the Union and repealing Directive 2013/32/EU [2024] OJ L2024/1348.

this connection requirement, which is not mandatory under general international law.[88] Thus, the Rwanda asylum arrangement could be pursued.

V. Conclusions: Implications of the *AAA* Judgment and UK–Rwanda Arrangement

Given the relative recency of the *AAA* decision and subsequent abandonment of the UK–Rwanda arrangement, their implications are difficult to assess. Clearly, 15 November 2023 was a good day for the international protection system, as the UK Supreme Court invalidated a bad faith attempt at unlawful externalisation of asylum responsibilities. The decision also dampened Danish interest in a bilateral arrangement with Rwanda, with Copenhagen looking to forge an EU response to the challenges of irregular migration, rather than a bilateral response.[89]

At the same time, the decision in *AAA* and failure of the MEDP do not invalidate all such arrangements and there remains significant interest in externalisation arrangements in Europe. The Italy–Albania Protocol, for example, which was finalised in the same month *AAA* was decided, seems to have learned some of the lessons from the failure of the MEDP. Rather than seeking to externalise asylum processing for all irregular arrivals, the Italy–Albania Protocol only applies to persons with likely unfounded claims from a list of prescribed safe countries of origin. Furthermore, the Italy–Albania Protocol is limited to asylum processes only, with those found to require international protection provided access to protection in Italy. Moreover, rather than delegating responsibility for these asylum processes to a third country, under the agreement Italian authorities are carrying out asylum procedures extraterritorially, on Albanian soil.[90] This is not to suggest that these distinctions render the Italy–Albania Protocol internationally lawful nor a form of responsibility sharing, but rather that destination states are moderating their approach to externalisation arrangements, in line with judgments like *AAA*, rather than abandoning them.[91]

Ultimately, then, the implications of the *AAA* decision and the collapse of the UK–Rwanda arrangement largely remain to be seen. What can be said with certainty is that *AAA* provides a key bulwark against unlawful externalisation arrangements. The judgment does not settle international law governing third country asylum arrangements, but it upholds cardinal principles of safety for protection seekers subject to such arrangements.

[88] UNHCR, 'Legal Considerations' (n 53) para 6.

[89] Tan (n 82).

[90] A De Leo, 'Managing Migration the Italian Way: The "Innovative" Italy-Albania Deal under Scrutiny' (*Verfassungsblog*, 29 October 2024), available at https://verfassungsblog.de/managing-migration-the-italian-way/.

[91] Nikolas Feith Tan, *Transnational Asylum: Toward a Principled Framework* (Routledge, 2025).

15

Ioane Teitiota v New Zealand [2020]: Meeting the Challenge of Climate Change Through International Protection Law

BRUCE BURSON

I. Introduction

One of the most significant legal developments in recent years has been the way in which courts around the world have, through litigation, been required to grapple with how principles embedded in different branches of the law relate to the context of climate change. What of the *non-refoulement* obligation under international law? Does the 1951 Convention Relating to the Status of Refugees ('the Refugee Convention' or 'the Convention')[1] apply in the context of climate change? How far can complementary protection extend to address the humanitarian impact of disasters, and if so, on what basis? These are some of the questions which confronted the writer of this chapter in early 2013, when as a member of the New Zealand Immigration and Protection Tribunal ('the IPT' or 'the Tribunal'), he had to decide an appeal filed by Mr Ioane Teitiota – arguably one of the most famous refugee claimants of all time. My decision – anonymised as *AF (Kiribati)* in accordance with the Tribunal's usual practice – and the decision almost seven years later by the United Nations Human Rights Committee (HRC) upholding its reasoning have become legal 'ground zero' in terms of sparking debate – often stridently expressed – as to the positions adopted in regards to the law and the facts.

This chapter will consider the *Teitiota* litigation as a whole. It traces the arc of the case though the IPT, situating it within the specific structure of New Zealand's international protection system, before traversing the narrower

[1] UN General Assembly, 1951 Convention relating to the Status of Refugees, United Nations, Treaty Series, 189:137, 28 July 1951.

grounds raised before the HRC. This focus on the litigation as a connected body of jurisprudence is important. Commentary typically fails to do this, yet such an approach facilitates a more accurate grasp of the IPT's analysis, and that of the HRC which by and large accepted the IPT's reasoning in making its own decision.

The chapter will argue that the *Teitiota* litigation – through the New Zealand courts and the HRC – is a landmark for three reasons. First, it settles the question of whether international protection law can, in principle, apply such that movement across national borders in the context of disasters and climate change can no longer be said to be wholly regulated by domestic migration policy. Second, it raises questions around the interpretation of Articles 6 (right to life) and 7 (prohibition against torture and cruel, inhuman, or degrading treatment or punishment) of the International Covenant on Civil and Political Rights (ICCPR) as norms shaping the scope of *non-refoulement* obligation beyond the climate change context. Third, it has brought into sharp focus critical issues around the nature of time in the forward-looking assessment of risk which underpins international protection law, and the evidence necessary to establish a sufficient degree of risk to warrant international protection in cases where the impact of disasters and climate change feature.

The chapter will conclude with observations on what the *Teitiota* litigation reveals about the role the international protection law can play in meeting, arguably, the most pressing humanitarian issue of the twenty-first century.

II. The International Protection Landscape in New Zealand

International protection law is operationalised in New Zealand by the Immigration Act 2009 ('IA 2009' or 'the Act'). This legislation established a statutory complementary protection mechanism to sit alongside a pre-existing two-tiered refugee status determination procedure and a right of appeal against removal on humanitarian grounds. The statutory bodies which had hitherto exercised discrete jurisdiction were disestablished, and the IPT was established in their place to provide a streamlined and efficient appellate process.[2]

This new architecture of international protection in New Zealand was mapped by the Tribunal in *AC (Syria)*.[3] After noting the drafting history and the scheme of the IA 2009, the IPT concluded that it was the Parliament's clear intention to ensure the primacy of the Refugee Convention, notwithstanding the enactment of a complementary protection mechanism. The IPT noted that entitlement to complementary protection – called 'protected person status' – was

[2] See discussion in *AU (Afghanistan)* [2017] NZIPT 502815 at [37]–[41].
[3] *AC (Syria)* [2011] NZIPT 800035.

grounded in a subset of the wider body of international human rights law which had long formed the metric by which New Zealand refugee law had interpreted the concept of 'being persecuted'.[4] This, the IPT reasoned, had two significant implications:

i. The protected person jurisdiction did not rest on some autonomous notion of cruel, inhuman, or degrading treatment or punishment (hereinafter referred to as 'CIDTP') or arbitrary deprivation of life which is different to that which operates under the refugee jurisdiction.
ii. The threshold level of seriousness of harm to amount to CIDTP for the purposes of engaging complementary protection was not lower than that required to engage refugee protection.[5]

The IPT also observed that New Zealand's protected person jurisdiction, although derived from the ICCPR, does not embrace all of the rights contained in the ICCPR. Its scope is limited to exposure to torture, as defined under the 1984 Convention against Torture and Other Cruel, Inhuman or Degrading Treatment or Punishment, arbitrary deprivation of life or CIDTP.[6] Further, the protected person jurisdiction 'is not an unlimited humanitarian free-for-all' but rather is 'a bounded protection regime' sitting between refugee protection and relief from removal on humanitarian grounds. The critical point to note for present purposes is that, so far as the IA 2009 is concerned, complementary protection in New Zealand is statutorily structured to capture in its orbit a narrower band of the harms which can arise in the disaster context than those capable in principle of falling under the Act's refugee and humanitarian mechanisms. As Mr Teitiota did not have a right to a humanitarian appeal, the capacity of the IPT to allow him to remain in New Zealand by taking into account his future circumstances in Kiribati due to climate change was substantially narrowed.

Two further elements of the configuration of international protection law under the IA 2009 are important to have in mind to understand how the *Teitiota* case was decided.

First, complementary protection in New Zealand is statutorily focused on qualifying treatment or punishment in the receiving state. It was not possible to follow the approach of the European Court of Human Rights (ECtHR) which has, when confronted with cases involving pressing humanitarian concerns such as those relating to the end of life, effectively, located the qualifying

[4] B Burson, 'Give Way to the Right: The Evolving Use of Human Rights in New Zealand Refugee Status Determination' in B Burson and DJ Cantor (eds), *Human Rights and the Refugee Definition* (Brill, 2016) at 25–48.

[5] *AC (Syria)* (n 3) at [77]–[78]. These propositions were re-confirmed in *JR (Fiji)* [2024] NZIPT 802308 at [58]–[63]. A recent challenge to this understanding of international protection law was rejected by the High Court in *AP (Chile)* [2024] NZHC 2424. They remain the bedrock principles of international protection law in New Zealand.

[6] *AC (Syria)* (n 3) at [90]–[92].

'treatment' as the act of removal/deportation by the host state where harm is a foreseeable consequence of the removal. In New Zealand, the language of humanitarian exceptionalism used by the ECtHR to justify the 'extension of an extension' approximates the test for humanitarian relief against removal under a separate section of the Act.[7] While difficult cases can raise issues as to which side of the protection–humanitarian boundary the circumstances of an appeal may lie, the existence of this stand-alone jurisdiction means that, in New Zealand, hard-edged protection law grounded in the *non-refoulement* obligation is not the only avenue by which the impact of hazards on appellants can be, and increasingly are, addressed. What is often overlooked in commentary is that this humanitarian mechanism is increasingly used by the IPT to grant relief, including grants of residence, in cases where concerns around disasters and climate change feature.[8]

Second, the IA 2009's complementary protection mechanism requires the claimant to be 'in danger' of suffering the particular harm.[9] Although expressed in different terms to that of the Refugee Convention's 'well-founded fear' test, the IPT has been clear that this likewise only requires a degree of risk which is more than speculative or remote.[10] As will be discussed, this bedrock component of international protection law in New Zealand has been routinely misunderstood, leading to an unfortunate foray into debates around 'imminence' as the relevant risk threshold.

Having mapped the bedrock propositions which underpin international protection law in New Zealand, it is now possible to better understand how the *Teitiota* case was decided.

[7] See discussion in *BG (Fiji)* [2012] NZIPT 800035 at [180]–[184]. The IA 2009, s 207(1) provides:

> The Tribunal must allow an appeal against liability for deportation on humanitarian grounds only where it is satisfied that—
>
> (a) there are exceptional circumstances of a humanitarian nature that would make it unjust or unduly harsh for the appellant to be deported from New Zealand; and
> (b) it would not in all the circumstances be contrary to the public interest to allow the appellant to remain in New Zealand.

[8] See, eg, *AD (Tuvalu)* [2014] NZIPT 501370–371, where climate change was expressly recognised as a humanitarian circumstance which was weighed alongside the presence of family in New Zealand. Residence was granted. This approach continues, including explicitly recognising the psychological harm associated with exposure to climate hazards; see most recently, *BM (Tuvalu)* [2024] NZIPT 506177–178; and *Tamatoa* [2024] NZIPT 506284–285. In *AV (Tuvalu)* [2022] 505532, the Tribunal weighed an appellant's differential vulnerability as a deaf and mute person to hydrometeorological hazards as an element of its assessment as to the existence of exceptional circumstances of a humanitarian nature. Residence was granted. In another, deportation liability was quashed to allow an appellant to remain lawfully in New Zealand to work to support his family who were still recovering from the impacts of a tropical cyclone in Fiji, in circumstances where government capacity was already stretched by the impacts of COVID-19; see *Tuiwainikai* [2021] NZIPT 505185.

[9] Immigration Act 2009, ss 130(1) and 131(1).

[10] *AI (South Africa)* [2011] NZIPT 800050–053 at [81]–[83].

III. The *Teitiota* Litigation

A. The Case before the Tribunal: *AF (Kiribati)* [2013] NZIPT 800413

The countries of the Pacific – and Kiribati and Tuvalu in particular – are rightly recognised as being on the front-line of climate change. While the 'sinking island' narrative which can dominate discourse around population movement masks a more complex picture, it is undeniable that climate change poses huge challenge for the populations of these countries and the wider Pacific. Recent research across the Pacific has revealed the extent to which concern about climate change is already and increasingly featuring in decision-making around whether, where and when to move.[11] For good reason, Pacific Island Forum leaders have for some years identified climate change as one of the most pressing issues for the region and are at the forefront of the developments adapting international law to meet the challenges.[12]

Unsurprisingly perhaps, Mr Teitiota was therefore not the first person from the Pacific to claim refugee status in New Zealand because of the impacts on climate change. In 2000, a number of claimants from Tuvalu argued that environmental factors such as inundation, coastal erosion, salination of the water table, combined with factors at the individual and household levels, meant that they should be recognised as refugees. Their appeals were dismissed by the IPT's predecessor body – the Refugee Status Appeals Authority – because the indiscriminate nature of these events and processes gave rise to no nexus to a Convention ground.[13] Similar claims brought in Australia by claimants from Kiribati and Tuvalu were also unsuccessful.[14] These decisions reflected the received legal wisdom at the

[11] B Burson, E Marsters and R Bedford. *Pacific Peoples and Climate-Related (Im)mobility: A Synthesis Report on Scale, Pattern and Impact, Now and Into the Future* (New Zealand Ministry of Foreign Affairs and Trade, 2024) at 21.

[12] Pacific Islands Forum, Declaration on Preserving Maritime Zones in The Face Of Climate Change-Related Sea-Level Rise (6 August 2021), available at https://forumsec.org/sites/default/files/2024-03/2021%20Declaration%20on%20Preserving%20Maritime%20Zones%20in%20the%20face%20of%20Climate%20Change-related%20Sea-level%20rise.pdf; 2023 Declaration On The Continuity of Statehood and The Protection of Persons In The Face of Climate Change-Related Sea-Level Rise (20 November 2023). Also see https://forumsec.org/sites/default/files/2024-05/2023%20Declaration%20on%20the%20Continuity%20of%20Statehood%20and%20the%20Protection%20of%20Persons.pdf.

[13] *Refugee Appeal No 72185* (10 August 2000), *Refugee Appeal No 72186* (10 August 2000), *Refugee Appeal Nos 72189–72195* (17 August 2000), *Refugee Appeal Nos 72179–72181* (31 August 2000), *Refugee Appeal No 72313* (19 October 2000), *Refugee Appeal No 72314* (19 October 2000), *Refugee Appeal No 72315* (19 October 2000) and *Refugee Appeal No 72316* (19 October 2000).

[14] N00/34089 [2000] RRTA 1052 (17 November 2000), N95/09386 [1996] RRTA 3191 (7 November 1996), N96/10806 [1996] RRTA 3195 (7 November 1996), N99/30231 [2000] PPTA 17 (10 January 2000) and V94/02840 [1995] RRTA 2383 (23 October 1995).

time – articulated by courts of high judicial authority – that 'persons fleeing natural disaster' cannot obtain Convention-based protection.[15]

It was against this unpromising legal background that Mr Teitiota lodged his claim for protection in May 2012. After being dismissed at first instance, his appeal came before the IPT in March 2013. For reasons which are not clear, neither his wife nor children lodged any claims, meaning their eligibility for international protection was not able to be considered by the Tribunal. The IPT received written and oral evidence from Mr Teitiota and his wife as to their lived experiences in Kiribati, and from an expert witness. It noted country information including Kiribati's 2007 National Adaptation Programme of Action. This evidence established that climate change impacts such as sea level rise, made existing environmental hazards (such as coastal erosion) worse, and compounded problems associated with rapid population growth and urbanisation. These conditions had impacted on the wellbeing of Mr Teitiota and his family: life was becoming more difficult for them, including through the salination of the fresh water supply, the destruction of crops through saltwater intrusion and damage to the seawall in front of their home by storm surges. Fearing for the future, the decision was taken to migrate to New Zealand for a more secure future for the family. The wife's concern for the safety of the couple's young children was also noted, despite neither she nor the children filing their own claim for protection.

While Mr Teitiota was not entitled to international protection as either a Convention refugee or as a 'protected person', the opportunity was taken to critically examine the legal status quo as it stood at the time. In arguing that the legal status quo should no longer be maintained, three core general propositions were articulated.

First, the predicament of 'being persecuted' rests on human agency. The legal conception of refugeehood, governed as it is by the refugee definition in Article 1A (2) of the Refugee Convention, is narrower than a sociological conception. It was not possible to regard environmental degradation and climate change as agents of persecution.[16]

Second, the need to identify human agency nevertheless potentially creates pathways into refugee or complementary protection. It was important to expressly recognise that broad generalisations about 'natural' disasters and protection regimes masked a more complex reality. The relationship between natural disasters, environmental degradation, and human vulnerability to those disasters and degradation is complex. It is within this complexity that pathways can, in some circumstances, be created into international protection regimes, including

[15] *Applicant A v Minister of Immigration and Multiethnic Affairs* [1998] INLR 1, at 19; and *AH (Sudan) v Secretary of State* [2007] 3 WLR 832, at 844.

[16] *AF (Kiribati)* [2013] NZIPT 800413 at [51]–[54].

Convention-based recognition.[17] Some (but not all) vectors by which international protection law could potentially become engaged were identified, namely:[18]

i. the 'political weighting of state response in which the recovery needs of marginalised groups are sometimes not met';
ii. the politicisation of the post-disaster humanitarian space;
iii. that 'environmental issues can pose threats to security and induce violent conflict and displacement, albeit in a highly uncertain manner and through complex social and political processes'; and
iv. environmental degradation being used as a weapon of war.[19]

Third, while disasters and climate change are a protection-relevant context, no special rules applied to this case load. Ordinary principles of international protection law were to apply. The IPT framed the point thus:

> [g]eneralised assumptions about environmental change and natural disasters and the applicability of the Refugee Convention can be overstated. While in many cases the effects of environmental change and natural disasters will not bring affected persons within the scope of the Refugee Convention, no hard and fast rules or presumptions of non-applicability exist. Care must be taken to examine the particular features of the case.[20]

As to what this all meant for Mr Teitiota, the IPT was satisfied that he was not entitled to be recognised as a Convention refugee. He could not establish a future risk of being persecuted. The conditions that he would experience in Kiribati did not establish a breach of his socio-economic rights, nor place his life in jeopardy. In any event, by his own admission, the effects of environmental degradation on his standard of living were faced by the population generally and he could not therefore establish the requisite nexus to a Convention ground.[21]

As required under the IA 2009, the IPT then turned its mind to the question of complementary protection, in particular, whether the facts established that Mr Teitota was 'in danger' of suffering the arbitrary deprivation of his life, or CIDTP in Kiribati. It found that he was not. The Tribunal noted that what was protected against under the IA 2009 was not risk to life itself but rather 'deprivation of life by state action or as a consequence of its omissions'.[22] Nevertheless, it accepted that the prohibition on arbitrary deprivation of life must take into account the positive obligation on states to protect life from risks arising from known natural hazards and that failure to do so may, in principle, constitute such an omission. The

[17] ibid [57].
[18] ibid [58]–[59].
[19] At the time of writing, there are reports that the Russian Federation has engaged in such a practice by deliberately poisoning a waterway on Ukrainian territory as part of its campaign of aggression.
[20] ibid [64].
[21] ibid [72]–[75].
[22] W Kälin and J Künzli, *The Law of International Human Rights Protection* (Oxford University Press, 2010) 273.

difficulty was that Mr Teitiota could not point to any act or omission by the Kiribati Government which might indicate a risk that he will be 'arbitrarily deprived' of his life within the scope of Article 6 of the ICCPR.[23] Recalling its orthodox approach as the level of risk required, and need for CIDTP-relevant 'treatment' to occur in Kiribati, the IPT found that Mr Teitiota had not established that he was 'in danger' of suffering such treatment.[24] The appeal was dismissed. As already noted, Mr Teitiota's wife and children had not filed claims, let alone appeals. The IPT was without jurisdiction to make any determination as to their entitlement to international protection.

B. The Appeals before the New Zealand Courts [2013–2015]

Mr Teitiota unsuccessfully sought leave to appeal to the High Court, the Court of Appeal and ultimately the New Zealand Supreme Court.[25] Each court found no error in the IPT's analysis of the law. The Supreme Court made clear, as had the IPT, that although Mr Teitiota had not been able to establish his claim, this did not mean international protection as legislated for under the IA 2009 did not apply to the disaster context and could not rule out the possibility that other cases may well succeed.[26]

C. The Communication to the Human Rights Committee [2015–2020]

Having exhausted his domestic remedies, Mr Teitota and his family were removed to Kiribati in September 2015. He filed a complaint with the HRC that, by doing so, New Zealand had violated his right to life under Article 6(1) of the ICCPR and that the IPT and courts in New Zealand had not properly assessed the risk to him. For reasons which are also not clear, no complaint was made in relation to a violation of Article 7. It was not until October 2019 that the HRC adopted its views on the complaint. Its decision was published on 7 January 2020, heralding substantial international coverage. As is customary, the HRC first set out the relevant principles extracted from (largely) its own jurisprudence.

[23] *AF (Kiribati)* (n 16) [83]–[88].

[24] ibid [91]–[95].

[25] *Teitiota v Chief Executive, Ministry of Business, Innovation and Employment* [2013] NZHC 3125, [2014] NZAR 162; *Teitiota v Chief Executive, Ministry of Business, Innovation and Employment* [2014] NZCA 173, [2014] NZAR 688; and *Teitiota v Chief Executive, Ministry of Business, Innovation and Employment* [2015] NZSC 107.

[26] *Teitiota v Chief Executive, Ministry of Business, Innovation and Employment* [2015] NZSC 107 at [13].

These included that:

i. The risk to life must be personal and cannot derive from general conditions in the country of origin except in the most extreme cases.
ii. The right to life cannot be understood in a restrictive manner and requires the adoption of positive measures by States.
iii. The right to life is to be read as meaning a right to life 'with dignity', free from acts and omissions which would cause an unnatural or premature death.
iv. The right to life extended towards 'reasonably foreseeable' threats and life-threatening situations that can result in loss of life.
v. Environmental degradation, climate change and unsustainable development practices are some of the most 'pressing and serious threats' to the enjoyment of the right to life by present and future generations.[27]

The HRC then engaged with the IPT's reasoning to determine whether there was a 'clear arbitrariness, error or injustice' in its evaluation of the claim such as to found the complaint that the removal action which flowed therefrom meant New Zealand had violated Mr Teitoita's right to life. Sixteen of the 18 members found no such arbitrariness, injustice or error. Nor had the IPT failed to provide him with an adequate and individualised assessment of the risk to his life. The two dissents are problematic. The first focuses only on safe drinking water, reverses the evidential burden which applies in IPT appeals and references the children who never had a protection claim lodged on their behalf as an available domestic remedy. The other entirely mischaracterises the IPT's reasoning as to risk in language owing more melodrama than persuasive legal argument. Insofar as it also references risk to 'dignity', it highlights, as discussed below, the problematic subjectivity of using 'dignity' as a criterion in this legal context.

Nevertheless, citing the Global Compact of Safe, Orderly and Regular Migration,[28] the HRC – like the IPT and New Zealand Supreme Court before it – was at pains to stress that the sudden onset events and slow onset processes associated with climate change can 'propel cross-border movement of individuals seeking protection from climate change-related harm' such that, in the absence of 'robust national and international efforts', violations of Articles 6 and 7 of the ICCPR might arise in the future, thereby triggering the *non-refoulment* obligation. It was not necessary that 'an entire country' be submerged before the right to life with dignity could become engaged. States were required to keep the situation under review.[29]

[27] Human Rights Committee (HRC), *Ioane Teitiota v New Zealand* CCPR/C/127/D/2728/2016 (7 January 2020) [9.3] and [9.4].

[28] United Nations General Assembly, *Resolution Adopted by the General Assembly on 19 December 2018, 73/195 Global Compact for Safe, Orderly and Regular Migration* A/RES/73/195 (11 January 2019), para 18 (h), (i) and (l).

[29] HRC, *Ioane Teitiota* (n 27) [9.11] and [9.14].

IV. International Protection Law in the Aftermath of the *Teitiota* Litigation

There can be little doubt that the single most important significant outcome of this litigation has been to move the legal paradigm from one in which it was generally understood that international protection law does not apply to the disaster and climate context to one where it is now broadly accepted as doing just that; indeed, this was the primary ambition of the author of this chapter in writing the decision in *AF (Kiribati)*.

In the years which have followed the IPT's 2013 decision, international protection has become recognised as a potential tool to address cross-border displacement in the Nansen Initiative's 'Protection Agenda', itself the product of a state-led consultative process endorsed in 2015 by 109 states.[30] That same year, states endorsed the Sendai Framework for Disaster Risk Reduction 2015–2030 which articulates as its first core principle that 'Each State has the primary responsibility to prevent and reduce disaster risk'.[31]

In the wake of the HRC decision, United Nations High Commissioner for Refugees (UNHCR) was moved in 2020 to issue a paper setting out its position as to how international protection law applies[32] and, in recent months, publish a working paper documenting global good practice.[33] The International Law Association's (ILA) Committee on International Law and Sea Level Rise published a number of reports on the protection of persons in which the *Teitiota* litigation anchors the discussion around the relevance of international protection law.[34] This work has more recently been taken up by the International Law Commission.[35] The decade since *AF (Kiribati)* was decided has seen an explosion in academic interest, with many journal articles and even books devoted to the topic. Globally significant research centres such as the Refugee Law Initiative at the University of London and the University of New South Wales' Kaldor Centre on International Refugee Law have developed guidance for decision-makers, including a new

[30] Nansen Initiative on Disaster-Induced Cross-Broder Displacement, *Agenda for the Protection of Cross-Border Displaced Persons in the Context of Disasters and Climate Change* (December 2015) at 27.

[31] *Sendai Framework for Disaster Risk Reduction 2015-2030* (18 March 2015), para 19(a).

[32] United Nations High Commissioner for Refugees (UNHCR), *Legal Considerations Regarding Claims for International Protection Made in the Context of the Adverse Effects of Climate Change and Disasters* (1 October 2020).

[33] W Kälin and H Entwisle Chapuisat, *Protection of Persons Displaced across Borders in the Context of Disasters and the Adverse Effects of Climate Change*, UNHCR Legal and Protection Policy Research Series PPLA/2024/01 (June 2024).

[34] For a summary of outputs, see J McAdam, W Kälin and B Burson, 'Statehood and the Protection of Persons in the Context of Sea-Level Rise: The International Law Association's Contribution' in *Yearbook of International Disaster Law* (Brill, 2025).

[35] International Law Commission (ILC), *Sea-Level Rise in Relation to International Law: Second Issues Paper by Patrícia Galvão Teles and Juan José Ruda Santolaria, Co-Chairs of the Study Group on Sea-Level Rise in Relation to International Law (18 April–3 June and 4 July–5 August 2022)* A/CN4/752 (19 April 2022).

Toolkit.[36] In 2023, the European Union Agency for Asylum included an entire section on 'environmental dangers' in guidance on international protection by courts and tribunals in the European Union[37] and, in 2024, the International Association of Refugee and Migration Judges established a working party looking at this issue.[38]

The pathways towards Convention-based protection identified in *AF (Kiribati)* are increasingly recognised as 'scenarios' within which international protection needs may arise. Although not expressed in identical terms, the identification of factual scenarios has become central to the process of socialisation of the paradigm shift in the law generated by the *Teitiota* litigation among lawyers, decision-makers and judges.[39] Some scenarios, such as the exposure of a claimant to state violence or to harm perpetrated by non-state actors such as trafficking – increasingly recognised as a risk in post-disaster settings – will be more familiar and thus more straightforward in terms of identification of an international protection need.[40] Others, particularly where a state is willing to protect but is simply unable to do so, less so.

The scenario relating to state (in)action which exacerbates disaster risk is a further area in which the law appears increasingly settled. Failure to discharge positive obligations, for example by not undertaking lifesaving evacuations, may constitute an arbitrary act for the purposes of the prohibition on the arbitrary deprivation of life under Article 6 of the ICCPR. The IPT has also recognised that the discriminatory denial of humanitarian relief, or the arbitrary withholding of necessary foreign humanitarian assistance where domestic state capacity is overwhelmed to undertake necessary relief and recovery phase operations are forms of 'treatment' of the affected populations for the purposes of Article 7. Where these have a sufficient nexus to a Convention reason, a pathway towards recognition as a refugee emerges.

While the *Teitiota* litigation has settled the headline issue, other critically important issues in determining just when international protection law may be engaged remain unsettled.

[36] The Toolkit is a joint publication involving the Kaldor Centre, UNHCR, The Centre for Gender and Refugee Studies and the University of Essex. See *International Protection for People Displaced Across Borders in the Context of Climate Change and Disasters: A Practical Toolkit* (February 2025), available at https://cgrs.uclawsf.edu.

[37] European Union Agency for Asylum (EUAA), *Qualification for International Protection: Judicial Analysis*, Second Edition (January 2023) at 261, available at https://euaa.europa.eu.

[38] International Association on Refugee and Migration Judges, *List of Working Parties*, available at www.iarmj.org.

[39] M Scott, *Climate Change, Disasters, and the Refugee Convention* (Cambridge University Press, 2020) 45–88. Platform on Disaster Displacement (PDD) and UNHCR, *Protection of Persons Displaced across Borders in the context of Disasters and the Adverse Effects of Climate Change: Good Practices to Support Implementation of the Global Compact on Refugees* Policy Brief (December 2023) s 2; UNHCR, *Climate Change Impacts and Cross-Border Displacement: International Refugee Law and UNHCR's Mandate* (December 2023); Refugee Law Initiative, *Declaration on International Protection in the Context of Disasters and Climate Change* (May 2024), para 8; and Kaldor Centre et al *Toolkit* (n 36) 6.

[40] For an example of a case involving trafficking, see *Tribunale Ordinario di Firenze, X c Ministero dell'Interno* ERG 6142 [2023] (5 October 2023), cited in Kälin and Entwisle Chapuisat (n 33) 12.

A. The Right to Life 'With Dignity'

As regards to Article 6 of the ICCPR, in *Teitiota*,[41] the HRC drew on its *General Comment No 36* which reasons that the 'right to life is a right that should not be interpreted narrowly' and included an entitlement to be 'free from acts and omissions that are intended or may be expected to cause their unnatural or premature death, as well as to enjoy a life with dignity'.[42] This general proposition was applied to the disaster and climate context.[43] In its subsequent decision in *Billy et al v Australia*,[44] the HRC again reiterated the relevance of right to life with dignity in the context of disasters and climate change.

While an unimpeachable ethical proposition and core norm of international law, using 'dignity' as a metric of the right to life for the purposes of international protection law is problematic. In New Zealand, there has been a deliberate avoidance of obtuse language such as 'reasonable toleration' of harm or the 'reasonable expectation' in favour of identifying the underlying objective factors which the decision-maker must weigh so as to minimise the room for the subjective perceptions of the decision-maker as to what is 'reasonable' to influence outcomes. The same problem inheres in using 'dignity' as a standard; just how is this to be objectively measured to determine when the *non-refoulement* obligation is engaged?

Insofar as the measure of dignified life depends on access to a bundle of socio-economic and cultural goods and services, it risks overreaching into the terrain of the 1966 International Covenant of Economic Social and Cultural Rights (the ICESCR) and presents problems in principle. This point, raised by Australia in *Billy*, was unceremoniously swept aside by the HRC by reference to the Preamble to the ICCPR and case law relating to the general obligation of domestic authorities to protect life from known environmental hazards, about which there is no dispute.[45] Regardless, the fundamental problem with this expansive configuration of Article 6 remains and was addressed by the IPT in *AW (Kiribati)*:

> [I]nsofar as the threshold requirements for dignified life are grounded in socio-economic entitlements for which the relevant human right is subject to progressive realisation or rights more generally which may be permissibly limited or derogated from, an extension of Article 6 to being one of an absolute nature risks rendering the right otiose. It is no doubt these concerns which have underpinned the very high threshold requirements in both *Teitiota* (at para 9.8) and the *Torres Strait Islander* decision (at para 8.6) as to when a right to life 'with dignity' is breached.[46]

[41] See HRC, *Ioane Teitiota* (n 27) at [9.4], [9.8] and [9.9].

[42] HRC, *General Comment No 36: Article 6: Right to Life* CCPR/C/GC/36 (3 September 2019) at para 3.

[43] ibid para 62.

[44] *Billy et al v Australia*, CCPR/C/135/D/3624/2019 (22 September 2022) at [8.4]–[8.6]. This is not a complaint relating to international protection but rather concerned the accountability of Australia for the impacts of its climate change adaptation policies on the human rights of indigenous populations living on the Torres Straight islands.

[45] *Billy*, ibid [8.4].

[46] *AW (Kiribati)* [2022] NZIPT 802085 at [124].

The concern regarding overreach has been echoed in the final report of the ILA Committee on International Law and Sea Level Rise which likewise expressed concern.[47]

This is not to deny the interrelationship between socioeconomic factors and safety, much less that disasters and climate change impacts routinely gravely undermine the safety and wellbeing of affected populations.[48] Moreover, some courts and mechanisms have extended the prohibition on CIDTP to include specific situations of severe socioeconomic deprivation.[49] Given lingering concerns around the justiciability of economic social and cultural rights, the impulse to expand Article 6 of the ICCPR in such fashion is understandable. However, in doing so, this approach arguably concedes too much from the standpoint of progressive development of international protection law.

An alternative, and more progressive but principled approach to that adopted by the HRC, is to reverse the legal telescope and view the issue through the lens of the underlying socioeconomic right. In 2012, in a case concerning the long-term impacts of the relocation of the Banaban population in the 1940s to Rabi Island in Fiji to facilitate continued phosphate mining on Banaba (now Ocean Island in Kiribati), the IPT recognised that for the purpose of international protection law in New Zealand, socioeconomic rights were to be weighed equally as their civil and political counterparts.[50] There is a dense architecture of widely accepted norms deriving from the General Comments of the United Nations Committee on Economic, Social and Cultural Rights relating to more objectively measurable metrics such as availability, adequacy and accessibility sitting alongside the notion of a 'minimum core obligation'.[51] Indeed, the General Comments relating to health and food have expressly referenced the disaster context.[52] These developments, noted by the IPT in *AF (Kiribati)*,[53] can be leveraged to argue that, where the impacts of a state failure to discharge positive obligation to respect, protect and/or fulfil socioeconomic rights is so grave as to imperil the life, the *non-refoulement* obligation can be engaged. Under this alternative approach, it is not necessary to resort to 'dignity' to ensure

[47] International Law Association, *Final Report to the Eighty-First Conference* (Athens, 25–28 June 2024) 39, available at www.ila-hq.org. The author is a member of this Committee and contributed to the writing of this Report.

[48] See J McAdam et al, *International Law and Sea-Level Rise: Forced Migration and Human Rights* (Fridtjof Nansen Institute, 2016) section 1.3.

[49] *BG (Fiji)* [2012] NZIPT 800091, [147]–[157].

[50] ibid at [90].

[51] ibid at [103]–[109].

[52] In *General Comment No 14: The Right to the Highest Attainable Standard of Health* E/C12/2000 (11 August 2000) at para 14, the United Nations Committee on Economic, Social and Cultural Rights stated that Art 12(2)(b) obliges states to take steps aimed at the prevention and reduction of the population's exposure to 'detrimental environmental conditions that directly or indirectly impact on human health'. In *General Comment No 12: The Right to Adequate Food* (Art 11) E/C12/1999/5 (12 May 1999), at para 6, the Committee states that 'States have a core obligation to take the necessary action to mitigate and alleviate hunger … even in times of natural or other disasters.'

[53] *AF (Kiribati)* (n 16) at [63].

protection is appropriately extended when socioeconomic harms imperil life. If anything, the HRC approach undermines the quest to have the ICESCR rights taken just as seriously as their ICCPR counterparts for the purposes of international protection.

B. The Question of Time

Just how far into the future does international protection reach? In the wake of the *Teitiota* litigation, this question has emerged as one of, if not the most, hotly debated issues. Regrettably, this stems from a misreading of *AF (Kiribati)* in the literature and, more problematically, by the HRC. Scott, for example, raises concerns that the IPT has taken 'an unduly narrow temporal scope of the notion of being persecuted'.[54] For its part, the HRC stated that the IPT required risk to be 'imminent' albeit meaning 'at least likely to occur'.[55] Both statements are incorrect and stem from a failure – and despite the IPT stressing clearly that no special rules applied – to locate the decision within the IPT's ordinary approach. The IPT was clear, citing its own relevant jurisprudence, that the degree of risk was akin to the Refugee Convention real chance threshold which does not require protection-relevant risk to manifest imminently.[56]

As McAdam rightly observes, 'imminence is not the appropriate test when it comes to the lawfulness of removal'.[57] The IPT revisited the controversy in *AW (Kiribati)*, noting that 'while an imminent risk of persecutory harm will certainly meet the real chance standard, this is not to say that it is only imminent risk which does so'.[58]

The proposition that risk need not be imminent does not, however, fully answer how more distant bands of time relative to the date of the decision impact upon the evaluation of risk. Building from the foundation laid out in *AF (Kiribati)*, the following year the IPT noted that:

> [G]iven the forward-looking nature of the inquiry, the nature of the hazard, including its intensity and frequency, as well as any positive changes in disaster risk reduction and operational responses in the country of origin, or improvements in its adaptive capacity, will need to be accounted for.[59]

[54] Scott (n 39) 87.

[55] See HRC *Ioane Teitiota* (n 27) [2.9].

[56] The Tribunal was merely making the point that the long-term lags in the climate system means that, as a decision-making context, cases brought on the basis of risk associated with future climate change impacts are imbued with greater contextual certainty than cases brought on a risk of nuclear holocaust. The latter is an assertion of future harm predicated, not on science, but the relatively less certain trajectories of international relations.

[57] J McAdam, 'Current Developments – Protecting People Displaced by the Impacts Of Climate Change: The UN Human Rights Committee and the Principle of Non-Refoulement' (2020) 114(4) *American Journal of International Law* 708, at 720.

[58] *AW (Kiribati)* (n 46) at [103].

[59] *AC (Tuvalu)* [2014] NZIPT 800517 at [69].

This approach has been echoed by the HRC in its decisions in both *Teitiota*[60] and *Billy*.[61]

That disaster risk reduction, climate change adaptation and sustainable development projects and programmes must be factored into risk assessment in this context must also now be regarded as a settled proposition. Nevertheless, these cannot be presumed to reduce risk of harm sufficient to fall within the scope of protection to below the relevant threshold: there are both hard and soft limits. In the Pacific context, the story of Pacific populations is a story of adapting to changes in the climate through innovation of traditional practices. However, there may yet come a time when the impacts of climate change are such that adaptation of customary practices cannot keep pace. It is for this reason that the IPT, the New Zealand Supreme Court and the HRC have stressed that the situation needs to be kept under review.

C. The Question of Evidence

The assertion that Kiribati 'is losing land mass and can be expected to survive as a country for 10 to 15 more years' referenced by the HRC in its decision was not asserted before the IPT in *AF (Kiribati)*. It does not appear that this claim was grounded in scientific evidence and/or customary or indigenous knowledge, but rather appears simply to have been asserted by Mr Teitiota as the author of the complaint.[62] As noted in *AW (Kiribati)*, this timeframe 'sits uneasily' against relevant reports by the Intergovernmental Panel on Climate Change which make no such claim and points to a potentially far longer timeframe for habitability thresholds to be reached.[63] The submission appears to have been made in December 2016, over eight years ago, and we are well into his suggested timeframe without there being suggestions that Kiribati is about to cease to function as a country no later than the end of 2031.

While such unsupported assertions are insufficient, nor do decision-makers need to become climate scientists. Rather, the focus must be on the underlying 'hazard-scape'[64] and how this has and will impact upon the claimant. There will be an abundance of evidence available, albeit from sources which may be unfamiliar. As is discussed below, in some jurisdictions such as Italy, there is a tradition of providing humanitarian protection to disaster-affected persons. This is an emerging practice in New Zealand. Other countries have general humanitarian migration pathways which allow for some degree of 'protection' to disaster-affected persons. There will be a body of evidence which sits beneath such interventions.

[60] See HRC, *Ioane Teitiota* (n 27) [9.12].
[61] See *Billy* (n 44) [8.7].
[62] See HRC, *Ioane Teitiota* (n 27) [7.2].
[63] See above *AW (Kiribati)* (n 46) at [109].
[64] See, ibid.

The unsettled issue is the extent to which this body of evidence will be sufficient to found a protection claim. The HRC position is that 'risk cannot derive from the general conditions in the receiving State, except in the most extreme cases, and a high threshold for providing substantial grounds to establish that a real risk of irreparable harm exists'.[65] The evidence before the IPT was held not to reach this high threshold.

The application of the HRC's general position to the disaster context is ambiguous given the realities of how a disaster unfolds. The focus on the general conditions in the receiving state arguably casts the gaze of the inquiry at the wrong scale. The focus needs to be more localised, particularly where not all parts of the state experience the same hazard. Moreover, it is not clear what is meant by the 'general conditions' and what counts as 'extreme'. Must the extreme circumstances affect the country as a whole? Must the extreme situation have a minimum degree of anticipated duration? These questions are important as their answers will shape just what evidence is needed to establish a claim for international protection before the HRC.

D. The Question of Application

Echoing the pre-*AF (Kiribati)* position in New Zealand, Scott and Garner's analysis of state practice in Sweden and Finland has demonstrated a similar judicial reluctance to apply 'innovative international protection categories introduced by Sweden and Finland in anticipation of large numbers of people being displaced across borders'.[66] The Swedish provision was suspended in 2016 and repealed in 2021 by which time some 102 persons had lodged claims based on exposure to disaster-related harm. The Finnish provision was removed in 2016. Neither resulted in a single grant of international protection.[67]

Looking to the future, the window for judicial reticence is surely closed. This chapter has already noted the significant change in the legal landscape post-*Teitiota*. Failure by judges and decision-makers to recognise this will cause a new 'protection gap' to emerge, a gap, not in the relevance of international protection law as a body of law, but in its practical application. There are encouraging signs that judges are becoming sensitive to this change.[68]

It is the case that the HRC extends some deference to national authorities as primary fact finder and limits its inquiry to whether the assessment of domestic authorities was 'clearly arbitrary or amounted to a manifest error or a denial of justice'.[69] While far short of an *ex nunc*, substantive review, this still puts national

[65] See above HRC, *Ioane Teitiota* (n 27) at [9.3].

[66] M Scott and R Garner, 'Nordic Norms, Natural Disasters and International Protection: Swedish and Finnish Practice in an International Perspective' (2022) 91(1) *Nordic Journal of International Law* 101, at 101.

[67] ibid 106 and 112.

[68] For an excellent overview, see Kälin and Entwisle Chapuisat (n 33) at 17.

[69] See HRC, *Ioane Teitiota* (n 27) at [9.3].

authorities squarely on notice that such cases need proper consideration. The ever-clearer reality of climate change means that exposure to hazards will endure as a context in which protection claims are brought; national authorities – like it or not – will need to assess them.[70]

While there is no longer place for presumption of non-applicability, this begs the wider question of just when international protection can apply. Reflecting differing domestic legal frameworks within which a court or administrative body is tasked with applying international protection law, state practice diverges to some extent. Arguably, the most expansive is that within Europe, where the ECtHR has countenanced the extension of international protection law into general humanitarian conditions where general living conditions are regarded as sufficiently 'dire'[71] or where suffering in the country of destination is found to be intense and/or to result in a 'significant reduction in life expectancy'.[72] This approach is not without its controversy. In *Teitiota*, the HRC seems to lean towards this interpretation, but a high bar is set.

As noted, in New Zealand, a separate humanitarian jurisdiction is part of the domestic landscape in which cases categorised as 'protection' cases in Europe is increasingly used to address the same issues.[73] So too in Italy, where a provision of the Consolidated Immigration Act relating to 'protection against calamities' has for many years been used to grant relief on humanitarian grounds to permit the stay of disaster-affected claimants.[74] While not drawing on the principle of *non-refoulement*, that these systems are in fact recognising climate change and disasters as a relevant factor justifying humanitarian relief against removal means that they are just as – if not more – effective in the short-term than hard-law, *non-refoulement* oriented cases in which the evidential requirements are so stringent that very few claims for protection from harm are successful.

V. Conclusion

The *Teitiota* litigation is indeed a landmark in international protection law: there is a before and an after. As much as this claimant failed, the litigation provides an architecture for future claims to succeed, albeit one which is not in all aspects fully sketched-out.

Nevertheless, given the reality of global climate change, and the increasing overlap of the climate crisis with conflict, poverty and other drivers of cross-border

[70] ibid [9.14].

[71] *Sufi and Elmi v United Kingdom* App nos 8319/07 and 11449/07 (ECtHR, 28 November 2011) at [291].

[72] *Paposhvili v Belgium* App no 41738/10 (ECtHR, 13 December 2016) at [183].

[73] See, eg, in relation to 'end-of-life' cases: *Tukunga* [2017] NZIPT 503288, *Palota* [2020] NZIPT 504783 and *DN (Tonga)* [2023] NZIPT 505853–854.

[74] See Kälin and Entwisle Chapuisat (n 33) 27–28.

population movement, it is likely that international protection claims featuring exposure to climate change and other hazards will become more common in more jurisdictions. Moreover, as crises overlap and/or recur, it is inevitable that state capacity to discharge positive obligations to protect life and progressively realise socioeconomic rights will be compromised in some, if not, many disaster-affected countries. Should the international community not support such countries to discharge these obligations though financial, technical and other support, the likelihood that some affected populations may move across borders and seek protection will only increase. Decision-makers in more national settings may yet be required to determine just when the *non-refoulment* obligation applies.

However, it is also the case that the use of international protection law to regulate movement of persons in the context of disasters and climate change will remain shaped by the availability of other legal tools at the domestic level. Looking to the future, some degree of differentiation in the form by which decision-makers and courts respond seems inevitable, particularly in more difficult cases such as those where risks occur over longer time-horizons and there is no suggestion of discriminatory state response. Even so, although different legal tools are being deployed, there is a burgeoning body of case law centred on the notion that the impacts of disasters and climate change can be sufficiently grave for an individual that they ought not be removed. Even so, further development depends on the willingness of lawyers, decision-makers and judges to become sensitised to the issues. It is this which will determine just how 'landmark' the *Teitiota* litigation becomes.

INDEX

www.ingramcontent.com/pod-product-compliance
Lightning Source LLC
LaVergne TN
LVHW011746250226
832549LV00003B/148